Trading Options to Win

Trading Options to Win

Profitable Strategies and Tactics for Any Trader

S. A. JOHNSTON

WILEY

John Wiley & Sons, Inc.

Published by John Wiley & Sons, Inc., Hoboken, New Jersey.
Published simultaneously in Canada.

Designations used by companies to distinguish their products are often claimed as trademarks. In all instances where John Wiley & Sons, Inc. is aware of a claim, the product names appear in initial capital or all capital letters. Readers, however, should contact the appropriate companies for more complete information regarding trademarks and registration.

Limit of Liability/Disclaimer of Warranty: While the publisher and author have used their best efforts in preparing this book, they make no representations or warranties with respect to the accuracy or completeness of the contents of this book and specifically disclaim any implied warranties of merchantability or fitness for a particular purpose. No warranty may be created or extended by sales representatives or written sales materials. The advice and strategies contained herein may not be suitable for your situation. You should consult with a professional where appropriate. Neither the publisher nor author shall be liable for any loss of profit or any other commercial damages, including but not limited to special, incidental, consequential, or other damages.

For general information on our other products and services, or technical support, please contact our Customer Care Department within the United States at 800-762-2974, outside the United States at 317-572-3993 or fax 317-572-4002.

Wiley also publishes its books in a variety of electronic formats. Some content that appears in print may not be available in electronic books.

For more information about Wiley products, visit our web site at www.Wiley.com.

Library of Congress Cataloging-in-Publication Data:
Johnston, S. A.
    Trading options to win : profitable strategies and tactics for any trader /
S. A. Johnston.
        p. cm.
    ISBN 0-471-22685-8 (alk. paper)
    1. Stock options.   I. Title.
HG6042 .J64 2003
332.64′5—dc21

2002153117

Printed in the United States of America

10 9 8 7 6 5 4 3 2 1

Contents

Preface

There are thousands of books about trading. Some books approach trading as an exercise in mathematics and focus on effective ways to turn the mathematics of the marketplace into a profit-generation machine. Some approach trading as an exercise in psychology and tactics, attempting to generate profit from a correct understanding and appreciation of what the other traders in the market are doing. Some are catalogues of strategies. Some apply economic, statistical, or logical principles to trading in the marketplace. Some are practical guides to the minutiae of markets.

This book either fits into none of those categories or is a mixture of all of them with several other topics included. I'm not sure which. What it is, at bottom, is my understanding of the whats, hows, and whys of earning a trading profit, acquired over 30 years of trading in all sorts of markets (*all* sorts—remind me to tell you sometime about the great caviar-for-condoms caper). I didn't become a steadily profitable trader until I came to understand some of the assumptions and conditions that underlie markets and to figure out certain practical and usually effective ways to combat the assorted risks that markets present; in short, to learn to deal effectively with the nature of the beast.

This book is informal, because I'm an informal guy. There's almost nothing I like better than talking with other traders about trading, and so the text is written in a generally conversational style. We will crunch a few numbers on occasion, to clarify various topics and as an aid in looking at practical examples of trading, but there are no formal mathematical demonstrations at all in this book for two very good reasons.

First, a number of fine analysts and remarkable scholars have published extensive compilations of the mathematics involved in quantitative analysis, numerical methods, and risk and price modeling, and there's no point whatever in even attempting to replicate their efforts. A motto of mine is, "Always go to the *best* source available," which is usually the original author. Who wants to read a rewrite of someone else's work, anyway, particularly a very good original work? Can you even imagine *Hamlet* as rewritten by, say, Danielle Steele? Ghastly thought.

Second, a whole lot of people (possibly including you) find formal mathematics either mind-numbingly boring, or impenetrable, or both. Cards on the table, I want you to turn the next page, not fall asleep or use the book to stoke up your barbecue. To this end, I figure that, in addition to providing what I believe to be useful and in the best cases profitable information, the text had darned well better be entertaining too.

This book is for traders, particularly retail traders. That's easy to say but tricky to accomplish, because the level of experience varies greatly among any group of traders. This is not a primer. I'm assuming first of all that you trade in some market, and that your principal interest is to look at ways to improve the profitability of your trading. In addition, I'm assuming that you are moderately familiar with what a futures market is and with its basic workings, and that you are at least comfortable with the *idea* of options, even if you believe you've never traded an option in your life. You have dealt in options, of course; you very likely deal in them implicitly every single day of your life . . . but we'll get into that subject a little later. Don't believe it? Care to bet against it? Read on, and save your money.

If you know the difference between a put and a call, and know what a premium, a striking price, and an expiration date are, you'll have no difficulty with the text. If you're a sophisticated and experienced trader in futures and options markets, you'll doubtless find some of the text to be elementary, even possibly annoyingly so. Sorry about that, but this result happens to be a condition of contest when writing for a wide (I sincerely hope!) audience about the subject of trading. Frankly, I think that any trader, no matter how sophisticated, will find a number of worthwhile ideas inside . . . but there's only one way to find out, isn't there?

Few books are the product of any single person's thoughts and efforts, and most certainly this one is not. It literally would not even have been written without the encouragement of Alex McCallum of INO, and without his introduction to my generous (and patient!) editors, Pamela van Giessen and Lara Murphy, at John Wiley & Sons. I also owe a considerable debt to Jay Shartsis and Bob McKenna at R. F. Lafferty & Co., for the enormous amount of practical advice they've offered, and explained, over the years. Many traders, including especially David H. Murray, Elaine Long Knuth, Janet diGregorio, John Anderson, and Mark Kelly were kind enough to read my original drafts, offer a variety of valuable suggestions, and point out and correct several instances where I had driven neatly off a literary cliff. Dan Reinhart, a marvelous statistician (among his other considerable talents), was gracious enough to check over the analyses in the text and correct several that I had fluffed. Thank you, Danimal.

Even though my principal business is the design of computer systems, I'm an absolute idiot when the subject is graphics, and I'm fortunate to have a very talented friend to bail me out of my fumblethumbedness. The tables and figures in the text were produced by the ultimate sweetheart, Lee Fleming, one of the masterminds behind InfoPulse LLC (www.infopulsellc.com), of Norwalk, Connecticut.

My long-time futures broker, Ken Margherio at REFCO, Inc., has contributed mightily to this little effort by applying his 30-plus years of experience to helping refine some of the strategies discussed in the later chapters. Mark Kinoff, a local trader at the Chicago Board of Trade, offered several creative ideas about useful tactics in interest rate markets. The noted currency analyst and author, Barbara Rockefeller, was extremely generous, both in offering constructive criticism and in introducing me to a bunch of folks who could, and did, clarify a number of points. I also want to thank Ed Rittershausen for taking his time to make several excellent and practical suggestions.

In theory at least, we learn from our mistakes. I know for a certainty I've learned much more from my errors in trading than from my successes. Books about trading or investing that focus on the author's successes, usually with at least an implied "Hey, look how wonderful this method (or this author) is!", exasperate me no end. Look, I already know how to win; what I *want* to know is how not to lose. Consistent with this view, the examples of actual or hypothetical trades throughout the text are generally negative examples—demonstrating what to do if a trade goes awry, how to deal with unanticipated risk, and even, occasionally, how to turn a loss back into a profit. After all, if a trade goes well, it goes well, we bank the profit, and there's little more to be said about it, right? There just isn't much value in yammering on about a wonderful trade I made last year or last month, and I want to provide as much value to you as I can manage.

I'm just a trader, a part-time trader at that. I realize that there are numerous ways to profit in trading. Unfortunately, there are a much larger number of ways to lose. Many of these losing methods are superficially appealing and seem to offer an advantage to traders, but turn out ultimately to be only expensive illusions. Larry McMillan, the inestimable author of, among his other works, *Options as a Strategic Investment* (New York Institute of Finance 1993), states on page 467 of the third edition, "There are certain investors who will enter positions only when the historical percentages are on their side."

He is exactly right, as usual, and his statement applies with equal validity to traders as well as investors. I'm one of those traders and, by George, I *will* have an advantage. Whether the advantage is historical, statistical, or one based on demonstrable fact, I will have some sort of advantage in hand *before* I enter a trade. Trading without some sort of definable advantage is gambling. Gambling is about amusement or ego. Trading is about making a profit.

This book is about attempting to recognize and gain advantages in our trading in a methodical fashion, but our flight through this world will not be non-stop. We must visit several interim topics, the practical and logical underpinnings of markets, before reaching our ultimate destination. May I suggest you get a cup or a glass of your favorite beverage and settle into a comfortable chair as we examine together a number of ways to view and understand and profit from the mechanism of the marketplace. Our destination? The ability to put and keep an advantage on *our* side when we trade, that is, when we engage in making money with money.

OFFICIAL WARNING: The author is about to commit heresy. Do not read further unless you are willing to consider revising at least some of your beliefs about markets, particularly about the desirability of trading in certain of them. The author disclaims any and all responsibility for the results of shattering any and all long-held illusions, particularly those about stock markets.

CHAPTER 1

Making Money with Money

If we win here, we will win everywhere.
—Ernest Hemingway, (*For Whom the Bell Tolls*)

I trade in the markets. I *expect* to win. I expect to profit handsomely by trading, over both the short term and the long term. And you can and should, also.

That said, I don't have any surefire "system" to offer, nor any original mathematical or analytical techniques to employ, nor any special knowledge of a market or markets. I concentrate on *method*, that is, an approach to the development of trading strategies that put the likelihood of profit on my side of the table. With your permission, I propose to illustrate several means by which you can do so, too.

Since time is money—and time absolutely is money when trading the markets—let's get right down to cases. Let's play a game, a wagering game. All games have rules, and here are the rules for this one:

1. I select all the wagers to be made between us.
2. You will pay me, in cash, an indeterminate amount of money that I will name before I will accept your wager.
3. Wagers are not settled immediately, but after some amount of time, and the net value of both our wagers fluctuates day to day.
4. Either you or I may transfer our wager to a third party of our choice at any time prior to settlement.
5. I can purchase insurance against a bad outcome of my wager at any time, while you may or may not be able to insure your wager satisfactorily.

6. You know at the start that if you see your wager through to the end, you will win only one time in four or five, but that winning wager may be enormously profitable, and that the other times you will likely lose your whole wager.

7. Other rules may apply from time to time, or there may be changes in the rules, according to circumstances over which neither you nor I have any control.

Do you really want to play such a game? Right, I didn't think so, and your decision to refuse this game is entirely accurate. Those who do play such a game lose, just as you almost surely would. Not all the time, certainly, but they lose, and steadily. Why would anyone kick his own shins by playing a game such as this? I really don't know. Misplaced hope, or greed? Possibly. Lack of information or failing to analyze the game properly? Perhaps. Outright stupidity is definitely in the running, too, as is compulsive gambling.

Believe it or not though, large numbers of people play a game highly similar to this every business day of the year. They spend a great deal of time and capital buying options that are exceptionally unlikely to return a profit to them, an activity that is functionally identical to the hypothetical game I just described. For the most part, I trade against these folks, which implies directly that I win some very large percentage of the time.

There is only one legitimate reason why someone might play our hypothetical game or any of its real-world analogs. He may be required to play by law, much as you and I must purchase car insurance in order to drive legally. We could be cynical here, and note that the game I've described is more than a little bit like my taking the part of an insurance company. The only rule that doesn't really fit is the rule about your possibly making exceptional profits from time to time. Making a profit is impossible when dealing with insurance companies, except, of course, if you can manage to defraud them successfully.

The point of this example is not that there is some terrifically profitable game waiting to be played, but rather to find a starting place. What is it, really, that we're doing when we trade? In the sense of the example, and as far as some mathematicians are concerned, we're playing a game. Many other people would answer, very reasonably, that we're trying to make money. Both answers, though, miss the mark to some degree, and this error is not only not unimportant, it is vital. What traders do is attempt to make money *with money*, within a societally defined game-like context.

Does this strike you as a bit odd? It should. Money is primarily a tool for use within the context of society. Suppose you have a huge stack of $100 bills right in front of you. Suppose also that you're in a house outside West Broken Glass, Montana, the pantry is bare, your car won't start, and the phones are out. A flood has just washed out the bridge on the road to town, your nearest neighbor is miles away, and, worse yet, there's nothing good on cable. How useful is that stack of bills now? Hardly useful at all (well, you could light them to keep warm for a little while). Other tools do not share this limitation of usefulness only within a specific context. A can opener works just as well at the North Pole as it does at the Equator, or in your kitchen.

Equally, no one would attempt to make a screwdriver *with* a screwdriver, a radial arm saw *with* a radial arm saw, or even a computer *with* a computer, although this last concept does have some interesting possibilities for futurists and cyberneticists. Money is unique among tools for these reasons. Therefore, if we intend to make money with money by trading, we would be well advised to take a reasonably hard look at other ways to make money with money and at what each of these may involve, and, even more importantly, to see what we can learn from them. And so we will, right now.

To my observation, there are just four generic ways to make money with money: gambling, bookmaking, banking, and trading or investing. Each has, naturally enough, advantages and disadvantages for their respective practitioners. With a view toward learning more about developing a successful methodology for making money with money, let's take a look at the characteristics of each activity in turn.

Gambling—Skill, Luck, or Something Else?

Gambling is an enterprise in which the entrepreneur, usually called the "player," attempts to profit by winning games consisting either of foretelling the outcome of a specific event or of beating an opponent at a contest. These games can be broadly separated into two groups: low-skill and high-skill. By "skill" here, I distinctly mean the ability of the player to alter the outcome of the game in his favor through the use of advantageous strategies. In the typical low-skill game, casino games for instance—craps, roulette, keno, what have you—there are no such strategies; the player may, through accurate play, only reduce the size of his expected loss over time. Indeed, in quite a number of casino games, various types of coin-operated machines for instance, the player may not even have the option of minimizing his loss through correct play, but must willy-nilly accept the pre-set negative outcome of the game.

Gambling in high-skill games, sometimes called proposition betting, involves the player accepting a partially predictable prospect of success or failure and will almost always contain a considerable mix of skill and non-skill factors relevant to the outcome. Examples of this form of gambling are commonplace. You might bet a friend that you will beat him at golf, tennis, cards, or any of thousands of different activities each involving some degree, sometimes a staggering degree, of skill. You might, alternatively, bet him that your favorite sports team will beat his favorite team in the upcoming game. "Wait a minute, where's the skill in that?" you may be asking. Have no doubt here; skill is and must be involved in this latter bet if the player intends to prosper over time.

In playing a golf or tennis match, the player's skill is applied; his strokes immediately affect the outcome. In a sports wager, the player's skill is implied. The player himself does not affect the outcome of the game directly, short of perhaps introducing strychnine into the other team's pre-game meal, but the player's outcome, win or loss, is a function of his skill in rating the relative talents of the teams involved. In addition, to succeed, he must accurately evaluate other conditions that will or may affect the outcome before the game takes place.

If you are a purist, you may object to the characterization of a gambler as "making money with money" by contesting a golf or tennis match, or by playing a card game, or by wagering on a hockey match. Such an objection is specious. The only important question is, "What is at risk?" The banker, the bookmaker, the gambler, and the trader all put their *capital* directly at risk. The physicist, the baker, the assembly-line worker, the teacher, the salesman, and the policeman put their time, talent, and effort right square on the line—but not their capital. To be such a purist here is equivalent to asserting that the only true way of making money with money is to play some form or another of flipping coins, wherein the only intermediary device used is actual currency or specie. That's much too formalistic a view.

The Starting Line

To make money with money, whether by gambling or through any other enterprise, first involves a selection process of profit possibilities. For the gambler, the selection process amounts to "Which game(s) shall I play?" In low-skill games, this selection is basically emotional, that is, the gambler likes the game. It's entertainment for him and he enjoys it, notwithstanding that some large percentage of the time he is going to lose. Likely enough, he's aware of this high probability of loss . . . and simply doesn't care. In high-skill games, though, the selection process is much more empirical, as well as much more important to the player's outcome. The high-skill gambler wants, in short, to maximize his confidence level methodically, either by selecting opponents he "should" beat or by choosing wagers that appear, empirically or intuitively, to be to his advantage. He will ultimately end up measuring his success or failure with the yardstick of careful selection of his profit possibilities, of opponents, or propositions. This success or failure will be modified only by the intrusion of non-skill factors, of something very much like Shakespeare's "outrageous fortune."

If the result for the gambler in low-skill games is more or less preordained, the result for the gambler in high-skill games is nothing if not highly variable. Part of the reason for such variability is that, in a disproportionate number of games the gambler might play, he will not know his profit expectation beforehand. He may perceive he has an advantage in a given proposition or in playing against a given opponent, and, based on experience, he may very well be correct. The notion of perceived advantage in propositions, however, is in most cases a subjective view. There's nothing wrong with subjectivity per se, but it has a notable tendency to work against consistency of success in any enterprise, the more so if subjective measures are employed when objective measures are available. When actual advantage can be calculated, the gambler who relies on perceived advantage is subjecting his profit expectation to unnecessary fluctuations. Even beyond skill of whatever type, the winning gambler must have or have access to the ability to calculate his advantage when such a calculation is available.

Risky Business

There are other factors contributing to his uncertain profit expectation. Players in high-skill games, as do we all, have the well-known bad day occasionally, whether self-induced or due to external circumstance. Perhaps you recall a famous scene in the film *The Hustler*. After a long night of shooting pool, Minnesota Fats steps away from the table, washes his face, re-combs his hair, re-knots his tie, generally refreshing himself and renewing his concentration on the match, while Fast Eddie Felson uses the time to make wisecracks and guzzle bourbon. Subsequently, of course, Fast Eddie gets cleaned out. This is a nearly perfect parable of the self-induced loss.

External circumstance can cause loss in any way imaginable. The golf ball hits a rock as it lands and kicks off into a bunker instead of going onto the green. An outfielder slips on a patch of loose turf while chasing a fly ball and the winning run scores. The pool player hits a perfect shot but an auto accident outside causes a car to come through the wall and wreck the table before the object ball drops into the pocket. The gambler will certainly try to and may well succeed at eliminating self-induced losses, but he is almost completely helpless against the occurrence of adverse external circumstances.

These external circumstances collectively are called *event risk*, and event risk is relatively large for the gambler in high-skill games. If you're not immediately persuaded of this, consider that a high-skill game, any one you like, is played over time and usually involves thousands, even millions of sub-events during the course of the game. What's a sub-event? It's any event that occurs within the context of the game. It might be the move of a rook, a pitched ball, a rainstorm occurring (or not occurring) on the 14th hole, the turn of a card, literally anything that happens over the course of a game.

The likelihood of any one particular sub-event occurring in such an improbable fashion as to alter the outcome of a game is tiny, yet the likelihood of *some* sub-event doing so during the course of a game is larger, sometimes much larger. Why? Because this likelihood increases multiplicatively over the number of sub-events to be considered. When the sub-events in a given game are numbered in the millions, the probability that some of them will materially alter the game's outcome is no longer insignificant and may even end up being the largest determinant factor in the outcome. Worse still, from the gambler's standpoint, he has no way of knowing either when or how often the feared improbable sub-event(s) will occur, and there is almost nothing he can do about it in any case. Therefore, in his attempt to make a profit, the high-skill gambler must accept a rather high level of event risk, and this level increases along with the complexity of the game.

It would be very useful to be able to quantify the amount of event risk for the high-skill gambler, but such a quantification is impossible in the general case. What is the probability before the fact that, say, an opponent will play an unexpected and effective move during a game of chess and that the gambler will be unable to counter it? What odds that a fly or some other insect decides to inspect the gambling golfer's inner ear in the middle of his backswing on an important shot? Before the game starts, how likely is it that the quarterback of the team on which the gambler bets, who hasn't thrown an interception all season, will throw five interceptions in today's game? Perhaps someone knows how to compute the probability of occurrence of events such as these with some degree of accuracy. I'm not that person, probably you aren't, and I somehow don't think the gambler is, either. The net result, and a very undesirable one it is too, is that the gambler must not only deal with event risk, but also has no objective measure of how large or small it may be at any particular point during the game.

The gambler faces other kinds of risk. Suppose that he wins his proposition bet and the opponent, for whatever reason, doesn't pay him? Or, suppose that he's wagered on a football game and won, but his bookmaker has been arrested before the gambler can collect? Without resorting to unlawful means such as rearranging someone's anatomy, the gambler is entirely dependent on the good will of the other party for his profit, and he has no worthwhile way to offset the risk of the other person not playing fair. This is a different and specific risk, called *counterparty risk*, wherein one party to a transaction does not perform as previously agreed. *Every* method of making money with money involves counterparty risk to some extent. If you consider the point for a moment, you'll realize that this statement must be true de facto. If we are engaged in making money with money, where does our profit originate? It comes from other people, some of whom, for various reasons, may occasionally fail to perform as agreed. The good news is that other methods of making money with money have certain built-in advantages in avoiding and offsetting counterparty risk which gambling does not.

Gambling in low-skill games as a way of making money with money is statistically a hopeless proposition, but even so we can learn something very useful from those who attempt to profit in this futile enterprise, that is, what *not* to do. Specifically, we can't take the short end of the bet and expect to profit over time. That sounds pretty obvious, doesn't it? I agree, but a little later on we're going to see that some people, even some sophisticated and informed people, fail to adhere to this seemingly obvious notion.

Gambling in high-skill games may indeed prove to be profitable, provided the player himself has sufficient skill, but his making a steady profit is subject to still other obstacles. Can the gambler find a continuous source of games to play, propositions to wager on, and opponents to contest? It's not exactly as if he can dig up profit possibilities in the telephone directory, after all. Further, with regard to opponents, won't the successful gambler need to continually locate new opponents? He definitely will, because sooner or later everyone gets tired of losing at the same game. If you're even thinking, "Heck, the gambler can go to Las Vegas or Atlantic City and find all the proposition bets he wants, and probably a lot of opponents besides," then sit right down and have another think. If he does so, he's going to find himself competing directly against another way of making money with money—bookmaking. And, if he does so, he's going to lose.

Bookmaking—The Art of the Spread

Bookmaking is a name for a class of enterprises in which the entrepreneur attempts to set both the purchase price and sale price for some event or set of events, or for a financial instrument. The entrepreneur, let's call him the "bookie," may or may not be able to set absolute buy/sell levels, but will in almost all cases have near-absolute control over the spread between the buy and sell prices, and he will earn his profit principally from this spread. There are all sorts of widely different entrepreneurs who use bookmaking as their method of making money with money. They range from the local guy who takes bets on football games, to the absolutely state-of-the-art sports books housed in casinos, to the specialists on the New York Stock Exchange (NYSE), to the market makers on the Chicago Board Options Exchange (CBOE), to every insurance company in the world. There are thousands of variations on bookmaking.

Terminology matters. Specialists, market makers, and insurance companies *are in fact* bookmakers by any reasonable definition. If you happen to be a little bit surprised at this statement, it's probably due to the unrealistic and negative connotation that the word "bookmaking" has acquired, particularly in America. Consider what the NYSE specialist firms do. At bottom, they guarantee liquidity to the market. The specialist guarantees to step up and buy shares when most are selling, and to make shares available when everyone wants to buy. In return for undertaking such a responsibility, specialists are allowed by the rules of the exchange to control the bid-ask spread for NYSE-traded stocks. Ergo, they are bookies by precise definition.

The function of the market maker on the option exchange floors is similar, although the rules under which the market maker operates differ considerably from those governing the specialist. Both these groups of entrepreneurs earn the bulk of their profit from the spread between the bid price and the offer price of the markets in which they participate, the markets they make. Naturally enough, they do have and will employ other means of increasing their earnings, certainly including trading for their own accounts, but we're concerned here with their primary function and method of making money with money.

Insurance companies are bookies also, but their bid-ask spread is much more complex and far less immediate than the spread to be found on the exchange floors. Insurers do not ordinarily make the bulk of their profit by buying policies at $1,000 and selling them at $1,100 in lots of five, a hundred, or ten thousand. Rather, they use what might be called a "deferred" bid-ask spread. An insurance company's bid is the sum total of all possible liability to the company as specified in the policies it writes for you, me, and who knows how many others. Their offer is the sum total of all premiums that you, I, and others pay them—but with a twist. While you and I pay the policy premiums on a known date, the insurance company, in some enormous majority of cases, pays out their liability for our auto crash or hospital bill or storm damage only much later, if at all. Therefore, in addition to the bid-ask spread, the company can (and does, you bet your life) also earn investment return on a tidy chunk of the premium dollars collected.

Now, all this is merely ordinary business practice for insurance companies, but this is once again bookmaking, just as sure as sunrise. The only differences here between insurance bookmaking and specialist or sports bookmaking are the time frame and number of variables involved, and the very convenient notion of being able to use other peoples' money to increase their profits. Nice work if you can get it, eh? To be sure, specialists are also highly leveraged. Specialists use other peoples' money, too, with the major difference that the people lending money to specialists will at least be making a market rate of return on the dollars lent.

Bookmaking Versus Gambling

In comparing bookmaking to gambling, it's useful to note that the profile of profit differs considerably in both amount and frequency. The low-skill gambler usually attempts to make a very infrequent profit well out of proportion to his stake, his capital. The high-skill gambler attempts to earn a profit generally proportionate to his capital over a healthy majority of (usually varied) propositions. The bookmaker, however, attempts and intends to make a small or smallish but consistent profit over a pre-defined set of propositions within a more or less specific time frame. The sports bookie, in particular, should and will usually know his profit on a given proposition very nearly to the exact dollar even before the game begins. The specialist and the market maker know from long experience how much they are likely to earn from each day's market activity. The insurance company relies on a statistical expectation of profit over time, which depends generally on reversion to the mean and the law of large numbers.

The bookmaker must select his own set of profit possibilities, and it is in doing so that the bookmaker enjoys a sizeable advantage over the gambler. The sports book, simply because of the gigantic number of sports events occurring in a typical week, knows where his profit possibilities are without even breathing hard. Probably he's known where most of them are for six months or more, since professional league schedules are published well in advance, and collegiate schedules years in advance, of the games being played. Sports bookies have no shortage of profit possibilities; they need only to attract players. Since total dollar levels of sports gambling have been rising for years worldwide, attracting players seems to be presenting no obstacle to them. They are in the enviable position of turning on the profit spigot by just opening their doors.

Specialists and market makers similarly know their profit possibilities right down to the nth degree. When the market is open, so also is their opportunity to profit by simply operating their business. Given the great bull markets of the 1990s in stocks and a huge expansion in trading in options and other derivatives, not to mention the continual media shilling (and their prattle that passes for commentary about stock markets), trading in these markets has increased fantastically. So have the profits of the specialists and market makers. With the advent of decimalization of prices and the rapid growth of electronic trading, the bid-ask spreads have shrunk considerably, but the exchange bookmakers are hardly taking out third mortgages. Their gains from the huge volume increases appear to have handily outstripped the reduction in per-trade profit.

The insurance companies have a more difficult time in selecting profit possibilities. The decision to begin offering insurance against some type of risk is immensely complex, time consuming, and expensive. Even if a company has the will, the time, and the capital to enter a new market, it may not be able to do so because state and federal regulations may bar the way. Furthermore, on entering a new market or offering a new type of insurance, the insurance company initially confronts a difficulty similar to that of the high-skill gambler: finding players who will take the other side of their proposition, in this case, buy their product. Insurers, of course, prefer to call these folks policyholders and are, unlike the gambler, able to advertise in order to attract them.

Not Such Risky Business

Bookmaking, just as all human activity, has its risks. Fortunately for the bookmaker, though, the risks in his enterprise are usually very well known in advance and can be controlled to a very high degree, even totally in some cases. Counterparty risk exists, but it is not a material factor for a competent bookmaker. The losing gambler might choose not to pay his bookie. A brokerage might go into receivership, or have several large clients go bankrupt, and be subsequently unable to pay off obligations to the exchange. The insurance company might have a disproportionate number of policyholders who for some reason become unable or unwilling to keep paying the policy premiums. How serious can these risks be?

Perhaps curiously, they aren't serious at all. In fact, these perceived risks are almost entirely a product of appearance, mere chimeras and straw men. Bookmaking, in all its forms, has been going on for thousands of years, and over the course of time each type of bookmaker has developed ways of making most counterparty risk about as bothersome to the bottom line as a stubbed toe. The traditional sports book, on having a player welsh on a bet, used to make a practice of introducing the player to groups of large gentlemen who were fond of demonstrating the proposition that wood and steel are much harder than the human kneecap. This approach tended to be very effective in getting the bet settled and guaranteeing no future backsliding on the part of the player, but it was costly both in salaries and occasionally in time . . . as in time served. Modern sports books insist on either prepayment of the player's bet or immediate settlement at the end of the game (that's why the chairs are comfortable and the drinks are cold, isn't it?). Increasingly often, the sports book will require the player to set up a bank-like account with the book, funded in advance of any wagers. Thus, counterparty risk for the modern sports book is at worst a tiny cost of doing business. Those comfortable chairs do have to be cleaned once in a while and the electric bill must be paid, but this form of risk poses no threat whatever to the sports bookmaker today.

The exchange bookmakers have a more elegant means of minimizing counterparty risk, although it may possibly be less effective in an absolute sense. If a member of the exchange defaults on a trade, the exchange itself will pursue the miscreant/unfortunate member (choose one), and, additionally, the exchange members self-insure; they contribute to a capital pool for just such a circumstance. The specialist or market maker will have a relatively easy time of it in getting matters put to rights. If actual fraud is involved (a very rare happenstance for specialists and market makers), the exchange bookmaker has the option, in some cases the duty, to yell for the cops, namely the SEC, the CFTC, or the FBI.

Naturally, once the bureaucrats get involved, efficiency goes straight down the tubes, but sooner or later the exchange bookmaker will either be made whole, or the fraudster will find himself explaining his actions to assorted authorities, or both. In any case, the exchanges take great pains to prevent fraudsters from plying their nasty little trade against the exchange members in the first place, and to sniff them out quickly when they do. Counterparty risk for the exchange bookmaker is, as a consequence, almost always a nuisance factor as opposed to a substantive risk to capital.

For insurance companies, counterparty risk operates differently. The first and most important form of this risk is plain fraud. Fraud is, regrettably, an absolute condition of contest for insurers. Part of the reason for this is, doubtless, human nature. Certain people apparently cannot resist an opportunity to attempt to swindle other people, and large profitable companies seem to be an irresistible target for these lowlifes. Another major part of the reason why insurance fraud is so common is the diffuseness and complexity of the industry. For example, of the thousands of auto repair shops in the nation, it's a statistical certainty that some are operated by dishonest individuals. Insurance companies can't possibly monitor all of them for occasional fraud, particularly in those instances where the mechanic and the policyholder work in collusion. Counterparty risk in the form of fraud runs to untold millions annually, and the insurers have little choice but to add the estimated costs of fraud into the policy premiums. By doing so, they *lay off* this risk, or a very large piece of it, onto the customer, the policyholder.

The second form of counterparty risk is less costly to insurers. If a policyholder does not pay his premiums, the insurer cancels his policy. Ho hum. Everyone knows this, so where's the risk? In the case of casualty insurance or term life insurance, the insurer suffers the cost and inconvenience of having to find another such policyholder if profits are to be maintained at the same level. Fortunately, from the insurer's standpoint at least, there is usually a very large pool of potential new policyholders for most types of insurance and the replacement of lapsed policyholders becomes just another cost of doing business. It would be fascinating to know what the per-unit replacement cost is, but insurers don't seem to want to talk about that subject very much.

The third and most interesting form is the nominal counterparty risk involved in ongoing types of insurance such as whole life or universal life. If a policyholder terminates or otherwise fails to pay the premium on one of these policies after several years, the analysis becomes quite intriguing. The company will pay out some funds in the form of benefits to the former policyholder, but, and this is the fun part, will also likely make a profit even doing so. These policies tend to be heavily backloaded in terms of benefit accrual; quite a bit of time must pass from the initiation of the policy until the policyholder actually has a significant level of payable benefits.

Insurers, having the advantage of employing the best actuarial minds on the planet, understand perfectly well that some percentage of their policies will be abandoned every year, and have most assuredly calculated very carefully the rate of abandonment to benefits due ratio, the better to approach maximum profitability. When the counting is done, counterparty risk for most insurance bookmakers is next to nothing and might even occasionally contribute, net-net, to a firm's profits.

The Real-World Risks

Just because one specific type of risk, counterparty risk, is rarely a significant factor in professional bookmaking doesn't for a moment imply that there are not very real types of risk involved. Some of these risks are due to the nature of the game. Let's face it, insurance companies, specialists, market makers, and sports books (the lawful ones, at any rate) are highly regulated by sundry agencies of various governments. Governments can and do change the rules of the game from time to time, sometimes arbitrarily and without much, or any, warning. Event risk, you say? Perhaps, but that's a stretch. By definition, event risk cannot be prevented, only insured against or transferred. *Regulatory risk*, contrarily, can be prevented. There's not a doubt in the world that the insurance, securities, and gambling industries spend millions each year on bribes . . . pardon me, campaign contributions in an attempt to forestall or scuttle outright the ever more onerous and costly regulation so dear to the hearts of so many supposed public servants. Occasionally they even succeed.

The great majority of the risks faced by bookmakers, though, do fall into the category of event risk, but the difference between event risk in the worlds of gambling and of bookmaking is breathtaking. The gambler can lose his stake on a specific wager due to event risk, but the bookmaker can lose, according to the famous dictum of Lloyd's of London, "everything, down to the last collar-stud in his shirt." Unlike the gambler, though, the bookmaker is able to do something about this. He can take positive action against "suffering the slings and arrows." *It is this opportunity, the ability to deflect or insure against the negative effects of external circumstance, which we as traders must seize upon and learn to apply to our machinations in the markets.*

Event risk used to be much more important to sports bookmakers than it is today, and the reason for this lies in the nature of the industry and the changes that have taken place within it over the last few decades. You see, event risk for a sports bookie is a very simple thing: it consists of having too much money wagered on one side of a proposition.

If and when this condition occurs, the bookmaker is at risk. If the wrong team would win, the team on which the bookie holds too many bets, he would incur a serious loss. As you certainly imagine, the bookie will resist such an outcome with every fiber of his being. In years past, the sports bookie applied several remedies to this situation. In order to put his betting book back into closer balance, he either changed the terms of the bet for future players, thereby encouraging players to wager on the other team, or he exchanged excess wagers with another bookie who had too much wagered on the other side of the proposition. In the case of extreme betting imbalances, he persuaded players to allow him to repurchase their previous wagers. For today's sports book, these remedies have changed very little in nature, but, due to modern communications, these can now be implemented much more quickly and accurately. A betting imbalance that would have taken an old-time bookmaker hours or days to correct via telephone and wire can now be rectified by a few clicks of a modern bookie's mouse.

Insurance companies obviously must grapple with event risk. That's why they exist in the first place. Suppose that an insurer, as a result of a well-designed product, good market research, and superior salesmanship and pricing, has managed to insure some very high percentage of all the homes in some county or group of adjacent counties. Suppose also that the company, through assiduous study of weather disasters, earthquakes, arsons—generally all the loss-producing external circumstances that have occurred in this area over the past 50 years—has determined that the chances of an unacceptable rate of loss are just 1 in 100 in any given year. The resulting insurance policy has been duly priced to generate underwriting profits, allow for accumulation of loss reserves, and leave enough over to permit generation of good investment returns. Homeowners have decided that the policy represents good value and have bought it enthusiastically. Everyone involved has behaved responsibly, and now the homeowners will pay their premiums and the company can just sit tight, manage its business carefully, publish glowing earnings reports each quarter, and live happily ever after, right?

As George Bernard Shaw used to say, "Not bloody likely." Given such a concentration of liability, the company *absolutely cannot tolerate* a huge disaster in this insured area. If such a disaster would occur, the company might very well not survive it. And such disasters do occur. The hypothetical situation just described is in essence the situation in Florida immediately prior to hurricane Andrew in 1992, except that Andrew's subsequent wrath bankrupted not one but several insurance companies and damaged numerous others heavily. What happened? How did the bookies lose?

The bookies lost, in this case, because they forgot they were bookies; they became players. Inadvertently or complacently so, perhaps, but nonetheless they did. They kept too much risk, had too many eggs in one basket if you like. Insurers have always been able to reduce their potential liability, to lay off portions of their risk while still earning a very good profit. For one thing, reinsurance, which is insurance for insurance companies against their underwriting risks, has been readily available for decades. Insurers have also historically been very active in lobbying politicians for improved building codes and standards, which, when adhered to (sadly, not always the case), directly reduce the possible insurable loss. More recently, insurers have gone directly to the capital markets and securitized, literally sold as financial instruments, various parts of their potential exposure, thus transferring some portion of their risk to investors and speculators. Reinsurance can ordinarily be acquired in a day or two. Securitization takes longer to put in place, due to underwriting rules in the securities industry and the unavoidable red tape of assorted bureaucracies, but it is such an efficient way to transfer risk that its use by insurers seems almost certain to grow rapidly henceforth.

Why didn't the insurers lay off their excess risk, only to end up stabbed in the knee by Andrew? I have no idea. You'll have to ask them. The obvious point here is that, if event risk can wipe out an insurance company, it can much more easily wipe out a trader. To avoid this sort of catastrophe as traders, we'll want to be constantly on the lookout both for the existence of potential high event risk situations, which we will shun like the plague, and for opportunities to lay off risk, event risk particularly, to other parties.

Event risk menaces the exchange bookmakers, too, and we have no further to look for a clear example of this danger than Black Monday, October 19, 1987. The Dow Jones Industrial Average, astonishingly, lost 508 points in a single day, more than 20% of its value at the time. The causes of this debacle were many and varied, and have been the subject of hundreds of books and articles, but these do not concern us just now. What happened to the bookies, our market making and specialist friends? In words of one syllable, they got creamed. Not all of them, certainly, but enough of them that Merrill Lynch and other huge investment firms had to open their checkbooks to the tune of hundreds of millions of dollars in order to recapitalize many specialists so that the market could open for trading the next day.

On the Chicago Board Options Exchange that day, traders were only interested in trying to buy put options or sell call options. With next to zero interest in the other side of these trades, the market makers' spreads became so wide that trading simply stopped for a while in many stock and index options. At the Chicago Mercantile Exchange (CME) where the S&P 500 Index futures contract trades, the arbitrageurs who had sold stocks short and had purchased S&P futures contracts against them were utterly destroyed. They were clipped for well over a billion dollars when the futures contract moved to a then unheard of forty-point discount to the cash S&P Index itself. This was more of a problem for CME than it would have been for, say, NYSE, because futures trades must be settled up daily, as opposed to stock trades that were then allowed five business days for settlement. How did they whistle up a cool billion-plus dollars overnight? The Federal Reserve, no less, had to open the discount window to let many of the people involved borrow the amounts needed to settle, or else the exchange probably would not have been able to open on Tuesday, October 20.

Nor were the exchange bookies able to lay off this inordinate event risk to other market participants. How could they? In the week preceding Black Monday, the stock markets had already been moving sharply lower. Most of the larger market participants who might under ordinary circumstances have been willing to accept part of the risk were, in fact, either already trading with a downward bias or had stepped away from the markets and, in some considerable number of cases, were cowering under their desks.

The Ultimate Risk—Capacity Risk

A curious sidebar to Black Monday is that, unlike the disastrous event risk that the insurers encountered with hurricane Andrew, the exchange bookies didn't do anything systemically wrong. They didn't abandon their roles as bookmakers, as did the insurers before hurricane Andrew hit. They weren't careless or complacent, merely overwhelmed by the vicious confluence of events. No matter. The results in each case were the same, differing only in the number of dollars lost. This event was an excellent illustration of yet another type of risk, called *capacity risk*. Defined bluntly, capacity risk is the probability that some obnoxious event will occur and, as a result, you (or I, or the gambler, or the bookmaker) will subsequently not have enough capital remaining to be able to stay in the game.

You may be saying to yourself, "Well, if this can happen to people who are in the markets for their living, whether specialists, market makers, or professional arbitrageurs, how the devil can I avoid being chopped to bits by these whirling swords of risk?" A fair question, and very eloquently asked. The answer to this question provides yet another guidepost toward a method of developing successful strategies. Specialists and arbitrageurs *require* a considerable degree of leverage to operate their businesses profitably. We traders have an advantage on this very point—we can take leverage or leave it, use a little or a lot, entirely at our discretion. Like money itself, leverage is a tool, and, as with almost any tool, if we use it improperly or carelessly, we may damage ourselves seriously.

Capacity risk only exists when leverage is used. If we wanted to avoid capacity risk completely, we would simply avoid using any leverage at all in our trading, but using zero leverage is a terribly inefficient application of our capital. Contrarily, using 5,000% leverage might well turn out to be a suicidal application of our capital. The right amount of leverage is, as is true in most things, somewhere in between.

Banking—The Balancing Act

Banking is an enterprise that lends capital to those who have a potential use for it, and profits by charging for its use over time. The entrepreneur, the banker, has a wide range of profit possibilities that vary by the type and duration of loans made, and he enjoys certain advantages not always available to bookmakers, and never to gamblers. One significant advantage is the collateralization of risk; bankers actively tend to insist that the borrower put up collateral security over the term of the loan. In the event of a borrower's default on repayment of a secured loan, the banker will liquidate the asset(s) pledged as security and thereby reclaim his capital, and, if possible, any interest due and other applicable charges. Again, all this is ordinary business practice, and the process of collateralization allows the banker to lower his risk and thereby also lower the rate of interest he charges the borrower on the loan.

Bankers, like bookmakers, typically select profit possibilities with a very high probability of success and accept in return a known and calculable positive expectation on their selections. But this expectation isn't necessarily as small as you or I might think. Just on a whim, I called my banker (an old friend) the other day and asked him what he and his bank deem an acceptable rate of default on secured loans, expecting him to say something along the lines of 1 per cent. Surprisingly, he very nonchalantly replied, "Not counting mortgages, 3 to 6 per cent on secured loans; 15 to 19 per cent on unsecured loans, sometimes a little higher."

With a bit more conversation, he disabused me of my (evidently!) very stodgy mental image of "conservative bankers." Of the 3–6% default rate, he pointed out that, in perhaps 85% of the cases, liquidation of collateral would make the bank completely or nearly whole. "What about the other 15% (about 0.67% of all secured loans)?" I asked. "Oh, we'll reclaim some capital from the collateral, maybe go through replevin (repossession, for instance in the case of automobile loans) or wage garnishment, whatever looks like the best way to clean up the loan. We have all the options. This isn't really a headache for us, just a cost of doing business." That phrase again!

Sometimes I don't know when to quit. "All right. What about the unsecured loans?" He actually chuckled. "Come on, Stu, why do you think the interest rate on unsecured loans is so high? We just raise the interest rate to accommodate the higher default rate, and we still have most of the options here. If a borrower skips town or a business declares bankruptcy we can have some losses, but a 10 to 15 per cent interest rate spread solves a *lot* of problems, wouldn't you say?" You bet I would.

Wait a minute. "Interest rate spread?" Now, this sounds more like bookmaking, doesn't it? Banking does indeed have similarities to bookmaking. The interest rate spread is comparable to the specialist's control of the bid-ask spread for stocks. The banker's bid is his cost of money; the interest rate the bank pays its depositors or pays to borrow funds from other banks or from the Federal Reserve. On certain types of deposits such as what you and I call checking accounts, the bid can actually be zero and the bank can find itself in the very enjoyable position of *using other peoples' money for free*, a better deal than even the insurance companies can create. The offer is the interest rate charged the borrower. Ten to fifteen per cent on this spread? Good grief, bookmakers would kill for a spread like that.

We must be careful not to push this bookmaking–banking analogy too far, however. In the first place, the banker only partially controls the bid side of the interest spread. He may or may not be able to attract new deposits at any given time, and he surely does not dictate to the Federal Reserve how much it can charge him for additional funds. In the second place, bankers provide capital to various markets. Bookmakers do not; they provide a service, be it the opportunity to back one's opinion on a sports event, the liquidity to trade easily in the markets, or a guarantee against excessive loss. More importantly still, the risk profile of banking differs from that of bookmaking.

The Banker's Risks

Ordinary counterparty risk, as my banking friend so thoroughly explained, is present but very manageable for the prudent banker. Hard counterparty risk for banks, as for insurance companies, consists of deliberate fraud and is not as manageable, although the typical bank is not nearly as exposed to fraud as is the typical insurer. After all, insurance fraud can be engineered without the insurer's knowledge, but those who would defraud banks almost always will have made the acquaintance of the banker, which fact offers another level of security for the bank.

The "five Cs" of moneylending are credit, capacity, cash flow, collateral, and character. Someone bent on fraud is clearly deficient in the character department, but bankers, not being psychic, occasionally do not discover this deficiency in time. If the banker happens to misjudge the character of a borrower or the value of the collateral, he will find himself standing hip-deep in a very black pool of counterparty risk. If such an error occurs, the banker can compensate by maintaining a proper loan-loss reserve, but, unless he sells the dubious loan to some other party, he can't completely eliminate the risk to the bank's capital.

The form of risk that bedeviled the exchange bookmakers on Black Monday, capacity risk, can easily be avoided. Capacity risk presents itself to the banker when the amount of capital sought by qualified borrowers reaches or exceeds the banker's available lending capital, and when depositors remove their funds from the bank en masse. The banker who wants to control capacity risk either can acquire more capital by borrowing from the Federal Reserve, borrowing against his loan portfolio, or by other means, or he can reduce the demands on capital by making his criteria for lending more stringent. Unlike the specialist and the market maker, the banker doesn't have to play the game every day with all qualified comers.

Regulatory risk is present, certainly, but bankers deal with it in the same way as regulated bookmakers do; they buy off the politicians. The banking lobby is one of the strongest in the nation, and the banking industry has learned, over the centuries, that *baksheesh* is a very effective device for dealing with governments and bureaucracies. Please note that I do not disapprove of this practice, merely call it by its right name as opposed to using euphemisms such as "campaign contributions" or "directed lending." If you and I were bankers, we would employ this tactic, too. We'd be completely mad if we did not.

True external event risk, short of an outright collapse of the financial system, is not really on the banker's radar screen very much any more. It used to be a huge consideration. American history is chock full of famous financial panics and runs on banks, sometimes originating from the flimsiest of rumors (and sometimes not!). Numerous writers, scholars, and economists have made a persuasive historical case that many or most panics, and the ensuing bank runs, were at their root due to persistent regional imbalances in the money supply. This analysis seems awfully reasonable to me.

If the supply of money in, say, a five-state area somehow becomes insufficient for the conduct of ordinary business, then money will tend to become more valuable to its holder than the utility or value he might otherwise gain from the purchase of goods or services. The holder of money, seeing how slow business is, may also decide that prices will soon be coming down somewhat, which will reinforce this notion of relative utility and further cause him to defer purchases. In such a situation, he and other people will likely tend to hoard money, or at best spend it very cautiously.

From its very nature, banking absolutely depends on economic activity in order to generate the profits, thence the money, necessary for a borrower to repay his loan and the associated interest. Such manifested caution or hoarding will in fairly short order tend to increase the number of loan defaults as the profits generated from business activity decline. Over time, and sometimes not very much time at that, the increase in defaults will increase resentment and distrust of banks, at minimum among the ranks of those whose loans have been foreclosed. At some point, someone will decide that his money will be really much, much safer under the mattress than languishing in the banker's vault. He'll tell a neighbor how clever he's been, and then he'll tell the barber, and others. And they'll do the same. And then the run on the bank begins.

Fanciful, you say? Gloom, doom, and Chicken Little? Hardly. This is exactly how many bank runs proceeded in American history, particularly in rural areas. Nor did all bank runs result from monetary imbalance or citizen paranoia; some were deliberately instigated by shortsighted competitors, by spreading rumors or gossip in order to destroy a rival bank. Frank Capra's film, *It's a Wonderful Life*, may have been fiction, but there probably wasn't anyone in the theatres' audience for whom the bank run scene didn't ring absolutely, and perhaps very painfully, true.

The Federal Reserve System was created for a variety of reasons. One of these was an attempt to diminish the occasional blips and dips in regional money supply by providing a framework within which money, or more precisely liquidity, could be quickly transferred to areas where an imbalance existed. The reappearance of fiat money in the 1930s and the stunning advances in electronics, information processing, and data transmission from 1952 through the present day have greatly assisted the Fed in this mission. Old-fashioned panics are probably a thing of the past, and bankers need spend few sleepless nights worrying about this external event risk.

There is still the little matter of self-induced event risk, though, and this turns out to be the approximate equivalent of bubonic plague for the banking industry. Bubonic plague is the handiwork of a bacterium named *Yersinia pestis*. Most of the time, it's a benign little critter, passing its time in the guts of several species of fleas, doing whatever it is bacteria do from day to day. Every so often, under certain conditions that medical science is as yet, sadly, unable to describe, one of *Y. pestis'* genes, the hemin storage gene, switches on and causes something not unlike a Jekyll–Hyde transformation. The formerly placid bacterium becomes incredibly virulent and the flea, frenzied, begins energetically biting anything with warm blood, generously spreading *Y. pestis* far and wide. The result is a plague epidemic.

This sequence of events is akin to what happens every so often in the world of banking. Most of the time, bankers are prudent folks who conscientiously go about their business, always on the watch for new opportunities. As these opportunities arise, especially if the profitability appears to be very high and the risk of default very low, more and more bankers pile into these newly discovered putative profit generators. Occasionally, the bankers' native prudence and caution becomes overpowered by optimism, and later on by greed. Some number of times, about once a decade or so, the seeming opportunity turns out to have unseen or underanalyzed or misunderstood inherent risk. When these two events converge, the result is what amounts to a banking epidemic.

Examples of this phenomenon abound. Did you ever hear of sovereign loans? These were very popular in the 1970s and 1980s at certain large banks. The premise behind the strategy of making such loans was that nations do not voluntarily declare bankruptcy. Walter Wriston, the chairman of Citibank, put this sentiment even more baldly, "Countries don't go broke." With interest rates rising in the mid-1970s and banks looking around furiously for safe, high-interest loans, this style of lending rapidly gained a following, first at international money-center banks, then at large regional banks. The banking industry moved a major chunk of capital into loans to these nations, sometimes even in preference to lending to current corporate and individual customers. The perception was that it was almost entirely risk-free to make huge high-interest loans to these governments, *unsecured by anything except the full faith and credit of the borrower*. For the typical nation under consideration at the time, the former part of this alleged security was mostly imaginary and the latter nonexistent. No matter. The bankers collected whopping loan origination fees, expecting to earn lots of interest and enjoy the Nirvana of years of high profits. After all, since the borrowing nation wouldn't ever declare formal bankruptcy, then, short of a revolution, what could go wrong?

What could go wrong became evident quickly. The borrowing nations in many cases simply decided not to pay. Ouch! The bankers were left without any recourse. There was no collateral to liquidate. There was no one to sue, or, at least, there was no court with jurisdiction. The bankers were just plain stuck until such time as they could get the taxpayers to bail them out or write these funky loans down or off the books. This entire little drama was a platinum-plated example of self-induced event risk throughout.

Other instances of this unfortunate and ugly phenomenon include the Mexican *Tesobonos* bond mess in 1995, the savings and loan fiasco-cum-fraud in the 1980s, and, waiting in the wings yet to be discovered, the exposure of banks to the dot.com/New Economy bomb of 2000–2001. In all these instances, the pattern of first incautiousness, then greed, then fear, then desperation, then—invariably over the last half-century—bailout has been remarkably consistent.

Grist for Our Mill

While all this information may be fascinating, we as traders are still more interested in the practical benefit we can derive from this examination of the other methods of making money with money. From the dealings of gamblers, bookmakers, and bankers, we can recognize several principles that we very much want to incorporate in our approach to markets. Successful bookmakers and bankers expect to win in the vast majority of their selections of profit possibilities because they have arranged their affairs so that each selection has a *high probability of success and positive expectation of profit*. We must determinedly seek out strategies offering identical features. Bankers, while generally conservative in outlook, are nevertheless ready to embrace a new opportunity provided that it meets their criteria for profitability and risk. Similarly, we must keep open minds regarding trading. It's likely enough that the trading strategies seemingly everyone uses are not superior in either the short or the long run, and it's a dead certainty that there are many more highly profitable opportunities in trading than those to be found at the NYSE and on NASDAQ.

Further, we should note that those who succeed at making money with money do not try to win by hitting financial home runs, choosing instead to try to earn a profit steadily and keep their expectation of return positive at all times. We must do so, too, and disdain the false lure of trying for the big score. Successful high-skill gamblers and bankers have an ability to seek out profitable opportunities (bookmakers, as a rule, have these opportunities pre-defined by the nature of their particular business). We must attempt to develop this ability.

We can also clearly see certain actions to be avoided. Unlike the low-skill gambler, we must avoid playing games (in our case, using strategies) that have a demonstrable statistical bias against us. To avoid the most serious fate that can befall the bookmaker, we must attempt to recognize external event risk and to stay as far away from it as possible. When some event risk is unavoidable, the typical situation in trading, we must both diversify away from it and lay off as much we can to other parties. To avoid the self-inflicted damages occasionally suffered by the banker, we must always be aware of the possibilities of encountering a gold brick masquerading as an opportunity. To avoid willful self-destruction in the fashion of the fictional Fast Eddie Felson, we must design and adhere to a discipline.

We now have in hand some ideas about which principles to incorporate into a method of making money with money via trading. It's time to examine the nature of trading and organize our thoughts about the types of risk involved therein. For traders, risk is a paradoxical beast—it must be present in order for us to have the opportunity to profit, yet if we embrace it too closely we may cut our own throats. Fortunately for us, there are a large number of ways to avoid or minimize the danger of excessive risk to our jugular vein . . . and to our pocketbooks.

CHAPTER 2

On the Trail of a Method

Risk, Leverage, and Markets

I'll take my chances . . . I'll risk it all.
—Bob Seger, "You'll Accomp'ny Me"

What a maroon!
—Bugs Bunny

Trading and investing, as we know from experience, are enterprises in which we attempt to forecast a change in the price of something over some period of time, and buy or sell that something accordingly. One reasonable view of the primary difference between investing and trading is the time frame over which we commit our capital to a position in the markets. From this condition, we might, as many do, consider Warren Buffett to be the ultimate investor, for his time frame seems to be nearly infinite. In the same fashion, we might look at Marty Schwartz as an example of the ultimate trader—his time frame for any given commitment of capital, by his own testimony, may well be measured in minutes. What amount of time distinguishes a trade from an investment? Any dividing line is likely arbitrary, so we'll just *be* arbitrary here and define a trade as a commitment of capital having duration of less than one year. If this isn't your favorite definition, feel perfectly free to boo, hiss, or throw a brickbat.

Risks Peculiar to Trading

Having examined the other ways of making money with money, our next logical step on the road to developing a successful methodology for trading must be to examine its comparative risk profile. The trader encounters the same types of risk as do the banker, the bookie, and the gambler, but risk operates rather differently for the trader. Certain types of risk are present in trading that are only sometimes or not at all to be found in the other worlds of making money with money. The first of these, which every trader encounters, is *contest risk*. When you or I enter a trade, we must expend a bit of capital in the form of a brokerage commission, much as the poker player must ante up before contesting the next hand. Commission costs, though, are only a portion of contest risk, and not infrequently the least portion. There is a good deal more to the notion of contest risk.

In terms of pricing, the trader's markets aren't like retail markets such as Armani, Bloomingdale's, Wal-Mart, or McDonald's. If the price tag at Bloomie's reads $399.50, then that's what we'll have to pay for the jacket or the chair or whatever (at least, that's what we'll pay today—the item might be on sale tomorrow), no choice and no haggling. In retail America, the seller quotes a single price. If we want the goods, we pay the stated figure, and that's the end of the discussion almost all the time.

Historically, this state of affairs is very unusual, because single-price retail markets have not been the norm for pricing in the bulk of the world over the centuries. The bazaars of the Middle East, for example, even today treat the stated price as only the starting point for negotiation between buyer and seller. The folks at McDonald's, by contrast, would frown rather darkly if we were to walk in and bid only $0.79 for a Big Mac.

The trader's markets, even though they are also retail markets in one sense, are never single-price markets. The price of any asset, whether IBM shares, Inco's 7.75% bonds of 2016, or November soybeans is always stated as current bid/current offer. The NYSE specialist might quote IBM at 107.05 bid/107.07 offered, just two pennies differential, but the trader who trades "at the market" will pay all or most of this spread. This is the exchange bookmaker's profit margin. When trading "at the market," we will pay the offer price in most cases, and the bid/ask spread or a large fraction thereof becomes part of our contest risk. This form of contest risk varies directly with the liquidity of the market in which we're trading. IBM shares are exceptionally liquid and trade in large volume most days and the bid/ask spread is tiny, but there is no practical upper limit to how large this spread can be in less liquid markets.

There's one other form of contest risk that occasionally dents our wallets, called *slippage*. If we buy or sell an asset at the market or use a stop order to enter or exit a position, some number of times we will experience the thrill of being "skidded." While our market order is making its way to the trading floor, the market may move suddenly and sharply, and whoops, here comes our order, and WHAM! it's filled at the now-current market conditions, which are rarely favorable to us. The difference between our intended entry or exit price and the price we ultimately obtain is the slippage, and we must include this amount in our contest risk.

We can readily limit contest risk by negotiating a lower commission rate with the brokerage or by shopping among brokerages for a lower rate. In addition, we can reduce the bid/ask and slippage forms of this risk by trading only in highly liquid markets, or by avoiding the use of market and stop orders except in the most liquid markets. At first glance, it would seem that we should apply these tactics at every chance, because, unlike the penalty exacted by other types of risk, when we incur contest risk, those dollars are gone forever. Paradoxically though, and unlike with other types of risk, it may not be to our advantage to be ruthless about minimizing contest risk. If we receive excellent service, good executions of our orders, accurate accounting, and prompt and fair resolution of the occasional account problems from a brokerage, we may quite reasonably decide that these advantages are easily worth a few extra commission dollars per trade. Regarding markets, a decision on our part to participate in *only* the most liquid markets may (and almost surely will, over time) conjure up other costs in the form of lost opportunity in the less liquid markets.

Information and Knowledge Risk

Mathematicians many times view trading in the context of game theory. If we examine trading from this perspective, then, because trading involves prediction and prediction requires information, we quickly come to the realization that trading is at bottom a game in which information would seem to be the most significant variable factor. *Nothing* ever happens in markets until and unless someone changes his mind. What is the principal cause of a trader changing his mind? The acquisition of new information, undoubtedly. If you do not own Microsoft shares or T-Bills or July corn at 10:00 A.M., but do own one or more of these at 1:00 P.M., then obviously *something* has occurred that changed your mind about the desirability of owning these assets. I'll lay heavy odds that this something was your acquisition of some sort of information concerning the asset(s) you subsequently bought.

Information comes complete with its own built-in risks, and these pose a serious difficulty for us. If a new piece of information comes into our possession, we must answer several questions correctly, and on occasion we must do this immediately or almost so. First, is the information *relevant* to our position in the market, and how immediately relevant is it? Fortunately, this question tends to be pretty easy to answer. If we're trading IBM shares, we recognize instantly that a screeching headline about, say, soybeans has no relevance to our situation. If the President proposes a new health care plan, this might be relevant. IBM might, down the road a piece, obtain a fat contract for the computers needed to manage the patient database or something similar, but the immediate effect of such an announcement on IBM's share price is likely nil. If IBM and Cisco Systems announce that they're exploring some sort of joint venture, however, it's a dead cinch that this news will affect our position materially right this minute, and for some little time to come. Unfortunately, not all information is as unequivocal as these examples may imply.

More important and less easily decided, is this new information *accurate*? Is the source reliable, has the information been confirmed, *can* it be confirmed? Might it be an honest error, for instance a simple typo in a newswire story? Even more problematically, might this putative new information turn out to be instead deliberate disinformation being spread around by another market participant? Naahh, that would never happen, would it?

As if these questions aren't sufficiently difficult, on obtaining a new piece of information we must ask ourselves whether this information is *timely*. Do most or all the other market participants already have it, too? Certainly we must assume that, if a large majority of participants in a market have had this information in hand for some time before we obtain it, they've already made their decisions and this market has already changed price to reflect any changes in the collective market view. When this is the case, we must as a rule discard this information as being useless for our subsequent market decisions. Here the difficulty is obvious: how can we possibly figure out how many other traders have already acted on our purportedly new bit of information?

This problem of evaluation becomes still more complex when we ask ourselves the remaining question, specifically, is this new information *complete*? Do we have the whole story, or is there more information pertinent to *this* information shortly to come? Is the source of the information playing the "good news/bad news" game by releasing a piece of mildly favorable news about a company, a company's debt, or a futures market, with some absolutely rotten news soon to follow? How can traders resolve all these questions about and vagaries of information?

We can't. At least, I freely admit that I can't. If you can, that's terrific and would you please send me a detailed how-to commentary! In the meantime, I've accepted as an axiom that I, as a trader, am at or near the bottom of the information chain. I firmly believe that I will never have information that is simultaneously relevant, accurate, timely and complete, and I trade according to this premise.

This viewpoint directly implies that I must stay away generally from very short-term trades, day trades, and scalping, and I do, with rare and very specific exceptions. Why? The shorter the term of the trade—any trade, any market—the more seriously the result of the trade will be affected by the indifferent quality of the information I have, and by the introduction of new information into the marketplace during the term of the trade. The arrival of new information relevant to a market is not predictable, except when its introduction occurs on a previously published schedule. Taken another way, the short-term trade has less time, hence less opportunity, to recover from the appearance of adverse information. I assume that the information I have in hand isn't topflight to start with, reasonably so because it almost never is. If I'll suffer losses when new information appears, then I would be taking much the short end of the odds to attempt a trade based on this information in the affected market over the very short term.

Perhaps you're saying to yourself, "Hey, new information can work in favor of your trade, too!" True enough, but this is a gambler's reasoning. When trading to win, we traders must continually work to minimize risk, and there's no long-term success to be had by employing trading strategies whose success depends on what is, to all intents, the toss of a coin. Will a company's earnings exceed market expectations in the quarterly report due out today? Moody's is about to announce new bond ratings; will the company's debt be downgraded? The USDA will release the *Cattle On Feed* report later in the week; will the numbers be down 3% or up 2%? I don't know the answers to any of those questions, and I don't give a hoot because I guarantee you that I won't be initiating a trade in that company's stock or in its bonds, or in cattle futures either, under these assumed conditions. These are instances of the purest form of information risk, and I want no part of that risk. Neither do you.

This is not to say that we should (or could) avoid the introduction of new information into the markets we trade, that we should stumble around in ignorant bliss. What a silly notion. It is, however, to say that we can in some large majority of cases substantially reduce information risk in our trading. There are at least three practical ways to do this.

First, if a news event is pending in a market in which we're considering a trade, we have the very obvious option of waiting until after the event to enter the trade. Not enough traders use this simple tactic, in my experience. Any number of traders I know will plunge right ahead, with the attitude "How bad can the bad news be?", to which I always respond, "Why would you ever consider *paying* to find out?"

Next, we can deliberately select trades of a longer term, two weeks instead of a day, a month instead of a week, five months instead of one. This adjustment allows normal market forces, however you prefer to define them, time to operate in our favor. After all, we buy something *because* we expect "the market," by which term we of course mean the participants in that market, to bid the price higher. Similarly, we sell *because* we expect other market participants to be selling in the future and drive the price lower. Ah, but neither process is instant for the most part. Both ordinarily require some amount of time in order to operate, and we are shortsighted indeed if we do not allow the other market participants a convenient amount of time to put dollars into our pockets.

The remaining way to cut information risk down to size involves our choice of broad markets in which to trade, and we look into this selection process in some detail later in this chapter. We can't do so just yet because there are still a number of types of risk in trading we need to examine.

Another structural feature of our set of broad markets generates an off-beat form of information risk. The more popular the market in terms of its total participants, the more information is generated. The more information we have (I'm tempted here to call the bulk of it "pseudo-information"), the more difficult it is to separate the wheat from the chaff, particularly when considering the financial press. Which media sources, which journalists reliably report fact untainted by opinion, and which are little or nothing more than gossipmongers with straight teeth and more hairspray than the law allows? How can we traders tell the difference? Should we even bother trying?

Notwithstanding the huge volume of indiscriminate bilge passing for information that is belched out by the financial media, we can for the most part dodge the risk it represents to our capital. Look, five zillion other people, some of them traders, are reading, hearing, or watching this same information at the same time we are, and the reporter had to learn it from another source well before we acquire it. Likely enough, the source who gave the information to the reporter had, in turn, received it from a prior source. Now, these prior sources didn't only tell one person, did they? Very unlikely. In short, far too many people already are aware of this information for it to be of any practical use to us in the short term. If we want to avoid being penalized by information risk here, the proper thing to do is to *take no short-term action whatever* based on information broadcast in the media.

There is one class of exceptions to this policy, involving what might be called "hard data." When a company reports quarterly earnings, when the Federal Reserve releases money supply figures, when the USDA publishes crop estimates or the DOE provides current petroleum storage levels, these are—usually—hard data. Most participants in markets affected by these presumably definitive data accept them as accurate and act on them as would seem to be warranted. Unless we happen to possess accurate and reliable contrary information, we should join the majority here and at least consider taking action based on these data, especially if the market reaction to the data threatens or might threaten our capital. Sure, we'll still be late, relatively, in our reaction but, as I'm certain you agree, in these cases protection of our capital must take priority over any doubts we may harbor regarding the quality or the source of the information. First things first, after all.

Stock markets being by far the most popular market in the United States, this phenomenon of what should likely be called pseudo-information risk is most dangerous to stock traders. Futures traders, I'd say, are next most at risk, followed by those who deal in bonds.

With a little care, the conscientious trader can effectively erase certain risks from consideration. One of these is *knowledge risk*, the occasional risk that a trader, for some reason, will not be aware of an *existing* condition in some market, will trade in that market, and will be adversely affected by this lack of knowledge. Examples of this type of risk are fairly infrequent, except for the crapshooter who is impersonating a trader, but when they occur they can be heartstopping.

In late 1999, I had sold several January 2000 NYBOT coffee put options. This trade was based on, among other things, the historically valid premise that the coffee market tends to have finished its harvest selloff by that point in the year, and prices typically do not proceed much lower through the expiration date of the options. At the time, I had believed the options' expiration date was the first Friday in the month preceding the named month, which had been the case for many years. With these January 2000 options, expiration was presumably the first Friday in December 1999. (I have absolutely no idea why this is, by the way. Listed stock options expire, reasonably, in their named month. Why not futures options too? A few markets' options do, but most don't. It's an enduring mystery.)

Whoa, not so fast. It became evident shortly, much later than I'd have liked, that the exchange had changed the expiration date to the second Friday in the preceding month, beginning with these very January 2000 options. In fact, they'd notified the exchange members of this change more than a year earlier. The trading calendar my brokerage sent out did not mention this change. The exchange websites themselves (both of them, www.csce.com and www.nybot.com) did not mention this change. Rats and double rats! All of a sudden, the conditions of the trade were different than I'd thought. The exchange kindly sent me a dated fax confirming the announcement of this change, which I keep as a reminder of direct experience with knowledge risk. Because I didn't have the facts in hand, I gave myself the rare privilege of sitting a week longer than intended in a time-based trade, thus accepting more market risk without any compensation for it. This is no way to profit in trading, I guarantee.

The trade had a happy, if highly annoying, outcome. During the term of the trade, coffee prices moved much higher, far, far away from the striking prices of the puts I'd written. In that extra week, the coffee market was completely berserk, trading over an enormous range, but luckily nowhere near my short puts. The options I'd sold expired worthless and a Merry Christmas was had by all. It didn't have to be that way, though, didn't have to be nearly that pleasant. And sitting through that extra week wasn't at all pleasant . . . but having to do so was my fault, no one else's.

This form of knowledge risk can be almost completely eliminated by following this maxim: "When in doubt, find out. When not in doubt, check it out anyway." Nothing but naivete or laziness can really expose us to knowledge risk, except when legal issues intrude on one of our trading positions. Brokers are fine; they'll certainly try to give you straight information when you ask, but you cannot rely on them to inform you of situations such as occurred in this nerve-wracking coffee trade. They simply may not be aware of such changes themselves, as here. Pick up the telephone, call the exchange, e-mail them, fax them, whatever you find convenient. It is entirely to the exchanges' advantage to see to it that the trading public has accurate information about the products traded on their floors, and most exchanges' personnel in my experience give a sincere good-faith effort to provide this.

Risk Me Once and Risk Me Twice and Risk Me Once Again

When we enter a trade, we become subject to yet another type of risk unknown to the gambler and the bookmaker, although our banking friends see a form of it from time to time. Being sensible people, we attempt to limit the dollar or percentage loss that an adverse market movement might cause us. To this end we set a loss limit either by placing a stop-loss order with our brokerage or by carefully watching our new trade and preparing to exit at a (presumably predetermined) point if the trade moves against us. The risk that may accompany these pragmatic tactics, called *wiggle risk*, occurs when we are consistently too conservative in setting our loss limit.

You and I both know from long experience that some markets' prices fluctuate more over time than other markets' prices do. If we would try to set our loss limits, therefore, at the same dollar or percentage level for every market in which we trade, it's unfortunate but unavoidable that in some considerable percentage of trades our fixed loss limit will end up being either too generous or too cautious. Now, no one in his right mind would advocate accepting, except infrequently and in very specific instances, "too much" risk in any trade, but demanding "too little" risk is often a worse poison.

If we systemically insist on too little risk, we will be taken out of our trades with a loss far too frequently, simply due to the ordinary price fluctuations of the market. We must expend some effort, then, to devise a means through which we can set acceptable and realistic risk levels market by market. If we don't, if we attempt to trade IBM shares with a 3% risk, or the wheat markets with a 7-cent stop, we will accomplish nothing except the loss of our capital and possibly becoming poster children for the Wiggle Risk Prevention League. I suppose it might be interesting to be on such a poster, but, on the whole, I'd rather be in Philadelphia.

Our unfriendly acquaintance, counterparty risk, is definitely present in the world of trading. Actually, this risk causes more headaches for the incautious trader than it does for the other parties who attempt to make money with money. First off, we have more total parties involved in our enterprise than have the banker, the bookie, and the gambler, and the very presence of these extra parties increases the likelihood of encountering one form of counterparty risk. We usually place our order with a trading desk, or with a broker who relays it to a trading desk, which in turn passes it along to a trader on the exchange floor. When our order is executed, both we and whoever has taken the opposite side of our trade must be informed, the two orders matched up and cleared, and the books of the brokerage(s) adjusted to reflect both our and the other trader's new position(s).

Simple mechanical errors in clearing our trade are rather common, but are easily fixed up after the fact with no threat to our capital. We call our broker and point out that we bought 800 shares of General Electric, not 300 as the confirmation slip says, or that we sold 10 December crude oil at 21.92, not 21.82. In the great majority of cases, our broker agrees straightaway with our viewpoint, sets to work putting matters to rights, and that's the end of it. We should, of course, facilitate this process, because both we and the broker will make inadvertent verbal or typographical errors once in a while. We'll just insist that the broker repeat our order before sending it off to the exchange floor, and we should without doubt maintain a written record of the orders we place. These practices will avoid all or almost all instances of misunderstanding, or what might be called accidental counterparty risk.

Like the banker and the insurance bookmaker, we may sometimes encounter plain fraud. There's no avoiding the fact that there are dishonest brokers and brokerages, notwithstanding the efforts of the SEC, NASD, CFTC, and NFA, and we deal with these persons at our peril. However, by exercising a little care and applying a bit of economic common sense, we should be able to elude the clutches of these slimy bottom-feeders. We have a couple of straightforward ways to do so.

The better and easier way to avoid a less than scrupulously honest broker is to know your broker personally and over a long period of time during which he has been a broker. Too obvious, you say? Perhaps, but some traders do not seem to agree. I'll tell you right now that I had known my present futures broker personally for 17 years before opening a trading account with him. Previously, I'd known my former futures broker for 19 years before dealing with him. To date, I can't recall any sort of trading dispute or account problem that wasn't resolved more or less immediately, within the week at worst. Just as for the banker, our having personal knowledge of the people with whom we deal lowers our risk. Still too obvious? All right, then tell me why boiler rooms and bucket shops prosper (ideally, only for a short time). A considerable number of traders and would-be traders must not share our reasoned view here, evidently.

If taking a long time to get to know a broker well is inconvenient, you've another good choice. The Internet is indispensable to traders, and one reason why is that all the regulatory agencies publish their customer complaint records, and their compliance and disciplinary actions involving brokers and brokerages, online, entirely free for your inspection and use. If you're considering opening an account with a particular broker, and this individual appears as much as once in these agencies' complaint files within the past five years, then find another broker. True, an honest broker might have been tarred by an idiotic or unfair customer complaint, but this is not our problem because we have fundamentally no way to determine whether the customer complaint was either utterly warranted or lunacy in action. Avoid this broker, period, unless he or she happens to be your brother- or sister-in-law, and doing so would cause severe domestic discord (in which case, good luck!).

Avoiding counterparty risk at the hands of a corrupt brokerage firm is a trickier proposition. Searching the regulatory agencies' files is absolutely an aid in throwing out of consideration a bunch of such firms, but we cannot apply the "one-complaint-and-out" standard here. The regulators, over two or three or x years, will have received customer complaints about practically every brokerage, including the most competent and straight-shooting ones. Some customers appear to be born to complain. (And by some curious circumstance, they seem very often, in my experience, to be lousy traders, too. Odd, isn't it?) Instead of looking around for one complaint when examining the regulators' files, look for a pattern. Corrupt brokerages and their principals usually sail as close to the regulatory winds as possible, which tends to result in a semicontinuous stream of complaints and official actions against them.

Another excellent filter for undesirable brokerages is your group of friends and acquaintances who trade. Likely enough, you talk trading with them some or a lot of the time, and it must be to your advantage to compare notes about brokerages with other traders whom you know and respect. The old adage "investigate before you invest" doesn't apply only to whichever stock or bond or future you may be considering. It applies with extra force to those with whom you may be considering employing as brokers.

Capacity Risk—It's All Archimedes' Fault

Traders, more frequently than bankers or bookmakers, can be and often are seriously threatened by the form of capacity risk specific to trading. Any trader who doesn't take this threat seriously to heart and doesn't keep a watchful eye every day for the possible approach of this risk is almost certainly doomed to failure, typically sooner than later. "Hold on here," some of you are thinking right now, "you said earlier that capacity risk only exists when I use leverage. Well, I don't, I buy my stocks and bonds for cash and put them right away in the safe-deposit box. Why do I even want to hear about capacity risk?"

If this is what you're thinking, or even screaming out loud at me, you're absolutely correct. I did say that, meant every word of it, and it's inarguably true . . . but look a little deeper, please. We're talking about trading. If you pay cash for your financial assets, the answer to your question is very simple: you're not a trader. You sound much more like an investor. You certainly do not care about capacity risk. Best skip on to the section about markets before you blow a gasket.

The *efficient use* of capital is necessary to success in any enterprise of making money with money. Zero leverage is not an efficient use of capital, and this is easily demonstrated by observation. Who are the most steadily successful at making money with money? Indisputably, they are the competent bookmaker and the prudent banker, and these folks are *leveraged to some degree all the time*, sometimes quite highly. If leverage is both useful and profitable for successful professionals, why would any trader or would-be trader avoid, disdain, fear, or even hate using this tool? Right you are. Traders don't. Instead, they use the tools at hand, leverage being one, and simultaneously look for effective ways to minimize the implied capacity risk incurred thereby.

As noted previously, the measure of our capacity risk is the probability that, at some time in the future, we will come to have insufficient capital to continue trading. This is related but not identical to the well-known statistical problem called "gambler's ruin." Due to the comparative complexity of the broad markets in which we might deal—specifically stocks, bonds, and futures—analyzing capacity risk is more difficult for us than analyzing its statistical cousin is for the gambler. Unfortunately, stock markets apply one set of rules governing leverage, bond markets apply a similar but not identical set, and futures markets a different set entirely. This needlessly prolix situation makes our efforts to evaluate capacity risk across different markets a little bit dicey, because we can't compare apples directly to apples. However, if the comparison of this risk among several markets poses problems, evading such risk does not.

Foremost, we can avoid a large amount of capacity risk by insisting on using the time-honored tactic of diversifying our capital into several activities, and by using several different trading strategies. Please note that the term "activities" does not necessarily imply "broad markets," plural. If one of the set of tradable broad markets offers or appears to offer us a healthy statistical edge as compared to the other broad markets, then the notion of diversification should here be taken to mean only diversification among various markets within that one broad market.

Those who believe in the philosophy of asset allocation are probably apoplectic at this last statement, for this concept is anathema to them. Sorry, but I'm not about to keep 5%, or whatever amount, of my capital in ersatz "precious" metals just on the off chance that the whole of the economic world will melt down some day. This is just silly. Why the devil should anyone hold an alleged "asset" that has steadily lost value for decades, whether AT&T shares or gold? Nor do I fancy clipping bond coupons and watching inflation and taxes take the bulk of the earnings. This isn't trading in any case, and it's unsound investing too, in my view.

Shortening the Lever—Trimming Capacity Risk

We have a second easy and effective way to reduce capacity risk. We can, and will, steadfastly *refuse* to use all the leverage that any market may offer. It's child's play to obtain gigantic amounts of leverage in any of the broad tradable markets, but it's almost surely to our disadvantage if we do this in our trading. One of the most spectacularly successful financial ventures in history, Long-Term Capital Management, used almost unimaginable leverage in their portfolio, by design. This organization had the advantages of enormous capital, probably the finest assemblage of traders, analysts, statisticians, and theorists in the entire history of markets, more trading experience than you and I will acquire throughout our lifetimes, and immediate access to more complete, timely, and accurate information than we'll ever see.

They went bust. Even with all these advantages, which you and I can only dream of having, *they* went bust. They were done in ultimately by nothing other than the capacity risk we're discussing right now, and by keeping the bulk of their huge portfolio in illiquid and not-very-liquid instruments. Their deliberate policy of maximizing leverage put them into a situation one day in which they didn't have and couldn't raise enough capital to stay in the game, *and* they couldn't get out of their positions without incurring monstrous losses, well in excess of their total capital. Uniquely (at least so far), none other than William McDonough, president of the New York Federal Reserve Bank, had to convene and persuade (or dragoon) a consortium of lenders to provide interim financing in order to allow an orderly liquidation of LTCM's portfolio. This portfolio was so large and involved so many diverse assets that the liquidation process took about two years to complete.

If, even after considering this example, the mortal danger of using too much leverage is still not perfectly clear, let me just embellish this point by citing the words of the late Harrison Roth. He wrote the book *LEAPS* (Irwin, 1994), an enormously entertaining, informative, and readable discussion about the uses of and strategies for trading long-term listed stock options (by the way, if you're a trader and haven't read this book, you owe it to yourself to do so). Margin requirement is the inverse of leverage, and minimum margin is maximum leverage, correct? He condemned the use of too much leverage elegantly and succinctly: "Minimum margin is a sign of minimum intelligence." And he was dead-bang right in that sentiment, then, now, and forever.

If we are pure asset traders, only trading shares and bonds and physical commodities, leverage is completely measurable. When we add derivative instruments such as options and futures to our trading, leverage is measurable only statistically, hence only approximately. In the text, we'll define the amount of leverage in a trade as the actual or statistical value(s) of the instrument(s) we trade, divided by the amount of capital we are required to have in hand before entering the trade, minus one, expressed as a percentage. If we pay cash for an asset, our leverage is zero. If Microsoft shares are trading at 60 and we buy 300 shares, market value $18,000, but we only commit $9,000 of capital, our leverage is 18,000 / 9000 = 2, minus 1, = 1, or 100%. By applying this definition of leverage and examining the risk profiles of the various broad markets, we'll gain more useful information concerning which of the set of the broad tradable markets may be most advantageous for our trading.

Which Hog Shall We Slaughter?— Selecting a Market

An essential part of developing a successful trading methodology is to select *which* broad market offers us a convenient and useful amount of leverage, contains fewer inherent disadvantages, and has the lowest relative levels of structural and external event risk. I only know of one way to make this selection, and that's to look at each of these conditions in each broad market in turn. Let's do just this with a gimlet eye and see what we can discern.

Checking on the amount of leverage available to us in each broad market is a straightforward proposition, and a good way to start. Using leverage in stock and bond markets is easy; we merely open up a separate account with our brokerage, universally called a margin account. The brokerage will cheerfully lend us up to 50% of the market value of the shares or bonds we purchase, assuming only that we're dealing in NYSE or AMEX or a majority of NASDAQ stocks, selected foreign stocks, or in a very broad group of corporate bonds. This 50% level is set by the Federal Reserve's Regulation T, hasn't changed in decades, and allows for leverage of up to 100%, a perfectly acceptable figure.

The problem when we trade stocks or bonds on margin is that the brokerage will also, even more cheerfully, charge us interest on this loan.

Whether we finally profit or lose on a margined trade, we have voluntarily increased our contest risk by paying interest dollars to the brokerage. This increase must be counted as a black mark against these two markets regarding our practical use of leverage. Also, as always, where there's leverage there's capacity risk, and when trading stocks or bonds on margin, the capacity risk point is defined exactly and by rule. If the price of the stock or bond moves in such a way that our capital stake in our position, our equity, falls to less than 25%, none other than the Federal Reserve will demand more capital from us. We can at that point either liquidate the position or open up the checkbook. Brokerages, being prudent enterprises, will rarely let our account equity fall to this level, and will issue their own internal demand for more capital well before the Fed gets into the act.

Trading in the futures markets offers us sizeable leverage automatically. We don't have to ask for a loan or open a separate type of account. The various futures exchanges set down a basic capital requirement for trading in each of their markets, thus defining the amount of leverage available to us. This requirement, usually if imprecisely also called "margin," is functionally a performance bond that we post as an assurance we will be responsible for any losses in our trading. Having set the basic capital requirement, futures exchanges then do something remarkably practical. They subsequently modify this requirement according to current market conditions by applying a formal mathematical model to evaluate the risk of our position(s).

In the late 1980s, the Chicago Mercantile Exchange developed a formal model for approximating the level of risk in any given portfolio and began the practice of applying the risk thus modeled to the margin requirements for traders. This model was named SPAN®, for "Standard Portfolio Analysis of risk" and has become universally used by major futures exchanges worldwide and, interestingly, by several stock exchanges (none of them, unfortunately, American). The SPAN model was derived from the work of the late Fischer Black, Myron Scholes, and Robert Merton, and is quite generous to traders in the amount of leverage it offers. Moreover, in futures trading, there is no lending of capital by anyone to anyone under any except one rare circumstance, and from this auspicious condition we gain a double-barreled advantage. We pay no interest on the levered amount, and we should actually earn interest on the amount of capital in our trading account that is not currently applied to margin our positions.

SPAN and SPAN-like methods of setting margin requirements, called *portfolio margining*, are advantageous to traders, but embedded within them is yet another risk. When the SPAN parameters—the values inserted into the various formulae in the mathematical model—change rapidly due to market movement or other conditions, our margin requirement will change correspondingly, and sometimes sizably. This is eminently reasonable because the purpose of a statistical model, SPAN or any other, is to attempt to reflect conditions in the real world. In the event of a significant increase in the SPAN requirement, whether or not the market(s) have moved against our position(s), we will again face the choice of liquidating some position(s) or committing more capital.

If a market is quiet, SPAN generates a lower margin requirement figure for a position in that market, and a higher one if that market is unusually active. This is the problem. We traders have no reliable way to tell when a market will suddenly become highly volatile, and when we hold a position in a market which has become so, our margin requirement might rise so sharply that we can be hauled off to the land of capacity risk quite involuntarily. In plain English, we can get blown right out of a position. The good news here is that we already know how to negate or minimize this risk. Didn't we agree a little earlier that we will not accept all the leverage available to us? If we follow this policy faithfully and use only some fraction of the maximum leverage offered, we will reduce our capacity risk radically, even cut it to zero at times.

Futures markets offer us leverage without direct cost, and this is a clear positive for trading in these markets. Stock and corporate bond markets limit leverage to a specific but useful amount, and U.S. government bond markets to a higher amount (900% at this writing). The leverage available in futures trading ranges roughly from 300% to 10,000%, and varies by specific market, as illustrated in Table 2.1.

Overall, we'll give stocks and corporate bonds a plus here for restricting the maximum leverage available, thereby making it more difficult for an unwary trader to fall into the clutches of capacity risk. A different plus goes to futures and government bonds for the flexibility that the larger leverage in these markets grants us, with the proviso that it is completely our own responsibility to avoid abusing such leverage. We have more to enter on our scorecard, though, and next on the list are structural risks, those native features of markets that threaten the trader's profitability by the simple fact of their existence.

Asymmetry Is Poison—We Want to Play the Whole Game

Some people assume that all the markets we trade are symmetric, that is, we can buy or sell assets with equal ease and the rules of trading are the same for all market participants. This is a reasonable assumption, theoretically. By the classical definition, a free market is a mechanism for the exchange of goods or

TABLE 2.1 Leverage Available, Selected Futures Markets, December 26, 2001

Contract Month	Contract	Closing Price	Contract Value	SPAN Init. Requirmt	Leverage Offered (%)	Equity (%)
Mar	Corn	2.08–6	10437.50	405	2477	3.88
Mar	Chi Wheat	2.84–4	14225.00	743	1814	5.51
Mar	Soybeans	4.28–2	21412.50	810	2543	3.93
Feb	Live Cattle	70.75	28300.00	810	3394	2.95
Feb	Lean Hogs	55.47	22188.00	1080	1954	5.12
Feb	Pork Bellies	77.65	31060.00	1620	1817	5.50
Feb	Gold	279.60	27960.00	1350	1971	5.07
Feb	H-G Copper	68.95	17237.50	1350	1177	8.49
Mar	Palladium	424.00	42400.00	6750	528	18.94
Mar	Silver	4.543	22715.00	1350	1583	6.32
Feb	Crude Oil	21.27˙	21270.00	3375	530	18.87
Feb	Heating Oil	59.46	24937.20	2700	824	12.13
Feb	Unld. Gasoline	60.67	25481.40	2700	844	11.84
Feb	Natural Gas	2.937	29370.00	5400	444	22.52
Mar	Cocoa	1283	12830.00	840	1427	7.01
Mar	Coffee "C"	46.65	17493.75	2100	733	13.64
Mar	Cotton #2	36.65	18250.00	998	1728	5.79
Mar	Orange Juice	95.50	14325.00	700	1946	5.14
Mar	Sugar #11	7.12	7974.40	700	1039	9.62
Mar	Can. Dollar	62.45	62450.00	608	10171	0.98
Mar	Eurocurrency	87.57	109462.50	2025	5306	1.88
Mar	Japanese Yen	76.75	95937.50	2025	4638	1.03
Mar	Swiss Franc	59.07	73837.50	1451	4989	2.00
Mar	30-Yr. U.S. Bond	100–11	100343.75	2700	3616	2.76
Mar	10-Yr. U.S. Note	103–305	103953.13	1890	5400	1.85

services between an informed seller and an informed buyer, both operating independently and able to deal without external restraint. In the practical world, though, this ain't necessarily so. In fact, it isn't so at all. While futures markets are almost perfectly symmetric, such is not the case in the stock and bond markets. This asymmetry is due to the rules governing these latter markets, and it constitutes a severe disadvantage for traders.

Because the price of anything fluctuates over time, during some portion of the time the prices of any asset or class of assets will be going down. If we trade assets during a falling market, we can generally profit only by selling an asset and repurchasing it later at a lower price, the tactic uniformly called selling short. If we cannot freely sell assets short when and as we wish in some market, this restriction directly implies that, some considerable portion of the time, we will have difficulty in making a profit trading in a downward moving market.

In stock and bond markets, the plain fact is that we *cannot* freely sell shares and bonds short as a means of initiating a trade. Selling short in these markets is actively discouraged by brokerages, unfamiliar to many (most?) brokers, restricted in practice by exchange and Federal Reserve rules, situationally impossible in too many cases, and all in all a major pain in the neck for anyone except very large traders. For the ordinary trader, therefore, for you and me, stock and bond markets are not symmetric. These markets are becoming less asymmetric, slowly, as the popularity of "basket" products like SPDRs, Diamonds, and QQQs, which traders can readily sell short at will, grows over time. Single-stock futures, which debuted in the United States in the last part of 2002, have also reduced asymmetry, all to the good as far as stock market traders are concerned.

Asymmetry still persists, though, and is really very undesirable. We've all seen price bubbles, most recently in several different groups of U.S. stocks from 1995 through about March 2000, when we watched the prices of numerous stocks bid to astonishing levels. Such market action is, of course, wonderful when we own shares (provided we took our profit at some point), but when the bubble ends, if we cannot even attempt, in many cases, to profit during the long-lasting deflation of the bubble, we've little alternative but to step away from the market. Regardless of whether now or any other time is or is not propitious for selling stocks or bonds short, the asymmetric structure of these markets is costly for us in terms of profit opportunities we must forego. The symmetry of futures markets, wherein we can sell short virtually whenever this tactic appears to be desirable, is a distinct plus factor for traders.

Your Tax Dollars at Work—Governmental Event Risk

In which broad market is event risk the highest? We've yet to consider the role of government regarding this question. Which broad market can government tamper with most easily, and which *does* it they screw up most frequently?

All the broad markets are distorted at times by arbitrary government action. We can take comfort only in that it is a little difficult for government to mess up the stock markets, because it must do so indirectly, at least in the United States. In stock markets, why look further for an example of political interference than the so-called antitrust prosecution of Microsoft Corporation? I'm not particularly a fan of Microsoft products, and I've never owned a single share of MSFT, but I'm not bloody blind, either. "Trusts" or "monopolies" or whatever today's fashionable misnomer may be, are in theory supposed to be engaging in practices that damage those who buy their products, the customer, the public. Well, I've designed computer systems for almost three decades, and I punch the keyboard in this pursuit for some hours every day. All I can tell you from experience is that Microsoft, whether I prefer their products or not, has done nothing but decrease my costs and increase my little company's productivity. If that's "damage," call me Oliver Twist. May I please have some more, sir?

My preferences are irrelevant. What *is* relevant is that it is indisputable that the government's politically bought-and-paid-for prosecution of Microsoft immediately and adversely affected every participant in the stock markets, especially those who owned technology shares. If this were a solitary incident, we might shrug it off as hard luck. Of course it wasn't, and we both know it. Political prosecutions have happened many times before and will again in the future. Should we even consider accepting the amount of risk such prosecutions represent?

The bond markets can be tampered with by government action both easily and directly. Which factors change bond prices? Certainly, the rate of inflation, sundry economic statistics, and the cost of money are at the top of this list. Would you care to guess who controls these either broadly or absolutely? Right you are. If we trade in the bond markets, by the way, we are also subject to a special form of knowledge risk. Bonds are a contract between a borrower and a lender, and the formal terms of a bond are called its *indenture*. Lawyers draw up these contracts. That's fine, and straightforward, except that lawyers are not required to write these indentures in any language resembling English. If you're not an attorney or a CPA and you've nothing better to do some afternoon, try deciphering a bond indenture. Afterwards, stand up and swear you completely understand what you've just read. Just let me bet against you, please.

Futures markets have no shortage of governmentally generated risk, either. Legislatures are very fond of tinkering with futures markets through subsidies, tariffs, tax rates and preferences, confiscation, declarations of *force majeure*, embargoes, and whatever other measures their tiny minds can concoct. In addition, governments love to collect and publish statistics, usually with the self-important presumption that these figures actually reflect conditions in the real world, and always with the blithe dismissal of Disraeli's famed and accurate observation, "There are lies, there are damned lies, and then there are statistics." If you disagree with this sentiment, please ask yourself why governments revise their own statistics so frequently after the fact. Might it be that they know the numbers aren't valid in the first place? Market participants act on them anyway, and voluntarily incorporate this risk of governmental error or incompetence in their trading decisions. We'd prefer to minimize this voluntary extra risk, wouldn't you agree?

The governmental risks discussed above are only occasional, but their existence is structural; they exist because of the nature of modern government. We must also consider the unfortunately permanent and pernicious structural risks of inflation and taxation. Inflation, after all, is only ever produced by government action—you and I, or Boeing and General Motors for that matter, can hardly manage to inflate the currency unless we are able to become highly successful counterfeiters. Similarly, you and I have no practical influence on levels of taxation, unless we would care to spend time, effort, and lots of capital to try to outbid the vast number of people who attempt, sometimes successfully, to buy off the political wolves.

To be fair, we should observe that when we trade specifically in futures, we are in fact trading in contracts, just as we are in bonds . . . but, what a difference! First, the terms of any futures contract are readily available on the exchange's Internet site or by calling the exchange or our brokerage. By contrast, try to obtain the indenture of, say, the NYSE-traded Inco 7.75% convertible bond maturing in 2016. Unless you're a professional bond trader or you get very lucky, getting that indenture will take, uh, just a little bit more effort than one phone call. Second, whether or not you know or care anything at all about, say, corn, any normally literate person will understand most or all of the CBOT corn contract without any technical assistance, and every competent brokerage is sure to have any required technical assistance available for the asking. Third, very much unlike corporate bonds, futures exchanges historically have almost never defaulted on the contracts traded on their floors. There are contracts, and then there are *contracts*, evidently.

The point of all this is that, and I hope by now it's completely clear, just as with fraud for insurance companies, governmental interference in any market is absolutely a condition of contest for us in our trading. Although government is the engine of most of the structural event risk that traders encounter, we also must contend with the menace of ordinary external event risk to our capital and profitability.

Eight Million Ways to Lose—External Event Risk

Disregarding particular markets for a moment, let's ask which other flavors of event risk we face. What about weather risks, droughts, hurricanes, or intemperate temperatures? No one controls the weather, surely. Such events will occur and we must have some means of dealing with the risk they pose. What about another risk generated by the legal system, that 12 ambulatory featherless bipeds with the proper number of chromosomes will decide out of the clear blue sky that something is a matter of "law" and thereby invade our pockets when we're merely innocent bystanders? We cannot anticipate or defend against willful morons. What about deliberate corruption, simple incompetence, or even unrealistic optimism on the part of the managers of a company whose shares or bonds we own? Any of these events will vaporize some amount of our capital, too often before we can even learn of them. Which of our set of broad markets offer us active means to protect ourselves to a considerable extent against these events and their kin?

The answer here is clear, and it eliminates one of the broad markets from our consideration. Much like insurers, from time to time we want an immediately available way to neutralize or mitigate our trading risk. Two of the broad markets offer us such a way, but one does not. This risk reduction mechanism is an options market, and moreover, an options market in which we can deal relatively easily. Options are available in the bond markets, but they are not feasible for us to use. At this time, bond options are customized to a trader's particular situation and request, are for all practical purposes completely illiquid, and are ordinarily available only to very large accounts. This situation compels me, at least, to limit my trading horizons to stocks and futures. If I cannot protect my capital by taking positive action either before or when a market moves adversely, as opposed to the simple supine action of willy-nilly accepting a loss, I see no reason whatever to trade in such a market. Invest in, maybe. Trade in, excepting pure arbitrage, no.

We can bring matters into sharper focus still by asking which remaining market, stocks or futures, offers us a better deal in terms of the frequency of and limits on occasional event risk. The logician's adage is "anything not provably impossible is possible," and this applies fully here. Any outrageous event you care to name will from time to time distort the markets in stocks as well as those in grains, meats, energy, interest rates, metals, and currencies. The occurrence of this form of event risk is probably equal over the long term in these two broad markets, but the *amount* of risk generated by any specific such event differs markedly between them.

Pick up a financial newspaper any day you like. Far more likely than not, you'll find some number of companies whose share prices have risen or fallen 15% or 25% or even 50% in a single day, due no doubt to news events or rumors about the company. Now, sometimes these events are avoidable. When definitive regulatory decisions are announced, for example an FDA decision to approve or reject a new drug, it's not uncommon to see a company's share price change by 60% or 75% or more in a day. Fortunately, the dates of most American regulatory decisions are announced well in advance, and we can dodge this sort of risk, as mentioned previously, by just staying away from the affected company's shares at the indicated time. However, there's not a single thing the trader can do to mitigate a loss caused by surprise events affecting a company, and these occur far too frequently, with too much variety, and in far too many companies' shares for my trading tastes. Just repeat "Arthur Andersen" to yourself 30 or 40 times, and if this point is not already quite clear, it will become so.

By contrast, the very nature of futures markets strongly inhibits these severe price shocks over a short period of time, barring the introduction of new supply/demand information (which, again, we can avoid by staying out of markets when such new information is known to be on its way). A 10% daily move is gigantic, and quite rare, in futures markets. Any futures market is by definition a market dealing in a standardized batch of goods, physical or financial, readily available in large amounts, and of specific quality, quantity, and/or term. These markets are therefore structurally much simpler than stock markets, thereby holding fewer undefined and opaque risks and substantially lower potential for external supply/demand surprises.

How so, you ask? Put bluntly, the Kansas City wheat market is *not* going to launch a surprise hostile takeover of the Chicago wheat market, ever. The Centers for Disease Control and Prevention are *not* going to issue a health warning about copper or 30-year bonds, ever. Nor is Indiana Jones ever going to discover the Lost Warehouse of Cocoa with ten million 62.5-kilo bags sitting inside. Yet any of these types of events, and numerous others, can and do affect share prices almost every day of the year.

The comparative impact of occasional external event risk between stock markets and futures markets changes even more when we consider the frequency of event risk stemming from the vagaries of the American legal system. Companies sue companies, people sue companies, governments sue companies (or indict them, witness again the astonishing Arthur Andersen debacle in 2002, with numerous others likely to follow down the same path). There is also exactly zero doubt that some people are working to allow a way for monkeys, cats, trees, duckbill platypuses, and probably even bacteria to sue companies. We traders cannot have any realistic idea, a priori, how such suits will be decided, because the concept of objective law, sadly, is as extinct as the dodo. We suspect, and rightly so in most cases in my experience, that we're likely to be popped in the chops when a company whose shares we own gets hauled into court.

The Philip Morris company has made cigarettes for a long time, but these are nowadays suddenly a "defective" product, so says the legal "system," and therefore this company should pay billions in "damages." Hilarious, considering that at least as far back as World War II era films, cigarettes were routinely referred to as "coffin nails." More hilarious still, every cigarette package in the United States has had an official government warning printed right on it since 1968. We traders must admit the risk of such politically driven nonsense, and it must be clearly to our advantage to avoid the risks emanating from this curious and extortive legal "system." As far as we can . . . sigh.

Contrarily, no one sues silver or Eurodollars or azuki beans or natural gas, not even the comically idiotic governor of California, who so pompously and corruptly bungled his self-created energy "crisis" in 2000–2001. Legal actions resulting from arguments over genetic modification of grains or from occasional paranoia involving supposed conspiracies (gold, crude oil, round up the usual suspects . . . yawn) may affect futures prices. However, these sorts of developments have had and will continue to have notably smaller effects on commodity prices per se, than on producers or users of commodity products. To be sure, legal flubdubbery will scorch a commodity producer or user every so often, but producers and users are usually companies, and this is not our problem unless we're trading their shares.

When we add in what might be called the human destruction factor, the answer crystallizes as to which broad market is most advantageous (or least natively disadvantageous) to trade. Corrupt or incompetent managers have wrecked more companies than you and I can name, as have periodic sudden and negative shifts in public opinion about a company. No company is immune here. Enron, famously wrecked in November 2001, had at one time the seventh largest income stream of any American company, and its managers bear, at least apparently to date, the bulk of the blame for its collapse. WorldCom, once the nation's second-largest long-distance telephone service provider, saw its share price fall to pennies and was forced to declare bankruptcy in July 2002 when it was discovered that its managers had conducted a colossal and not very subtle fraud on the shareholders and the public.

Between us, we've read or heard of hundreds of such trainwrecks. While futures markets undoubtedly have some corrupt major players, and public opinion is at least as volatile regarding commodity markets, crude oil and gasoline being obvious examples, we will never see any futures market trade at the equivalent of penny-stock levels. The sudden price moves seen when traders stampede in futures markets, in either direction, are ultimately restricted because the goods underlying a futures contract have both a demonstrably positive and also demonstrably limited economic value. The only limit on the price of a common stock is zero.

What We Want, We Have . . . And What We Have Is the Future

Successful trading is a matter of understanding and dealing effectively with risk, managing capital, and selecting favorable markets in which to trade.

Risk? When we're trading to win, we must attempt to minimize it in almost all cases. We've examined several risks we must take into account when trading, and several methods of avoiding or neutralizing or limiting them. We have much more to do here, though. Capital? We must attempt to use it efficiently, and to this end some leverage is essential, but leverage comes complete with the caveat that its careless use will—not *can*, but *will*—sink our trading ship without a trace. Markets? We want the ability to enter long and short positions freely, the ability to adjust our leverage according to the opportunity at hand, and, without any question, the ability to deal in the broad market having the lowest available levels of both structural and occasional external event risk. We also insist on being able to take positive action, through the existence of an options market, to protect our capital when we perceive that such action is desirable.

Investing in shares over the long term, particularly in U.S. shares, has been an enormously profitable proposition, but trading in shares over the shorter term is simply not the best we can do. Futures markets come much closer to offering the full set of conditions we desire for trading in a broad market, especially when regarding the essential notion of reduced event risk, and this broad market will be our principal focus henceforth. However, until now we've only looked at what amounts to a mug shot of risk on the Post Office wall. Interesting, certainly, but hardly profitable. Let's begin considering how to collect the reward.

CHAPTER 3

Profitability 101

Expectation and Options

Statistics are like bikinis. What they reveal is suggestive, but what they conceal is vital.
—Aaron Levenstein

I've used the term *expectation* frequently here, and now is a good time to define it properly and to examine how to enlist it firmly in our cause. Have a look at Figures 3.1 and 3.2, will you?

These illustrate profit and loss when we simply purchase or sell any asset to initiate a trading position. Figure 3.1 illustrates the profit and loss for a purchase and Figure 3.2 for a short sale. In these figures, the horizontal axis measures the change in the price of the asset. The vertical axis measures our profit and loss. The point labeled P_p is the price at which we prefer, before the fact, to enter the trade. The point labeled P_n is our net entry price, which differs from our preferred entry price by the amount of our contest risk, the sum of commissions, exchange fees, whatever portion of the bid-ask spread we have to pay, and any slippage that occurs. The area under the line, but above the horizontal axis, represents our potential profitability, the area above the line and below the horizontal axis, our potential loss. The solid black wedges illustrate our contest risk.

There's something pretty ugly about these diagrams. Sadly, our potential profitability is smaller than our potential loss, and this is an extremely undesirable condition in any trade. This excess loss potential, our contest risk, is trading's equivalent of the house advantage present in all casino games, and we know what happens to gamblers in casinos, don't we? Our first question must thus be how we can eliminate this initial disadvantage, this initial negative expectation of the outcome of our trade.

45

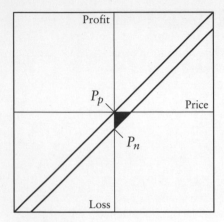

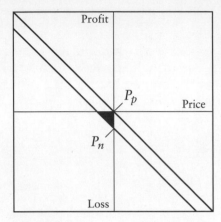

FIGURE 3.1   Profit and loss for a
purchase.

FIGURE 3.2   Profit and loss for a
short sale.

Statistically, expectation is a completely straightforward concept. It's simply the probability of success multiplied by the gain realized when successful, minus the probability of failure multiplied by the loss realized when unsuccessful, added up for all possible outcomes in a game or enterprise. In activities such as most dice games, expectation can be calculated very easily. In others, for example, bridge and backgammon, such a computation is considerably more difficult, but still usually available given a bit of effort. Sometimes, as in trading, expectation cannot be precisely calculated at all and we must instead settle for an approximation. If the result of our calculations turns out to be a positive number, we say we have a positive expectation, and vice versa.

Traders use an amazing variety of methods in an attempt to eliminate the initial negative expectation when buying and selling assets. Some traders analyze economic data to try to anticipate a market's likely future movement and trust that their analytical skills will overcome the initial negative expectation represented by the contest risk. Some traders watch for one or another pattern of price movement to appear on a chart, arguing that when a certain pattern appeared previously, a market subsequently moved in such-and-so a fashion, and will likely do so again. Some watch the activities of the traders on the exchange floors or those who manage funds, with notions of riding the coattails of the big boys. Some look for demonstrable errors in the price of an asset and try to construct an arbitrage between the mispriced asset and another one.

If there are eight million stories in the Naked City, there are at least that many ways to attempt to gain an edge in the markets. There is nothing innately wrong with any of these methods, provided only that the trader can make them work to his steady profit, but most methods share a common weakness in my view. They tend to begin a trade with a known and measurable negative expectation and depend on future events to overcome this initial risk. Is there some rule etched in stone commanding that our only choice when we trade is to depend on future events for a profit? Not a bit of it. We can easily erase that nasty little wedge of contest risk when we want to, and this is where options come onto our playing field.

Flexibility—A Powerful Edge

Trading in pure assets is not the most flexible of activities. When we buy an asset, we profit if the price rises and we lose if it falls, and the opposite result occurs when we sell short. There is little the pure asset trader can do to protect himself from loss during or in anticipation of an adverse move in the asset's price, aside from exiting the market. He might attempt to use other assets to obtain some insurance, paired stocks and intramarket spreads in futures being two common insuring tactics. These tactics are, overall, a tricky proposition because the "protective" asset may be subject to its own adverse price move for reasons unrelated to the original asset, and the relation in the price of the two assets may itself change adversely over time for a wide variety of reasons.

From the standpoint of flexibility, the pure asset trader is similar to a football quarterback whose playbook has only four plays: buy, sell, sell short, and short cover. No matter how skillfully we may trade, having the flexibility to protect and enhance the expectation of our trading positions when and as we please must be nothing but advantageous to us. Options offer us this flexibility. More usefully still, options offer us the opportunity, literally, to *design* trades with desirably high positive expectation.

Suppose the price of some asset, a stock or a future, is 60. Suppose also that the asset has a regularly traded and reasonably liquid market in its options, and further that, through whatever type of market analysis we prefer, we believe this asset's price is likely either to rise or to do nothing in the near future. Having looked at all these conditions, we decide to buy this asset. In the interest of eliminating our contest risk and moderately expanding our range of profitability, we might consider selling ("writing" is the usual term) a 65-strike call option expiring at some time in the future. Suppose that we do write this option and receive, arbitrarily, a premium of 4 for it. Figure 3.3 shows the comparable profitability curves of this trade versus a simple asset purchase, on the date the option expires. The hypothetical dollar profit/loss on the vertical scale is what would result if we would execute such a trade in the "C" coffee futures traded on the New York Board of Trade (NYBOT). The straight diagonal line is the same as the line through the point P_n in Figure 3.1, the profitability curve of an asset purchase. The

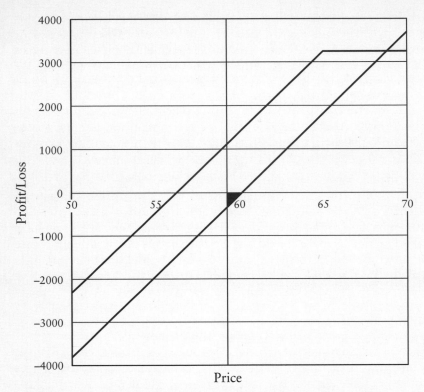

FIGURE 3.3   Profitability curves for buying an asset and writing a call (flattened diagonal line) versus a simple asset purchase (straight diagonal line).

other line, which begins as a diagonal and then flattens out, is the profitability curve of buying an asset and writing a call option against it, as in the present discussion.

First Things First—Reduce the Risk

Throughout the text, we'll assume that we pay a one-way or half-turn commission of $15.00 for all our futures and options trading. For the sake of discussion, we'll also assume we've paid 5 points of the bid-ask spread in the futures contract and 10–20 points of the bid-ask spread when writing an option. Bid-ask spreads in futures options can be sizeable, because liquidity in these options tends to be relatively low, so we are correct to assume a conservative, that is, high, bid-ask cost when trading these options. Just for fun, we'll assume no slippage (lucky us) from our intended purchase and sale prices respectively.

The commission portion of our contest risk is just $30.00, so let's compute the bid-ask portion. The New York "C" coffee contract involves 37,500 pounds of Arabica coffee and is priced in cents per pound. Again, by assumption, our cost of the bid-ask spread on the future is 5 points. In the coffee market, there are 100 points to the penny, so the bid-ask cost on the future works out to $0.0005 × 37,500, or $18.75, and our bid-ask cost on the option is four times that, or $75.00. Summing these figures, our total contest risk is $123.75. Against this, we sold the call option for 4 cents: $0.04 × 37,500, or $1,500.00. Less our contest risk over the whole trade, this puts $1,376.25 net in our pocket, and the brokerage will require us to leave this sum in our trading account. However, these dollars earn interest (or if they don't right now, we can and should arrange matters so that they will), so this requirement is not entirely unfavorable.

At this point, after we've written the call option, our initial contest risk has vanished. We have dollars in hand and are sitting in a trade we like at prices we wanted. Balancing this good news is our necessary acceptance of a now limited profit potential. If the price rises above 65.00 prior to the expiration of the call option we wrote, we will still make the 5 cents profit, $1,875.00, less a $15.00 exit commission, $1,860.00, due to the price movement from 60 to 65. We'll keep the net premium, $1,376.25, we received from writing the option. When the market has moved above 65.00 cents, the trader who bought the option we wrote will, of course, exercise it, call our coffee contract away from us at 65.00 cents, and claim all the subsequent profit if the price of coffee continues to rise. That's perfectly all right with us, for we granted the other trader this right when we wrote the option.

By writing the call option, we have in reality made *three* trades: one in the asset itself, a second in the call option, and a third involving risk. We've traded some amount of possible future profit for a direct reduction in the risk of the position. Whether the market moves in the fashion the other trader prefers or in the fashion we prefer, we've laid off two chunks of risk. The contest risk is gone completely, and we can now also suffer some adverse movement in the price of the asset without incurring any loss of our initial capital. Put very baldly, for us to end up with a loss on this trade, the other market participants must now come and *take* money out of our pocket instead of the usual case of us voluntarily paying them to enter the trade. This is a hugely useful advantage, especially when considered over a long time frame involving a large number of trades.

This hypothetical but perfectly plausible trade requires a little commentary regarding capacity risk and capital. How much capital have we applied to the trade? The exchange, at tonight's close, will allow us to deposit just $1,806.00 plus our entry contest risk as our initial capital commitment, our initial "margin" . . . if we wish to. While we certainly could enter this coffee buy-write trade by having just $1,806.00 plus actual contest risk in our trading account, we would be thoroughly and irredeemably irresponsible to do so, for our capacity risk if we would do so is absolutely off the charts. If we would employ just this minimum amount of capital, we would essentially be stating that our market view is correct, and it's correct right this minute, and it won't ever become incorrect over the term of the trade. This would be pure insanity on our part, and some considerable number of times would lead to our getting absolutely pummeled by an adverse move in the market price. I won't speak for you, but if I have to get beaten up, I'd much sooner step into the ring against the heavyweight boxing champion. It's much more profitable.

Minimum margin is a sign of minimum intelligence, correct? Let's demonstrate that we're well above minimum intelligence simply by making a firm policy of committing a good deal more capital to each trade than the exchange may require. As a starting point for controlling the capacity risk present in this or any futures/options position, committing 300% of the required initial margin is an excellent idea.

Sometimes, and it's well worth your time to ask your broker about this, your brokerage will agree to formally set your account's margin requirement at some multiple of SPAN. Whether they'll do so or not depends ultimately on their back-office computer systems. Brokerages have every positive incentive to do this, though. Offering such a disciplined auto-caution margining policy is good marketing, aids the trader in proper money management, and undoubtedly increases customer satisfaction, all for just pennies in cost. In fact, the brokerage should actually turn a profit by offering this sort of margining policy because they'll earn interest on the nominal excess amount of margin we will apply to every trade.

Diversification of our trading positions may allow us to reduce this 300% figure somewhat. If we should subsequently enter a number of other positions in different markets, we may very reasonably consider that all the markets we're trading are unlikely to move against our several positions in concert on any particular day. Diversification, depending on our selection of markets, might reduce our gross capacity risk sufficiently to allow us to reduce our capital commitment to perhaps two or two and a half times the initial SPAN requirement. Whether well diversified or not, we cannot take any reduction in our capacity risk for granted. Market factors, sudden changes in supply or demand, weather, governmental action, or an emotional tidal wave striking other participants in one of our markets may indicate that we should prudently allot four or five times the SPAN requirement for our trade in that market, conceivably even more.

The comfortable ratio of capital to margin requirement in futures markets isn't easily definable. It varies with the markets we're trading, with our prior experience in these particular markets, and with our personal emotional makeup, but when it comes to capacity risk, erring on the side of caution can never be wrong. Put another way, nature saw to it that your butt is well padded because you'll fall down on occasion and the padding will lessen the pain. Keep your trading account well padded, too, for the very same reason.

Approximating Expectation

In our hypothetical trade here, as in any other, we have to look at what will happen if the market moves against us. We've partially insured against such a move. Our dollars in hand from the start of the trade cushion us from some adverse movement in the underlying asset's price, but there's nothing at all to prevent our asset's price moving sharply lower, much lower than the amount of insurance we hold. The question now becomes, "How much insurance is enough?" and the answer is: we don't have sufficient information to deal with this question—yet.

By definition, expectation is not only a matter of profit and loss, but includes the probability of occurrence of the profit and the loss. So, what is the probability that our asset's price moves from 60 to 65 in 60 days' time, or from 60 to 40? Good question. It's so good a question, in fact, that it and related questions baffled mathematicians for centuries. Finally, beginning in the 1950s, a number of exceptionally talented mathematicians and statisticians figured out a few methods of answering this question. The original reasoning toward these early solutions proceeds approximately as follows.

In any market, the next "tick" of the price of any asset is random. Might be up, might be down, might be neutral, and, other things being equal, if we take a huge sample of a market's ticks, we will likely find out that the counts of upticks and downticks will be close to equal at the end of the trials. This randomness is intuitively appealing. The next tick on Ford Motor stock might be due to the Ford Foundation offering a big block of stock and thereby taking out all the bids on the specialist's book, thus pushing the price lower. Or, a mutual fund might come in and bid for a million or more shares, swallowing up whatever shares are offered at that time and bumping the price higher. We have no way of knowing which of these or other events will occur before any particular tick. We can therefore argue that the direction of a single tick is random, a straight fifty-fifty proposition if we disregard no-change ticks.

What about a large series of ticks? What about the next 100,000 ticks in, say, gold futures? If the next single tick is random, then the result of a long series of ticks should logically be some sort of sum of all possible outcomes of these random events. Indeed it is, but we must be satisfied with an approximate answer, a *model*, rather than an absolute chalkboard sum. One of the most frequently used models for the summing up of large numbers of demonstrably random events is the Gaussian or normal distribution, a.k.a. the famous bell curve. There's a problem with using the normal distribution for our model in trading, though.

The normal distribution curve is symmetric and extends infinitely in both directions, as illustrated in Figure 3.4. But, in the world of trading, it represents a distribution of linear price changes, for example, +7 or –5 points. This representation is useful, but not quite what we want. We are interested in the *ratio* of price changes. By way of example, consider an asset having a price of 100. A 10-point move upward and a 10-point move downward are not equal here, for modeling purposes. These are linear price moves (or additive, if you prefer), and that's fine, but we must compare apples only with apples. When dealing in ratios, we must apply multiplication, not addition, to the upside and division, not subtraction, to the downside. A 10% upward price move in our asset gives us the proper ratio of change, 100 times 1.10, or 110, thus a 10-point gain. The price at the end of an equal downward move, in the model, is 100 divided by 1.10, or 90.909, a loss of only 9.0909 points.

Cutting through the mathematical implications of all this, the normal distribution curve isn't the one we want; it is suited to linear changes, and 10 points is 10 points is 10 points as far as the normal curve is concerned. What we require is its first cousin, the lognormal distribution curve, which reflects the ratios of price change that we need. It is not a symmetric curve, and rightly so, since we surely agree that 10 is not equal to 9.0909. To further illustrate that we're on the right track, the left-hand side of the lognormal curve terminates at zero. This is obviously reasonable, since asset prices cannot trade below zero (although we've likely enough occasionally owned shares that *should* have traded below zero; someone should have paid *us* to

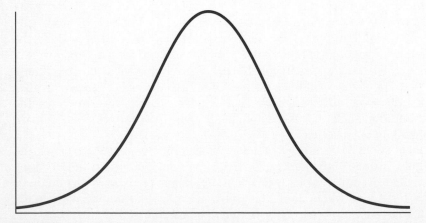

FIGURE 3.4 A normal distribution curve.

own these dubious assets).

The lognormal distribution, as illustrated in Figure 3.5, and another statistical relative of the normal distribution called the binomial distribution, are the bases for a sizeable number of risk and pricing models. Good. We now have at least a theoretically sensible way to begin our attempt to measure the probability of the price of an asset moving from A to B over a stated period of time.

In Figure 3.5, P_0 marks the current price of an asset. P_f is some possible price in the future about which we're curious. Now, the probability of any event ranges between zero (it's impossible) and one (it's a certainty), so the whole area under the curve is equal to 1, for purposes of probability. The probability that the asset's price will be at or below price P_f at some time in the future is represented by the shaded area, taken as a decimal fraction of one. The size of the shaded area is easily computed by using the cumulative normal density function, which formula can be found in any statistical textbook or in the many fine books dealing with the mathematics of trading.

No matter what pricing model we choose, the purpose of the model is to make the calculation of this probability available to us, and the lognormal model certainly accomplishes this end. Even if we don't want to take the trouble to crunch a bunch of numbers in order to calculate this probability ourselves, there are lots of ways to obtain it, whether from commercial services, numerous Internet sites, our brokerage, or our fellow traders.

We're not out of the modeling woods just yet. We're looking at the lognormal curve as a way to represent the distribution of future prices of an

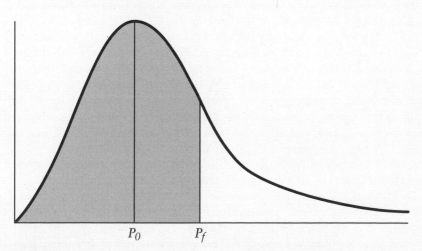

P_0 P_f

FIGURE 3.5   A lognormal distribution curve.

asset *after a very large number of ticks*, perhaps 100,000 or more. That's all very well, but in the real world we aren't likely at all to see, let alone hold a trade through, a hundred thousand ticks in any market except, rarely, the very most active ones. The COMEX/NYMEX market in gold futures, for example, only sees several hundred ticks on a normal day. We must ask ourselves, then, whether it is valid to assume that any model, and particularly in our case the lognormal distribution, realistically represents the probability of price movement over only the next 5,000 or 10,000 ticks? After these smaller sets of ticks, the distribution of the real-world prices will differ by some amount from those indicated by the lognormal model, not a doubt in the world, but the lognormal curve will still be a reasonable approximation of market reality, and so is worth our attention.

Applying a Model

While this is an interesting topic, what we really want to know is how to gain an advantage by applying this (or any) model of potential future price distribution to our trading. Taking the line of least resistance, let's just combine a profitability curve with the lognormal price distribution curve, as in Tables 3.1 and 3.2, and see what we might discover. These tables are derived from real-world prices in the New York coffee market on June 17, 2002. December coffee futures settled at 52.10 and the December coffee 55-strike call option at 3.10 cents, worth therefore $1,162.50 before considering contest risk.

These are tables describing large portions of two expectation curves. If we graphed them, they would be pictorial representations of the definition of expectation. Each line in the tables contains the profit or loss at points on the curve (fourth column) multiplied by the probability (third column) that the indicated price will be reached. In theory, such tables would have one line for each 0.01 change in price, but such detail is very difficult to display in a readable fashion. Please pardon the abbreviation. Completely unsurprisingly, Table 3.1 confirms that negative expectation is present in the simple purchase or sale of an asset, and also illustrates the asymmetry of the lognormal curve. Table 3.2 shows the shift in the trade's expectation when we write a mildly out-of-the-money call option against the purchase of an asset. These tables are useful enough for indicating our approximate expectation in a couple of types of trades, but they hardly tell the whole story. Embedded within the numbers in the tables is a vital assumption.

The values in expectation tables, whether we consider them proportionally or as absolutes, are *not* constant from market to market. The other way to say this is that the price distribution curves, both real-world ones and modeled ones, vary significantly among different markets and in any single market over time. These variations are due to the fact that the *volatility* of any

TABLE 3.1	Expectation for a Purchase			
Object Price	**Probability Below Object Price**	**Probability of Range**	**Profit/Loss at Range Midpoint**	**Expectation in Range**
39.00	0.0133	0.0133	−6817.50	−90.67
40.00	0.0216	0.0083	−4567.50	−37.81
41.00	0.0335	0.0119	−4192.50	−49.92
42.00	0.0499	0.0164	−3817.50	−62.54
43.00	0.0715	0.0216	−3442.50	−74.44
44.00	0.0989	0.0275	−3067.50	−84.22
45.00	0.1326	0.0336	−2692.50	−90.51
46.00	0.1723	0.0398	−2317.50	−92.19
47.00	0.2179	0.0456	−1942.50	−88.56
48.00	0.2686	0.0507	−1567.50	−79.49
49.00	0.3235	0.0548	−1192.50	−65.39
50.00	0.3812	0.0577	−817.50	−47.20
51.00	0.4405	0.0593	−442.50	−26.24
52.00	0.5000	0.0595	−67.50	−4.02
53.00	0.5584	0.0584	+307.50	+17.95
54.00	0.6144	0.0561	+682.50	+38.27
55.00	0.6672	0.0528	+1057.50	+55.85
56.00	0.7161	0.0488	+1432.50	+69.94
57.00	0.7604	0.0443	+1807.50	+80.15
58.00	0.8000	0.0396	+2182.50	+86.44
59.00	0.8348	0.0348	+2557.50	+89.04
60.00	0.8650	0.0302	+2932.50	+88.42
61.00	0.8907	0.0257	+3307.50	+85.14
62.00	0.9124	0.0217	+3682.50	+79.84
63.00	0.9304	0.0180	+4057.50	+73.16
64.00	0.9452	0.0148	+4432.50	+65.66
Overall expectation:				$−63.34

market differs from that of another. Also, the volatility of any single market varies over time, due to changes in market factors and traders' sentiments.

Volatility—One Measure of a Market

There are lots of ways to view and compute the volatility of a market. One frequently used is called either *historical* or *statistical volatility*, typically abbreviated as HV or SV. I prefer the term statistical volatility and that's what we'll use throughout the text. This is a simple if mildly tedious calculation.

TABLE 3.2   Expectation for a Purchase and Call Write

Object Price	Probability Below Object Price	Probability of Range	Profit/Loss at Range Midpoint	Expectation in Range
39.00	0.0133	0.0133	−5880.00	−78.20
40.00	0.0216	0.0083	−3630.00	−30.05
41.00	0.0335	0.0119	−3255.00	−38.76
42.00	0.0499	0.0164	−2880.00	−47.18
43.00	0.0715	0.0216	−2505.00	−54.17
44.00	0.0989	0.0275	−2130.00	−58.48
45.00	0.1326	0.0336	−1755.00	−58.99
46.00	0.1723	0.0398	−1380.00	−54.89
47.00	0.2179	0.0456	−1005.00	−45.82
48.00	0.2686	0.0507	−630.00	−31.95
49.00	0.3235	0.0548	−255.00	−13.98
50.00	0.3812	0.0577	+120.00	+6.93
51.00	0.4405	0.0593	+495.00	+29.35
52.00	0.5000	0.0595	+870.00	+51.75
53.00	0.5584	0.0584	+1245.00	+72.66
54.00	0.6144	0.0561	+1620.00	+90.83
55.00	0.6672	0.0528	+1995.00	+105.36
56.00	0.7161	0.0488	+2062.50	+100.70
57.00	0.7604	0.0443	+2062.50	+91.46
58.00	0.8000	0.0396	+2062.50	+81.68
59.00	0.8348	0.0348	+2062.50	+71.81
60.00	0.8650	0.0302	+2062.50	+62.19
61.00	0.8907	0.0257	+2062.50	+53.09
62.00	0.9124	0.0217	+2062.50	+44.72
63.00	0.9304	0.0180	+2062.50	+37.19
64.00	0.9452	0.0148	+2062.50	+30.55
Overall expectation:				$417.80

When we want to find the 30-day statistical volatility of an asset, we start by taking the daily change in the price of the asset, expressed as the closing price divided by the previous day's closing price, for each of the past 30 days. To satisfy the lognormal nature of the model, we then take the natural logarithm, log_e, of each of these 30 price changes, and next compute the standard deviation of the set of these logarithms.

The result of this calculation is the immediate 30-day statistical volatility. Volatilities are almost always stated as annual figures, though, so we've one final step yet to go. To annualize our calculation, we must multiply our result by the square root of the number of trading days in the year. Some authors, Larry McMillan among them, use 260 for this figure in every year. Some use 256, whose square root is 16 (very conveniently), some count up the actual number of trading days in the current year. All these work well for our purposes, so just choose your favorite.

I know some very masochistic people, but I've yet to meet any trader who actually sits down and manually performs these calculations each day (or each week, or ever for that matter) for all the markets that might be of interest at any given time. SVs are available from commercial quotation services, from many brokerages (be sure to specify the *term* of the volatility to your broker, 20-day, 60-day, 6-month, or whichever you prefer), and from a considerable and growing body of Internet sites. Some of these sites provide volatility figures at no charge, some have nominal fees, but a few will try to take a hefty bite out of your wallet and are to be avoided. Traders whom you know personally and who use volatility calculations in their trading will surely have them available.

If you're comfortable with spreadsheet programs, you can easily and cheaply acquire your own database of historical prices, a means of acquiring each day's closing prices (even at no cost, on sundry Internet sites), and whip up the appropriate spreadsheet. You'll have all the SVs you want every day, with just a few clicks of the mouse. There are also several worthwhile commercial software packages, ranging in price from modest to ridiculous, that include historical price databases and volatility calculators, among a large number of other features.

Some Fruits of the Volatility Tree

One of the many profitable implications of volatility is the concept that we can calculate the *theoretical fair value* of an asset's various options. Granted, the values we'll obtain from this calculation are, again, only approximations, and almost assuredly will not match the actual prices of the options that we see in the marketplace. We can easily trade and prosper with these approximations, though, because "the market" is the sum of the actions of people over time, and, in broad, it bears no resemblance whatever to a precision instrument. In addition, we must remember in the first place that the lognormal curve is only a model of the future distribution of prices, an approximation to be respected and applied as we find useful . . . but not worshipped.

Let's be candid with each other, shall we? The real world is *not* lognormal. It would be terrifically convenient if it were, but it isn't. Just because the theoretical prices of a market's options don't match the actual prices we observe in the market, does this imply a failure of the model? It does not, for the actual price of any option at any time represents the various market participants' collective view of what the price of that option "should" be at that specific point in time. For clarification of this point, we can look to the heating oil market.

Everyone who trades heating oil is well aware that heating oil distributors begin building their inventories in the late summer and that consumers, particularly homeowners, tend to buy the bulk of their heating oil in the autumn. Most years, due to this concentration of demand, heating oil prices tend to rise during one or another portion of the time from July through early October. In anticipation of this, option traders in heating oil will on occasion be bidding rather eagerly for these months' call options even earlier in the year, and the actual market price of these calls will acquire a premium, sometimes a very large one, over their computed theoretical fair values.

In order to use the disparity between an option's theoretical fair value and its actual market value to our advantage, we first need to measure this disparity. Fortunately, there is a measure ready-made for us. When we compute the theoretical fair value of an option, we use the SV of the underlying market, among other inputs. When we observe that the actual market price of the option differs from its computed fair value, we very rationally conclude that the volatility of the option must be different from that of the underlying market.

Before, when we were computing the option's fair value, we wanted to know a price; now, we know the price of the option by observation, but not its volatility. To obtain this number, we just apply the fair value calculation backwards, so to speak. The result of our calculation is the famous implied volatility, the IV of the option, so called because it is the volatility the underlying asset *should* have in order for a fair value calculation to yield the actual option price we observe in the market at this time.

If you're familiar with options trading, you may be saying to yourself, "Stu, everybody knows this stuff, let's get on with making a profit." I must respectfully disagree with you here. The large majority of non-professional traders, in my experience, do not have nearly enough exposure to or appreciation of the concept of volatility, for there are few other fields of human activity in which it is so immediately significant and so prominent.

The experienced options trader knows full well that volatility and its implications are essential considerations, whether using options to reduce risk in an existing position or designing high-expectation trades using options in their own right. It is every bit as important to the trader to be familiar and comfortable with the details of removing risk and putting expectation in his favor as it is to the banker or to the bookmaker. Options are one of our tools for accomplishing this, and understanding the basics of volatility and its related topics is necessary to the effective use of this tool.

Everything Changes over Time, Including Volatility

Volatilities change over time, just as prices do. The SV of a market and the IVs of its associated options react to the same news and market developments as does the price of the asset, but they do not necessarily react in the same way or to the same extent. When SV and IVs diverge considerably, as for instance they sometimes do before an important supply/demand report is issued, we can listen for the sound of opportunity knocking. In such a case, the IVs of the options may rise well above the underlying market's SV and we can look around for cautious ways to sell this excess volatility, which will be represented in the market by relatively high option prices. Conversely, when SV is depressed and the IVs of the options are even more depressed, it's generally profitable to look at buying some selection of longer-term options, which, given the low volatilities, will tend very strongly to be underpriced to some degree.

If we trade only in assets, we are completely dependent on the movement of the asset's price for our profit. This is *not* the case when trading options, whether by themselves or in combination with their underlying assets. Trades are commonplace that reap a tasty profit solely from changes in IV, even when the price of the asset does nothing or moves in slightly the wrong direction over a period of time. Further, when we use options in our trading, we can on many occasions enlist the most inexorable force in the universe on our side. That force is time, and it is a very powerful ally indeed.

One enormously pleasant thing about volatilities, SV especially, and especially in futures markets, is that they tend to persist within a measurable range for long periods of time, and during these periods they tend even more strongly to revert to the mean semiregularly. When a market's SV has varied from 8% to 14% consistently for years, under a variety of market conditions, through euphoria and calamity, the trader who observes SV approaching either end of the range can, much more often than not, construct a trade having a high positive expectation.

Figures 3.6 through 3.10 illustrate the persistence of SV ranges in five widely different futures markets from 1998 into 2002. For these examples, I chose the 60-day SV of the nearest contract, but it doesn't make a whole lot of difference what term of volatility we examine. Figure 3.11 is the 120-day SV for Swiss franc futures, and you'll notice a clear degree of symmetry between that figure and its 60-day cousin, Figure 3.10.

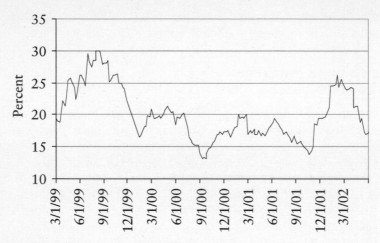

FIGURE 3.6   COMEX high-grade copper 60-day statistical volatility, 1999–2002.

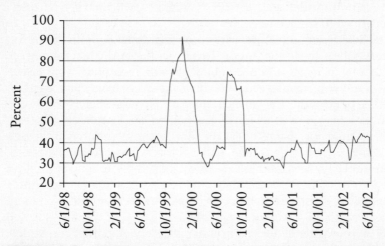

FIGURE 3.7   NYBOT coffee "C" 60-day statistical volatility, 1998–2002.

Implied Volatility and Delta

The study of volatility doesn't only suggest possible trading strategies and potentially advantageous situations. We're interested in figuring the expectation of trades we might enter, are we not? Absolutely we are, and the notion of volatility provides us with a couple of ways to do this. The more complex way is to perform a series of calculations using the various formulae of whichever model we may be using. The simpler way is just to use

FIGURE 3.8   CME lean hogs 60-day statistical volatility, 1998–2002.

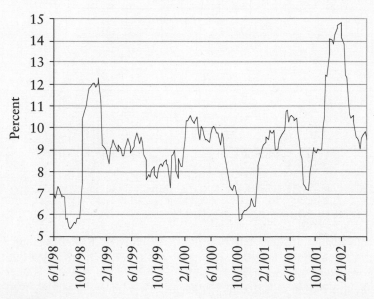

FIGURE 3.9   CBOT 30-year Treasury bonds 60-day statistical volatility, 1998–2002.

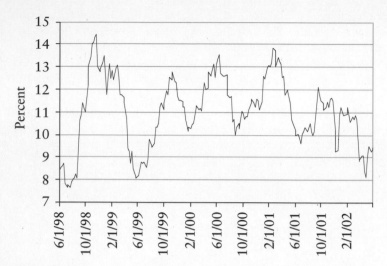

FIGURE 3.10   CMME/IMM Swiss franc 60-day statistical volatility, 1998–2002.

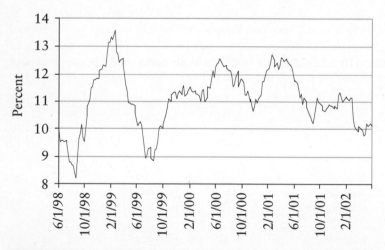

FIGURE 3.11   CMME/IMM Swiss franc 120-day statistical volatility, 1998–2002.

a couple of the results of these calculations, which are almost universally available from the same folks from whom we obtain SVs (if we don't calculate them ourselves, of course).

To find an approximate probability of an asset's price moving from A to B over a known period of time, we can first apply the measure called *delta*.

In the simple lognormal pricing model, the delta of the X-strike call option turns out to be a decently close approximation of the probability of the future price of an asset being at or above X when the option expires. Suppose that the price of an asset is 50, and that the actual price of a 90-day, 60-strike call option is 1.00. If we calculate this option's 90-day IV, along the way we obtain the delta of the option as a free bonus. If the delta of the option turns out to be 0.20, then we can say that the rough probability of the asset's price being above 60 in 90 days' time is equal to 0.20. Stated another way, the asset price 90 days from now can be expected to be below 60 in about 80 cases out of 100.

Delta has another practical use. By its definition in the model, it is the measure of how much an option's price can be expected to change if the price of the underlying asset changes by one unit. In the preceding example, if the price of the asset would move from 50 to 51 tomorrow, the model would predict the price of the 60-strike call to move to 1.20. If the asset price moved down to 49, this option's delta indicates we would expect the price of the call to fall to 0.80.

If you're wondering about the delta of the underlying asset itself, it's always 1.00, and this is perfectly sensible. Every time the price of an asset moves one unit, it moves exactly one unit, whereas the price of any of its options will only move a fraction of one unit (with rare exceptions). When we buy an asset and write a call option against it, we obtain the delta of the whole position by adding up the deltas of both parts of the position. In our example here, the total position delta is 0.80, which is just another way of saying that if the asset were to move to 51, we'd gain 1.00 point on the asset and expect to lose 0.20 point on the option, gaining 0.80 point net.

Computing any position's total delta is a snap, no matter how complex the position may be. If we buy an asset, buy a call option, or write a put option, the delta of any of these is a positive number. If we sell short an asset, write a call, or buy a put, these items' deltas are negative numbers. Add up the deltas of each position in the trade and we're done. If this result is a positive number, we will almost always profit if the price of the asset rises; if the total delta is negative, we'll nearly invariably profit if the price of the asset falls. Delta, however, changes from day to day (and even from minute to minute), and must be recomputed for any position at least daily, lest we find ourselves in what amounts to a very unprofitable time warp.

As you undoubtedly and rightly suspect, there's a whole lot more to the subject of IV and delta, and for that matter a whole bunch of related topics. Perfectly true, but all things in good time. The good news is that, after all this preliminary, we finally have enough information in hand to take a good, hard look at the expectation of a real-world trade.

The Toxic Waste of Markets—Using Expectation to Avoid Hype and Nonsense

Regardless of whether you've ever traded an option in your life, if you've traded in any market for any length of time, you almost certainly have run across the claims of some number of promoters, usually titled something like "Fantastic Profits in Options," or something equally flatulent. These types of claims and promotions too frequently employ, as their "secret strategy" or "lesson of a lifetime" or some such bilge, the tactic of buying call options whose striking price is way the heck away from the underlying asset's current price.

If some month's crude oil futures are at $25.00/bbl, a way-out-of-the-money option, or WOOM as I always call it, might be the 31.00- or 32.00-strike call. The types of promoters I'm talking about don't deal in WOOMs, though. No, no, they rave about WTBOOMs, options that are way-the-BLEEP-out-of-the-money, the 39.00- or 40.00-strike calls, or even higher-strike ones. Typically, they'll "recommend" that the suck-, uh, trader buy such options with a term of six months or nine months or a year.

All right, let's play these sleazeballs' little game—on paper only, of course, since we really don't want to contribute to their upkeep. Let's crunch the numbers on a trade this type of lowlife might advocate and keep a sharp eye on the expectation of the trade throughout. "Hey, why bother with these clowns?" someone is asking. Fair question. For a very good reason: it's not enough to look at a prospective trade and say, "That's a loser" or "That should be profitable."

We want to understand *how* traders lose by ignoring expectation and using disadvantageous strategies, and also learn to construct strategies that eliminate or reverse these disadvantages. More than this, we want to know how to recognize the difference between a profit opportunity and an accidental purchase of the Brooklyn Bridge, and the way to do so is to watch expectation in action. As a side benefit of this little analysis, we will also permanently vaccinate ourselves against these types of hyped promotional viruses. Here we go.

"Upcoming Iraqi War Threatens World Oil Supply!" "Experts Say Supply Deficit Can Exceed 3 Million Barrels A Day!" "During Desert Storm, Oil Prices Rose 200%!" "$70.00 Oil? It Will *Happen When The Bombs Fall!"*

So rave the headlines in the promotional mailer or on the Internet site, both of which doubtless prattle on for quite a while, with lots and lots of exclamation points (I'm actually skimping here on the number you're apt to see in such a promotion). The hype hints strongly at astonishing profits to be made in anticipating political developments by buying six-month call options in crude oil with a striking price of 40.00. Well, well, WTBOOM, boomity, boom. As I write this on May 17, 2002, the market in NYMEX December 2002 crude oil, ticker symbol CLZ, settled at 26.15 and December crude oil's 6-month SV is 32.4%. Table 3.3 shows the pertinent data for the expectation of this trade, evaluated according to the lognormal model.

One fact, not included in the table, about the CLZ call options tonight is that they're right near their theoretical fair value until we get into WTBOOM-land. The other way to say this is that the calls' IVs are about equal to the SV of CLZ itself. Evidently, option traders in crude oil don't seem to share our hypester's optimism right now. The WOOM and WTBOOM calls are a tad pricier than they *should* theoretically be, so if we purchase these, we'll be paying up a notch—not necessarily a sin, but hardly advantageous either. We'll assume that we can buy the CLZ 40 calls with just 1 point of slippage, so we'll be paying 0.11, or 11 points, $110.00 plus a $15.00 commission, thus $125.00 including our unavoidable contest risk.

The main portion of our expectation in this trade is easy to compute. If CLZ is not above $40.00 when the December options expire, we'll lose our entire purchase price and contest risk, so this portion of the expectation in

TABLE 3.3 Expectation of Buying CLZ 40.00 Calls on May 17, 2002

Strike Price	Option Price	Delta × 100	Probability Below*	Probability of Range	Profit at Range Midpoint	Expectation in Range
40.00	0.100	4.40	0.9664	0.9664	−125.00	−120.80
41.00	0.060	2.93	0.9778	0.0114	350.00	3.99
42.00	0.040	2.17	0.9837	0.0059	1350.00	7.99
43.00	0.035	1.93	0.9857	0.0020	2350.00	4.70
44.00	0.032	1.80	0.9868	0.0011	3350.00	3.74
45.00	0.030	1.67	0.9879	0.0011	4350.00	4.64
46.00	0.023	1.33	0.9905	0.0026	5350.00	13.94
47.00	0.018	1.14	0.9919	0.0014	6350.00	9.06
48.00	0.014	0.95	0.9933	0.0014	7350.00	10.11
49.00	0.012	0.85	0.9941	0.0008	8350.00	6.46
50.00	0.010	0.73	0.9950	0.0009	9350.00	8.55
51.00	0.009	0.71	0.9952	0.0002	10350.00	1.86
52.00	0.008	0.64	0.9957	0.0005	11350.00	5.62
Overall expectation:						$−40.15

Notes: CLZ = 26.15; Z options expire 11/17/2002.

*Probability of being below the striking price on the same line.

this trade is perfectly clear. As Table 3.3 shows, the delta of the CLZ 40 call is 0.042 tonight. Hmmm. Only about 42 times out of 1,000 will the market theoretically be above 40.00 when our options expire? We'll lose all our capital and costs in this trade roughly 95.8% of the time? Geez, that's terrible. I don't know about you, but I want a second opinion on this deal! We can easily get one, too, but to do so we must digress for a moment.

The Bad News Only Gets Worse

In fact, the situation is actually worse than this for the option buyer in this or any purchase of WTBOOM call options. The delta figures of WTBOOM call options are over-optimistic, proportionally too high. Why so? The unmodified normal distribution curve is perfectly symmetric, but we aren't using that curve, are we? We aren't, and the lognormal curve we are using is *not* symmetric; it has a measurable bias to the right-hand side, the "upside" in terms of markets. In plain language, the right-hand tail of the lognormal curve is too fat, implying too high a probability that the market will reach any of the points way out on the curve within a specified time. Not shockingly, the lognormal curve also slightly understates the probability of a sizeable fall in price (hey, the fat tail had to be taken out of some other part of the curve, didn't it?).

The works of a French mathematician and an English botanist offer us a reasonable method for adjusting the computation of the probability of a market attaining any particular price over a known period of time, presumably generating a probability more in line with reality than delta offers. You may have read, in chemistry or physics class when you were at school, of the phenomenon called "Brownian motion." This effect originally was the result of the observation of the total motion of tiny grains of pollen in water over time. Robert Brown, evidently a remarkably persistent scientist, concluded after long study that this motion was random, and the distance these grains moved from their starting point varied with the square root of the amount of time elapsed during the observation.

Some decades after Brown's study, a student of the remarkable mathematician Jules-Henri Poincaré, a fellow named Louis Bachelier, wrote a thesis demonstrating that the movements of stock prices on the Paris exchange bore considerable resemblance to the movements of these grains of pollen. Poincaré, rather surprisingly in retrospect given his brilliance as a mathematician, thought Bachelier's thesis was not up to snuff. Poincaré was undoubtedly his nation's leading mathematician at the time; his opinion was not to be questioned. Bachelier's thesis was ignored, and he subsequently could not even obtain a university professorship.

Time heals many wounds. Half a century later, the Nobel-prize winning economist Paul Samuelson rediscovered Bachelier's paper, and publicized the concepts within it, and the notion of random motion varying with the square root of time became, *mirabile dictu*, a topic at the forefront of economists' discussions about the movement of market prices.

It's heartening to see a good piece of research being honored and applied, even if far too late to bring the researcher any benefit, but how do we turn this evidently useful discovery to our advantage? I've found it to be practical, when figuring the expectation in writing (*not* buying!) WOOM and WTBOOM options, calls particularly, to use a square root of time calculation rather than delta in order to estimate the likelihood of a market going to such-and-so a price within a known time frame.

This square root of time calculation, SQRTT as I call it, is straightforward and can be found, again, in the numerous books dealing with the mathematics of trading. (I particularly like McMillan's discussion of this calculation and its implications in *Options as a Strategic Investment*, 3rd edition, New York Institute of Finance, 1993). SVs and IVs are ordinarily computed as annual values, then reduced according to the actual amount of time we want to consider. This reduction occurs automatically, as it were, in the calculation of delta, but we must do this minor piece of work ourselves to obtain the SQRTT figure.

Now, back to business. Our negative dollar expectation is the probability that CLZ will end up below 40.00 on option expiration day, times the amount of the loss we'll realize: $0.9664 \times -\$125$, or $-\$120.80$. Computing our positive dollar expectation requires a series of incremental calculations, the results of which are illustrated in Table 3.3. The probability that CLZ will end up between 40.00 and 41.00 is by definition the probability that CLZ moves at least to 40.00, minus the probability that it moves no higher than 41.00. We calculate the profit for this increment by figuring the profit in the trade at the midpoint of this range, in this case $350 at 40.50. The probability of CLZ ending up between 41.00 and 42.00 is the probability that CLZ moves above 41.00 but no higher than 42.00, the profit for this increment is $1350 at 41.50, and so on, right up the line. We stop calculating when our SQRTT probability falls below 0.0050.

The minimum tick in crude oil and its options is 0.01. How then can we have option prices such as 0.018? We can't. Entries like this represent the computed theoretical fair value of an option that has not yet traded. There is also some rounding error in the right-hand column values, which are the product of the corresponding values in the two columns to its left. The column showing the delta of the options is just for comparison to the next column, the SQRTT-generated probability that CLZ will be below a specific striking price on expiration.

There's one more thing to note, too. What about the last 0.0043? We stopped calculating at 0.9957, and isn't there is more calculable dollar-positive expectation in the remaining tiny chunk of the curve? There is indeed. This seemingly wanton discarding of the last bit of the curve is another means of compensating for the fat-tail bias in the curve. We're not being negligent by doing this, not at all, because we've taken the calculation out to almost three full standard deviations of the curve, most certainly a good enough approximation to completeness for practical trading purposes.

One entry in Table 3.3 requires comment. The range between 40.00 and 41.00 technically would encompass partly profit and partly loss. The breakeven point for the option buyer in this trade is about 40.16, and, technically, we should perform two calculations for this range: one for the loss from 40.00 to 40.16 and a second for the profit from 40.17 to 40.99. Go right ahead if you like. It's a straightforward proration over the 100 points in this range. It's also a waste of time, pure and simple.

We're *not* going to exercise our option if CLZ is between 40.00 and 40.16. Pay another commission, another chunk of the bid-ask spread, and maybe more slippage? What are we, crazy? We'll just sell the option back for what few points we can get. In short, in calculating the expectation of this trade, we're going to ignore this small range and lump 40.00–41.00 into the positive dollar column. Purists hate this attitude. That's all right with me, I find purists a little bit tedious. What they refuse to admit is that we're dealing with a model, an approximation, and 10–15 point ranges, when they're way the devil out on the lognormal curve, don't mean beans. (As an aside, if we *would* perform this computation, it would change the total expectation by . . . are you ready? . . . 15.4 cents. Yawn. Let the purists knock themselves out; we have better things to do.)

Well, well, well. Given current market circumstances, if we purchase the CLZ 40.00 calls tomorrow, we can expect to *lose* $40.15 each time over a series of identical trades. That's 32.12% of our initial capital of $125.00! This is a real sweetheart of a deal, isn't it? Bah! We'd do much better for ourselves by visiting a casino. Hell's bells, we'd do better even by playing some states' lotteries.

In fairness, we must observe that our calculations only apply to the whole trade, from date of entry through option expiration. If CLZ spiked upward to, say, $32.00 in 45 days, the premium of the CLZ 40.00 call would doubtless increase even if its IV did not (although its IV likely would rise, too). The option buyer would have a chance to cash out a profit at that point. Additionally, the IVs of CLZ call options generally might go higher either with or without a corresponding price move in crude oil, perhaps on economic news or increasingly clamorous sentiment about a war in the Middle East, and the option buyer might be able to turn a profit here also.

This type of option purchase is exactly the game I described in Chapter 1. As I asked back then, "Do you really want to play this game?" I can't imagine that any marginally sane trader would, and certainly not when much better alternatives and expectations are readily available. While there are some chances for profit in this trade, they are pretty remote, and in any case a rather spectacular event must occur, or be rumored to be about to occur, somewhere along the way. The option buyer in this case is *dependent* on such an occurrence to put a profit in his pocket; he is hoping for event risk to intervene in his favor. Good luck, pal. That way lies, if not madness, then definitely poverty. Luckily, I was inoculated against this type of unprofitable and frankly silly trading long ago (not without, ahem, some cost), and now you are too.

Well, so much for those who promote this sort of hype-over-hard-facts trade, but there's another good question to ask. If buying this sort of WTBOOM option doesn't offer us a positive expectation, what about writing it? Can we earn a good profit by selling instead of buying in this situation? In theory at least, a negative expectation present when buying an option should imply a positive expectation when writing the same option instead. Is this really the case? Table 3.4 shows the expectation of writing this same CLZ 40.00 call if we simply write it and take no action whatever before the option expires.

This is marginally a better idea because the expectation of the trade is slightly positive, and we have in hand a minor additional advantage in writing this call. When the option expires worthless, as this one will do in a gigantic majority of cases, our trading costs when exiting the trade are close to zero.

TABLE 3.4 Expectation of Writing CLZ 40.00 Call on May 17, 2002

Strike Price	Option Price	Delta × 100	Probability Below*	Probability of Range	Profit at Range Midpoint	Expectation in Range
40.00	0.100	4.40	0.9664	0.9664	85.00	82.14
41.00	0.060	2.93	0.9778	0.0114	−430.00	−4.90
42.00	0.040	2.17	0.9837	0.0059	−1430.00	−8.43
43.00	0.035	1.93	0.9857	0.0020	−2430.00	−4.86
44.00	0.032	1.80	0.9868	0.0011	−3430.00	−3.77
45.00	0.030	1.67	0.9879	0.0011	−4430.00	−4.87
46.00	0.023	1.33	0.9905	0.0026	−5430.00	−14.11
47.00	0.018	1.14	0.9919	0.0014	−6430.00	−9.00
48.00	0.014	0.95	0.9933	0.0014	−7430.00	−10.40
49.00	0.012	0.85	0.9941	0.0008	−8430.00	−6.74
50.00	0.010	0.73	0.9950	0.0009	−9430.00	−8.48
51.00	0.009	0.71	0.9952	0.0002	−10430.00	−2.08
52.00	0.008	0.64	0.9957	0.0005	−11430.00	−5.71
Overall expectation:						$1.79

Notes: CLZ = 26.15; Z options expire 11/17/2002.

*Probability of being below the striking price on the same line.

What would have been the exiting contest risk expense stays in our pocket, where it belongs. (Side note: this is not entirely true when we write options in markets on some exchanges. These exchanges have the curious practice of charging a small fee just for removing the expired option from their books. We should expect this sort of practice to become more common over time, as exchanges increasingly become profit-centered corporations instead of mutual/partnership organizations.)

Unfortunately, writing the CLZ 40.00 call here isn't a good trade either. First, we have exactly zero interest in entering a trade with a positive expectation of, basically, pennies. Even if the expectation were, say, +$80.00, this still wouldn't be a worthwhile effort. Why? We haven't yet considered, have we, how much capital we we'll be required to commit to this trade. We haven't looked at what our return on capital (which I'll call ROC in future) might be. When we write the CLZ 40.00 call for 0.10, $100.00, less $15.00 contest risk, the NYMEX exchange will require an initial margin of $288, or $864 when we multiply it by 3 to provide our required cushion. Our notional ROC is 85 / 864 = 9.84% over six months' time, a mere 1.64% per month. This calculation is notional, because it doesn't include the additional capital we'll have to commit if CLZ would move sharply higher during the trade.

We won't be writing these options, period, because we can and should do much better with our capital. And we will . . . but by using other strategies and different tactics. Irrespective of the strategies and tactics we will subsequently examine, keeping the expectation of a trade in our favor must be our first concern.

First a Foundation, Then the First Brick in the Wall

There are several reasonable measures we can employ to evaluate the potential desirability of an option trade. Expectation is not unique to this task; it is, however, the one I prefer and use. Adopting a useful measuring stick for risk and reward, though, is only the first part of creating a profitable trading methodology.

We've long since agreed, haven't we, that one factor necessary to successful trading is the acquisition of information about markets. There isn't, as far as I know, any yardstick for evaluating the usefulness and potentially profitable implications of a single specific piece of information other than experience, but there is an extremely useful question we can ask ourselves concerning information in general. What happens if some of the information we acquire is *bad*, pure and simple? Also, can we determine if such information *is* bad, in a general way? One good way to do this is . . . well, come along and see for yourself.

CHAPTER 4

Just the Facts, Ma'am

Avoiding Moonshine, Morons, and Myths

No one stays here by faking reality in any manner whatever.
—Ayn Rand, (*Atlas Shrugged*)

D epending on whose figures you believe, somewhere between 75 and 95% of *all* traders lose when they trade, in any market you care to name. They lose capital over time! No matter what the exact percentage is, this is a horribly high figure and a completely unacceptable result. It's a perfectly believable proportion, mind you, if we assume that traders (as opposed to longer-term investors) are all gamblers at heart. However, it's an utterly unbelievable figure if we assume that this same huge majority of traders apply any sort of favorable methodology with some amount of discipline. You and I must conclude, therefore, that a very large proportion of all traders either use consistently inferior methods or lack consistent discipline, or both.

This chapter isn't about method. It's about acquiring one essential part of a trading discipline. Specifically, we must avoid or ignore or reject outright the bad information, the sundry misconceptions, misperceptions, and myths that a sizeable number of market participants, would-be gurus, and self-styled experts, including, of course, the alleged financial media, attempt to foist upon us. This class of so-called information, in broad, represents a sub-type of the pseudo-information risk we saw in Chapter 2.

Staying Out of the Trickbag—Reality Rules

Philosophers have argued for millennia over the nature of the real world, over whether reality is an objective truth, a subjective one, some combination of the two, mystical, or merely an illusion. As traders, we don't have a dog in this fight, but we must nonetheless form a world-view about trading. We can accept any of these viewpoints we like and design a methodology in accordance with our chosen one, but we cannot even hope to prosper in trading by embracing a false perception of trading reality, that is, attempting to delude ourselves or allowing others to practice fakery on us.

Whatever our own world-view may be, trading itself is largely a subjective activity. Please observe that it must be so. If there were a hard, objective, mechanical method to employ in order to guarantee profitable trading, those who know or knew of such a method would have applied it to markets by now. Objective knowledge is impossible to hide over a long period of time (consider all those throughout history who have tried and failed at this endeavor). Perforce then, such a method would at some point have become widely known, and it would have come to be ineffective at some point, as traders who formerly lost to the users of such a method changed their own methods over time. Ergo, there isn't any such purely objective method.

In trading, there are few certainties and far too many opinions, maybes, possiblys, and perhapses. One of the few hard and objective realities in trading is our net equity, our bottom line after each day's market movements. Does it seem reasonable that you and I should entrust our objective trading results to the tender mercies of supposition, superstition, and in many cases plain stupidity?

Well, that was a no-brainer, wasn't it? Now, tell me why so many traders do exactly this, because I haven't a clue (no jokes, please). Why do lots of traders believe in and trade according to half-truths, delusions, the *diktat* of self-anointed gurus, and outright myths? Don't get me wrong here; I surely don't have and don't pretend to have all or even most of the answers to the problem of trading in a consistently profitable fashion over the long haul, but I didn't just fall off the watermelon truck last Tuesday, either. I'll guarantee you this much; shedding all this type of mental baggage in favor of hard fact and disciplined methods can do absolutely nothing but improve our trading results. As the old satiric songwriter Tom Lehrer used to say, with *just* a trace of irony, "I have a few modest examples right here."

Models Are Useful, but . . . There's No Holy Grail

The first myth we must dispose of is that any model of future price distribution is consistently accurate. Even though this statement may sound contradictory given our discussion previously, it is not. In the first place, no model can predict the unpredictable, and the unpredictable event occurs with disturbingly higher frequency than *any* model indicates. Even aside from obvious examples such as weather calamities and wars, the number of possible unpredictable or imponderable events is enormous, and some of these will—not might, but will—intrude on our trades from time to time. No model can warn us that such events impend, and the trader who believes otherwise is headed for an appointment with a bankruptcy judge.

Looking at the matter objectively, all we traders can really do is to keep our likelihood of success, our expectation, in the plus column. Models are useful because they provide a means of calculating our approximate expectation in a trading position. Sometimes the calculated figure is rather rough, sometimes it's very close, but it is *always* only an approximation. This approximation can be dead wrong at times, too. When our trading model indicates one thing but our own eyes perceive something else entirely, we must resolutely junk the model, at least temporarily, and not bother with a visit to the optometrist. Part of Long-Term Capital Management's downfall was due to their outright refusal to discard certain of their risk and pricing models that were being proven more and more inaccurate with each passing day by the markets' movements. This is an error we *must* avoid: falling in love with a model is just deadly to our profitability (no disrespect to Elle MacPherson or Cindy Crawford, of course).

Aside from the plainly egomaniacal notion that we can somehow model future price movements with near precision, there are other reasons we must use models cautiously. Many famous models, Black-Scholes-Merton and Rubenstein-Leland (better known as "portfolio insurance") to name two, include one or more highly dubious assumptions. Please understand here that I'm not in any way criticizing any of these wonderfully talented theoreticians. I'd pay hard cash, any time at their convenience, to sit down with Robert Merton or Mark Rubenstein or Myron Scholes over a long lunch and discuss modeling and trading with any of them, or with numerous others. I admire these gents enormously, but notwithstanding that, some of the assumptions included in pricing models are quite suspect.

The primary suspicious assumption is that markets are continuous. Models many times (please keep in mind that I'm not familiar with all the models now in use) assume the mathematical continuity of markets, that is, that prices in markets move in small amounts, 0.01 or 0.05 or ⅛ or something similar. It would be delightful if this were the case, but it isn't at all, and you and I and anyone who has traded for longer than a month know this to be a fact. Markets frequently have ticks with large jumps, or gaps— the interjection "Duh!" must come in here someplace—and this awkward fact damages the usefulness of any model that assumes mathematically continuous markets.

These gaps are by definition discontinuities, and the effects they may have on our trading results are simply not included in any model of which I'm aware. If I were feeling bold, I'd say that they *can't* be included. How could anyone model the likelihood of occurrence of a 10-cent gap in soybeans, say, next Thursday? Or a 30-cent gap? The frequency of such occurrences we can easily calculate by looking at historical price movements, but there is no way to model when the *next* such gap will occur.

Can we compensate for the risk this and other dubious assumptions embedded in models pose to our capital? Indeed we can, and we can do so in at least two distinct ways. We've touched on both of them before, but we can now appreciate another reason to apply these tactics. Diversification of our trading positions is desirable from the standpoint of limiting capacity risk, and it becomes even more so as a means of dodging the risk that our trading model will be spectacularly wrong at some point. Certainly it must pose much less risk to us to have our model become radically inaccurate regarding one of our positions if we hold 10 or 12 positions than if we hold only 2 or 3.

We can also compensate in another manner. In addition to our firm commitment to avoiding the use of more than a fraction of the total leverage available to us, we can take another bite out of the potential risk when a model becomes erratic by keeping the size of each of our positions small.

Old advice, you say, nothing new here? Not really, for there's a very practical twist to this second tactic within the context of models. The SPAN margin requirement is derived from the lognormal model; therefore, unlike traditional keep-your-positions-small advice, we can actually quantify the answer to the question of "How small is small?" Here, "small" is, to a limited degree, a matter of personal preference, but there's a nice, easy rule of thumb to help us quantify the notion of "small." Assume that we're considering entering a position in a pure asset trade. For the sake of caution, let's postulate that a sizeable adverse price move will occur within a few days or a couple of weeks, in the market we're considering. We can generate quite a decent real-world estimated maximum size of the initial position to take in that market.

Suppose we're trading an account of $50,000, we have nine different positions in various markets, and our current margin requirement, as computed by the SPAN procedure, is $9,200 (yes, my skeptical friend, this is entirely possible, even normal for cautious traders). By our own rule from Chapter 2, we'll treble the actual margin requirement to $27,600, leaving $22,400 in theoretical free capital. Suppose that we're interested, for whatever reason, in selling April unleaded gasoline (ticker symbol HUJ), which has an initial SPAN margin requirement of $2,700 as I write this. Given our situation, what is a reasonable and risk-controlled maximum number of HUJ contracts for us to trade?

We can almost certainly agree that a move of 7.00 cents in one week's time is a significant move for a contract now trading at 60.00 cents. A 10% or larger move in a week's time? Oh, yes, we can agree on this, I do believe. Fine, the initial margin requirement on HUJ tonight is $2,700, times 3 for our initial safety cushion, or $8,100, plus 700 points, or $2,940, of postulated potential adversity risk, giving a total of $11,040. According to our free capital figure of $22,400, we would just have room to sell two contracts, which would involve $22,080 of assumed capital commitment encompassing the exchange margin figure of $5,400, plus the 1400-point postulated loss, plus the extra cushion we give ourselves when entering the trade.

However, we aren't going to sell two contracts of HUJ in this hypothetical situation; we'll sell exactly one. The other way to say this is that we will divide our current free capital by 2 before beginning our calculation. I can already hear the objections to this properly conservative notion of initially selling just one lot of HUJ. "You joker, I'm not going to sit for 700 points risk in HUJ!" and "How can you allot $11,000 for one lousy contract of gasoline and claim you're only using $9,200 for nine other positions, what a con job!"

Think it through, my friend. Neither of us will often tolerate anything like 700 points risk in the real world given our choice, *but we might not have the choice*. We're talking about model failure here, the possibility of occurrence of large gaps in a market, typically resulting from some outrageous or highly improbable event. Will you guarantee me that some terrorist loony-tune doesn't blow up a refinery or a pipeline, or that a for-real full-bore live shooting war doesn't erupt in the Middle East, either of which might result in much more than a 700 point move in HUJ, even perhaps within one day?

No, you won't do this, because you can't. Such events are possible, and your guarantee would be worthless. We'll be both conservative and practical to acknowledge these possibilities, and others unnamed, and to insure right now, if and as we can, against the risk their occurrence would pose to our capital. In this instance we can, and the insurance is so reasonably priced that we'd be fools to decline it. All we need do is refuse to take too heavy a position.

The point here is that if the model, and hence our trade, fails because of external event risk, I'll still be here to trade another day. You might have difficulty surviving such an event if you would trade 8 or 10 lots, which you notionally could do in our hypothetical account. One more time. It's called capacity risk, and to avoid it we must make as certain as we possibly can that we have the capital capacity to deal with a random outrageous event and not get blown out of the water like a torpedoed rowboat.

If you protested against the theoretical capital allotment of $11,040, as compared to the margin figure stated for our hypothetical pre-existing positions, please check the discussion again. By adding a position of 1 contract in HUJ, our initial margin as required by the exchanges, per the SPAN margining procedure, will only rise to $11,900. The rest of the figure we calculated is *cushion*, that amount of the insurance we voluntarily and gladly accept in order to provide against a potential failure of our model. The gambler in Chapter 1 may lose his stake due to external event risk, but he cannot lose more. We are using a considerable amount of leverage and we *can* lose more, a lot more, and we cannot breezily dismiss the possibility of occurrence, however remote, of the outrageous sub-event. As our assorted positions begin to move in our favor, we can and definitely should reduce this per-trade cushion, in the interest of efficient usage of capital, but we quite literally cannot afford to undertake such a reduction *before* we enter the trade.

So, You Don't Deal in Options, Eh?

Some traders apparently believe a number of myths about options. They break into cold sweats and begin twitching uncontrollably when the subject of options is raised. This reaction is remarkable to watch and difficult to understand, because every American who has capital or good credit, whether he trades in any market or not, implicitly deals with options almost every day of his life, one way or another.

Do you own a car? Do you own your home? Do you own rental property? Unless you bought these assets for cash, you deal or have dealt in options. Don't shake your head at me, you do deal in options. Can you pay down, or pay off, your loan on these assets any time you wish? If not, you have my sympathy, and I retract the preceding statements (and you really should have someone advise you, before taking out another such loan). If so, however, whichever lender financed your purchase of any of these assets also sold you an option to prepay all or part of the loan you made. It's your choice to prepay or not, correct? This is the precise definition of an option.

In this case, the lender sold you a put option on your interest payments, and a very interesting one, too, because it's a variable option. To exercise your option, you don't have to pay off the whole amount of your loan; you may do so in pieces, month on month as you find convenient, merely by paying an amount above the required monthly payment. When you elect to prepay a loan, you lower your capital debt immediately, but you also effectively sell back some amount of future interest to the lender for the intriguing price of *only* the time value of money, the expected interest rate over the remaining term of the loan. If interest rates, which by definition are the time value of money, are beginning to increase generally at some point, and if you've no other use for your capital for the moment, you might well consider prepaying part or all of your loan. Naturally, your decision to prepay will be influenced by the current interest rate charged on the loan, and whether this interest rate is fixed or variable, but you absolutely own an option here, because it's your choice to prepay or not.

You've paid for this option, certainly; it's not a free lunch at all. Lenders used to charge hard-dollar prepayment penalties as a matter of ordinary business, but no more. With the deregulation of interest rates and the fuller disclosure of lending practices beginning in the late 1970s, lenders cannot these days freely pick our pockets just because we wish to reduce our level of debt. Instead, they fold the cost of the prepayment option into the interest rate of the loan. So, what does this option cost? The practical way to discover its cost would be to approach two lenders and ask one for a standard loan, however defined and of a specific term, which we can prepay when and as we wish, and ask the second for an identical loan that we specifically cannot prepay. It would be very instructive to learn how much the second lender would discount the interest rate on his loan.

Loans are just one way in which you deal in options. Very possibly, especially during the recent bull market in stocks, your company might have granted options to you on its own shares, many times with an exercise price below (or way below) the current market price of the shares. These are call options by definition, of course. You have the right but no obligation at all to purchase your company's shares, under stipulated conditions, and prior to a certain date. The cost of these options to you is the expenditure of your time working for the company. Obviously, you will make your own decision as to whether this is a fair and worthwhile expenditure, and whether these options, in combination with your wages and any available non-wage benefits, represent good value regarding your time and effort. Regardless of the decision you ultimately make, though, you are dealing in options.

Do you use retail stores' coupons? You deal in a type of call option if you do. A store will sell you merchandise X at a reduced price Y on or before a particular date if you hand in the coupon when you buy X. These coupons are partial call options having the wonderful immediate price of zero. If you've a coupon in hand, you have the right, but no obligation whatever, to buy that merchandise at that store at the named price or with the named discount, on or before the named date. Your actual cost of this option is the incremental time and expense of going to the store that honors the coupon, which may well be zero if you had intended to go to that store anyway. The retailer or the manufacturer of the underlying product is writing this type of option in the hope that you'll purchase other products while you're in the store.

You don't deal in options, eh? Pardon me, but that's simply a false belief, if you still hold on to it at this point. These are but a few examples. The more interesting question is, since you already deal in options, why not use them to your advantage in your trading? Lenders do quite nicely by writing a prepayment option into your loan and charging a higher rate of interest. Companies retain good employees by writing nominally cheap calls on their shares, which the employees, presumably, will exercise for a profit at some point in the future as the company prospers. Groceries and retailers generally, and lots of manufacturers, do very well by writing discounting calls, coupons, or special offers, against your purchase of the products they sell, as an inducement for you to purchase more of them.

Isn't there something rather curious here? In each of these everyday cases, someone writes an option in order to achieve or help achieve a profit or business or marketing goal. These option writers gain by your acceptance and use of the options they write, even if you are (sorry, "have previously been") unaware of their existence, true? Is there some reason that you and I and the trader down the street should decline to use a similar tactic of writing options in our markets when and as we find this tactic to be advantageous to us? The only rationale that I can see for not applying various forms of this tactic to our trading is a combination of (many) traders' unfamiliarity with options trading and the presence of yet another myth.

Unlimited Risk, My Foot—An Amazing Myth

One of the most pernicious myths ever propagated by ersatz experts, and, oddly, by not a few thoroughly real experts too, has to do with one specific tactic that we might employ in using options in our trading. This is the myth of "unlimited risk" when a trader writes an option without also having an offsetting position in the underlying asset. This tactic is usually called writing a "naked" option, and this myth is incredibly pervasive. Some of the world's finest writers on the subject of options, Larry McMillan and Sheldon Natenberg among them, use the phrases "unlimited risk" or "unlimited loss" when discussing naked option writing in their books. This viewpoint just boggles the mind. Let's take a very stern and objective look at this myth, with the clear intention of putting a case of dynamite and a fast fuse right smack underneath it.

Pick a market, any market, stocks or futures or, for all it matters, nineteenth-century bowling balls (although we should suspect that the liquidity in this last market is a trifle too low for us to trade successfully, and option trading in this market is likely extremely thin). Take two positions in this market that will profit if this market moves up (or down, we can just as easily construct an example for the other direction). Let's say that today is July 7, and we buy December Chicago wheat at tonight's price of $3.33¾ per bushel for one position, and write a December wheat 330-strike put for 17¾ cents for the other one, temporarily pocketing the option premium. If the price of December wheat goes up between now and November 22 when the option expires, we will profit on both positions. If the price in November is within a few cents either side of tonight's price, we'll profit by writing the option and will make or lose a few cents on the purchase of the futures contract. Obviously, our trading risk shows up when the wheat market goes down.

Fine. Suppose July wheat goes to $2.00 between now and November 22. If we take no action in either position, we'll lose 133¾ cents on the future, plus contest risk. Now, the put option will be in the money (ITM), by 130 cents and will be priced almost exactly at that number, call it 130½, showing a loss of 112¾ cents (130½ – 17¾), plus contest risk. My, my . . . how odd. The dollar loss in the option position is less than that in the futures position. Looks like the option trade, in terms of pure dollar loss, is slightly less risky.

"Wait just a dang minute," I hear you shouting. "I'm not gonna stay long December wheat all the way down to $2.00! You think I'm nuts? I'll have a stop-loss order in there right away, and if it goes down 20 cents [or whatever amount you choose to risk], I'm out." Sure you will, you're not crazy. I will, too. So will Tom Clancy, Derek Jeter, the President, and General George S. Patton, Jr. . . . and he's been dead for 58 years.

And—guess what—so too will the trader who wrote the put option. The assorted commentaries concerning the so-called unlimited risk involved in writing naked options all appear to assume that a trader, just because he uses this tactic, has an extra strand of the stupids embedded in his DNA. Does an option writer spontaneously fall into a coma or something when a position goes against him? What nonsense! Just as those who trade in the underlying asset, the option writer will take some appropriate action to limit his loss, unless he happens to be a certifiable idiot. While there is no formal stop-loss order available to option traders, you, I, or anyone *will* liquidate the option trade (or possibly defend it, as we'll discuss in Chapter 7) at or near a pre-determined loss point, just as the asset trader would.

When we write a naked option, we accept a known maximum potential profit and an indeterminate loss if the market moves against us, but the horrific prospect of unlimited risk is simply false to fact. The risk in writing naked options is the *change in the ratio* of potential profit to potential loss, compared to the potential profit/loss ratio when we either trade assets or purchase options, considered over all the prices to which the underlying market might move until the option expires. Sound familiar? It should.

This so-called unlimited risk turns out to be nothing other than our old acquaintance, expectation. If our expectation in writing an option, either naked or covered by an offsetting position, is positive, we'll consider undertaking the trade. If not, we'll find something else to do. If our expectation is initially positive, but begins moving toward negative territory during the term of the trade as the market moves hither and thither, we'll either liquidate the position or take defensive countermeasures, certainly before the expectation of our trade actually becomes negative.

This mythical and widely vaunted notion of unlimited risk turns out to be just a variation on the logical fallacy of assuming one's own conclusion, to wit, that the potential loss is unlimited because an option writer won't take action to limit his loss, but an asset trader will. Please excuse me for a moment while I light this little fuse. There we go. . . . hissssssssssssssssssss. . . . BOOM!

Fanatics Are, Well, Fanatics

The preceding commentary, sadly, does not (and I've had this discussion many times) deter the true unlimited risk fanatic at all. He, she, or it will ask, rather stridently as a rule, "What about the December S&P Index futures on October 19, 1987?" "What about December Japanese yen on October 6, 1998?" or "What about April 2000 platinum on April 20, 2000, or July 1973 corn on July 17, 1973?" These dates saw some of the largest one-day moves in futures markets in modern history.

Yawn. Oops, pardon me. Dealing with fanatics is a little tiresome. Assuming only that our hypothetical option-writing trader has even a little discipline, avoids writing options in markets having excessive native event risk (palladium, to name just one), and hasn't recently been lobotomized, none of these exceptional moves were, would have been, or *could* have been more than a minor problem. Only one of these extreme price moves, the Japanese yen debacle, held *any* more risk for a naked option writer than for an asset trader. The risk to an option writer in two of these cases was exactly zero. No risk existed, no matter how much the underlying market might have moved. In the remaining case, a naked option write would never have been undertaken in the first place by any marginally rational retail trader, and surely not by you or me. Let's break these four examples down, right now.

July 1973 corn? On July 17, 1973, the market went up fully $1.30 per bushel during the trading session, the largest single percentage intraday move I've ever been able to find in modern futures markets. This date was the last trading day for the contract, and this was one heck of a move, about 60% of the corn contract's value the night before. There's just one *small* problem here for our unlimited risk fanatic. Options on futures were illegal in 1973. There were no such things. There was no unlimited risk because there were no options. Scratch one example.

Please allow me a small digression here. There's one point to make about trading late-in-the-life futures contracts, options aside. Any trader who holds a long futures position into the contract's notice period (wherein the trader may be assigned delivery of the goods described in the contract) and is not prepared to accept that delivery needs to reexamine his dangerously flawed ideas about risk, reward, and expectation. In the plainest possible English, don't even think of staying in a long position into the notice period, no matter your position or market view, unless you're prepared to settle the contract via delivery and a subsequent redelivery.

The experienced futures trader may say, "Big deal, I get delivery. So, I re-deliver, what's the problem?" While it's true enough that redelivery is generally a straightforward process, and your brokerage has surely handled many thousands of such transactions, the fact of the matter is that it's expensive. How does a minimum cost of $600 per contract in live cattle sound to you? Other markets are less confiscatory in terms of their delivery/redelivery costs, to be sure, but in every market you will be voluntarily increasing your trading costs, your contest risk. This isn't penny-wise and pound-foolish; this is plain old pound-stupid. Don't do it. By hook or crook, exit any long position you hold before the notice-of-delivery period begins.

The opposite case, holding a short position into the notice period, may or may not pose a related problem. Delivery is not an issue here—you, as the short-seller, are the party who decides whether or not to make delivery, and you and I most certainly won't be doing that—but the approach of expiration of the contract is of serious concern occasionally. Suppose the shorts in a market have difficulty acquiring the goods to deliver, or the goods are in the wrong place (for example, San Diego instead of New York in the case of unleaded gasoline, and a swap can't be arranged for some reason).

The shorts, in this situation, may get hammered by a short squeeze. The longs, the owners of the futures contracts the shorts have sold, can demand very nearly any price for the contracts that they want, and the short-seller will have to pay it in order to clear off the short position. July 1973 corn was a classic example of this situation, with some shorts having to pay upwards of $6,000 extra per contract just to get out of the position. You and I can't stand the gaff in this game, and the lesson here is completely clear. Don't stay short when there are only a few days left in a delivery-settled market (this is less risky if we're discussing a cash-settled market such as lean hogs, but it is still an undesirable tactic). Enough digression; let's return to blowing up the mythos surrounding unlimited risk in naked option writing.

What of our second example, the April 2000 platinum market? It ran up a tidy 41.59% on April 20, 2000. Sorry, Mr. Fanatic, but this alleged example was just a variation on the July 1973 corn theme, a classic short squeeze on the contract's last day of trading. Now, options did exist on the April 2000 platinum contract, but, terminally fatal for your argument, they had expired fully a month before the squeeze materialized. Whether platinum option traders had profited or lost when the April 2000 options expired, these traders certainly weren't put at risk by the last-day shenanigans in that market. They weren't even in the market at that time. Scratch two.

Black Monday? The date of the downfall of portfolio insurance and the 23% drop in the Dow Jones Industrial Average? If you had written naked put options on S&P futures sometime before that date, you have my sympathy, but wait just a minute here. You had all the *previous* week to remove your position, and you must have been quite mad if you wrote or sat with naked short puts during that previous week, too, because the various indexes had moved straight south throughout. Is this 20-20 hindsight? Not a chance.

Kid yourself if you wish, but don't kid me. The three trading days prior to Black Monday had already constituted one of the most severe short-term market drops in history. Who wanted to write or hold short the index put options during that week? Only bottom-fishers. Greedy bottom-fishers. Formerly solvent bottom-fishers. Taking or holding such a position, indeed *any* position, under the circumstances in force at that time and in that market, was nothing other than gambling at its utter worst. An old Chinese proverb applies fully here, and traders should always keep it in mind: when elephants fight, hope for the shade. Frankly, I'd say, *run* for the shade.

If you believe that event risk when trading stocks is disproportionately large compared to event risk in other markets (and I hope by now that you do), then why in the world would you as a disciplined trader consider writing naked index put options, then, now, or at any time? The historical return on your capital when writing these options, then as now, is rarely better than mediocre when compared to employing the same tactic in many other markets. I've asked this question of a number of traders, and usually the answer is something like "Well, indexes are less volatile than individual stocks, they rarely have large gaps in prices, so it's safer to write options on indexes than on individual stocks." Sigh. The continuous market fallacy rides again, and again, and again.

Aarrghh! True, America's stock markets rarely crash, but when they do crash, they crash more viciously than many other broad markets do *because* of the asymmetry between buying and selling short that we examined earlier. This asymmetry creates an ongoing and variable amount of pent-up desire to sell that cannot find expression in the normal market mechanism. Call it a selling panic waiting to happen. Furthermore, the histories of all stock market crashes that I can find are identical in one respect at least: the bear eats *everything* at the picnic, indexes included, and well before the dessert course, too. This notion of the relative safety of indexes during a crash is the merest moonshine, and it's 200-proof corn squeezins', too; it's downright deadly.

What rational trader, particularly a retail trader, wants to attempt to earn some very ordinary return on capital by accepting such a risk? Who, barring a very greedy, almost lunatic, trader would even consider jumping into a potential market crash situation and write puts? I don't care if these market crashes only occur as often as the Arizona Cardinals win the NFL championship (they're considerably more frequent, of course), this risk/reward situation is ridiculous. Do as you like, certainly, but *this* trader, your humble author, absolutely never writes, nor ever has written even once, naked put options against stock indexes. If we don't play a particular game, our risk in the game is zero. Scratch three.

The marvelous run-up of the Japanese yen against the dollar on October 6, 1998, in overnight forex trading, and in the Globex futures traded on the Chicago Mercantile Exchange's IMM, may appear to be a conclusive case against naked option writing and for unlimited risk, but it isn't. From the Asian currency meltdown of 1997, the Russian default in August 1998, and the so-called contagion that hit a bunch of Latin American currencies throughout the same time frame, the currency markets were pretty well screwed up. This wasn't any secret to anyone. Even those persons who claim to have learned how to trade cattle futures by reading *The Wall Street Journal* probably (no guarantees from me) had this one figured out. Nobody knew what the blazes would happen with a number of nations' currencies, and everyone was running scared.

I won't waste my time and yours weeping for the demise of a gold, or any other, standard, but the plain fact is that *every* national currency today is money only by fiat and at the point of a gun. Stripped of lofty-sounding frippery, currency trading was then, in 1998, and is still today a gigantic and complex variant of the card game we used to play as children, "pass the trash," sometimes called "screw your buddy," which is an accurate if mildly cynical description of currency policies among nations.

No longer is any nation's currency, to quote one classical definition, "a measure of value and a storehouse of wealth." These days, currencies are only units of account, economic constructs to facilitate commerce, and levers to be used as convenient against one or another of a nation's trading partners. All right, fine. If governments want to trade paper, traders will accommodate them. And, when government financial authorities, figuratively speaking I presume, start snorting PCP and smoking crack, as when the Bank of England attempted to maintain a fiction about the pound's value in September 1992, traders will tear them to pieces. But, we're discussing the astounding yen move in October 1998, so let's return to that.

As it happened, I had had an attack of the stupids and was short a few contracts of 1998 IMM December Japanese yen futures at the close of the day session on October 6, 1998. The position was mildly profitable at that point. I'd thought about writing a few put options to protect the position, but I hadn't (and I certainly should have, too, from the essential standpoint of reducing risk in a wildly volatile market). Early in the Globex overnight futures session, yen exploded just upward against the dollar. The sequence of action was amazing. Up and up yen moved, stopped for a cup of coffee, and then moved up some more. No one seemed to know what was happening except that a number of large market participants were unwinding the famous "carry trade," the arbitrage between Japanese and other nations' interest rates, which unwinding required the purchase of yen and the sale of other currencies. LTCM was rumored to be involved, and at that time, when many traders were at least vaguely aware that its collapse was imminent, even the mention of that name being active in a market was enough to shiver anyone's timbers.

The only thing I was absolutely certain of during that night was that I didn't have the faintest idea of what was going on, and I got the heck out of Dodge City. Not very gracefully, either, because I cleverly (cough, choke) managed to sit still too long and turn the existing profit into a loss. About 3 A.M. local time, disgusted with myself for having been slow to exit the trade, I bought a single contract of December yen (another very stupid decision, considering the risk—*never* trade when you're tired), entered a stop limit order 110 pips below the market, and went to bed. The next morning, I learned that yen had continued zooming higher and that my earlier loss had mostly been recouped. Huzzah! . . . mutter, grumble. I sold back the 1-lot and that was the end of that trade. Lots of aggravation, due to a good deal of incaution on my part. Not a penny of profit—and I didn't deserve any, either, having been some combination of stubborn and stupid along the way.

Now, suppose instead of being short yen futures, a trader had been short an equivalent number of naked calls. Options trading on IMM/CME currency futures is non-existent during the overnight Globex market, so what could an option writer do to protect himself, to limit or rid himself of risk? He might buy some quantity of the futures, sit still until the day session opens, and then liquidate the entire trade or adjust it further so that the expectation of the trade is again to his liking. He might execute an EFP, an exchange for physicals, which, depending on the terms of the EFP, might serve as well or better in the cause of risk reduction, but which would typically involve extra costs and wider bid-ask spreads. He might go to the interbank foreign exchange market to hedge his risk, but in doing so might and very likely would create other different risks, and would absolutely incur extra trading costs. He might try to purchase calls, similar to those he had previously sold, during the Irish session on the FINEX exchange, but usually the bid-ask spread is very wide in that market, and on that particular night the spread must have been nearly unbelievable.

Of these tactics, the first usually involves the lowest cost and is definitely simpler than the others, and probably would have been the best available way to proceed. This tactic reduces the remaining overnight risk to that of the occurrence of a sharp reversal, a whipsaw, and in wild markets such as yen was that night, a whipsaw was a distinct possibility. We'd always prefer to avoid such a risk, of course, but first things first—when we're under the gun in an existing position, we must deal with the risk at hand before worrying much about risks in the future.

Even supposing a trader had been short naked calls on yen on that explosive night, where's the unlimited risk? All trades except certain arbitrages involve some risk, but is a risk unlimited simply because a trader employs one tactic instead of another? Sell that stuff to the financial press if you will, but don't try to sell it to anyone who can add. The ultimate point here is that, as long as *some* countermeasure is available, whether to exit a trade, hedge it, or employ some other tactic, the risk in any position can be limited or eliminated, *assuming only that the trader is alert to the risk*. In this ferocious yen move, the naked call writer did indeed have more risk than the trader who was short the futures, said extra risk being more contest risk and the added potential risk of a whipsaw when defending the position overnight, but *unlimited* risk? What arrant rubbish! Scratch four.

The next time an unlimited risk fanatic crosses your path, don't waste your time trying to persuade him, her, or it of the error of its ways. After all, the fanatic just might be the person to whom you and I may be selling options in our next trade, and we can both use the money, I'm sure. Let the fanatics savor their own delusions undisturbed.

Stocks Good, Futures Bad—Shades of "Animal Farm"

Shortages of various goods occur occasionally, but there is not now nor ever will be any shortage of myths and moonshine about markets. Here's another common one. How many times have you heard someone pontificate about markets, something along these lines: "The stock markets create wealth. When you buy shares, you assist a company in raising investment capital that the company will use to build plants, employ people, or make better products, and profit thereby. Mathematically, stock trading is a positive-sum game, but futures markets are a zero-sum game that only transfers capital from one person to another." If you've traded in markets for any length of time, I'd be willing to wager hard cash that you've heard or read these or some highly similar sentiments. If you have, memorialize the occasion on which you did, for you've actually run across a truly world-class moron. These are scarcer than you might think, if we exclude politicians from consideration.

Remarkably goofy statements like this are factually incorrect in all particulars but one. Stock and bond markets are absolutely mechanisms for raising capital, but you and I, and that famously cited pair, Mr. Smith of Portland, Maine, and Mr. Jones of Portland, Oregon, never have contributed more than the tiniest pittance toward this process. Why? Companies raise funds only through the issuance of new shares or new bonds. For our part, unless we happen to purchase shares during an IPO or a treasury offering, the company itself will never see a penny of our capital, and the same is true when we deal in bonds. The rest of the time, these shares and bonds are exchanged among specialists, market makers, traders, investors, investment bankers, and mutual funds. The company in whose shares or bonds we trade is simply not in this loop, as regards raising new funds after the initial issuance of the instruments in question.

More laughably yet, our pontificator or anyone who utters a sentiment like this one either never took or flatly failed his university courses in game theory. Trading in any market is *always* negative-sum, in and of itself, because some fraction of capital is removed from the game with every single trade we make, unless we can somehow trade completely cost-free. In a positive-sum game, some external source would be continuously injecting capital into the game, by definition, and in a zero-sum game no capital would ever enter or exit the game, *by definition*. Pontificators who utter nonsense like this deserve nothing more than a polite invitation to have another drink.

Next, the stock markets create no wealth whatever. Wealth is created by the application of capital, effort, and management skill to a business enterprise over time. Prices of shares reflect this process in theory, but they neither initiate nor maintain it, and this actuality is all the difference. Finally, of course, the purpose of a futures market is not to create wealth, but to allow for the transference of risk from the producers and users of various goods and financial instruments to traders who will accept that risk in an attempt to make a profit. Our pontificator might as well whine about the President not being a competent left tackle. That's not his job, just as creating wealth is not and never has been the task of the futures markets.

You may very reasonably wonder why I would even bother becoming annoyed with phantasmagoric statements like the one at the beginning of this section and with the people who make them. What effect can such silliness have upon our trading results? That's an easy one. The first part of the answer is, "None, unless we let it." The problem is that you and I may hear or read such a statement, or any comparable potful of drivel, uttered by someone who has a large reputation as an expert in investing or markets or trading. We all are subject from time to time to being beguiled by the pronouncements of people whom we may perceive to be experts, and we may occasionally forget to analyze their statements objectively.

The second part of the answer is, whether our pontificator intends to or not, he is engaging in psychological warfare against us. Our pontificator obviously favors dealing in stocks over dealing in other markets. That's fine, and more power to him in his view, but instead of offering coherent reasons why trading in stocks is more advantageous to us, he merely recites erroneous platitudes and disparages other markets that he dislikes, expressing his view by mumbling pseudo-academic twaddle. Statements such as his are attempts to introduce doubt, or even some weird sort of guilt, into our minds regarding the relative risk advantage that we careful traders enjoy in trading in markets other than the pontificator's favorite. Our pontificator is the personification of information or knowledge risk, and we must utterly ostracize him and his ilk at all times. We'd do much better listening to Typhoid Mary discussing modern hygiene.

Profit Depends on Minds, Not Markets

Trading is about making a profit, in the best case by applying a disciplined method and an organized set of strategies over time. The markets in which we traders may deal are irrelevant to the activity of trading, except regarding the relative level of advantage we may obtain by dealing in one market and shunning another. I'd be perfectly happy to trade tiger shrimp, tiger lilies, Bengal tigers, or Kellogg's Frosted Flakes if I thought I understood how to profit by doing so.

Consider. If you and I would restrict our trading horizons by heeding the views of every purported expert to come down the pike, we'd very quickly find ourselves not trading at all! It's a lock cinch to locate an expert who dislikes any given broad market, any specific market within that broad market, or any given trading strategy we might employ. All other considerations aside, we should elect to trade in *any* market in which we can demonstrate to our own satisfaction that we can generate an advantage, and we should use whatever strategies will facilitate our claiming that advantage. Devil take the ersatz experts, the moonshiners, and the mythologists.

No part of this chapter is about bashing any other trader or any particular methodology. If a trader is successful in applying his methods, I cheer, whether I understand the methodology or not. I *like* winners. In his book *Pit Bull* (HarperBusiness, 1998), Marty Schwartz explained his methods in a general fashion, and his methods assuredly work for him. The same is equivalently and obviously true of other successful traders—their methods work . . . for them. You and I may or may not be able to put these other traders' methods into profitable use, or we may develop our own over time. However, we cannot possibly prosper until and unless we take the time to examine, and the more closely the better, the claims and underlying assumptions of *any* of those who would advise us, and to sort out the profitable from the unprofitable. And, make no mistake about it, you should absolutely apply this same standard to your favorite author.

Being cynical never earned anyone a dollar as far as I know, H. L. Mencken excepted. Discard any cynicism you may have about those who discuss trading, strategies, and methods. Some highly popular market pundits contain more crap than a Christmas goose, as you and I know (or should know) from experience. Fear of lawsuits prevents me from specifically naming a number of these folks right now, but consider all those financial experts, those clowns who ranted on about the "Y2K" event threatening a market disaster of Biblical proportions. Dang, I musta missed it! I hate it when that happens. Or, maybe these folks hadn't any clue in the first place?

Rather, and much more profitably, retain a healthy skepticism about such alleged experts and about any of their methodology, until such time as you can profitably apply portions of their advice or their strategies to your trading. When the mythologists, the moonshiners, and the morons crawl out of the woodwork and make all sorts of pronouncements about this, that, and the other thing, just give their views a withering look with a jeweler's eye. Smile at them and say "Thanks!"

Then fade them, and bank the profits. It's a *very* high expectation trade.

CHAPTER 5

No Hammer, No House

The Tools of the Trader

The house doesn't beat the player. It just gives him the chance to beat himself.
—Nick "The Greek" Dandalos

C apital and knowledge by themselves aren't sufficient for successful trading. We must also have a methodology for locating profitable opportunities, a discipline for limiting loss, and, unquestionably, continuing access to relevant and useful market information. I'd be shocked, however, if any two traders would agree on exactly what types and pieces of information are most valuable. Clearly, a useful set of information varies according to the markets we intend to trade and in our strategic approach to those markets. In addition, we require the means to obtain and process this information. We need a set of tools.

The trades I want to locate are generally longer-term than most futures traders prefer. These trades will have, as we'll continue to see, a definite positive expectation when entered and as high a theoretical probability of success as I can generate, consistent with a well-above-average return on capital. The approach I take to markets is broadly statistical, conditioned by historical price movement and the current and putative future supply/demand situations in the assorted markets. I'm not a technically oriented trader at all. Nothing against technical methods, but if you don't understand how and why certain methods work, you're surely better off not applying them to your trading. I know for an absolute fact that I don't understand how and why most technical methods operate, and therefore I don't employ them except in infrequent one-off situations.

Ignore History and Lose—No Exceptions

All right, what information do I require? First on the list, without any doubt, is a database of historical prices for a broad set of markets, perhaps 60–70 in all. Historical databases are available from numerous vendors, but be alert: the quality of the data varies *widely* from vendor to vendor. The best and most error-free end-of-day data I've found for futures markets comes from Pinnacle Data, at www.pinnacledata.com. The databases this company offers also have the merit of being very reasonably priced.

(Side note: you can be absolutely certain of three things when I mention any company's or person's product in this text. First, I use it. Not, "I have used it"; I use it and it's a very good product, for my purposes at least. Second, I don't receive and wouldn't take any compensation of any kind from any of these companies or people, period. Third, the number of such mentions in the text will be small; I'm not here to write advertising copy. Now, back to our exciting tale.)

In some instances, brokerages will provide price history data for some sort of fee, or even at no charge for good clients. Policies vary from brokerage to brokerage, so if you propose to use historical data as a tool in your approach to trading (which I believe strongly that most traders should), you would certainly be missing a bet if you didn't learn what your brokerage offers along these lines.

I trade futures options, mainly, and it would be entirely reasonable of you to assume that I also need a database of historical option prices. I'd *love* to have one, but I've never yet seen one in which the data were sufficiently error-free to use for analysis and didn't also cost approximately the French national debt. By all means, if you know of a company offering historical option price databases of good quality at a reasonable price (doesn't have to be cheap, just reasonable), would you please let me know?

Present-Day Information—The Sine Qua Non

For obtaining supply/demand and other worthwhile current market information, there's no one to match cash market brokers and professional market analysts, but—let's be honest here—not all analysts are created equal. I trade with REFCO, Inc. and with Salomon Smith Barney, and between them they've quite a number of very experienced and well-informed analysts. Better even than that, these analysts are all accessible to traders who have legitimate questions, and they typically also offer useful pre-market and post-market commentaries on their companies' Internet sites. Even if your brokerage doesn't maintain a staff of analysts, if they clear your trades through a firm that does, you can likely enough talk with the clearing firm's analysts. Again, the only way to find out is to ask. Talk about missing a bet, I know a flock of traders who have *never* asked this question, for reasons completely beyond me.

I said it earlier and I'll say it again: the Internet is indispensable to traders. If you don't use it for acquiring information, you are putting yourself at a dreadful disadvantage to other traders. While I freely grant you that a heck of a lot of the so-called information floating around the Internet is pure horse puckey, it's fairly easy to sort the gold from the pyrite with a bit of patience. The amount of useful and immediately valuable information available is simply staggering, and any trader would have to be purblind not to seek to take advantage of it.

Analytical Service

Now, we ourselves can manually wade through all the information we acquire, but that's just a little impractical, not to mention way too time-consuming. If you have any intention of applying historical data analyses or comparative supply/demand analyses to your trading, either use a computer and a spreadsheet program or find a commercial service that will perform your preferred analyses for you. I've only ever found one really convenient source for some of these analyses, but I haven't looked around as vigorously as I probably should have done.

That source is Moore Research, Inc., www.mrci.com, whose principal is Stephen Moore, and which offers a enormous amount of historical data, numerous different analyses, and a good deal of commentary. They keep all the information on their site nice and current and charge the reasonable sum of $344 per year for their basic service, which is dirt cheap at double considering all the information available there. One extra valuable feature of their service, from my perspective, is a continually updated presentation of specific seasonal tendencies in various markets. Having this information at hand is quite valuable in locating potentially profitable situations because I don't have to expend time and effort replicating Moore's research.

This is not to say that there aren't other equally fine or even better services available, whether on the Internet or elsewhere, it's to say that I'm simply not aware of them at this time. For that matter, as long as I'm admitting things, you should also know that I don't use a spreadsheet. I don't even know how to add up a column of numbers using a spreadsheet (I'll get around to spreadsheets one of these days . . .). My business is computer systems design, and over the decades I've written some hundreds of programs that analyze price databases, and, naturally, these are very easy to use . . . for me. In the wide world of trading, though, my personal situation is just a fluke. Either purchase or gain access to commercial analysis software or

Internet sites offering whatever types of analyses you favor, or use a spreadsheet. If you don't want to purchase a commercial analysis product and you aren't comfortable with spreadsheets, take some time to become comfortable with them. You can't afford, literally you cannot *afford*, to concede the analytical advantages of this tool to the other market participants.

Where *Is* My Capital? PC-SPAN

Every worthwhile book ever written on trading discusses capital management at some length, and this one will be no exception. We've touched on this topic earlier, in the notion of refusing to use the maximum leverage available to us in any market, and that's fine, as far as it goes. We need to go further, however, for there is another thoroughly indispensable tool for proper capital management when trading futures and futures options. This tool is PC-SPAN, the computer program developed and sold by the Chicago Mercantile Exchange. This program, using cost-free downloadable files as inputs, will keep you abreast of your current margin requirement and inform you when capital considerations indicate that a modification of your position(s) might be a good idea, and it does much more. It offers you the ability to view your capital and margin position in the future as prices and volatilities in the markets change, the well-known "what-if" analysis. This sort of forewarning is worth rubies to any trader.

At this writing, PC-SPAN version 4 costs $500.00, and it's worth every penny and then some to the serious trader. I don't care if you can get your brokerage's margin department on the phone on demand (and I'd wager you can't, these days!), without PC-SPAN, you simply cannot obtain all the information you need to manage your capital in a careful and practical fashion. Frankly, I've lost count of the times that PC-SPAN has either warned me of an impending margin problem, or indicated a sensible adjustment in an existing position, or pointed the way toward the most efficient use of capital in a new position I'm considering. It has easily paid for itself 20 times over or more, and I can't imagine trading as profitably without it.

Even if you principally trade in stock markets, you should still acquire PC-SPAN. Numerous overseas stock markets use the SPAN model to determine margin levels right now, and more are adopting this procedure all the time. U.S. stock markets are the primary holdout to date, and their resistance is entirely due to the inertia of legislators regarding the repeal of Federal Reserve Regulation T, which prescribes allowable margin levels for these markets. Given the development of modern risk analysis and its subsequent application to margin requirements, the technique usually called portfolio margining, Regulation T is a dinosaur and the next Ice Age is on its way. The advent of single-stock futures, which are backed by every major exchange in the United States except the NYSE, will further crank up markets' and traders' demand for elimination of Regulation T. Being familiar with the SPAN procedure through the use of PC-SPAN will be entirely to your advantage when the dinosaur bites the dust and the stock markets in which you trade do finally adopt portfolio margining.

Markets Are Made Up of People

The Rolodex, computerized or otherwise, is nearly the ultimate tool for the trader who intends to become and remain steadily profitable. Aside from your brokerage's market analysts, make a deliberate effort to acquire the phone numbers and e-mail addresses of successful traders you meet. Keep track, too, of people who write about trading, as well as industry analysts, cash market dealers, floor traders, theoreticians, and generally anyone who can provide accurate information on markets. I'm an absolutely shameless brain-picker, and being willing to brain-pick is the only way for a profitable trader to be. If a trader needs information on a particular topic, he must go to where—which is almost always to whom, in the practical sense—such information can be found.

There's good news to be had here, too. You might be thinking something like, "I can't impose on such people. They're way too busy to talk to me." Perhaps they are busy, but write this down: traders love to talk about trading. Professors love to talk about their theoretical work, although mere mortals like you and I have to be careful in these conversations lest we find ourselves getting onto esoteric topics far removed from trading and about which we haven't a clue. Authors absolutely adore talking about their books and articles. People are proud of what they do, and in the huge majority of cases are more than happy to respond to serious questions concerning their respective areas of expertise. We traders would have to be stark mad not to use this feature of human nature to improve our knowledge base and our trading.

There's a caveat here, of course. We cannot reasonably expect other people to operate on schedules convenient to us, and we must therefore learn to time our inquiries properly. Calling a trader near the opening or closing of his favorite markets is pure lunacy and will guarantee his placing you on his list of idiots-to-be-avoided. Calling someone at 10:00 P.M. (their time, in the United States) who writes an overnight newsletter on forex trading is a sure way not to acquire a valuable source (hint: that person is probably asleep at that time, because of the time frame in which forex markets trade). Calling an academic is a tricky business at all times, unless you've acquired a direct phone number. A cold attempt to penetrate a university bureaucracy and locate Professor X is almost invariably a futile endeavor.

Don't even think about calling an author of a daily or weekly commentary or newsletter at or near his deadline.

What about e-mail? It's terrific, as long as you don't need the information you're asking about right away. If you're considering a trade in sugar sometime in the next week or so, then e-mailing those whose brains you wish to pick is a perfectly reasonable action and will probably yield the commentary you want. If you're considering a similar trade in the next hour or two, though, e-mail is just a Dirty Harry proposition: "Do you feel lucky?"

In almost all cases, though, you will and should—out of pure politesse and undiluted practicality—also attempt to find out from, and if at all possible provide to, your various sources the kinds of information useful to them. We are traders, are we not? We cannot expect other traders, or analysts or whomever, to pave all of Information Avenue at and for our convenience; we must be willing and able to shovel some asphalt and drive the steamroller for their benefit from time to time, too.

There's one more tool you really should use in order for your attempts to acquire information from other people bear more fruit. Some healthy percentage of the time when you call an out-of-town source, he or she is not going to be available that moment, for any of a long, long list of reasons. They'll have to call you back. Don't ask them to contribute their money, in addition to their time, effort, and expertise, to your cause. Some people are unbelievably nice about this, but you've gotta know what's going through their minds when they dial your number, don't you? Get an inbound 800 number. It's cheap to start, and will pay for itself over and over again because it completely removes one reason why a source might not return your call. The easier you make things for those from whom you want assistance, the more you'll get.

No Recipe, No Omelet—Be Prepared to Learn

Trading is an extremely curious activity in one sense. Would you attempt to perform a tonsillectomy on a friend tomorrow morning, having had no previous medical training at all? Extremely unlikely, I'd say. Would you care to try to compete in the Daytona 500 next year? Not to worry, even if you'd like to, NASCAR very prudently wouldn't let you anywhere near the track without substantial prior experience, and no racing team would even return your calls. Absent thorough legal training, would you consider attempting to plead a case before the Supreme Court, or even before a local magistrate?

Barring the occasional egomaniac or psychotic, no one would attempt any of these activities. Yet, some tens or hundreds of thousands of people every year enter the world of trading with the same lack of training and experience. They plunk down some capital and away they go, dollar signs in their eyes. Well, I'll be happy to take their money, but this is purely unreasonable on their part. Trading isn't the most complex activity in the world by a long chalk, but trading profitably in a consistent and disciplined fashion, from scratch and without any experience, is just a trifle more difficult than most activities requiring specific skills. Granted, there are so-called natural traders. There are natural plumbers, too, and natural athletes and people with green thumbs who can grow anything. I'm delighted at these folks' abilities, and more than a little envious, wish I had them, any of them.

All of these naturals, though, are a tiny minority of the set of people engaged in their respective activities. For the rest of us, acquiring knowledge and experience about an activity is essential before we can rationally expect to succeed at the activity. If I were to want to re-wire the circuitry in my house by myself, I'll guarantee you that I'd acquire every book on practical applications of the principles of electricity that I could find. And, you bet your sweet ol' grandma that I'd bend the ear of every electrician who would give me the time of day. Why? A priori, and absent learning about the subject at hand, and in the best case obtaining a good deal of practice at it, I know that I don't know how to succeed, how to do it right, or even how to do it in a marginally acceptable fashion.

The would-be instant trader, however—and I've met hundreds, and likely so have you—doesn't ordinarily hold this view. They'll say something like, "Hey, I'm a successful lawyer (or pediatrician, or professional athlete, or businessman), I know what it takes to make a buck!" They ignore or forget how they came to be successful in their own field—through study, practice, and experience—and they assume their future success in trading because of their success in their own field. Oops. When they turn to trading, they have exactly one advantage, namely, that there is no one right way to turn a profit in trading, and they might get lucky. This advantage doesn't help them much, though. This is philosophically a very interesting topic. After all, have you ever met a successful trader who believes he'd also be a successful beekeeper or doctor or, for that matter, a successful chef, just by purchasing a toque and an apron, snapping his fingers, and saying, "Shazam! Now I'm a chef!"? I can't think of a single one, can you?

The would-be instant trader will do what he likes. Perhaps he will discover his information and experience deficit in his own time. Traders, meaning specifically you and I, will continue to study our craft. Out of nothing less than pure self-interest, I try to find something worthwhile about trading or markets to look at and to learn from every week (it's tempting to say every day, but that would be an exaggeration in fact). In short, *read!*

It would be silly in the extreme for me to try to name exactly which books to read in order to improve your trading. You'd be entirely within your rights to tell me to get stuffed. You and I are unlikely to have the same strategic views about markets or the same preferences as to markets in which to trade, and that's fine. I would, however, like to suggest several works that have improved my profitability significantly.

On the subject of options, the world's most popular writer (and with very good reason) is Larry McMillan. Get out the stone tablets and your engraving tools right now. Thou shalt acquire the current edition of *Options as a Strategic Investment* (NYIF, 2002) if thy wish is to prosper in options trading, no matter thy strategies. His other major book-length work, *McMillan on Options* (Wiley, 1996) should definitely be on your bookshelf, too.

If the traders on the exchange floors swear by a certain book, I know I want to read it. Sheldon Natenberg's *Options Volatility and Pricing* (Irwin–McGraw-Hill, 1997) is one such book. Some of the mathematics in the book is a bit daunting to non-mathematicians, but his discussions of numerous facets of options trading are very clear and he has quite a knack for getting right to the heart of matters, in my view. As a nice bonus, he offers a useful list of works on options by other authors and conveniently ranks these works by their relative degree of difficulty. On a whim, I bought one of the books he rates as "advanced," and, while I'm certain that that author knows very well whereof he writes, I got lost on about page 36 . . . and I used to be a, er, half-slow mathematician in my youth. To Mr. Natenberg, "advanced" means *advanced*. Just be advised.

One of the most helpful books I've ever read, mentioned previously, is the late Harrison Roth's *LEAPS* (Irwin, 1994). Harry Roth was concerned only with stock markets, and his book only deals with long-term stock options, but his thorough discussion of option strategies (written in a wonderfully readable and enjoyable style) is an excellent precis of the nuts and bolts of strategizing and applied tactics in options trading. One additional quality of Harry's writing is that he is occasionally hilarious—and there's nothing like a good laugh to keep the mind clear, is there?

A gent named David Caplan has written about options for years. He may have offered one of the best shortcuts for options traders ever written. One of his works, essentially just a long article with lots of graphics, titled *Trade Like a Bookie*, is very worthwhile for option writers to read. I've never met Mr. Caplan, but I can tell you right now that some of his strategies are highly similar to those we'll be examining a little later on in this text.

The Internet comes into our picture yet again regarding the subject of useful tools. There are several popular discussion and commentary forums that are Internet-based. This is not to say that we can wantonly jump into any of these forums and expect to be told all or any of the secrets of the universe. That's just not going to happen. The sundry forums I've visited, and the one I participate more or less actively on, though, do offer us a clear contrary indicator occasionally. If you visit one of these forums, and you observe that some large fraction of the contributors are talking about gold, or wheat, or soybeans, or coffee, it's time to look around for a statistically or historically profitable way to trade *against* these enthusiasts in the current supposedly hot market.

Cynical? *Moi?* Not a chance. Skeptical? Absolutely, because, once again, *most traders lose*, and the louder the voice, the more likely the loss, in my experience. Ask yourself: who posts messages on Internet forums, stating that such-and-so a market will or will not behave in thus-and-such fashion? A few of those who do are individuals of good will and considerable trading or analytical skill and experience, offering the best information and ideas they have. Most are not, however. These others range from the inexperienced trader with good intentions, to the consistently losing trader who for some perverse reason wants to see other market participants share his fate. Doubtless, too, there will be some political ideologues, conspiracy theorists, and DNA-damaged people in the mix. Stated very baldly, the presence of such unfortunate individuals tends strongly to work to our advantage, provided we regard these latter folks as contrary indicators. We take our advantages anywhere we can find them.

Time Waits for No Man . . . or Trade

There's one more tool in our kit, one that may not seem obvious. It's enormously powerful, but many traders apparently have some difficulty in using it to their advantage. This tool is *time*. It's just sitting there waiting for us to use it, we don't have to spend a dime to acquire it, and all its power is available to us just for the price of understanding.

When we trade options, we can usually put time on our side to one degree or another, and we are utterly negligent if we don't at least try to claim this trading edge. Options are famously described as "declining assets" because they lose value over time. Look at any table of striking prices and market prices on the options available in any market and you'll see one absolutely constant condition. Go ahead, pick up a copy of *Investor's Business Daily* any day you like. Or, visit quote.cboe.com for stock option prices or check the futures options' closing prices each day at www.bohlish.com (a remarkably useful, and free, Internet site, by the way, provided by a very savvy introducing broker named Bernie Bohl) after about 4:15 P.M. Central time.

One thing is absolutely plain, every single day. The price of any option, per unit of time remaining in its life, is highest for the shortest-dated and lowest for the longest-dated options. Option premiums also vary directly with their IVs. The general principle of time with regard to options trading is this: when buying options, buy as much time as you can conveniently afford, and prefer buying options with lower IVs to options with higher ones. When writing options, sell the smallest chunk of time you can manage (consistent with caution and a satisfactory notional return on capital, of course), and prefer writing higher-IV options over lower-IV ones.

Please note that, regarding options, this buy-the-long-date, write-the-short-date, buy-the-low-IV, write-the-high-IV advice is nothing new. One way or another, virtually every book or article ever written has acknowledged these basic principles of options trading. One thing is puzzling, though. How is it that there are *still* so many traders who willfully misapply these principles in their trading? More curiously yet, there is another sizeable group of traders who, for whatever reason, simply refuse to exploit the advantages that a proper consideration of time would offer them. I've no idea why these camps don't use time to their advantage, but I've a very good idea of how to relieve them of some of their capital as they fail to do so. Don't emulate these folks in your trading, okay? Get accustomed to enlisting time as your ally to whatever degree possible, all the time.

There are numerous Internet sites that offer lots of data about option IVs. A Google search using +"futures options" +"implied volatilities" as the search key will turn up quite a few very interesting sites (along with, sadly, a lot of brokerage sites which usually require a lot of time and effort to navigate successfully). One particular page on one of these sites is an excellent time saver regarding option IVs. The multifeatured service site, www.optionetics.com, publishes a summary page of futures options' IVs every day. If I'm in a hurry or away from the office, the Web page http://platinum.optionetics.com/cgi-bin/oamergef/www/tablesf/rank6mo has a nice table of 6-month ranges of IVs for most of the major American futures markets. Within the table, the various markets are ranked from most expensive to least expensive, in terms of the relative level of the options' IVs within their recent range. Option IV ranges for other lengths of time are presented on related pages at this site. Additionally, by clicking on a specific market, you can view all the current information about *every* individual option in that market. Theoretical fair values, option deltas, all the so-called "Greek" figures are all there, right in one spot. Very convenient indeed.

If information is the key factor in making trading decisions, then our toolkit must be designed with a view toward facilitating our ability to gather and analyze information, on both an immediate and a long-term basis. Any tool that advances our efforts here is a worthwhile one, and we should spend some amount of effort to acquire new tools over time, while also improving our current ones when we can. We should distinctly also realize that information is directional. Most information is positive in that it fills a gap in our knowledge, clarifies a situation in a market, or assists our decision-making process in other ways. Negative information, that which allows us to draw accurate negative inferences about a market, should not be allowed to fall off our radar screen, though. It's every bit as useful to fade a losing trader, provided we can identify him, as it is to ride the coattails of a successful one.

What we haven't explored yet is the application of all this information and the principles I've mentioned to profitable real-world trading. Which strategies among thousands of possibilities offer us top-notch opportunities to profit, and which tactics can be used gainfully within the context of these strategies? Why haven't we done this? Because that's what we're going to do for the rest of our time together, starting right now.

CHAPTER 6

Thomas More's Revenge

A Strategy for All Seasons

"Is there any other point to which you wish to draw my attention?"
"Only to the curious incident of the dog in the night-time."
"The dog did nothing in the night-time."
"That was the curious incident," remarked Sherlock Holmes.
—Sir Arthur Conan Doyle (*Silver Blaze*)

One thing that most traders do almost all the time is to try to anticipate where a market is likely to move in future, be it in an hour, a day, or a month. There's nothing inherently disadvantageous in doing this. It might even be called normal in some sense. However, as we've observed previously, most traders tend strongly to lose, so we must conclude that most traders are considerably less than accurate in forecasting where a given market will move over some period of time. We have two alternatives here: we can either learn to improve our forecasting methods, or we can try a different approach.

Have you ever considered trying to anticipate and profit from where a market is *not* likely to go, what the dog won't do in the night-time, so to speak?

It turns out that this is a relatively easier task, for several reasons, than predicting future market direction. First, some large amount of the time, any given market does nothing. It goes sideways, up a day, down the next two, up the next four, then down for two more. You and I have certainly entered many trades and waited for the market participants to make up their collective mind, true? This decision never occurs until the market acquires enough information to move in one direction or the other, and this acquisition process can easily take weeks, even months. During such a period, if a market is mired in, say, a 5% range for months and there's little prospect of market-shaking developments on the horizon, it's reasonable to consider that a 15% move within the *next* month is an unlikely proposition, barring, as always, the advent of the unpredictable.

Next, there is the more complex case of a market that is strongly trending in one direction or the other. As you and I have seen frequently in this type of market, during the course of the trend there will occur one or more countertrend moves, "corrections" if you like, sometimes very sharp and extensive ones. This isn't news to anyone, but when the countertrend move has apparently stopped and the original trend has resumed, we can ask ourselves a potentially very profitable question. Are the market factors that fueled the original trend still in place? Naturally, the answer to this question is indeterminable in many cases, but when it *is* determinable—as, for instance, when there is a known supply shortage that will not and cannot be eased for some time—opportunity awaits. In such a case, we can select or design a trade that will be profitable *unless* this market resumes its zippy countertrend move within a known period of time.

We are also able to design similar trades when a market is about to enter a period of the year in which it tends firmly to move in one or the other direction. This is a very valuable strategy for our purposes, because such seasonal tendencies occur much more frequently than do countertrend moves in trending markets. Seasonally based strategies have been used ever since there have been markets, and with good reason. The Earth revolves around the sun after all, supplies of agricultural products increase when they're harvested, obviously, and harvests occur within a broadly predictable period for any given crop.

When I was a futures broker in the 1970s, there was a surprisingly accurate and therefore popular set of seasonal trades, so popular in fact that some brokerages marked these trades' entry and exit dates on the trading calendars they gave to their clients. These were called collectively "The Voice From The Tomb" and were the creation of a remarkable person whose name I've never known. Whoever he was, with only pencil and paper, mind you, he kept track of decades of grain prices and figured out a set of optimized entry and exit dates for trades in a considerable number of futures contracts. He directed that his calculations not be published until well after his death, thus the colorful name for these trading ideas.

As you rightly suppose, the advent of the personal computer has given this type of analytical capability to anyone who wants it. There are now books and Internet sites and newsletters, electronic or otherwise, devoted to the analysis and discussion of seasonal trades. With a database of historical prices, a computer, and a spreadsheet program, anyone can perform as many seasonal entry/exit analyses as desired in a very few minutes, and for a ten-thousandth or less of what such capability would have cost only 30 years ago. If you're of a mind to perform this sort of analysis yourself, let me strongly encourage you, because studying these seasonal entry/exit analyses is an absolutely wonderful method of learning about market tendencies over time, and a good way to turn a trading profit, too.

The Non-Seasonal—Being Not Wrong Is Easier Than Being Right

We can easily use a seasonal-following strategy when we want to, but such a strategy is hardly flawless or without its own considerable risk. Seasonal trades, let's face it, don't always behave this year as they did in previous years, for a large variety of reasons. Actually, we can build the proverbial better mousetrap if we examine what markets *don't* do at specific times of the year, looking in effect for a seasonal non-tendency, or, as I like to call it, a "non-seasonal" tendency. If a seasonal tendency is valid over the years, traders will trade it, and probably profitably too, but the amount of profitability and the interim risk will vary widely from year to year (or else everyone would trade it every year, right?). All right, that's perfectly clear, but let's ask a different question. Pick a market, any market, during some portion of the year. What are the largest moves upward and downward for that market within that period, over some reasonable number of years?

For an example of the non-seasonal strategy, take a look at Table 6.1, will you? These are the historical market prices for the NYMEX August unleaded gasoline (ticker symbol HUQ) contract from June 17 through July 26 over 12 years. The first column is the putative entry date, and the second is the market-on-close (MOC) price on that date, which we'll name as our theoretical entry point. The third and fourth columns are the interim highs and lows reached by the market during the named period. The sixth column is the MOC price on the end date of the period or the next business day following, which is the fifth column. The seventh column is each year's result if one had held the trade from the start date through the end date, ignoring all trading costs and not setting any stop-loss point. The last column is the cumulative result achieved over the years by undertaking this trade on the start date and holding it through to the end date unless the stop-loss point (shown below the table, at right) has been hit. This last column's figures do take our estimated contest risk into account.

August unleaded gasoline closed at 79.40 on Monday, June 17, 2002 (which by a huge coincidence is the date I'm writing this). From Table 6.1, it would seem to be the case that this market's price tendency is moderately downward in the period we're examining. Whether trading this very modest seasonal tendency is a good idea is not of immediate concern to us. But,

TABLE 6.1 Seasonal Buy Study, August Unleaded Gasoline, 1990–2001

Entry Date MOC	Entry Price	Interim High	Interim Low	Exit Date MOC	Exit Price	Gross Result	Cumulative Net Result
90-06-18	56.12	65.55	54.10	90-07-26	65.26	+9.14	+9.000
91-06-17	61.45	66.70	59.80	91-07-26	65.80	+4.35	+13.210
92-06-17	66.05	66.25	57.20	92-07-27	61.89	−4.16	+9.270
93-06-17	55.31	56.10	49.90	93-07-26	52.06	−3.25	+5.330
94-06-17	55.32	57.30	51.75	94-07-26	57.16	+1.84	+7.030
95-06-19	57.56	58.70	51.50	95-07-26	52.89	−4.67	+3.090
96-06-17	60.41	65.56	56.70	96-07-26	60.16	−0.25	+2.700
97-06-17	57.84	65.50	54.65	97-07-28	64.84	+7.00	+9.560
98-06-17	47.45	49.70	41.10	98-07-27	42.82	−4.63	+5.620
99-06-17	53.56	62.60	51.40	99-07-26	61.75	+8.19	+13.670
00-06-19	98.27	104.00	86.00	00-07-26	89.25	−9.02	+9.730
01-06-18	84.09	86.00	69.70	01-07-26	76.36	−7.73	+5.790

Average on 12 buys: +0.482 cents; stop w/loss of: 3.80 cents

Interim Movement
Avg Up 4.211   Max Up 9.430   Avg Dn 5.803   Max Dn 14.390

Notes: August unleaded gasoline (NYMEX), HUQ; buy on 06-17, sell on 07-26.

what about the non-seasonal tendency, that HUQ doesn't rise strongly during this period?

HUQ historically has never risen 17% in price over this period, and the maximum gross price rise has been 9.43 cents, 943 points. We want to ask ourselves, "Is there some reason that HUQ might move upward more than this in this period *this* year?" What are the current market factors that might propel the price of gasoline well higher?

Well, the Middle East situation is as muddled as ever. OPEC is meeting next week, and the "wise men" are saying, to a man, that OPEC members will not raise their production quotas this summer. With West Texas Intermediate (the American benchmark grade) crude oil above $25.00 and the OPEC "basket" of several crudes almost to $24.00, OPEC appears to be perfectly satisfied with oil's price level, and its members likely won't lower the production quotas either. The homicide bombings in Israel are at an all-time high, but this fact doesn't seem to be affecting energy prices so far. This situation rates to get worse, though, principally because no one seems to have any idea how to stop it, and the Palestinians sound as if they've no intention of desisting.

After a spring season of refinery problems due in part to 2001's heroic production runs, refiners seem to have hit a steady stride, and the big Citgo refinery in Illinois is back on line (very important for supplying the custom blend of gasoline required in the upper Midwest). The EPA, notably and for once, hasn't issued new onerous regulations concerning summer gasoline. Supplies of motor gasoline are a touch higher than last year, although this figure is down from a 7% year-on-year increase six months ago. Demand is about nine million barrels per week in America, fairly typical for the Memorial Day–Fourth of July period over the past few years. Norwegian oil workers have just opted not to strike, removing one potential disruptive factor, and Norway and Russia (who aren't OPEC members) have stated that they won't honor the OPEC production cutbacks in the next quarter, beginning July 1. The price of gasoline, after a spring run-up, has been whopping and flopping in the 75–80 cent range for a couple of weeks.

In terms of supply and demand, there doesn't seem to be a strong bull or bear case to be made in gasoline right now. This situation can change in a heartbeat, without doubt, if one of the players in the Middle East does something sufficiently stupid, but, as the guy who jumped off the Empire State Building said as he passed the fiftieth floor, "So far, so good."

Who Needs a Trend to Profit? Not Us

Now, how do we propose to profit from all this wonderful information about this apparently neutral market? It looks like there's little to choose between buying the market and selling it, but who says we must do either? Why not profit by writing an option whose striking price is *most* unlikely to be reached within a very limited time? Given that the HUQ options expire in five-plus weeks, on July 26, let's just crunch a few numbers.

HUQ's price tonight is 79.40. Seventeen per cent, just a trifle more than the maximum percentage upmove from June 17 to July 26 in our study, of 79.40 is 13.50, which added to 79.40 gives 92.90. We can reasonably assert that HUQ is historically unlikely to reach the 93.00 cent level. Is this analysis good enough? Should we therefore write the 93.00 HUQ calls? We could do so and have a fine expectation of earning a profit, but first we want to consider some other implications from our historical price study.

When did HUQ have its largest upmove in the period we're examining? In 1999. What was happening in the energy markets in 1999? After years of bickering, back-stabbing, and cheating, and after the price of crude oil had collapsed in 1998, OPEC finally started getting its act together. It became, for the first time in a long while, a reasonably effective cartel. Crude and its products were wildly oversold throughout 1998, for one reason because various of the OPEC players were fighting for market share to the detriment of prices. The major non-OPEC producer, Russia, was trying desperately to restore its financial credibility after its horrendous currency devaluation and bond default in 1998. Russia simply hadn't the capital to invest in upgrading its oil industry's infrastructure and increasing production of its staggeringly huge oil and natural gas reserves.

The other 16+% rise in HUQ during our sample period, in 1990, was of course due in large part to some market participants' anticipation of Iraq's reckless action on August 1, 1990, leading ultimately to the Gulf War. In theory, this sort of thing can recur at any time, but Iraq's military posture offers no hint at the moment that they are preparing for a general mobilization, and certainly not in the next five weeks.

It seems that neither of these sets of factors will affect the energy markets this summer. HUQ, particularly, is nearer its yearly highs than its lows and isn't oversold at all; some analysts even consider gasoline to be overbought at this time, and, if actually so, this factor would likely work to our advantage in writing call options. Gasoline supply is ample, considerably improved over the past three years. Capital, in limited but still significant amounts, is flowing back into the Russian oil industry, and the President is clearly making overtures to the Russians, presumably with a view toward establishing long-term supply agreements. Even OPEC has finally seemed to realize that crude oil at $30.00/barrel when the world economy is relatively slow is *not* to their longer-term advantage.

The practical implication of this supply change from 1999 for us traders is to allow us to be slightly bolder than we might otherwise be. Another way to say this is that the lack of evident threats to supply such as those that impelled large upward price moves in 1990 and 1999 lowers our potential event risk somewhat. We ordinarily prefer to select a striking price well past the extent of the largest historical price movement. In this HUQ example, such a strike would be calculated as 13.50 (17% times tonight's closing price) times 1.15, or 15.53, plus tonight's price of 79.40, or 94.93. Achieving this price would require a 15% greater upmove than has ever occurred during the period. The 95.00-strike HUQ call would, by this process, be our candidate for writing tomorrow morning. Historically, and absent some off-the-wall event, we should bank a profit by writing this option some enormous percentage of the time, perhaps as often as 99 cases out of 100.

We might gain an additional perspective to aid in our selection of the strike of the call to write. Have another look at Table 6.1. Check the couple of years when HUQ prices were high at the start of our sample period. Interesting, no? If we accept this very limited set of data as indicative, upmoves in our named period are quite small when prices are high at the start of the period. This is understandable. The dynamics of any market change along with its price. Cocoa prices don't behave the same when the market is at $1700/tonne as when it's $750/tonne. An $8.00/bushel soybean market behaves nothing like a $4.50/bushel market. And so with gasoline, too, no matter how much some academic types may yap about the price inelasticity of demand that is peculiar to gasoline.

With these additional supply/demand and market history considerations, writing the 95.00-strike call becomes a little conservative, but still a very good selection. The overall set of factors, though, leads me to prefer writing HUQ calls with a strike of 91.00, 92.00, or 93.00, likely the 92.00. It settled at 81 points tonight, and, given a steady opening tomorrow, we can probably write it for 72–76 points net of contest risk. The SPAN initial margin requirement tonight for writing one HUQ 92.00 call is $1,355. Because I'm trading a number of other markets right now, fourteen to be precise, I consider that the portfolio is sufficiently diversified to allot only 2.5 times the SPAN requirement, or $3,387.50, for each call that I'll write. If I can manage to write the call for 74 points net, that will represent 74 times $4.20/point, or $310.80 gross in pocket, suggesting a notional ROC of 9.17% over 40 days, or 6.88% per month, a perfectly acceptable figure.

Am I at risk in this trade? Sure. This isn't a pure arbitrage, and there is always some statistical risk and, in energy markets, event risk is never absent. Are the odds of success substantially on my side? Oh, yes. If our model is to be believed at all, this trade will be profitable about 93% of the time, a little bit under two standard deviations in the lognormal distribution of prices (see Table 6.2). The only thing that beats the trade is a rise of 34% in the price of HUQ in 40 days' time.

Now, there are traders who do have such an apocalyptic view of the energy markets, and have staked and will continue to stake their capital on the occurrence of extreme short-term upward price movements. Who are these optimists (or are they really pessimists, an interesting philosophical question)? That's easy enough; these are the folks who have purchased HUQ 92.00-strike calls recently, and who will buy them from me when I write these options tomorrow. I love these guys. Everyone should have such a positive view of life and the markets—such a view makes it *so* much easier to put a smile back on your face after you've helped someone else pick your own pocket.

So, How Often Do We Win?

Before we make any decision about whether to help ourselves to a chunk of the optimists' capital, we've a little bit more work to do. We naturally want to learn what our pricing model has to say about the probability of success if we write WOOM August unleaded calls at this time. Table 6.2 is our usual incremental analysis of the expectation for writing the HUQ 92.00-strike call options, expiring on July 26.

The SV of HUQ is a measurable number, but it reflects the recent past. The deltas and the IVs of its call options, as ever, represent the current sentiment of all the market participants regarding the future price of HUQ. Evidently, sentiment is relatively modest at this moment, because the IV of the

TABLE 6.2 Expectation of Writing HUQ 92.00 Calls on 6/17/2002

Strike Price	Option Price	Delta × 100	Probability Below*	Probability of Range	Profit at Range Midpoint	Expectation in Range
92.00	0.81	13.87	0.9196	0.9196	+310.80	+285.81
93.00	0.71	12.44	0.9310	0.0114	+84.00	+0.96
94.00	0.61	11.01	0.9418	0.0108	−336.00	−3.63
95.00	0.53	9.86	0.9502	0.0083	−756.00	−6.27
96.00	0.46	8.69	0.9583	0.0081	−1176.00	−9.52
97.00	0.43	8.05	0.9626	0.0043	−1596.00	−6.86
98.00	0.34	6.79	0.9706	0.0079	−2016.00	−15.93
99.00	0.29	5.87	0.9760	0.0055	−2436.00	−13.40
100.00	0.25	5.15	0.9801	0.0041	−2856.00	−16.71
101.00	0.22	4.77	0.9822	0.0021	−3276.00	−6.88
102.00	0.19	4.19	0.9852	0.0030	−3696.00	−11.09
103.00	0.16	3.67	0.9877	0.0025	−4116.00	−10.29
104.00	0.14	3.24	0.9897	0.0020	−4536.00	−9.07
105.00	0.13	3.01	0.9908	0.0010	−4956.00	−4.95
106.00	0.13	2.95	0.9911	0.0003	−5376.00	−1.61
107.00	0.11	2.60	0.9926	0.0015	−5796.00	−8.69
108.00	0.10	2.35	0.9936	0.0010	−6216.00	−6.22
109.00	0.09	2.18	0.9943	0.0007	−6636.00	−4.63
110.00	0.09	2.05	0.9948	0.0005	−7056.00	−3.53
111.00	0.08	1.86	0.9955	0.0007	−7476.00	−5.23
112.00	0.07	1.73	0.9959	0.0004	−7896.00	−3.16
113.00	0.06	1.55	0.9965	0.0006	−8716.00	−4.99
114.00	0.05	1.31	0.9973	0.0007	−8736.00	−6.12

Overall expectation: $127.97

Notes: HUQ = 79.40; Q options expire 07/26/2002.

*Probability of being below the striking price on the same line.

**The option is assumed to expire worthless if HUQ is exactly 92.00 cents.

HUQ options has ranged from 33.2% to 55.1% over the past six months and tonight's IVs are down toward the low end of this range, at 38.0%.

Oddly, even given the lowish call IVs (we prefer to write options with relatively higher ones, per their recent 6-month range of volatility) and considering the theoretical possibility of severe supply disruption due to wars or related occurrences, we should have a high degree of confidence in this trade. The non-seasonal tendency of this market at this time is solidly on our side, as indicated by Table 6.1, and we've also enlisted in our cause our favorite ally, time. When a trader buys a short-dated WOOM option, he not only must be correct in his view about the direction of the market, he must be correct P.D.Q., and he has taken *much* the short end of the odds, in this case roughly 93-to-7 against. Do you want to trade along with the option buyer in such a situation? Very likely not, I'd wager. Each day that passes without some amount of market movement in his favor is another nail in his coffin, and we who have sold him this option find our trading capital increasing merely by courtesy of the passage of time. A very painless process, I assure you.

When we write short-dated options, we have a useful measure for approximating our potential rate of dollar gain. This measure is *theta*, the rate of decay per day of the time premium remaining in an option. Other considerations being equal or roughly so, theta increases steadily for near-the-money options toward the end of an option's life. Theta's rate of daily increase actually accelerates going into these last few weeks, if the market remains fairly close to the option's striking price. When the option moves or stays WOOM as it nears expiration, theta becomes more or less irrelevant—there's little time premium left to decay. For those of us who write options, especially short-dated WOOM options, theta is easily the best friend we have other than the price of the underlying asset moving smartly away from the striking price of the option we're writing.

All the numbers generated by our pricing model are approximations, as we've seen, and we must keep in mind three other things. First, the probability of the success of our trade will change daily, as the market moves up and down. Second, and this point cannot be overemphasized, any computations using the lognormal model to measure expectation and/or success/failure apply *only* to the whole term of the trade, only if we sit until the expiration of the options. Third, the numbers in Table 6.1 do not consider the amount of loss we can incur if HUQ moves outrageously higher. This is, again, why we must perform the incremental analysis of expectation as shown in Table 6.2. To skip this step would be at minimum careless and self-deceiving, and we would be plainly stupid for putting our capital at risk by simply ignoring potentially useful information . . . creating in effect a sort of voluntary knowledge risk.

The first and second points are related. The typical lognormal model treats a trade as something to be examined in one big chunk; it says nothing at all about what may happen *during the term* of the trade. If we wanted to analyze a trade thoroughly, we would perform an analysis similar to our preceding incremental analysis for each day remaining in the trade and compute what amounts to a cumulative sum of each day's expectation. Doing such an analysis is quite possible (such an analysis is the heart of the Cox-Ross-Rubenstein and Whaley quadratic models, for instance), but the analysis is somewhat involved and is, in my view, better suited and more useful to institutional traders. We can—and we will—put and keep profitability on our side without such an extensive analysis.

Conditions of Entry—The Criteria for a Non-Seasonal Trade

The practical preconditions involved in applying the non-seasonal strategy are as follows:

1. The underlying market we're examining must have an historically valid non-seasonal tendency over an upcoming period. A non-seasonal is fully valid if it was not violated at minimum 9 years in the past 10, 18 in the past 20, and so forth, with the more recent years' results being more indicative.

2. The non-seasonal must persist for an absolute minimum of 2 weeks, 3 to 10 weeks is more desirable, longer occasionally, and 4 to 7 weeks is the typical case.

3. Immediate supply/demand factors that might operate against the success of the non-seasonal must be moderate or remote, as far as we can tell, and the market we're examining must not be in the midst of a strong trend toward the striking price of the option we write.

4. The maximum counterseasonal move during the period under consideration must be known (that is, we have to do our homework) in order to select an advantageous striking price to write.

5. In the best case, the average interim price move for the regular seasonal asset trade in our favor (away from the strike we write) over the whole period should be at least 1.5 times the average interim price move toward the strike we write.

6. In the best case, the maximum interim move in the direction of the seasonal should be at least 1.75 times the maximum contrary move.

7. The theoretical ROC of the trade at the start, net of all costs, should be not less than 7% per month, compounded, of double the initial SPAN margin requirement of the trade. Using a standard of 5% of treble the initial SPAN requirement is better still, from the essential standpoint of caution.

8. The distance from tonight's closing price to the striking price of the WOOM option we're considering writing should usually be at least 10% larger than the maximum historical contrary move over the term of the trade, although present day supply/demand considerations may, as in the HUQ example, suggest modifying this condition.

9. The non-seasonal tendency should persist until the option's expiration in the best case, and without exception to at least within 1 week of the option's expiration, unless we, by design, intend to exit the trade at some point during the option's life.

Why These Criteria? What's Our Advantage in Adhering to Them?

Now, that's quite a list of conditions, and rarely will all of them fall into line for us. That's all right. They don't have to be *all* aligned for us to earn a healthy profit and still be sensibly cautious in the process. Some conditions are much more important than others. Conditions 1, 3, 4, 7, and 9 are vital or nearly so, but the various markets meet these five conditions frequently enough. Let's look a little more closely at these conditions.

Fooling with less than 90% successful non-seasonals means that, more than 1 time in 10 historically, the non-seasonal trade will either aggravate us or be an outright loser. I prefer better odds than that, thanks. If we don't do our homework regarding condition 4, thus remaining unaware of how far an adverse move might persist, we're juggling chainsaws in the dark, and I strongly suspect that this cannot be profitable unless we've arranged double or triple indemnity on our medical insurance. Concerning condition 7, if the ROC isn't fairly handsome, why should we bother entering the trade in the first place? These are all straightforward enough, but condition 9 wants a little more comment.

If we should trade what I call "shorties," in which the non-seasonal tendency evaporates more than a week before option expiration, we foist upon ourselves an extra market decision. Should we wait for expiration and cash out the whole trade, or simply take our profit now (at the end date of the measured non-seasonal tendency) and thereby incur extra trading cost and accept a diminished profit? The principal factor that prompted our use of this strategy is now gone. Why stick around and make an extra decision, one that has a distinct component of guesswork in it? Match the term of the trade to the option's expiration before entering the trade, and save yourself the implied risk of this extra trading decision.

Condition 2 is a restatement of a point made earlier. We must allow the market participants some amount of time to put dollars into our pockets. The notion of a 6- or 9-day seasonal, although some traders favor these and seek them out, is dubious at best from a supply/demand standpoint and our success in such a trade might well depend on an external event. This is acceptable if we know what the external event is, but do we? Why is there a short-term tendency for the S&P 500 Index to rise over the last two trading days of a month and the first four trading days of the succeeding month? I don't know, do you? There are hundreds of such shorties available, but I stay well away from them unless and until I come to understand the reason for and mechanics of such price movements. Which, by the way, occurs rarely.

Condition 3 is partly obvious. If a market is trending the wrong way for our proposed trade, then proceeding with the trade is clearly akin to playing on the railroad tracks, but there's more to it than that. This condition also brings back our old nemesis, information risk. For an example, we can examine a seasonal in the NYBOT "C" May coffee contract. There is a long-standing, pronounced, and quite reliable seasonal in May coffee from early- to mid-March into April, and it is downward.

In this period in 2002, May coffee went more or less straight up. What happened? The daily/weekly explanations from the pundits were so much blah-blah, fund buying, technical rally, rata-rata. What seems to have occurred, as things turned out, was a change in an important supply condition. The Central American coffee harvest (which includes Colombia, oddly) was some 15–20% lower than the previous year, due largely, so it was said, to high levels of crop abandonment in the face of historically very low prices. A huge Brazilian crop, perhaps 50 million 60-kilo bags, or more, was on the horizon. Ah, but, most Brazilian coffee is not deliverable against NYBOT's "C" contract, and the "C" certified stocks in storage were shrinking rather rapidly at the time. Call it a window of opportunity for those who were bull-ish on coffee. With no *immediate* threat from the putative enormous Brazil-ian crop, and temporarily declining supplies even with a known overall surplus hanging over the market, May "C" coffee became very well bid dur-ing a time when ordinarily its price would have been falling.

What's the point of the example? Simply this: some traders latched on to the possibility of a temporary mini-reduction of supply very early and took a bullish stance, whether with futures or options, and reaped a fine profit for themselves. Other traders, your humble servant included, traded according to the historical tendency. Those who did so and who dealt in futures were beaten up badly. Those of us who had applied the non-seasonal strategy by writing calls with striking prices well above the market went through some amount of aggravation. At one point we had the, er, privilege of sitting with an untidy paper loss, but Father Time and his option-dealing sidekick, Sister Theta, showed up just like the U.S. Cavalry in an old Western film. We gave ourselves an extra chance to be successful by using the non-seasonal strat-egy, and it came in very handy, too.

Nonetheless, my capital in this trade became threatened purely because I, and probably also the majority of seasonal/non-seasonal traders, either didn't acquire the pertinent supply information, didn't realize its significance, or ignored its implications. In the plainest possible English, we stupidly ac-quired an extra portion of information risk. I plead "guilty as charged, your Honor," and am delighted to have emerged from the trade with a profit. How-ever, this was definitely *not* a competently executed trade, and it illustrates with crystal clarity that, even in the most statistically favorable non-seasonal trades (and this one is and has been hugely favorable), we must constantly be alert to the implications of new information on the market.

Extra Advantages, and a Little Common Sense

Conditions 5 and 6 are ideal when we can find them, but are not essential for profitability in a non-seasonal trade. Lower figures are certainly acceptable, especially when the principal conditions are all in place. Too, there's the possibility that one aberrant year has skewed the maximum and average up-move or downmove figures. Even so, we want these ratios as high as we can find them. Conditions 5 and 6 also presuppose the existence of a legitimate regular seasonal tendency, which is fine if it happens to exist, but is by no means necessary for our success in using the non-seasonal strategy.

Let me clarify a bit. Every time a market has a seasonal tendency over some period during the year, there exists by definition a corresponding and likely worthwhile potential non-seasonal trade within that same time frame. However, the existence of a seasonal tendency is *not* a precondition for the existence of a non-seasonal trade. All that is required for a non-seasonal trade is that the market, whichever one we're examining, regularly does *not* behave in some fashion. If a market, say from June 1 through July 28, drops sharply in some years, usually stays in a restricted range in most years, and rises only modestly in the remaining years, there is no visible seasonal tendency. Nonetheless, this market is a candidate for writing WOOM calls on a non-seasonal basis during this period, because of what it does not do, or rather, has not done historically. There are therefore many more legitimate opportunities for non-seasonal trades than for seasonal trades, and this fact represents a terrific opportunity for us.

Condition 8 is merely applied common sense. If a specific market has never behaved in a specific fashion over a named period of the year, why should we even think of challenging history? Just as with our capital usage, it can never be anything but advantageous to us to be conservative in choosing the parameters for our trades. Assume there's a possible non-seasonal trade with a potential 6% ROC over a month's time and a striking price 40% beyond the largest contrary move in history. Assume also that there's another trade available in the same market having a potential 15% ROC and an option strike only 20% beyond the maximum contrary move. I'll take the former trade every single time, other things being equal. Pardon my proselytizing, but so should you. Be the bookie, not the player. Maximize the occurrence of the profitable outcome, give yourself an extra measure of safety, and let the optimists take all the risk to their capital.

Condition 8 is framed in terms of "usually," not "always," for a good reason. Consider again the presence of a really aberrant year in the history of a market over a particular time period during the year. Suppose that a particular non-seasonal trade would meet our preconditions if it weren't for the presence of that one year's price movement. If we can learn that the aberrant move was due to conditions that simply cannot occur this year, we may safely discard that year from consideration. If the resulting analysis excluding the aberrant year indicates that a non-seasonal trade is warranted, we've no reason not to undertake the trade.

The Non-Seasonal Advantage—Frequent Opportunity and Wide Variety

The non-seasonal strategy is advantageous for another reason. Unlike numerous other strategies we might employ over the same 3- to 10-week term as the non-seasonal, this one offers us opportunity in almost every actively traded market at some time or times during the year. This happy circumstance enhances our ability to diversify our trading, allowing us to reduce model failure risk, the overall risk to our capital that exists when we only trade in one, two, or three markets.

Agricultural markets have had for centuries more or less obviously defined seasonal tendencies, but even currency and interest-rate markets have some well-established non-seasonals that, objectively, we might not otherwise expect. After all, since governmental action is a—sometimes *the*—major determinant factor in which way and how far the value of currencies and the level of interest rates move, why should a currency or interest-rate market behave in a very consistent fashion at specific times of the year? For example, there's a notable tendency for the longer interest rate markets, the 30-year bond and the 10-year note, not to rise very much from about the first week in April through the middle of May. Swiss franc and British pound do not tend to fall very far against the dollar during certain times of the year; the franc from mid-August through the end of September, the pound during the autumn. There are surely reasons for such tendencies, although many times we haven't any idea what they are. We'd like to know about them, but even if we don't, and if the non-seasonal is historically reliable and we can garner a profit by trading it, we should absolutely keep these markets on our list of possibilities.

Am I advocating some sort of cult of willful ignorance here? Hardly. I'm just being practical. Can you explain down to the last detail the working of your car's engine? I certainly can't, but this doesn't prevent either of us from driving, now does it? It's really the same in trading. We must acquire a useful and reasonable base of knowledge about a particular market's workings in order to begin attempting to trade in it successfully, no matter what strategies we may employ. It must also be correct to acquire more and more information over time, but we quite literally cannot afford to defer *all* trading until our knowledge is complete, for it never will be.

Acceptable Results—The Risk and the Reward

There are a few other topics we want to examine concerning non-seasonals, and option writing in general. It's all very well to talk about ROC in the abstract, but I'm not abstract and neither are you. We'd like to know what sort of return on our capital we can reasonably expect to see in a typical carefully selected non-seasonal trade, and what levels of percentage and dollar risk we should consider tolerating.

The fact of the matter is that there aren't hard and fast answers to these questions, for a couple of reasons. We know perfectly well that the markets are going to move around to some degree during the trade. By definition, then, the SPAN margin requirement (plus our comfortable margin cushion, which is absolutely essential) is going to float around also. If the trade is what I call a "flier" and works in our favor right from the starting gate, the average margin and cushion we'll have to employ will be well less than indicated by our pre-trade analysis, and the ROC will be correspondingly higher. If the market behaves contrarily, we will certainly employ more capital than originally anticipated and our ROC will fall, sometimes a lot, if the adverse market move becomes extended. Short of keeping detailed daily records of margin and cushion levels and crunching quite a few numbers at the end of the trade, we cannot obtain a precise ROC for a particular trade.

Now, I'm not lazy (well, not too lazy), but this amount of record keeping is more trouble than it's worth, as far as I'm concerned. I'll compute the capital usage and cushion figures once a week or so, more often if the trade even seems as if it may work against me, and live with the approximate ROC result very happily. This is probably a sensible way to go about it, but if this is too Bohemian for you, then by all means track your capital-usage-per-trade on a daily basis. I'll wager you'll change your mind about doing this within 60 days. Or less.

As for the general question of typical or average ROC over a series of disciplined non-seasonal trades, this will be a function of the markets in which we actually do make a trade. ROC will tend to be higher in markets that normally have higher volatility on an absolute basis: coffee, natural gas, possibly gold or cocoa, lumber, crude oil and its products not infrequently, soybeans when they're active. Equally, we'll anticipate a rather lower ROC when trading non-seasonals in currencies, bonds and notes, and usually the metal markets. Except when the goldbugs have one of their occasional the-world-is-about-to-die-and-we'll-all-be-poor-forever-unless-we-buy-gold-right-now orgies . . . in which case, if we simply wait until their own fervor and their trading losses tire them out, we will see our ROC dancing at stratospheric levels.

In any market, 5% net potential ROC per month is the least I'll accept, and 7–9% for carefully selected and disciplined non-seasonals is a perfectly normal prospect. If the non-seasonal trade should happen to begin right when the market's options' IVs are to the high end of their 6-month range and option premiums are correspondingly high, such a trade can easily return 13–15%, even more, per month. This is sort of the best-of-all-worlds case, though. I'll tell you this right now: if you undertake non-seasonal trading and consistently take out 12, 15, 18% net ROC per month for a while, first, I'm delighted for you and, second, you are selecting striking prices that are too close to the market price when you enter the trade. Back it off some, be more conservative in your selection of the option strikes to write in future. You're tempting fate, my friend . . . and that's just never a good idea.

So much for our goals for profit. What about risk, much the more important consideration in the long run? The Duchess of Windsor once famously remarked that one can never be too rich or too thin. In trading, one can almost never be too cautious, and, speaking for myself only, I try to be a professional coward. To this end, I must match an approximate potential dollar risk and its likelihood of occurrence against the theoretical positive dollar return. In short, I have to keep the old eyeball on, what else, expectation.

At the end of our example HUQ trade, Table 6.2 shows that we have a nicely positive expectation on option expiration day. Fine, and we certainly wouldn't even undertake the trade if the expectation weren't positive, but this approximate figure is only valid at the very end of the trade. During the life of the option, suppose HUQ rises, say, 6.00 cents in the first 10 days of the trade and our short options rise in price from, say, 80 points to 190. Should we exit the trade? What is a reasonable level of interim dollar risk to assume?

Wiggle Risk Redux—Timidity and Recklessness Are Equally Deadly

The answers to these questions vary with our personal temperament and our trading capital. Some traders are terribly risk-averse and wouldn't dream of ever risking more dollars than they could possibly make in a trade. Bluntly put, if you are one such trader, change your attitude or don't use this strategy. There is no third alternative. No matter how carefully we select a non-seasonal option write, no matter how disciplined we remain, in some number of these trades event risk will turn up, the trader's ultimate nemesis. Extreme events will work in our favor more or less half the time, but we're not concerned when they do. We'll bank the profit and smile at the world.

However, when even a minor event risk intervenes and works against our position, a straight risk-no-more-dollars-than-we-can-make policy is 100% guaranteed to cost us dollars in the medium run and in the long run. This policy is essentially a wiggle risk generator, and I can't see any reason to introduce a higher, and completely avoidable, component of risk into our trading.

In our HUQ example, our odds of success, of ending up profitable, are roughly 93-to-7 in our favor at the end of the trade if our pricing model is reasonably reliable. We stand to make about $300 net per option when we're successful. Suppose we would accept a dollar risk, during the trade, of up to four times our potential profit, or $1,200. Outrageous, you say? Complete lunacy? Not so. Assuming only that our model is merely in the same neighborhood as reality, in seven cases we'd lose $1,200, an $8,400 total. In 93 cases, we'd make $300, a $27,900 total. Over a nominal series of 100 identical trades, even accepting what some would consider an outrageous risk amount of four times our potential profit, we'd end up with something like $19,500 dollars in pocket, all contest risk paid, at the end of this series of trades.

Admittedly, this figure is too rosy. A sharp price spike will likely occur more frequently than 3 times in 100, but will it be sufficient to cause us to exit the trade, given our generous dollar-risk level? Please note that such a spike will have to be really quite sharp in order to drive the price of the HUQ call option we wrote up to 358 points. That's right; we lose the $1,200 if and only if the premium of the option we wrote for 73 points net should subsequently move up to 358 points. If the gasoline market's volatility moves right up along with the price of HUQ, this would probably occur in our example if HUQ rose 8 or 9 cents, 800 or 900 points, within a week or two days of our entering the trade. If this wild little move occurs later in this 5-week trade, Sister Theta will likely gobble up enough time premium to prevent the option from reaching this price, bar the historically non-existent case in which HUQ actually moves above the strike of the WOOM call we've written.

Let's say, being *actively* pessimistic, that a wicked spike as described occurs 10 times in 100, and that we exit immediately when such a spike occurs, losing $1,200 each time. Adding these occurrences to our original presumptive 7 statistically expectable losses, we will lose 17 times $1,200, or $20,400, and profit in 83 cases times $300, or $24,900, yielding $4,500 through all 100 trials. We're still very solidly in the profit column, correct?

Clearly, whether or not we like the notion of risking four times the potential profit in a trade, we must match the dollar risk per position to our trading capital. If our account equity is, say, $15,000, this level of risk is too high, representing as it does fully 8% of capital. In such an account, it would be more practical to set the interim dollar risk level at three times potential profit (and it is probably correct also to refrain from employing the non-seasonal strategy in markets having volatility above 35%, too. Don't fret, you won't lack for other opportunities).

Exiting a Non-Seasonal Early—When the Real World Meets the Trading World

As an ordinary thing, when we write options in the non-seasonal strategy, we'd like to sit on them until expiration and avoid the trading costs of exiting the trade via repurchasing the option. That's fine when we can conveniently do so, and I support this policy completely, with exactly one exception. There's such a thing as making money *too* quickly.

Suppose we undertake a longer-dated non-seasonal trade having 14 weeks until option expiration, and we write some number of WOOM options we select, with full discipline, for 140 points each. Suppose also that the market tendency operates perfectly and vigorously right from the get-go. The premium of the options we've written falls all the way down to 9 points or even 5 or 2, within 6 weeks. Repurchase these options *now* if you can possibly do so. (Side note: a lot of times, WOOM options will show a settlement price of 2 or 3 points, but when you try to repurchase them there, you'll find the market quoted at something like 2 bid/14 offered. Nonetheless, try to repurchase them for just a few points if expiration is a more than a month away.)

Why do this? Because the risk/reward picture of the trade has changed, and this change is radical. In the case just described, we'd be sitting in our trade and waiting six, seven, eight weeks to collect 6 whole points. If our trade is in, for example, heating oil, 6 points is a big, bad, bold $25.20 per lot. "Well, what can happen?" you're asking. "Geez, if I wrote November heating oil puts (ticker: HOX) in July to take advantage of strong demand going into the fall, and they were 10 cents OOM then, and heating oil has moved sharply higher, say 9 more cents, why am I worried? They're 19 cents out of the money, 1900 points! Hey, I'm better off risk-wise than I was when I got into the trade. Thanks, but I'll just sit and wait for expiration."

Good luck. You are now in roughly the same tactical position as the folks at LTCM were, attempting to "pick up nickels in front of a bulldozer," as Nicholas Dunbar quotes one of LTCM's principals in his book *Inventing Money* (Wiley, 2000), (wonderful book by the way, great reading). If somebody starts up the bulldozer, if the one-off event, the impossible-to-predict catastrophe occurs, you'll rue this decision very rapidly. Why did I choose heating oil in July–October for this example? Easy. I was in that exact trade, in that exact circumstance, and thought exactly as you do . . . in 2001. I had written the November 62.00 puts for 140 points in July, straight non-seasonal trade, actually anticipating a typical seasonal rise in heating oil. Here's a snapshot of what happened when those jerks played kamikaze with the World Trade Center (my apologies: my editor doesn't want me to use a much stronger and far more appropriate term for those alleged humans).

The markets closed for the next few days, very honorably so in light of such a fantastic atrocity. Upon reopening, the energy markets went up, presumably on war fears, for precisely one day, with HOX closing at 82.00 (!) on Monday, September 17. The short HOX puts settled at 6 points on September 14 and at 5 points on the 17th. And then the energy markets just collapsed. One week, just five trading days later, HOX settled at 62.52, having made an intraday low of 61.50. I'd blundered into one of the sharpest moves in the history of the heating oil market—event risk at its most virulent.

I had protected the position somewhat by selling futures (which I hate doing) in the overnight NYMEX ACCESS session on Sunday the 23rd. I'd sold one future at 67.00 for every four 62.00-strike put options I'd written, and another at 63.30 (dumb and dumber, sigh) on Monday the 24th. The whole mess was not an outright disaster, but I still had brilliantly transformed a profit into a loss by simply not *accepting* the lovely profit available, which represented 90 or 95% of the absolute maximum profit that I could ever have made. And, no rest for the wicked, if I wanted to try to let the trade return to profitability, I was now faced with trying to keep up a defensive position for a month or so, while heating oil prices would probably be gyrating furiously.

Ultimately, with HOX trading at 64.90 or so some trading days later and margin requirement going through the roof, I exited the whole position, losing about $1,380 on each 4-lot of options written, and pocketing a small profit, $300 on average on each short futures. There's a term for trading in this fashion: rank stupidity. Trading genius at work . . . ri-i-i-ight.

Usually, I add very well. Occasionally, somebody should grab me by the collar and yank my stupid butt off to remedial math class. By not wanting to spend perhaps 10 or 12 points plus a commission, call it $65.00 per lot, I gave away about $480 profit per option and oh so cleverly (choke, wheeze . . .), turned it into a $300+ loss to boot. Moron! One of the great sins in trading is sitting still while the market takes your profit away. Learn the lesson, save yourself time, aggravation, and capital. If a non-seasonal trade works ferociously in your favor early in the trade, and the options you wrote have traded down to pennies, *buy them back now*. If you can make 85–90% of the original intended profit over just 40–50–60% of the life of the trade, then exit gracefully, pay the extra commission, and go and make another profit somewhere else. It doesn't pay to stay in such a trade, for the only things that can happen while you wait are bad.

Staying Alive—Skipping the Suicide Seasonal

There's one final consideration concerning our selection of markets for non-seasonal trades. We must avoid what I call the "suicide seasonal." There are several markets that have enormously reliable seasonals, but, when the seasonal does go wrong, it goes wildly and bizarrely wrong, and the risk becomes far too large to manage. Perhaps the classic such market is coffee, for the period of roughly May 22 through July 22, and for most of the Southern Hemisphere winter in general. Its 28-year seasonal tendency is shown in Table 6.3.

Hey, look at all those nice pluses in column seven. This seasonal works three years out of four or better, and the associated non-seasonal has even a higher rate of success. The cumulative and average yearly results are impressive, too. Oh, really? Now, focus on the asterisked years. Ow! That's right, in a straight seasonal trade, if we simply sold coffee, in three of these years, we might have had to contend with somewhere between 50 cents and 150 cents of risk, between $18,500 and $56,000 of adversity *per contract*. That's way too much. Gigantically too much. Unthinkably too much.

Uh, uh—I know what you're thinking. "Well, with a non-seasonal approach, I'll just write the call options 100 or 150 cents away from the current market price, and I won't have to be threatened by huge moves as occurred in 1979 or 1994 or 1997." Don't even think about it. These enormous run-ups in the price of coffee occurred when freezing weather, which coffee trees can't tolerate, visited the prime coffee-growing states in Brazil. Mark it down in big, black letters: when a freeze hits Brazil's coffee states, there is effectively no upper limit on prices in the short term. Bill Gates can weather this type of extreme move, but you and I cannot, and there's absolutely no reason to risk having to do so. Non-seasonal traders, and option writers in general, want no part of writing coffee calls from late May through the end of July—not if they want to stay solvent. As the baseball players say, it only takes *one*, and you don't want to even get close to *this* one. You'd rather gargle with nitric acid.

Few other non-seasonal trades embody as much risk. Some historically very risky ones are soybeans in May–July when prices are high, and corn from mid-June to early August under the same condition. When the goldbugs are having one of their scare parties, non-seasonal trades in gold can be very dangerous (although we'll have another look at these in connection with the *Picador* strategy in Chapter 12). No sane trader wants any part of non-seasonal trades in the NYMEX energy markets (possibly excepting natural gas) when there's a war or the immediate threat of war in the Middle East, and sure as sunrise there will be a few of these in the next decades.

The non-seasonal strategy is about normalcy, about things occurring more or less as they usually do. This implies directly that, the higher the likelihood in a given time frame of some wild event occurring—be it involving weather, war, or something else—the less desirable a non-seasonal trade is in the markets such an event would affect.

We can't predict the one-off event, of course, but we can and must avoid non-seasonal trades during periods of the year when such events, either

TABLE 6.3   Seasonal Sell Study, September Coffee "C", 1974–2001

Entry Date MOC	Entry Price	Interim High	Interim Low	Exit Date MOC	Exit Price	Gross Result	Cumulative Net Result
74-05-21	75.88	77.80	67.80	74-07-22	69.50	+6.38	+6.22
75-05-21	55.00	65.00	52.65	75-07-22	65.00	−10.00	−1.94
76-05-21	138.35	158.40	120.35	76-07-22	126.35	+12.00	−10.10
77-05-23	305.25	307.65	208.33	77-07-22	208.33	+96.92	+86.66
78-05-22	153.11	179.52	113.02	78-07-24	113.63	+39.48	+78.50
79-05-21*	157.50	221.54	151.10	79-07-23	208.29	−50.79	+70.34
80-05-21	206.87	210.40	159.84	80-07-22	165.69	+41.18	+111.36
81-05-21	118.17	118.75	83.75	81-07-22	116.63	+1.54	+112.74
82-05-21	120.12	134.30	117.00	82-07-22	124.75	−4.63	+104.58
83-05-23	127.75	131.75	124.15	83-07-22	128.76	−1.01	+103.41
84-05-21	155.03	155.87	139.10	84-07-23	143.68	+11.35	+114.60
85-05-21	146.03	150.20	134.10	85-07-22	135.48	+10.55	+124.99
86-05-21	218.21	219.75	157.00	86-07-22	187.36	+30.85	+155.68
87-05-21	123.49	125.00	99.50	87-07-22	104.65	+18.84	+174.36
88-05-23	133.85	143.15	130.35	88-07-22	137.72	−3.87	+166.20
89-05-22	128.59	130.00	84.75	89-07-24	84.83	+43.76	+209.80
90-05-21	98.73	99.95	84.50	90-07-23	87.15	+11.58	+221.22
91-05-21	89.85	91.35	82.75	91-07-22	83.05	+6.80	+227.86
92-05-21	66.25	67.45	56.80	92-07-22	61.35	+4.90	+232.60
93-05-21	67.20	74.95	58.90	93-07-22	72.90	−5.70	+226.74
94-05-23*	136.65	274.00	114.00	94-07-22	219.40	−82.75	+218.58
95-05-22	165.10	169.50	120.00	95-07-24	146.70	+18.40	+236.82
96-05-21	123.30	125.30	101.50	96-07-22	104.05	+19.25	+255.91
97-05-21*	225.05	277.00	156.00	97-07-22	169.10	+55.95	+247.75
98-05-21	131.85	135.25	105.00	98-07-22	114.80	+17.05	+264.64
99-05-21	120.25	128.00	91.35	99-07-22	98.10	+22.15	+286.63
00-05-22	105.80	122.00	82.40	00-07-24	86.30	+19.50	+278.47
01-05-21	67.80	68.60	53.25	01-07-23	53.95	+13.85	+292.16

Average on 28 sells: +10.434 cents; stop w/loss of: 8.00 cents

Gross Movement (cents/lb)
Avg Up 14.336   Max Up 137.350   Avg Dn 25.421   Max Dn 96.920

Notes: September Coffee (NYBOT), KCU; sell on 05-21, buy on 07-22

*Refer to text discussion.

historically or due to present-day conditions, might occur. Fortunately for our sanity and our capital, we can observe many historical time frames in which we might unsuspectingly commit *seppuku* in a particular market. Also, in the vast majority of cases, we can quite easily dodge current-year potentially suicidal non-seasonals.

We can make the process of dodging present-day risks easier for ourselves by being very, very scrupulous about a market complying with our preconditions before entering a trade. We'll refuse outright to even consider writing call options using this strategy when a market's volatility is high and rising, or during runaway bull markets (again, more on this topic in Chapter 12, The *Picador*). Make a note: the barest visible possibility of catastrophe trumps both seasonality and non-seasonality every time.

We really have only one more topic to examine regarding non-seasonals and other option-writing strategies, and trading strategy in general. What happens when our trade starts going wrong, as once in a while it will? This subject is more important to profitable trading as I understand it than any other, and it requires its own chapter.

CHAPTER 7

Apocalypse Never

The Uses of Defense

The best defense is a good offense.
—Adage

. . . and vice versa.
—SAJ

Trading is an enterprise of offense. When we enter a trade, we are taking positive action, taking the initiative if you like, to lighten another trader's wallet. Naturally enough, the other trader is up to the same tricks, and whenever our trade begins to go wrong and we can feel the other trader's grubby little fingers starting to reach into our pocket, we have three choices. We can sit quietly and look for (hope for, more likely) the trade to resume working in our favor. We can exit the trade and accept our loss or our diminished profit. Or, on many occasions, and particularly when we're in an option position or in a position involving a combination of futures and options, we can *defend* the trade.

Hope may spring eternal in the human breast, but Alexander Pope would have gone bust if he had attempted to apply his famous words to his trading. Write it down: the trader who *hopes* to win, won't. Dante Aligheri phrased this principle even more elegantly. Traders really ought to post his words, slightly modified, on their desk or above their trading screen: "Abandon all hop**ing,** ye who enter here." Hoping is purely poisonous to profitability, representing as it does the triumph of emotion over discipline, and it can play no constructive part in a successful trading methodology.

This circumstance removes one of our choices when a trade begins to work against us. Presumably, prior to entering any trade, we have fixed in our mind some loss point or dollar amount past which we don't want any further part of the trade. As the trade moves against us and approaches this loss point, we may decide to wait until this point is reached and just accept the loss if and when the market gets there. Nothing wrong with this policy at all, it's perfectly disciplined in that we're keeping to our previously designed plan. Of course, we will frequently take this loss when the market persists in moving in the undesirable direction, but we have in fact allowed for such a loss in our trading plan, and in any case we cannot profit in every trade.

For most traders of my acquaintance, this tactic—the simple exiting of a losing or threatened position—represents their total concept of protecting their capital. They're very serious about it, too. They'll agonize over exactly where to place a stop or over what type of order to use and so forth, sometimes for hours. (Hard to believe? It's absolutely true, and I can name the date, the trader, and the market. His agonizing over the placement of a stop-loss order for about $2\frac{1}{2}$ hours was in retrospect hilarious, because the trade moved in his favor handsomely later in the day.) While this fretting is good in that it represents a devotion to disciplined trading, it's not so good in that it distracts the trader from other possibilities. Under many conditions, we can take positive action to protect our capital as opposed to passively accepting a loss. We can give ourselves the opportunity to eliminate or reduce the threatened loss, to buy ourselves some extra time, or to convert the potential loss into a profit with the passage of time.

There are five general types of defense in option or options-with-assets trading. In no particular order, they are hedging, rolling, flipping, spreading, and moving the goalposts. Each is situational in nature. Any one of these defensive tactics may or may not be applicable at any given time, depending on what we're trading, current market conditions and prices, and the strategy we employed in the original trade.

The Hedge—Trading Potential Profit for Lower Risk

A *hedge* is the purchase or sale of some instrument, usually not an asset, in order to protect against an adverse price move in a market in which we're involved. A perfect hedge is a hedge that removes all the risk of adverse price movement. Wheat growers sell futures contracts and write call options as hedges against downward price movements in their market, and bread makers buy these same futures or write put options to lock in their cost of the raw material used in production. These are the two traditional hedges, and they can be perfect hedges against price risk in numerous cases. While we traders cannot usually apply perfect hedges in our trading, we can definitely reduce our risk in many instances by using similar tactics.

In the general case for traders, a risk-reduction hedge consists of establishing a second position that is in some fashion opposite to our current position in a market. Ordinarily, we use options as our instrument of hedge defense. If we own 10 July wheat futures and are concerned about a possible price decline, we might hedge the trade and provide some protection against such a drop by writing 10 July call options against our position. This is a common hedge, usually called a *covered write*. We might write only 5 calls and establish a partial hedge. We might write 15 or 20 calls, typically somewhat OOM, and hedge with a *ratio-write*. On a different tack, we might buy some number of wheat put options to aid in minimizing the risk we'd incur if the wheat market moves lower. This is an insurance hedge and, as with all insurance, requires us to pay dollars out of pocket. Hedging tactics that involve option writing, contrarily, provide comparatively less risk reduction but put dollars into our pocket. All these are reasonable hedges, provided only that current market conditions and the expectation of the resulting position indicate their use at a particular time.

When we trade pure assets, as opposed to trading assets in combination with options or options by themselves, the hedge is maximally useful if we apply it at the very start of the trade. If the (unhedged) asset price moves in our favor after entering a trade, we could write some appropriate options and put part or all of the trade's open profit back into our pocket at that time. This can be an inferior tactic in asset trades, though, because we might create the undesirable situation of having to stay in both parts of the trade until the options expire or at least until their time value has declined to a pittance, regardless of subsequent market developments. Hedging an asset trade after entering the position reduces our risk by some amount by definition, but simultaneously costs us a good deal of flexibility should the underlying asset price move unfavorably after we apply the hedge.

If the (unhedged) asset price has moved against our position, applying a hedge after entry is even less desirable. Why? For the same reason. To gain the full advantage that a hedge offers, namely, protecting against adversity and pocketing and keeping the premium on the options we write as hedges, we must remain in at least one part of our trade until the options expire or become worth only pennies. If we buy 10 July wheat contracts at $3.02/bushel, taking a 14-cent risk and intending to hold them for, say, 50 days or until wheat reaches $3.30, and wheat thereafter declines 10 cents, applying a hedge at this point becomes downright dangerous. Suppose that, after this 10-cent drop, we write the July 300 call options for 6 cents apiece, and they expire in 40 days. We've cut down our open loss in the position from 100 cents to 40 (excluding contest risk here, for simplicity), and that's fine as far as it goes. It doesn't go very far, however.

If wheat moves lower still, our hedge actually creates a new problem for us. If we leave our original 14-cent stop-loss order in place and do get stopped out of our long position, we are now short unhedged, or naked, calls in a market that we thought was bullish only a few days or weeks ago. Oof! If we're not stopped out, we will constantly be in doubt whether to liquidate the entire trade and accept our loss or to sell back the futures and try to recoup some of the loss by waiting until the calls expire. Either decision might be correct, but in both cases we're trying only to reduce loss, not to make a profit—because we have almost no potential profit remaining to us. The maximum profit now available to us has shrunk to just four lousy cents per contract minus all the contest risk (when wheat moves above 3.04), and, speaking candidly, this situation is just awful. It's also no way to succeed in trading.

If we look at this trade from the perspective of expectation, what do we see? We entered a pure asset trade when we bought wheat futures. This trade was dubious to start, because the initial expectation of such a trade is negative, as we saw very clearly in Chapter 3. We watched the price of our asset decline and *only then* took action to protect our capital. Now we find ourselves sitting on a 40-cent-plus-costs open loss with a maximum possible 40-cent-minus-costs profit if wheat rises, and the market must move in our favor for us just to break even. There's nothing to say about this situation except "ugh."

It gets worse. The belated hedge presents us with some prospect of having to take yet more action in future, to make yet another decision, or to have a decision made for us courtesy of our stop-loss order. This situation is undesirable, too, especially since our first two trading decisions have been incorrect, as demonstrated by the market's movement. Why should our third action now and perforce be correct?

There are two valuable principles to observe in this example. First, using a hedge to defend a losing asset trade is simply a bad idea. Let's cross that tactic off our list right now. Second, if we intend to trade assets and we want to hedge the trade by design, the right time to establish the hedge is when we enter the trade. Writing moderately OOM calls in a 1-to-1 ratio against the asset(s) we own eliminates our contest risk, protects against some decline in the asset price, and still makes us a nice profit when the asset's price moves in our direction. For these advantages, we pay the price of forgoing a huge profit if the asset price moves sharply in our favor, and we acquire the risk of possibly having to stay in the trade longer than we'd like.

Hedging Options with Options—More Reward, Less Risk

If we enter an option trade instead of an asset trade, whether by buying options or writing them, hedging becomes more useful. We can again apply a hedge when we enter an option trade if we wish, and we have remarkable flexibility in how we may employ this tactic. If we believe that May silver will rise and its price is now at $4.30/oz., we might consider buying May silver 4.25-strike calls, or perhaps the 4.50 calls. We can, of course, just buy these options and hope the market moves in our favor, but we are not statistical favorites to profit if we do, other things being, again, equal. If we hedge the trade when we enter it, possibly by writing the same number of 4.50- or 4.75-strike calls, we create an option spread, in this case what is usually called a bullish call spread. This tactic has its advantages. As we prefer to do, we've eliminated the contest risk in the trade by writing the options, but we're still dependent on the market moving in our desired direction, in this case higher, if we want to claim a profit.

The truly pleasant thing about applying a hedge to an option trade is that, unlike in an asset trade, we can still do so usefully after the market has moved somewhat higher or lower. Suppose it's July 24 and we've just bought a March Chicago wheat 3.40-strike call, with March wheat (ticker symbol WH) now trading at $3.37/bushel. We paid 23 cents for this option, and it will expire next February 21. Suppose now the case that WH moves up to $3.60 by October 1. Our call will have moved up rather nicely, to roughly $35\frac{1}{4}$ cents, and we're sitting on about $11\frac{5}{8}$ cents profit net of costs.

We can take our profit right now if we wish, or we can sit still and enhance the profit if the market will oblige by continuing higher. We have a third choice, though. We can retain chances for enhancing our profit and simultaneously reduce our capital risk, in the case of WH moving back lower, by writing a different strike December or March wheat call against our now-profitable position. December wheat is probably trading around $3.56 when March is at 3.60, and the December 3.50 call is probably trading for 18–19 cents. If we write this call and net 18 cents for doing so, we will have established a position that will be profitable from approximately $3.40/bushel to infinity between now and the expiration of the December options on November 22. In short, we've insured against the wheat market giving up the bulk of its gains, and we'll make a few more cents if wheat proceeds higher or stays right here until Thanksgiving Day. If we were more bullish but still wanted to exercise some caution and protect part of our gain, we might alternately write the December 3.70 call at this point.

If WH instead moves lower, let's say down to $3.20 by October 1, the 3.40-strike call we bought is now only worth perhaps $13\frac{1}{2}$ cents. We can accept the loss, or we can sit and hope that wheat turns back around and moves higher, or, again, we can take action. The December 3.40-strike calls are now trading at 8 cents. We could write one of these calls and reduce our current loss without adding any trading risk, but we will curtail our profit potential unless we are very lucky with timing and market movement. We could write two or even more of the December 3.50-strike calls, now trading at $5\frac{1}{4}$ cents, and eliminate our loss entirely (for the time being), if we decide that December wheat will not move well above $3.50 before its options expire. This latter tactic embodies some risk, definitely, because various events might propel the price of wheat way over $3.50.

The point here is entirely that, when trading options rather than assets, we have more useful tactics available to lay off some or all of our risk, or to reduce or erase our open loss in a position, and risk reduction is the goal toward which we always must work. Unlike establishing a hedge against a losing position in an asset, the fact that we initially chose an option position removes one major disadvantage. We no longer have to worry about the possibility of choosing between a continuing adverse move in prices or morphing our position into a new one that is the effective opposite of our original market view. All we can possibly lose from here is the remaining value of the initial option purchase less the amount we pocket by applying the hedge. The trade may even return to profitability at some point, but we certainly won't be counting on such a result.

Hedging an Option Write—It's a Process, Not a Single Action

The hedge can be a useful defense when purchasing assets or options, but it really comes into its own in tandem with several option-writing strategies, particularly the non-seasonal and the ratio-spread (see Chapter 11). If we've entered a non-seasonal trade, we have a couple of different ways to defend the trade via hedging.

For a detailed example of a defense, let's suppose the date is January 22, May unleaded gasoline (ticker symbol HUK) is 63.60 cents, each contract representing 42,000 gallons of RFG II unleaded gasoline, and the May options expire on April 25. We've looked at price histories and discovered that the price of HUK has had a very reliable upward seasonal tendency from this date through the expiration of its options. We also observe that the maximum interim decline ever recorded for HUK between now and April 25 is just 14.64%. This year, with HUK trading at 63.60, that degree of decline would represent 931 points, or 9.31 cents.

We've done our homework regarding the expectation of the trade and have satisfied ourselves that it is satisfactorily positive at this time. We've also seen in our look at the behavior of this market during this period that, because of a generally warm winter throughout the United States, demand for motor gasoline has stayed atypically high so far this year. The longer-term weather forecasts, for whatever they're worth, indicate that there is little probability of a reversion to severe winter conditions and temperatures, and, sure enough, we can't see anything at all immediately wintry on the horizon.

The HUK 48-strike puts, which are 24.53% OOM, or 67.55% further away than the price that would be represented by the largest observed percentage downmove in history in this period, are quoted in today's market at 70 bid/ 90 offered. We elect to write five of these at 75 points, our order is filled, and we find ourselves with $1,500 net in pocket, about 357 points

The term of the trade is right at 12 weeks, a little longer than we'd like, but we've been impressed by the historical reliability of the seasonal tendency and the current supply/demand situation in this market. We've decided that these factors justify accepting a little more time risk present in the slightly extended term of the trade. Our trade will be profitable when HUK stays above approximately 47.35, contest risk included—anywhere above it. That's nice enough, and to defeat our trade the market will, again, have to move about 68% further downward than it has ever done before during this time frame. This market's history complies handily with one of the vital conditions for a non-seasonal that we examined earlier, and this is a very encouraging factor.

For the first month, things go well. The weather stays temperate, and Americans are out cruising around burning up gasoline at very un-seasonal rates. A not-completely-unexpected scandal materializes involving the now-federalized cretins who imitate inspection personnel at airports, and polls show that the citizens have become even less enamored of air travel than formerly, and are increasing their auto miles driven. HUK rises 4.82 cents to 68.42 and we note with some satisfaction that our short 48-strike puts are now trading at just 21 points.

That's great, but now things start to go wrong. Over the next four weeks, the Russians decide to buck the OPEC cartel and export as much crude as they want. The President persuades the Congress to relax certain rules involving refineries, and a late-season Siberian Express weather pattern develops and threatens to put Detroit and points east into the deep freeze. All of these developments clearly either increase supply or potential supply, or decrease demand. HUK sells way off, all the way down to 58.40 cents, and we ruefully note the price of our short puts at 105 points. We're looking at about a $710 open loss. We still like the possible profit we may earn, but we don't want to deal with the possibility of a further immediate decline and a sharply rising open loss. It's time to defend the trade.

Starting the Defense

We have two ways to defend this trade using a hedge. We can either sell some number of futures or buy some number of puts having a strike higher than 48.00, perhaps the 53.00 strike. As far as I'm concerned, *the first principle of defense is always to use options for defense when feasible*. There is a very good reason for this principle when we defend both non-seasonal trades and WOOM option writes in general. If the market should whipsaw, in this example turning back higher, our cost of defense will be much, much lower. Here, if we defend by selling one single futures contract against our five short 48 puts and the market moves back up 300 points, 3.00 cents, we're in deep, er, weeds. We will have an additional open loss of $1,260, less whatever amount the short 48 put options decline during the whipsaw. Sheesh, we're now utterly dependent on the market to move *lower*—against the putative seasonal tendency—merely to regain even minimal profitability. This, putting it mildly, is rotten. We are back to hoping that things will work out, that the market will move in the desirable direction . . . and with a month remaining in the trade as originally conceived. Very bad business.

If we adopt the other style of hedge defense, buying a different strike put option, the result of a whipsaw is vastly less unpleasant. Here, by purchasing our hypothetical 53-strike put, probably for about 180–200–220 points, if the market whipsaws the same 3.00 cents, we will sell back the defensive put we purchased, incurring a loss of perhaps 50–70–90 points, and our trade will still be well profitable under our original market view. Let's say we buy a 53.00-strike put for our defense and pay 210 points for it.

This comparison of futures versus options in defense leads to a second principle of hedge defense, one which may be intuitively obvious but is still well worth stating. Unless we come to believe that all the market factors that prompted us to enter a trade have become invalid, then we will absolutely *not* spend more to defend than the amount of the initial credit we realized from the option sale . . . at the *first* line of defense. If the initial defensive hedging move we're considering violates this condition, then we'll select a different strike put to buy, or accept the loss in the trade, or apply a different defense, about which we'll have more to say in short order.

All right, we've hedged our original trade by purchasing a put. What next? We'll likely have more potential risk to confront, with a month left in the life of the options we wrote. If the market turns back higher, we'll sell back the defensive put and accept our smallish loss, as we previously decided. If the market becomes range-bound, whopping and flopping for a couple of weeks in a 3- or 4-cent range, we'll just sit still. We'll also reexamine, throughout, the seasonal tendency for the remainder of the original trade to see if any other profitable action might be indicated, including even selling back the defensive put without an upmove in the market. In either of these cases, we still retain a clear positive expectation for the trade, and we've pushed our loss point down to about 46.65 in the bargain. Not bad.

"Now dadgummit, hold on there, hotshot," you may be saying to yourself (or out loud) if you're not too familiar with options trading, "Whaddaya mean the loss point has moved? If HUK falls further than 75 points below 48.00, we'll still be looking at a loss." Uh, no, we won't. If the market falls to, say, 46.75 by expiration day, our short 48 puts will be worth 125 points, and probably be trading at 140 or so, and we'll be losing 65 points each, or 325 points loss plus all our trading costs. The 53-strike put we bought, though, will be worth at least 625 points (53.00 – 46.75), showing us a gain of 415 points (625 – 210) less costs, so at worst we'd be profiting by about 60 points net, at 46.75. Therefore, 46.65 is a perfectly honest estimated loss point (or break even point, same thing), and it has indeed moved down from its original level of 47.35.

More Defense? Yes, If Necessary

However, the real question is what to do if HUK keeps falling from here. We'll defend again. We won't particularly like it, but we will . . . as long as we can find a reasonable defense. We must be careful on establishing a second line of defense, though; we'll need to be rather more precise in how we go about it. First, we will absolutely not undertake a second line of defense until the notional upward seasonal tendency of the HUK market has been formally violated. Violation will occur in our example if HUK moves lower than our entry point minus the historical maximum interim percentage decline, in this case 63.60 – 9.31, or 54.29.

Let's say the gasoline market tanks another 4.30 cents to 54.10 in 10 days' time, thus rendering the seasonal tendency invalid for this year and tempting us to reach for the Maalox. Such a move happens in considerably less than 1 in 10 times for all disciplined non-seasonal trades in my experience. We see that our short 48-strike puts are now trading at 160 points and the defensive 53-strike put is now 340 points, so our open loss is 295 points plus costs, call it $1,380.00, and there are still 20 days until expiration.

We check the weekly supply figures published by the American Petroleum Institute (API) and the Energy Information Administration (EIA) and find that supply has increased somewhat more than is typical at this time of year, and the weekly refining utilization figure has moved smartly higher, up to 94.5% of capacity. Refiners are cranking out gasoline more or less as fast as they can, evidently. The weather nationwide has moderated and demand is still considerably higher than usual at this time of year, but these factors evidently haven't helped the price of gasoline much.

We'll look around for a second put to purchase. For the first defense, we selected an option about 5½ cents OOM, with 30 days left in the trade. Now, though, time is beginning to press firmly on the option premiums (thank you, Sister Theta!), but we haven't the luxury of as much space in which to defend. The 50-, 51-, and 52-strike puts settled at 186, 224, and 275 points, respectively. Because we still must be cautious about a whipsaw move, by policy we will prefer to spend the least amount for the second defense that we can manage.

Thus, it appears that the 50-strike is our candidate now that HUK has fallen below 54.29. We'll likely be paying something on the order of 190–215 points for it, let's say 210 points again, just to have a number (please understand that there will be few bargains on the NYMEX option floor after such a substantial move). Purchasing this put leaves our capital position at a small debit, which is undesirable. We've spent 210 + 210 = 420 points plus all trading costs, less 375 points originally sold, putting us in debit in our capital account for this trade. This debit is not a problem, however. We don't intend to hold both defensive puts through to expiration, at least not yet, and the proceeds from their resale ultimately will put our capital account back into the plus column.

If the market persists in working lower over the next two weeks, things may get interesting, and that's the last thing we want. Still, we must deal with this adverse movement if it occurs, and our choice of methods for doing so will have become limited. Suppose the market declines to 51.30 over these two weeks, what will we do? In this situation, nothing at all. Theta is busily munching on the time premium of the short 48-strike puts and their price will almost surely have declined considerably, given they now have only 6 days to live. Our defensive 53-strike put in now in-the-money, and we can expect its price to have risen a bit over the 2-week period given the market's further downward action. Our second defensive put, the 50-strike, probably shows a loss. We're almost certainly better off now with 6 days remaining than we were at the 20-day mark, even though the market has kept moving lower over these two weeks.

If, however, the market has fallen further than this, to, say, 49.75, the old Chinese curse has come true, for we are now living in interesting times. From a profitability standpoint, we're again better off than we were at the 20-day mark. The 48-strike puts are likely trading between 125 and 155 points by now. Our two defensive puts are around 370–400 and 200–220, respectively; in short, our open loss is approximately 180 points plus 7 commissions, $860 or thereabouts. Even though our situation is unfortunately "interesting" (we want our positions to be extravagantly boring when we write options), we have a dandy little edge on our side. With time having become so short in the life of the options, each passing day or any sort of bounce upward in the market price, even 100–200 points, will eradicate great chunks of the remaining premium remaining in the price of our short puts.

Please pardon another mild digression. Observe that, to get to this point, we have made entirely negative assumptions about market movement. We've postulated here that this trade has gone just crazily wrong. The hypothetical behavior of the gasoline market in this example is, frankly, aberrant, although it might of course occur. We've assumed that HUK has moved essentially straight down for 54 days . . . a pretty rare occurrence. It's even rarer, much rarer, to see a qualified non-seasonal trade become a one-way market in the contrary direction. *Notwithstanding all this negativity*, our open loss is small, certainly less than our original intended profit, which we still may very well earn.

In plain English, we've kept the probability of success on our side throughout by applying a reasonable defense to the trade. No genius in it, no "boy, are we lucky," none of that—in fact, we've been quite unlucky. We have simply behaved in a practical manner. Wouldn't you consider that this result to date isn't far better, no matter how it ultimately turns out, than our having let the other traders reach into our pockets by passively accepting a loss earlier in the trade? We're still heavy favorites to end up with their money in our pocket, are we not?

So, how does the trade finally turn out? Choose any outcome you like. If the market moves up, goes nowhere, or moves moderately lower into expiration, we clearly end up with a profit. We may have to repurchase the short 48-strike puts below 48.00 if the market moves there, or they may just expire quietly. We'll sell back the defensive puts we purchased whenever we consider doing so to be to our advantage, probably at the same time we resolve the 48-strike puts. Better still, we have excellent chances to be profitable on both the puts we sold *and* the puts we bought. Consider what happens if, on expiration day, the market price is right where it is now, or 100–150 points lower. Run the numbers—you'll be quite pleased.

One way or another, even though the original trade has gone *very* wrong, we are still highly likely to end up with the other trader's money where it belongs . . . in our pocket. In four of five cases from here (sharply up, up, nowhere, down), and in the three most probable (up, nowhere, down), we'll show a profit. Indeed, in two or maybe three of the cases, we'll end the trade with a greater profit than we anticipated when we entered it. I won't speak for you, but as far as I'm concerned, this is an excellent result, even if the fifth case comes along.

In the fifth case, a sharp drop from here, we can still very easily end up on the plus side of the ledger if we're alert, although we may have to wait another month to pocket the profit. "Huh?" I hear you saying, "If HUK drops another 500 points from here in 6 days, you've got a major problem, there's no way to escape a big loss!" Oh, really? Care to bet on that (he asks with an evil grin)?

Who says that a defense must end coincidently with the end of the original trade? Nobody, that's who. We have at least two perfectly satisfactory tactics available to evade such a loss or convert it into a profit, if we wish to employ them. "We ain' takin' no steenken loss on thees trade, señor" . . . and certainly not here and not yet when excellent and useful tactics for retaining profit still exist, and the expectation of our position is still very positive. Let's examine this notion of extended defense.

The Roll-Out and the Flip—Not So Fast, Jack, It's Still *My* Money

One tactic we might employ in an extended defense is the *roll* or *roll-out*, a straightforward, intuitively appealing tactic that has been thoroughly discussed in the literature on option trading. In its basic form, a roll consists of repurchasing the options we originally wrote, and then writing one or more options of the same series (puts if we originally wrote puts, calls if we wrote calls) that expire in the next month, or even 2 or 3 or more months further out. The striking price of the options we'll write, or roll into, may or may not be the same as the strike we originally wrote and subsequently repurchased.

The *flip* is the other side of the roll, the converse tactic. We put it into practice exactly as we do the roll-out, except that we write the *opposite* series from the options we originally wrote and repurchased, writing calls if we originally had written puts and vice versa. As a practical matter, good opportunities (by which I mean statistically favorable ones) for a flip defense seem to occur less frequently than they do for a roll defense. There's probably some perfectly good reason for this, but I'm hanged if I know what it is.

An example of a straight roll-out defense might occur in the Canadian dollar. The "Loonie" has been weak for a number of years and has been a favorite of some traders for writing calls. Suppose we wrote the February 63.00-strike calls on March Canadian dollar (ticker symbol CDH, but the option's symbol is CDG) when CDH was at 62.20 on January 4. Suppose it subsequently moves to 62.95 with just 2 or 3 days left in the life of the option. We should have a look at rolling our option write into March.

Suppose we wrote the CDG 63.00 calls for 18 points and they're now at 17 (typical premiums, by the way, just what they actually were in 2002). This current price for our options is ho-hum normal, even after CDH has moved almost to our striking price, because these options have become extremely short-dated. We might buy them back and roll into the March 63.50 calls. The 63.50 strike is the next higher striking price available, and let's say these calls are at 22 bid/25 offered. Alternately, we might just repurchase the CDG 63.00-strike calls at a tiny loss, trading costs included, call it a day, and look for something more profitable to trade. Which course we take will depend on current market indications of whatever kind we favor and an historical evaluation of CD's movement over the next month. Similarly, for a roll defense in our HUK example, we'd buy back the 48-strike puts and write some number of WOOM June unleaded gasoline puts. We might select one of the 43-, 42-, or 41-strikes, depending on current premiums and the results of the new historical and expectation analyses we will surely perform before taking any action.

Choosing Our Defensive Tactic

Which strike and which month we actually do elect to roll into or to flip into will depend on the relative level of advantage we can observe for the options under consideration. There are a few preconditions for and tactical points in implementing either a roll-out or a flip defense, and these apply without regard for the strategy we employed in the original trade.

1. The historical tendency of our option's market over the next period must not be notably in the wrong direction, must not be up if we're rolling calls or flipping puts, not down if rolling puts or flipping calls.

2. Present day supply/demand considerations, insofar as we can tell, should not indicate that our market is likely to move toward the strike we're rolling or flipping into.

3. Roll-outs and flips must always be at a credit, net of costs. We must sell more premium than we repurchase.

4. In the best case, the time remaining in the life of the option we're rolling out of or flipping out of should be as short as possible.

5. In the best case, we prefer to apply a roll or flip defense for exactly one month, with the clear realization that this may not always be possible.

6. Both our bid to repurchase the written option(s) and the subsequent offer when we write the option(s) we're rolling or flipping into should be to the offer side of the bid-ask spread.

7. The striking price of the option we're rolling or flipping into should be as far away as possible from the striking price of the option we're re-purchasing, consistent with maintaining an acceptable ROC, *even if* this requires us to write more options than we're repurchasing.

If we're rolling out of a short call option position and our market historically tends to move higher during the next month (assuming we're rolling out just the one month), we're thumbing our nose at the market, in effect daring it to come and get us. This action is plainly wrong-headed, because it will, it will. There is no good reason to violate condition 1. If you want to show your *machismo*, go run with the bulls in Pamplona next summer; you'll save money. This is the spot for a flip defense.

The same sentiment applies to condition 2. Traders seem in my experience to err regarding this condition most frequently when writing puts in agricultural markets during or just after a good harvest. Seasonal tendencies aside, when a good crop is coming in (or has just finished coming in), it's very difficult to estimate how far the market price may drop. Why should we bother trying? We might get it right, but are the odds of our doing so highly favorable? Hardly. In these situations, again, I strongly advocate that we opt for a flip if we intend to extend the defense.

Condition 3 is vital. Once more, time is money, and if we're going to sit in a trade for another month or more, we must absolutely insist on earning a profit. We will roll out and/or flip *only* at a net credit, always and every time, or else we're kidding ourselves. Here's a proposition for you: would you like to enter or continue a trade with exactly zero possibility of (further) profit, but some measurable probability of loss? Right, you wouldn't think of such a thing—but that's precisely what you're doing if you execute either of these defenses at a net debit. Don't do this.

Condition 4 is variable. The shorter-dated the option is when we repurchase it, the better the result of our defense is likely to be, because our favorite ally, Sister Theta, will be doing a number on its time premium. Perhaps a more important question is *at what point* to elect to roll out or to flip. In a straight WOOM option write, how close should the present market price have moved to the striking price of the options we've written? This is where personal taste enters the picture. I use a very arbitrary rule of thumb, and I'll warn you right now that it's too conservative, or seems to be. It's effective enough, but I've ended up wiping egg off my face any number of times by having to sit in a trade for another month when, as things turned out, no defense was necessary. That's right; a little egg never hurt a professional coward.

Subtract the closing market price on the day you wrote the option from the option's striking price. Make this a positive number if it is not (take the absolute value). Divide it by the number of trading days remaining in the option's life on the day you wrote it. Call this number A. Then, from tonight's closing price, subtract the option's striking price, and take the absolute value. Divide that figure by the number of trading days remaining and call this number B. Multiply B by 1.36 and call this C. If C is less than A and there are less than two weeks remaining in the option, defend the trade with a flip or a roll, which one to use being dependent on your market view for the next time period. If more than two weeks remain, consider a hedge defense instead, if feasible.

Yes, you will defend more WOOM option writes than you might do otherwise. Yes, you will curse at me once in a while for initiating a defense, only to find that the market suddenly stops threatening the trade and you get to sit for an extra month or two and only earn a diminished ROC. And yes, when a trade continues going wrong in the original direction, you will protect your trading capital, retain good chances of profiting ultimately, and undergo one heck of a lot less aggravation. I told you before that I'm a professional coward. We cowards have one outstanding trait: we sleep *very* well at night.

The fifth condition is a trifle obvious. By defending for a single month, we generally obtain the best value on the per-month time premium of the options into which we roll or flip. Caution considerations, and the illiquidity or non-existence of the next month's options, may dictate that we move out further than one month, and that's perfectly acceptable. If a two-month defense using a more distant strike increases our expectation of ultimate profitability in defending, we should be perfectly willing to accept a lower per-month ROC. This trade-off, caution versus ROC, appears constantly in option trading, and I'll take the more cautious stance or action every single time.

Condition 6 is subtler. If we decide to apply a roll-out or flip defense, the first order of business is to buy back the short options, and we should be rather eager to get this business done. To this end, if the market for our strike is quoted at 30 bid/50 offered, we should probably make our first bid at 45, or even 50 if this market's options are thinly traded. If you happen not to be in a hurry, then by all means bid 40, even 35, but how is it that you're defending this trade and are simultaneously not in a bit of a hurry? Sounds a little inconsistent to me.

Contrarily, having repurchased the threatened short position, we can and should be a little patient when we offer the options into which we want to roll or flip. If their market is 90 bid/115 offered, then our (first) offer should be 110, or perhaps 105, but somewhere above the midpoint of the bid-ask spread in any event. If there is any volume at all in the strike we're trying to roll or flip into, we should have good chances of being filled toward the offer side of the bid-ask spread. We can always lower the offer later if our order isn't filled.

If the market moves away from our offer, which it will do some percentage of the time, shrug it off. That's life, that's the market. Absolutely, we detest such a result, but the market dictates to us, not the other way around. We'll charge it off to experience gained, and the next time we'll be a bit more aggressive in implementing a defense. Even if we can't complete the defense and are dollars out-of-pocket, we still have benefited by exiting the losing/threatened position. Our trading risk no longer exists.

The final condition may at times be a little awkward for us, but be assured that I did not write it down for practice, because it's nearly vital. Let me emphasize once more that we only defend a trade if the market's movement has demonstrated that our original market analysis, whatever kind we performed, was wrong. The roll-out defense and the flip defense both require a market view. We wouldn't be defending the trade unless our previous market view has been proven inaccurate. We must therefore recognize the possibility that our second market view may be every bit as incorrect and compensate for this possibility by rolling or flipping into options whose strike is as far away from the current market price as is possible *and* that meet our other criteria.

By rule, we must write more premium than we repurchase, and, especially in a declining market, obeying this condition will occasionally require us to write a larger number of options when defending than the number we repurchased. This requirement is yet one more reason why we must keep a comfortable capital cushion in our trading account at all times: we might need to commit part of our current free capital during a defense.

Defense Is Rarely Perfect

Returning to our earlier HUK example, we see that we can—for the immediate term—dodge the potential bullet of a further sharp drop in the price of HUK over the remaining 6 days of the trade by either rolling or flipping. What we'd rather do is to wait a day or two and let theta chew up as large a chunk as possible of the remaining premium in our short puts. Therefore, because we have the enormously potent ally of time immediately on our side, we should at least *try* to sit still for a bit. The merest upward move will solve our modest dilemma swiftly and handily. Even a couple of days of the HUK market doing nothing will put our trade right back into the profit column.

I'll save you some time here. It's a blue moon when expectation, ROC, time remaining in our current short options, the market's distance from the striking price we originally wrote, and the next period's historical tendency all fall into line for a roll or a flip defense. We're back to, sigh, approximations. Said another way, we will accept the best arrangement we can find that encompasses these factors to the best degree possible . . . or we'll use a different defense, or we'll fold the trade and take the loss. Our usual tools, the computer and the spreadsheet, will help to inform us which of these actions is likely the most advantageous. Our object in an extended defense is to reduce immediate risk and to maximize the range of profitability in our altered new position. Clearly, we must compare the relative expectation of sitting in our present trade to that of shifting to the new position and remaining in the market for another 30 or 60 days.

When we're examining the desirability of applying a roll or a flip defense, it's a given that our original market view has been proven incorrect by the market's actions. When we apply one of these defenses, we are in the general case stating that our analysis won't be wrong twice hand-running, or three times, or four, or even more. Roll-out and flip defenses can be implemented any number of times, sequentially, until we finally cash out or dispose of the entire position. It's both somewhat costly and very aggravating to have to repeat a defense, though, and I'll leave the question of whether to undertake multiple sequential defenses to your good judgment. If we can manage to whittle the loss in our position down to some very small level or to sneak back into the profit column, the intelligent and efficient thing to do is to end the trade right then and find something more profitable to trade.

All the tactical points relevant to the roll-out defense apply equally to the flip defense, except one. Applying a roll defense to written calls in strongish or developing bull markets is problematic. We might, by using the supply/demand or technical indicators we favor, be able to detect the possibility of the bull market becoming a runaway market, but we have no guarantee whatever. Holding a short call position when a market threatens to or actually does go berserk to the upside, a recent instance being 2001 January natural gas in December 2000, can and usually will seriously damage our trading capital. Therefore, we should adopt the policy of being relatively more conservative in selecting OOM calls to roll into when the market shows more than a modest bullish inclination. We'll miss an occasional fine defense, but who cares? We'll also avoid being strung up by the ankles when the bulls go crazy.

Defense Is Not a Boxing Match

Whether we're using the non-seasonal or other option writing strategies, and no matter with a bullish or bearish stance, it goes without saying—or it should, but I'm going to say it anyway—that we don't want to put ourselves in the position of fighting the market. I don't suppose you and I would ever do this voluntarily, but we might accidentally get thrust into such a position if market conditions change rapidly after we've entered a trade. In our continuing HUK example of a longer-dated WOOM option write, we initiated a hedge defense when the market had moved roughly one-third of the distance between the market's price when we entered the trade and 48.00, the strike of the put we wrote. Are we fighting the market by doing this?

No, we're not. We're a little suspicious about why the market is behaving in the fashion it is, to be sure. We're distinctly worried about a further decline, too (or else we wouldn't have defended the trade), but our principal reason for entering the trade, its non-seasonal tendency, is still completely valid at our first defense point. When it comes to the second defense, buying the 50-strike put after the tendency *has* been violated, a case could be made that we have begun fighting the market to some extent. You can get into very interesting debates on this topic, but I'm of the view that the second defense is a perfectly reasonable action. Why? We are now in doubt about the market's short-term direction. To address this concern, the second defense represents net risk reduction for our trade over *either direction* the market might move during the next short period of time. Yes, we will cost ourselves some money if HUK turns back higher, but we can control this loss closely in almost all cases. What we can't do, and absolutely don't want to do either, is expose ourselves to excess (or "gigantic," choose your favorite adjective, just don't choose "unlimited") risk in the downward direction, which outcome *can* occur if we refuse to undertake a second line of defense.

Combining Two Defensive Tactics

When defending, we aren't in any way bound to a single defensive tactic. Many times, two different defensive tactics can be combined quite usefully, or a second tactic can be employed to enhance the first defense after the fact. A combination defense that frequently offers us excellent capability is the application of a roll-out and a flip simultaneously. I call this a "fission" defense because it resembles what occurs when a neutron splits an atom.

Suppose we've written OOM options in a relatively high-volatility market whose options are fairly or very liquid. Suppose also that the market moves in the undesirable direction for our purposes, and time is running out on the options but the market is threatening our trade. Whether or not we have already undertaken a defense for our trade isn't relevant here; maybe we have, maybe we haven't. This is probably a fine spot for a fission defense, and you'll find a detailed example of the application of this defense in the real world a little later, when I'll be inviting you to "Pay Me After Lunch" in Chapter 13.

Spreading—How Accurate Do You Want to Try to Be?

When we apply a hedge defense to a written option position, we are actually engaging in a form of spread trading. We've written some options, we've purchased some others against them, and this is the basic definition of a spread. Spreading or, more precisely, conducting a price arbitrage between two related markets, has been a popular strategy for a very long time, dating back at least to the Dutch tulip mania centuries ago.

Spreading is easy to employ as an offensive strategy. We might come to think that, due to summer weather developments or for other reasons, August soybeans will gain in price relative to November beans, and we'd therefore buy the August contract and sell short the November contract against it. We might believe that the price differential between British Royal Dutch (Shell Transport) shares and Dutch Royal Dutch shares will change, and trade accordingly. Right now, however, we are concerned with the notion of spreading as a defensive tactic if one or another of our option positions becomes threatened, or when a position becomes profitable and we want to protect our gain to some extent.

A spread defense for written options that involves buying options in other months than the month of the options we wrote is difficult to use, barring pretty specific conditions. If we buy the same number of options in a further-out month than we originally wrote in the (presumably) nearby month, we convert our original net credit into a net debit, usually an impermissible action for a first defense, and we also sharply reduce our range of profitability.

I will only employ this kind of spread, called a *time spread* or *calendar spread*, for defense if two separate conditions exist. We want the options we originally wrote to be very short-dated, to have a *very* short time until expiration, and we insist that the IV of our written options be *much* higher than the IV of the options we purchase for defense, 15–25% higher or more. Even when the market meets these conditions, we'll be taking on a good deal of risk of an unfavorable market move. If we apply a spread defense and the market moves sharply against the defensive long side of the trade, we may not have any means to recover the loss. We will be in a position, again, of hoping that subsequent market movement will be in our favor.

If we buy fewer options in the further-out month than we've written in the near month, in order to keep our position at a net credit, this is a better idea. If, also, the IVs of the short options are well higher than the IVs of those we purchase for defense, we might end up doing very well for ourselves, converting our temporary loss into a nice profit if the market trades in a moderate range until the short-dated options expire. Our plan here is to sell back the options we bought if the market stops threatening the strike of those we've written, and to sit still if the market persists in its threat. This is still far from an optimum tactic, though, because in many cases we may be required to keep adjusting our position as the market bounces around, as a rule much more frequently than when adopting a hedge defense. When defending, the more trading decisions we make, the lower will be our ultimate profit, *almost all the time*. Write it down.

We could take a more exotic stance regarding spread defense, say, by examining diagonal defenses or delta/gamma-neutral defenses. What are these? These are tactics we retail traders want to avoid using, that's what they are, and, no, I'm not going to discuss them here. We can only manage these types of defenses successfully if we're willing to monitor our trade more or less all day every day, and likely make lots more trading decisions. More work, more contest risk, and probably less profit? Uh, gee, no thanks. We don't need to make life so difficult for ourselves. In defending written options, avoid a spread defense in favor of a roll or a flip, or of accepting a loss when it's modest, unless the IVs of the options you intend to purchase are *way* lower than the IVs of those you've written. Problem solved.

Institutional traders are able to apply complex spread defenses for written options if they wish, because they have the computing power, the lower trading costs, and the personnel resources necessary to manage these defenses successfully, at least in a statistical sense. You and I do not enjoy these advantages. Go ahead, try a spread defense one time, under less than the precise conditions mentioned previously, when you've written some option(s) and the position becomes threatened. You'll soon see what I mean, if it's not already very clear.

Moving the Goalposts—Difficult but Effective

There's one last general defensive tactic to examine. Opportunities to apply it are somewhat scarce, and it embodies a little more risk than we'd usually prefer to accept. However, when we observe a situation where a market has moved against our position in a written option and other defenses are unavailable or undesirable, this defense is highly effective in reducing a loss or in returning our trade to profitability over time.

Suppose we've written an option and the market moves adversely. Suppose also that we don't want either to roll the short option out or to flip it into the next month. There are a number of situations in which we might prefer not to adopt an extended defense. The next month in our chosen market might involve some large weather risk, as in summer coffee or grains. Equally, we might be aware that the next month is historically much more auspicious for buying options than for writing them, as, for example, if we had written August CME/IMM currency options and it became necessary to defend the position. Moving the goalposts is a good way to reduce the immediate threat to our trade, regain most or all of any paper loss we might have, and possibly return to profitability . . . and all within the same time frame as our original trade.

There are two ways to apply this tactic, which I call respectively "the single" and "the double." The single move-the-goalpost defense consists of repurchasing the options we originally wrote, and for each repurchase writing two or sometimes three options whose striking price is further away from the current market price, but having the same expiration date. The double defense consists of repurchasing the options we wrote and then writing two OOM strangles (see Chapter 9) for each option repurchased, again with the same expiration.

The operational preconditions for moving the goalposts, as far as I understand them, are:

1. Other defenses aren't suitable to our current position and situation, or their preconditions cannot be met, or they are undesirable for market-specific reasons.

2. The IVs of the options in this market at this time are not at the low or the high end of their 6-month range.

3. In the single version of the defense, we must be able to replace the premium we repurchase by writing no more than three options further away

from the market. In the double version, we must be able to replace the premium repurchased by writing no more than 2 OOM put-call pairs (strangles), and we must make the width of the strangle (the striking price of the call minus the striking price of the put) as wide as possible.

4. We do not, ever, extend when we defend. We only move the goalposts in the same expiration month as the original option we wrote.

5. We prefer that the time remaining until expiration be short, but, *in extremis*, moving the goalposts is acceptable as a defense in a longer-term trade. In a longer-term defense, we will strongly prefer the single defense to the double.

A good example of a move-the-goalposts defense occurred in one of my accounts in April–May 2001. On April 16, for what seemed like very good reasons at the time (cough . . . an optical illusion that I was too nearsighted to see through), I wrote several June coffee put-call pairs (ticker: KCM) that were to expire on May 11. I chose the KCM 55.00 puts and 67.50 calls, with July coffee (against which the June options offset) trading at 60.15, and received 110 points gross for each put-call pair. Coffee, although a long-standing bear market at the time, had indicated that, heading into summer and hence the usual possibility of weather dramatics, it had stopped going lower for a while at least.

That indication was proven out pretty quickly. Two weeks later, July coffee touched 65.00 cents and closed just under that, at 64.45. When it opened above 65.00 the next day, it was clearly time to defend, given that there were $10\frac{1}{2}$ calendar days and $8\frac{1}{2}$ trading days left until the options expired. I had *zero* intention of rolling the June calls into July or any other month. One freeze event in coffee equals three strikes and out, possibly out forever. Nor did I want to flip the calls into July puts, because in most years, when Brazilian coffee doesn't freeze, it moves well lower from mid-May onward. The market was within one striking price of the calls I'd written, so no hedge defense was possible. The IVs of the market weren't suitable for a time spread defense. This, my friend, was a dandy spot to try to move the goalposts. The "double" version looked particularly attractive.

I repurchased the 67.50 calls for 210 points apiece (very ugly!) and wrote in their stead the 72.50 calls for 80 points and the 62.50 puts for 55. This move was opportune, because the option premiums were such that I didn't even need to write two put-call pairs for each repurchased call. Writing three of these for each two calls repurchased replaced almost all the cost of repurchase very adequately.

Certainly, I'd changed a 12.50-cent wide strangle into a 10-cent wide one, but counterbalancing this modest negative was the fact that the original trade was of 25 days' duration, while the defense, theoretically, was to be in place for just 10 days. I was still short the 55.00 puts, and a severe market downturn would have been both costly and difficult to defend, but—and here's something to remember—when the coffee bulls have the bit in their teeth, even modestly, short-term downside risk is anything *but* severe.

July coffee traded up as high at 69.70 over the next 10 days, finished at 67.65 on May 11 (oops! all I had to do in retrospect was sit still, rats!), and all the remaining options expired worthless. For each two original put-call pairs written, the scorecard looked like this: wrote 2 KCM 55.00–67.50 put-call pairs for 110 points gross each, total 220; repurchased 2 KCM 67.50 calls for 420 points total; wrote 3 KCM 62.50 puts for 165 points total; and 3 KCM 72.50 calls for 240 points total. Receipts before commissions, +205 points, or $768.75, less 12 commissions @ $15.00, or $180.00, for a net result of about +$580.00, allowing for exchange and other fees.

Not a poor defense at all, as thing turned out. We expect that defending a trade will cost us something, either hard dollars or potential profit forgone, but here the cost was tiny. The original pair of written strangles, had they expired without defense being required, would have shown a profit of 220 points, $825.00, less four commissions and fees, or about $760.00. We'll have to rate this defense as pretty successful. And, we'll take as the moral of the trade that writing coffee strangles only 12.50 cents wide, no matter how the trade may look statistically (it looked very good prior to entry, by the way), is a good deal more risky than it may seem.

Defense in General—Other Considerations

In my experience, the longer we try to defend a trade, the less likely we are to achieve a desirable outcome. We prefer to defend, particularly in the case of straight option writes, for no longer than a month, two months at the outside if very specific market conditions are present. Longer-term defenses, whether using a hedge, a flip, or any other tactic, tend rather solidly to end up being too expensive. These are expensive not only in terms of absolute dollar cost, but also in terms of aggravation, more trading decisions required, and a possible resultant loss of opportunity in other trades because some of our capital is tied up. This increased expense is why condition 2 exists in the chapter on non-seasonals (Chapter 6), and the disadvantages of long-term defense are broadly present in any option-writing strategy.

How do we tell when the time is right to defend a trade? This decision involves some degree of personal taste, clearly, but there are several principles that are universal, as far as I'm concerned. First, if the market moves sharply against our trade immediately or almost immediately, say within the first week, and the trade is a standard-term WOOM option write, we have just two reasonable choices. We can exit the trade and accept the loss or we can accept more risk and move the goalposts. The practical questions we must ask here are, one, *how far* can we manage to move the goalposts and, two, has some important supply/demand factor undergone a sudden change?

If the answer to the second question is yes, we exit the trade right now. Our original information about supply/demand conditions in this market, or our reading of them, was evidently in error, and we almost certainly have no practical way to determine how far the changed market condition will move the market. Nor is it correct to execute an early flip or roll defense in this situation, for again we are in the position of *not knowing*, and any defensive decision we might make has a nasty component of guesswork embedded within.

If, however, the answer to the second question is or appears to be no, then we've some work to do in order to determine whether to fold the trade or defend it. Using the previous June coffee trade as an example, we can see that one key facet of applying the move-the-goalposts defense was the relative ratios of the width of the straddle to the time remaining in the trade, before the defense and after its implementation.

One other broad point about defense needs to be mentioned. You've probably noticed that all the example or putative trades we've looked at have involved positions of at least five option contracts. There is a very good reason for this, but be prepared to accept another chunk of heresy regarding traditional trading theory. Unless you are willing to use only roll and flip defenses, you will do better overall when writing options to set a minimum position size of three contracts, and five contracts is better still.

"Huh! What are you saying, that I should trade a position larger than I want? Nobody recommends that I should take too big a position for my account size, that's just insane." You're right, of course, about one thing. It can't be correct to enter positions that *are* too large for your account size, but I'm advocating no such thing. In the first place, the SPAN margin requirement is usually pretty low when we write WOOM options. Even with a smallish account, we should be able to handle two or three 3-lot positions comfortably. In the second place, we *by design* commit three times the SPAN requirement to the trade, therefore, if we don't have sufficient free capital in our account to support a new 3- or 5-lot position, we don't enter the trade. It's called discipline, my friend. Why fret about missing a trade? Another good opportunity will come along shortly, no matter what.

The reason we'd like to set a minimum position size of at least three options is that, if we don't, if we only trade one or two lots at a time, our *defensive* choices become limited. A disciplined hedge defense that adheres to the preconditions is literally impossible, for we will spend too much capital, by definition, for the first defense. A spread defense, which is rarely our best effort, is also difficult here, though less risky in absolute terms. Moving the goalposts will involve writing more than one or two options in almost every case, and if we don't want to trade more than one or two lots in a market at a given time, we can't use this tactic either. The roll and the flip are the only two defenses remaining to us. There's nothing wrong with rolling or flipping; they're excellent defensive tactics, but why are we voluntarily surrendering our ability to use other equally fine tactics? Where's the advantage in that?

Defense—It's Indispensable

We've only scratched the surface of the subject of defense here. Just as there are an enormous number of strategies we might employ in trading, there are a whole flock of different defenses, and combinations of defenses, that we might usefully apply during a trade in any particular strategy. We can learn about and apply these and other defensive tactics, or we can passively accept a loss when a trade goes against us. If we choose the latter road, we will end up surrendering an enormous amount of capital and practical advantage over time, and to absolutely no purpose. The alternatives *are* there, and we must learn to use them, for our own sake.

Part of success in trading is the acquisition of a disciplined method for the selection of trades to enter, but the market will prove our selections wrong in some number of cases, no matter what. Another, and correlate, part of our success is the application of organized methods to protect our capital when adverse market movements occur, when we have undertaken a—temporarily—losing trade. If we simplistically and morbidly accept a capital loss whenever a trade begins to go awry, we should probably take up beet farming or politics (nothing against beet farmers, certainly). Our ultimate success in trading if we do not develop defensive skills will be *highly* problematic, and we'll be at a completely voluntary disadvantage to other traders who do apply defensive tactics to protect their capital.

CHAPTER 8

Don't Just Stand There, Do Something

The Straddle

The markets will *fluctuate.*
—John Pierpont Morgan

I'm not much of one for buying options. Being correct about the direction of a market is difficult enough, and having additionally to be correct within a known and limited period of time, and by more than a named amount, is usually a little more than I can manage to do successfully. Besides, I want a demonstrable historical or statistical edge on my side before entering a trade, and ordinarily there's a strong statistical edge on the other trader's side when we buy options. There have been several studies compiled that analyzed the percentage of options that ultimately expire worthless in particular markets. One of the sharpest options experts I know, Jay Shartsis, the director of options trading at R. F. Lafferty & Co. in New York, pegs this figure at 82–83%. David Caplan cites an 80% figure. The options department at the Chicago Mercantile Exchange indicates that, historically over the past four years, this number has ranged from 61% to 68%. Contrarily, Larry McMillan indicates that his studies show that 60–65% of all options are worth half a point or more at expiration, definitely not worthless.

Which view is correct? Both Shartsis and McMillan are principally concerned with securities options, but, when dealing in futures options, I'm pretty comfortable with the CME's figure, and take as a rule of thumb that two out of three options will expire worthless. That's one heck of a disadvantage for option buyers, especially those who persist in buying WOOMs.

Nevertheless, if we rationally approach the subject of purchasing options, we come to realize very quickly that there must exist some number of profitable strategies, else sooner or later no trader would buy them at all.

Far from that happening, though, options trading is and has been for years undergoing a stunning growth worldwide, so clearly lots of traders are buying lots of options, and some fraction of these traders are definitely profiting by doing so. How do we go about joining the ranks of the profitable?

Simplifying the Game

One positive step we can take is to simplify the game. Why does any trader trade in a market? He expects, sometimes rightly, sometimes wrongly, that the market's price will move in his favor over some period of time. This expectation is completely reasonable. Why would we trade anything if we did not anticipate some sort of profit from the movement of its price? I certainly wouldn't, and I somehow don't think you would either. Of course, if the market moves in the undesirable direction, our trader is going to lose capital. Now, card-carrying capitalists that we are, we must ask "OK, how can we turn a profit from this information?"

Our initial simplification process consists of removing the concept of direction from consideration when purchasing options. I'm confident you'd agree that the more variables we are able to eliminate from our trading considerations, the better off we apt to be. The straightforward way to profit from the simple gross price movement of a market without fretting about its direction is to buy a *straddle*, a call and a put having the same striking price and expiration date.

The naïve view of a straddle is that it will become profitable when the underlying market moves one direction or the other by more than the total premium we paid for the straddle. The price points (one higher, one lower) at which this occurs are sometimes called points of absolute profitability, but the view itself is incorrect. The underlying market doesn't have to move anywhere nearly that far before we begin to profit. For a quick and entirely typical example of this phenomenon, let's take a look at the CME/IMM Japanese Yen. On November 8, 2001, I bought a few March 2002 yen straddles with a strike of 84.00 when the March yen contract was trading at 83.90. We'll look at the rationale behind this purchase shortly, but right now we want to see how long it took and how far the futures contract moved before the trade became profitable. It did so more quickly than usual, a lucky outcome, but the amount of price movement March yen underwent was in no way extraordinary.

The straddles cost 368 pips apiece, $4,600 plus two commissions, and, courtesy of the bid-ask spread, they settled at 360 pips the day I bought them, contest risk having been present as always. March yen (ticker JYH) edged down 108 pips to 82.82 over the next five trading days . . . by which time the straddle was at 376 pips, a touch better than breakeven after allowing for commissions paid on the exit side of the trade. In the next two days, for what reason I can't recall, JYH moved down another 90 pips, to 81.93, and the straddle was now well profitable. I made a note during the day session that the straddle was quoted at 390 bid/415 offered when JYH was trading at 82.53, so I suppose it's fair to say that the straddle had moved legitimately into the plus column approximately when JYH was trading at that point.

March yen had moved just 137 pips, 1.63%, in a little less than seven trading days and the straddle had already become profitable? Exactly. Granted, this almost-immediate move doesn't and certainly won't always occur (it was a bit of good luck), but that's not the point. The point here is distinctly that a market in which we buy straddles does not have to move more than a decent fraction of our purchase price for our straddle to become profitable.

Now, sometimes this apparently too-quick profitability occurs because of markedly rising IVs in our market's options. Not this time; yen's 6-month IVs were 9.2%, and were just 0.4% off the low point in their recent historical range. The yen option IVs did rise later on in this trade, but when the straddle became profitable, IVs were still sitting at a lowly 9.7%. March yen subsequently went on an extended cruise downriver, and the trade ended up very nicely in the profit column. That's all very well, and hurrah for the home team, but the question to answer is "How do we select straddles having a high theoretical probability of success?" Our procedure for making this decision turns out to be a direct and fairly easy one. We'll decide which markets' straddles may present an opportunity, then we'll see if the history and the current volatility of one or another of these markets look as if they'll cooperate in putting dollars into our pocket.

Which Straddles to Look At, and Why—Setting Up Our Advantage

In any market we examine, we'll have a wide choice of straddles to consider for purchase. There are lots and lots of different option strikes out there. We can save a whole bunch of time, and no little aggravation, by adhering to a couple of principles regarding our selection. First, while I dislike using the word "always" in connection with trading, as far as I'm concerned, we will *always* buy the at-the-money straddle, the ATM, and no exceptions. This is one of very few tactical points in trading about which I'm (nearly) a fanatic. Furthermore, this is one of the very few times in option trading in which we should attempt to be as precise as possible. The term ATM in ordinary usage means "the striking price closest to the current market price." Well, "closest" just isn't good enough. I want the market price to be right smack on top of the striking price, certainly no more than a very, very tiny amount away from it, before I'll even bid for the straddle.

Why insist on this precision? Because to do otherwise, to buy a straddle at a near-the-money strike but some distance away from the market, say a September soybean 4.60-strike straddle when the market is trading at 4.69 in March, wastes some amount of the putative historical or statistical edge we have. I want every blasted bit of every edge I can get, and I want it all the time. "Wait a minute," you may be thinking, "why not buy the 4.70-strike straddle? That's plenty close enough, isn't it?" That's a fair question, and it would definitely be close enough, but the fact is that, for most of its life, the September soybean contract doesn't *have* any 4.70-strike options. They don't exist. This strike only comes into existence a couple of months before the expiration of the futures contract. The Chicago Board of Trade may change this situation at some point, but that's the way things stand today.

"All right, so you can't buy the 4.70 straddle. Why does buying the 4.60-strike surrender some part of our advantage here?" Another reasonable question. When we buy straddles, we absolutely don't care about the direction the market moves, just so it does move some decent amount within our selected time frame. In our example, if we buy the near-the-money 4.60-strike straddle with the market trading at 4.69, we *do* care about direction. We definitely prefer that the market go higher, because we will start to profit right quickly in that event, probably after a move of only 10 cents or thereabouts, which might occur on any given trading day. If the market instead moves lower, it must move approximately 17.5 cents lower *before we're even back to the same relative position in which we began the trade*. Worse still, some of the life of the options, ergo some amount of the time premium, will have been burned up while the market moves down these putative 17-odd cents.

This is downright ugly. Not only are our tactics here provably inferior, but we're also deluding ourselves (a definite no-no, right?) that we've undertaken a market-neutral, don't-care-about-direction trade when, in fact, we're bulls. If we have a bullish view on beans, fine, then let's use an appropriate strategy. Buying this 4.60 straddle isn't it, my friend, not in this case, not at this market's current price. If we want to buy soybean straddles, we'll just wait around for the market to move very close to either 4.60 or 4.80, then reexamine the potential of the trade.

Other Selection Conditions

Our pre-selection process has other conditions, just as important as the first one. When we write options, we love the decay of the option premium over time, and Sister Theta is our very good friend. When we buy them, she presents a mortal danger to our trading capital. Sadly, we can't kill her right off, but we can keep her usefully at bay for awhile. In options of a longer term, time decay operates slowly, sometimes very slowly, and the slower the better, as far as straddle buying is concerned. We will therefore consider only straddles having an absolute minimum of 3 months remaining until expiration, and a term of 4–12 months is much to be preferred, assuming that satisfactory opportunities over this longer term can be located. Simple enough, so far.

The process of selecting the term of our straddle isn't entirely straightforward, however, because an additional factor comes into play: the liquidity of the options. Except in the most liquid options markets such as Eurodollars and (typically) crude oil, natural gas, corn, gold, S&P 500 Index, 30-year bonds and 10-year notes many times, and a few others on occasion, the liquidity of longer-term options tends to be pretty low. This unlucky fact immediately implies that the bid-ask spread will be wider than we'd like, and, further, that the market for the long-dated striking price that we're interested in is likely to be completely made by the local traders (or trader, singular) on the exchange floor. There's nothing wrong with this situation, it's a condition of contest, and let's have no yowling about "thieves" and "pit sharks," please. The local traders have an immediate advantage, not a doubt in the universe of it, but hey, they've paid hard cash for this advantage in the purchase or lease of their exchange seat.

The way to compensate for less-than-liquid markets and the locals' advantage therein is to maintain our trading discipline. In direction-neutral straddle trading, just as in any other strategy, call your broker and get the current bid-ask spread on the straddle from the floor. Then, make a bid somewhere just a tad under the midpoint of the quoted range. Probably, the order won't be filled straightaway . . . and that's actually a very good result for us. Surprised? Don't be. When there are only one or two traders making a market in a thinly-traded option strike, we don't want our order filled quickly. If it is filled fairly quickly (or worse, almost immediately) on our first bid, I guarantee you like the sun rises in the East that we've either been dead lucky or we've paid too much. If some other off-floor trader like you and me happens to offer our longish-dated straddle at our price right now, that's great, but it's infrequent. If, however, the floor (the local trader) takes the other side of our straddle on our first bid, bet your life we've paid up for our trade.

We do have a small advantage regarding liquidity when we buy straddles, even longer-dated ones. We're always and only interested in the ATM strike, whichever month's straddle we're bidding for. The ATM puts and calls tend to be the most liquid strikes most of the time, but double nothing is still nothing. If the straddle doesn't trade, it doesn't trade. If a couple or three hours pass without the order being filled, and if the underlying market is still smack on or right next door to the strike whose straddle we're bidding for, let's call the broker and get a fresh quote. Why?

Perhaps the volatility of the market has changed somewhat. Perhaps the local who is making the market in our month and strike had to leave the floor for some reason. Perhaps the principal market maker was off the floor the whole time and another market maker, less active than the main man, had set his bid-ask spread too wide for us, whereas the principal market maker, on his return, will quote a narrower one. We've no way to know which of these situations may be the case today, and we've absolutely no reason to guess. Find out where the market is quoted right now.

If the original quote for our straddle was 650 bid/800 offered, and it's quoted identically when we get the later requote (never mind in which market, that's a pretty wide spread in any market), we'll almost certainly be filled by a local, if at all. If we had originally bid 710 for it, we might decide to change our bid, perhaps to 740. Our potential change of mind will depend on how long we've had the order in, where the underlying market is now, and how much we want the trade. A good straddle is like a good steak, though— there's a better one out there somewhere, so let's avoid being overeager and willfully overpay the floor just to get into the trade.

Generalizing this principle, let's make a firm policy that, when entering an option position, whether buying or writing, and irrespective of any particular market, we'll trade at *our* price without exception. If we don't get filled on our order, we don't get filled, and ho hum. Tomorrow is another day, and we might have another try then if market conditions still meet our specifications. We certainly will reserve to ourselves the decision to bid a little more when buying or offer at a somewhat lower price when writing, but there will be no dearth of potentially profitable trades turning up tomorrow, or next week, or whenever. We never, ever, *have* to enter a trade, okay? Sure, we'll miss out on some fine trades under this policy, but who cares, because there's another profitable trade coming along in due course. Speaking broadly, this is the same policy that the local traders employ. Locals must either profit or leave the floor, and they most certainly don't have to take the other side of *our* trade unless it's to their liking, so it's entirely logical to conclude that this policy works to their advantage. Why not to our advantage, too?

A Practical Consideration

Changing an order is perfectly legitimate and a common action, but we must once again be courteous about doing this—if we want to get and keep getting our orders filled. If we should change our orders around frequently during the day, and especially by small amounts, 5 or 10 points in this example, at some point the good nature of our brokerage's floor men is going to snap. They're working every bit as hard as we are, or harder, and they're doing a very demanding job both physically and mentally, the more so when we enter a multi-part order such as a straddle.

Change an order three times in an hour by 10 points each time (in this example), and your brokerage's floor man will start saying to himself, "Aw, geez, not this clown again," and you can forget about his exerting any effort on your behalf in future to fill that order. It will be filled at his convenience only, and your further trading in his market will become substantially more difficult. Likely enough, he'll mention your account to his colleagues, and you might start to experience difficulty trading in other markets on that exchange floor. This reaction isn't a conspiracy or anything like it. This is human nature in action, and markets are made up of people, true? (Side note: I am thoroughly indebted to Bob McKenna of Lafferty & Co. for taking me aside like a Dutch uncle and explaining this practical lesson to me, very forcefully, some years ago. And he was absolutely right to do so. Thanks, Bob!).

Historical Movement—When Does the Market Like to Boogie?

As you probably knew well enough before you picked up this book, and as we saw in some detail in Chapter 6, many futures markets tend to move upward or downward during specific times of the year. That's just fine with us, and you and I certainly should be prepared to exploit the opportunities these tendencies present. When we buy straddles, however, we are by definition not interested in direction, but rather only in the amount of movement the market is likely to see. This attitude is advantageous to us because such movement, historically, is easily calculated. We can, if we like, employ good old SV as a possible measure of the likelihood of X amount of movement, but I prefer a simpler tool. Let's just examine the gross movement of a couple of markets during each month for the last few years. Tables 8.1 and 8.2 present such examinations of the NYBOT frozen concentrated orange juice (OJ) contract.

To produce these tables, I've used the closest futures contract that spans a whole month, no partial months allowed. The reason for constructing the study in this fashion is that orange juice futures expire in the middle of the month. Sticking to whole months allows us to avoid any skewing of the data by omitting any price shenanigans that may have occurred during the last few days of a contract's life. The orange juice market's futures contracts open every two months, in January, March, May, and so on. Therefore, for the March 2000 futures, the studies have used the price data from January 1,

TABLE 8.1 NYBOT F.C. Orange Juice—January 1990 through July 2002

	Average Up	Average % Up	Average Down	Average % Down	Average Range	Average % Range
Jan years 13	9.85	8.85	8.20	7.92	18.05	16.78
Feb years 13	8.52	7.47	9.64	9.39	18.16	16.86
Mar years 13	7.63	7.72	1.82	1.78	9.44	9.50
Apr years 13	6.95	7.08	4.43	4.48	11.38	11.56
May years 13	8.85	9.18	3.54	3.12	12.38	12.31
Jun years 13	7.55	8.01	6.95	5.65	14.49	13.66
Jul years 12	4.74	4.50	6.53	6.18	11.27	10.68
Aug years 12	6.41	6.82	7.66	7.16	14.08	13.98
Sep years 12	4.65	4.62	7.17	6.43	11.82	11.05
Oct years 12	9.97	9.44	10.89	9.51	20.86	18.95
Nov years 13	7.14	7.33	4.25	3.80	11.39	11.13
Dec years 13	10.12	10.56	8.72	7.79	18.83	18.35

TABLE 8.2 NYBOT F.C. Orange Juice—January 1998 through July 2002

	Average Up	Average % Up	Average Down	Average % Down	Average Range	Average % Range
Jan years 5	5.59	6.59	6.06	6.70	11.65	13.30
Feb years 5	6.14	7.18	8.23	8.78	14.37	15.96
Mar years 5	4.59	5.18	1.38	1.70	5.97	6.88
Apr years 5	3.59	4.28	5.51	6.13	9.10	10.41
May years 5	7.42	8.60	1.44	1.54	8.86	10.13
Jun years 5	6.62	8.05	1.68	1.65	8.30	9.71
Jul years 4	2.61	3.12	6.99	7.81	9.60	10.93
Aug years 4	9.23	10.73	6.06	7.22	15.29	17.95
Sep years 4	3.90	4.41	7.19	6.88	11.09	11.29
Oct years 4	7.49	7.81	9.19	9.20	16.67	17.01
Nov years 5	7.99	10.08	0.98	0.97	8.97	11.05
Dec years 5	10.17	13.63	4.62	4.18	14.79	17.81

2000 through February 29, 2000, and the same construction applies for all the other contracts in the studies.

From the longer-term study in Table 8.1, it's very easy to see over which months the OJ futures historically have had their largest gross movement. Obviously, we want to own November straddles going into the fall, the August–September–October period showing a high gross movement. Similarly, we'd like to own March straddles into the December–January–February period. The shorter-term study (Table 8.2) confirms this, generally. And, I believe that we can fairly say that owning July straddles over the April–May–June period is probably quite unsatisfactory. However, as you correctly suppose (you know my methods by now, Watson), there's more to it than this. We can extend our advantage by looking at two more factors, one of which is specific to the year in which we are trading.

Selecting Volatility—Avoiding the Dreaded Premium Sag

As we saw in Chapter 3, the volatilities of a market change over time. This applies to both the market's SV and its options' IV. The present level of a market's volatility is of considerable concern to straddle buyers. If it happens to be up in the clouds when we purchase the straddle, we are accepting the risk of a decline in volatility. IV is the important one here, because we are dealing in options, and IV *is* a representation of the level of options' time premiums. There's no need for us to accept this extra risk and doing so would be just plain careless, in addition to likely being costly. Prior to buying the straddle, we must examine the relative IVs of the market we're considering.

If the IVs of the options on the market we want to straddle are to the high end of their historical range (and I always use the previous 6-month range of the IVs of the options for this analysis), then we'll look at another market. There's no point and little profit to be made in buying straddles in a market with lofty IVs, unless we've some outstanding reason to expect a *continuing* high volatility in that market. When we buy straddles that have IVs at skyscraper levels, we might ultimately profit if IV stays up or moves higher. If, though, especially early in the term of our trade, these high IVs (and hence the option premiums) develop a case of Cooper's droop, we are largely helpless. We'll become dependent on a sizeable move in the underlying market to return our trade to profitability. Now, such a move might indeed occur, but I intensely dislike "might" as a parameter of trading. "Is likely to" is much, much more friendly to our trading capital.

We'd strongly prefer, in fact I make it a condition of entry, to buy straddles in markets whose options' IV is specifically in the lowest quintile, the lowest 20% of their 6-month range. This policy eliminates the great bulk of the so-called sag risk from declining volatility and gives us the additional possibility of being aided by a rise in IV during the term of the trade, a very profitable double advantage when such a rise occurs. We could easily be more conservative still, and only consider buying straddles when IVs are in the bottom 10% of the recent range. This policy is fine, and very disciplined, but will unfortunately and smartly reduce the number of good straddle opportunities we see, perhaps by as much as two-thirds. It's your call here. The further the IVs from the bottom of their range, the more likely we should purchase an extra month or two of time when we enter the trade.

Naturally, there is utterly no guarantee that we'll see a favorable rise in our options' IVs. The IVs of a market's options can stay in the dumps for months and months, but, luckily for us, this is relatively rare. Volatility is cyclical in fairly regular degree, and over a 4- to 12-month period we realistically can expect some considerable change in it, within the particular market's recent historical range. If we insist on only considering markets whose options' IVs are well toward the low end of their recent 6-month range, more often than not over our chosen term of trading we will encounter a helpful rise in IV and a resultant boost to the value of our straddle.

Again, all this discussion of IVs assumes that we can either compute or obtain them. If for whatever reason you cannot do either, I strongly recommend avoiding the purchase of straddles. Historical studies are extremely useful (we've one more valuable use for them, too), but being able to observe a low relative IV in a market's options is probably the handiest immediate trigger for our decision to buy the straddle. Comparing the importance of IV in straddle buying to its importance in non-seasonal option writing as described earlier (I've no mathematical basis for this view, merely experience), I'd rate the importance of the existence of a proper IV when we buy straddles at 50–60% compared to 10–15% in a non-seasonal trade.

Ignoring a Higher IV—Where's the Suicide Seasonal When We Want It?

Using basic seasonal tendencies in our selection of straddles is clearly to our advantage, and a necessity when we're trading to win. The good news is that we can try to ratchet our advantage from seasonal analysis up another notch—and we should certainly, at least, try. By agreement previously, we will avoid writing an option in some market, using the non-seasonal strategy or any other, which option is subject to enormous external event risk if some extreme event occurs. Wouldn't it be just plain common sense for us to look for opportunities to buy options in that same market over the same period, catering to the possibility of occurrence of such an event, in effect buying into what for option writers would be a suicide seasonal? Oh, yes. Yes, indeed.

We can easily find such opportunities, but, sadly, we face another two-edged sword when we attempt to trade them. Let's be candid here; every trader who applies seasonal considerations to his trading is perfectly well aware of the periods of the year when a particular market is apt to have a higher than normal probability of seeing an outrageous event. The immediate result of this awareness is that the premiums of the options that expire after this period of putative volatility will, almost without exception, be very well bid. In other words, the IVs of the options we would like to purchase for our straddle may be too high, relative to their recent 6-month range, and be unsuitable for us to use, by rule. What to do?

If we do decide to bend our precondition about the options we purchase in a straddle having to have IVs in the lowest quintile of their recent range, we can compensate for the disadvantage we incur through this decision. We'll simply move the expiration of the straddle further away; in short, we'll buy more time. This tactic compensates us in two ways. First, our per-unit cost of time drops, and this always works in our favor to one extent or another when we purchase options. Second, we push Sister Theta further away from our wallets, invariably an excellent idea. The negative side of this tactic is that the straddle might be *awfully* expensive in dollar terms.

If, for example, we would be interested in taking on the supreme suicide seasonal, summertime coffee, when coffee options' IVs are moderate (not low—we should be so fortunate!), the considerations might be along the following lines. Say it's February 14, and we prefer to buy straddles with a term of 4–8 months, as a rule. Well, the September coffee options will expire on the second Friday in August, about 6 months from now, so we might ordinarily be tempted to buy a September straddle. Bad idea. Prime freeze season in Brazilian coffee is late June through late July. If we purchase the September straddle, then, to give ourselves the best chance of seeing a freeze or freeze scare, we might have to sit until the options only have two or three weeks of life left. *Real* bad idea. Sister Theta will be on the rampage by then, and will be gobbling time premium like that Japanese fellow who can eat 41 hot dogs in 15 minutes.

The way to snap our fingers right in Sister Theta's face is instead to buy the December straddle, if possible waiting until the IVs of coffee's options decline somewhat, a likely enough occurrence in late winter. Sure, if no radical event turns up by late July, we will probably end up with a loss in the trade. However, coffee is coffee, the utterly untamed market, and like as not there will be a period during our trade where the coffee bulls' noses will be scenting the air and pushing up the option IVs. Additionally, as noted before, absent the appearance of a freeze or frost threat, coffee prices can take a hefty dive in the summertime (which is why we buy the straddle, not just the call option). If none of our three desired eventualities occur, then, when we go to sell back our losing straddle, our percentage loss in the trade will be much smaller if we've purchased the December straddle than if we bought the September. Once again, coffee is coffee—and in late July there will still be upwards of three months before the December options expire, with lots of premium left in them.

"So, what is the cost difference between buying the September and the December straddle?" I hear you asking. Well, this year the respective costs of ATM straddles on February 14 happened to be 16.36 cents for the September and 21.07 for the December, or $1,766.25. Is buying the December straddle a good trade from a risk standpoint if no weather event occurs? Should we go for the gusto and try to catch either a freeze or glorious price-destroying summer weather? I personally wouldn't, it's not my style of trade—but that doesn't necessarily make buying the December straddle a poor idea. History indicates that this straddle should have been profitable *at some point* 12 or 13 years out of the past 17, but how profitable? And, what would our accrued loss have been over those years when the weather did not oblige us in the trade? Without a history of coffee option prices, answering these questions fairly is guesswork. Therefore, as a guess, buying the December straddle has been fairly profitable, oddly, *mostly* from large down moves. Contrarily, buying the September straddle has been breakeven, perhaps a little better, even granting the trader (generously) very good exit prices in the huge bull years.

Oddly enough, this sort of trade, buying perhaps-high-IV straddles in anticipation of a potential outrageous event, is likely to be more successful in stock markets than in futures markets. The way for a careful trader to profit from this type of trade in stocks is to study governmental information releases, especially those from the FDA. Suppose the FDA indicates that a decision on a new drug is to be made on May 15. Supposing also that today is November 18 or December 12 or January 3, I very much like buying ATM straddles in the shares of the company that makes the drug, selecting a June or July expiration for the trade. *Caveat emptor!* If you do decide to try such a trade, enter the trade *immediately*, ASAP, after the FDA (or whichever) announcement. Don't wait around, because options on the affected company's shares will start to become expensive right quick—you and I are hardly the only folks looking for this sort of trade.

Performance Above All—How *Has* the Straddle Behaved Before?

A careful selection process for buying straddles, as with almost every other trading strategy we might employ, must include an examination of the history of the straddle over its entire term in some number of years. Just as for the non-seasonal strategy, if the market we're straddling has not moved around satisfactorily during our intended trading term, historically, for whatever reason and no matter how otherwise attractive it may appear, let's give it a miss. Let's find something else to trade, because any statistical advantage we may believe we have to this point is too possibly only a mirage. We may or may not understand all the factors involved in this market's poor historical performance in this portion of the year, but, frankly my dear, I don't give a damn . . . and neither should you.

A study of only the historical price movement of the underlying market over the life of our intended straddle is a slightly inferior tool, but it does seem to be sufficient to the task. As mentioned, I haven't yet acquired an historical options price database, which would be very nearly the definitive tool for backtesting a straddle-buying strategy, and yet I've been quite profitable in buying straddles according to the preconditions described previously. Simple good luck? Possibly, and I wouldn't discount it. I'd love to have the remaining piece of the analytical puzzle for this strategy, but I can hardly complain, for these entry conditions seem to work both well and consistently.

A Selection Analysis—November 2002 Orange Juice

While looking over the markets as I do a couple of times a week, in late April of 2002 I happened to notice that the IVs on the November orange juice (ticker symbol JOX, or OJX sometimes) ATM options were at the dead bottom of their 6-month range. Nothing necessarily indicative about this—OJ can be a very slow market in the spring—but I took a further look. Was it time to buy straddles on JOX? You decide—Table 8.3 provides the relevant data for JOX and its options on the first day of May, 2002 (which by the way is the date I'm writing this).

How say you, ladies and gentlemen of the jury? Do we have the advantage we desire in this market? Shall we lighten the other traders' wallets? This trade looks to be historically very advantageous to us. Never a year in the last 12 with less than a 12-cent move one direction or the other in the price of JOX from now until its options expire. The straddle costs us, allegedly, only 710 points, 7.10 cents (but we should always add a minimum of 40–75 points to compensate for general mopery and dopery on straddles in the thin OJ options, trust me on this). The IVs are kissing the bottom of their 6-month range, and that's favorable, too. We even get a hefty chunk of hurricane season into the term of the trade. Hurricanes, though they rarely harm the Florida OJ crop significantly, can get the bulls' juices flowing, and there have been numerous dandy hurricane-scare rallies over the years.

Grab it! These conditions are nearly perfect for this approach to straddle buying. The term of the trade is sufficiently long, about 5½ months, and virtually everything is on our side. The 90-strike options are tradable, but they are thin markets even though 90 is the ATM strike, which implies that we'll have to pay to play, maybe as much as 30–60 points over the midpoint

TABLE 8.3	Snapshot of Orange Juice, May 1, 2002

	Striking Price	Premiums	
		Calls	Puts
	70.00	19.60	0.00
JOX2—November Orange Juice (NYBOT)	75.00	14.60	0.15
05-01-2002 close = 89.60	80.00	9.90	0.55
option expiration = 10-18-2002	85.00	5.90	1.35
	90.00	3.35	3.75
	95.00	2.10	7.10
6-month range of 6-month IVs	100.00	1.20	11.25
13.2–35.4%	105.00	0.85	15.70
tonight's 6-month IV	110.00	0.60	20.40
13.4% (bottom decile)	115.00	0.40	25.40

Historicals—JOX, 1990–2001, between May 1 and October 18

Entry Date	Close Price May 01	Interim		Close Price Oct. 18[*]	Maximum Period Move
		High	Low		
05-01-1990	180.25	188.40	107.75	108.65	72.50
05-01-1991	116.80	166.30	113.45	165.10	49.80
05-01-1992	112.70	121.00	96.10	101.10	16.60
05-03-1993	95.25	134.00	93.25	114.75	38.75
05-02-1994	110.25	111.00	85.00	105.20	25.25
05-01-1995	107.15	119.80	97.00	117.45	12.65
05-01-1996	125.50	127.40	103.00	111.65	22.50
05-01-1997	81.00	90.00	65.00	68.70	16.00
05-01-1998	111.20	131.95	94.50	121.50	20.75
05-03-1999	84.65	99.90	73.30	86.65	15.25
05-01-2000	83.50	87.90	69.25	71.15	14.25
05-01-2001	82.80	96.60	77.70	86.95	13.80
Mean Interim Upmove		15.267	Mean Interim Downmove		17.979
Maximum Upmove		49.500	Maximum Downmove		72.500

[*]Or next business day.

of the bid-ask spread. On a steady or higher opening tomorrow, I'll be bidding for the November 90 straddle, without a doubt.

What's our expectation in this trade? What kind of risk to reward ratio can we putatively establish, assuming we can purchase the straddle for 760 points, 50 more than tonight's settlement price? Historically, we can reasonably expect to make 4 to 6 cents, less all contest risk, call it $650–$750 net, a perfectly acceptable ROC on our initial cost of $1,170, commissions included. The ROC with this level of profit over the whole term of the trade is 59.8% or 10.9% monthly, but practically never will we stay in this trade until the October 18 option expiration. It's probable that we'll exit sometime in August or September, and the simple monthly ROC if we exit on September 1 is 14.9%. The compounded monthly return (which many traders prefer to use, your humble servant included) is 12.4%. Either figure should be highly acceptable to any but the most, uh, optimistic traders.

What's our probability of success? As in one of the examples in Chapter 6, the undesirable outcome has never occurred throughout the term of our historical study (and only once going all the way back to 1980), so we'll use an arbitrary 0.10 failure rate, implying 0.90 probability of success. Our positive dollar expectation is, therefore, roughly $700 times 0.90, or $630 per straddle. Interestingly, we could theoretically risk every penny of our initial capital and *still* be net profitable in the long term. If we enter this trade in 10 consecutive years, 0.10, the estimated probability of failure, times $1,170 is just $117, and our total theoretical expectation would therefore be $630 – $117, or +$513 per straddle per year. Risking our entire initial capital when purchasing options is spectacularly bad policy, though, so let's do something just a little more practical.

It may sound odd (or absolutely heretical), but here we do want to risk a relatively high percentage of our initial capital, in the interest of not letting Sister Theta force us out of the trade if the market goes dead in the water for a couple of months initially. Wiggle risk operates within the framework of time, too. Suppose OJ continues to be a very dull market for the next couple of months. Sister Theta will have lightened our wallets to some extent, but there will still be quite a bit of time remaining until expiration. If we decide to accept only some traditionalist minimal risk level, perhaps 10–15% of our capital, we'll get bounced out of this trade far too frequently . . . and we'll have only ourselves to blame. When buying straddles in which our historical expectation of profit is very high, as in this case, I use a figure of 35% of capital as the loss point. Is 30% a better figure? Is 40%? Any figure we choose is a rough approximation and pretty arbitrary. As far as I'm concerned, if the figure we set is sufficient to avoid self-induced wiggle risk, it's good enough, and 35% works very well. There's one more factor in deciding about our loss point, though.

When the Straddle Isn't Working—Liquidate or Defend?

Once we're in a straddle trade, our position doesn't require any immediate management. Essentially, we're waiting around for the underlying market to move somewhere, or for option IVs to increase, preferably both. About the only thing we need to do is to set a loss point, but the process by which we set this point is noticeably different than when trading pure assets, or when writing options. When we enter these kinds of trades, if the trade goes wrong (in the case of asset trading) or if it moves considerably against us quickly (the first week, say, in the case of an option write), we'll exit the trade at our previously decided loss point. This is mostly a one-dimensional decision process and our only usual concern is dollar loss.

When buying straddles, setting a dollar or percentage loss point isn't sufficient. Deciding on a loss point in this strategy is at least a two-dimensional problem and therefore trickier. Our concern is not entirely the gross amount of loss, as previously discussed, but also at what point in the trade we reach this level of loss. The great thing about buying straddles is that it's almost impossible to lose a lot of capital quickly, assuming only that we were disciplined in our original selection methods and trade only according to the criteria above (or other criteria that you may discover and find useful). If our straddle's underlying market goes dead in the water for roughly the first third of the straddle's life, we will surely be looking at an open loss, and we'll be facing our usual question: stay in the trade or accept the loss?

The first thing to do at such a pass is to re-examine the current conditions in our straddle's market. Has the market simply reached equilibrium? Equilibrium occurs at various times in any market, and is obviously a rotten development for straddle buyers when it does. Can we obtain an indication of market equilibrium? Maybe, and I'll warn you right now that the method I use is suspect. It's usually helpful, but can be laughably wrong at times. Assume our straddle is at or very near our pre-decided loss point with two-thirds of the trade's life still to go. If the trading volume in our chosen market has been pretty steady and the open interest, the number of contracts outstanding, has also been steady or declined moderately, the market is likely at or near equilibrium. In such a case, we probably should exit our trade, because we have exactly no way of knowing how long this unfortunately balanced market may persist, and each week it does persist will remove dollars from our pocket.

In contrast, if trading volume or open interest, or better still both, are rising (keep in mind, we're only at the one-third mark of the straddle's life) over this period, we should hold our straddle a while longer. Why? Traders expect markets to move, correct? If new traders are entering the market now, which is the case if open interest is rising, they doubtless have this expectation, presumably for some good reason, and we should wait around a bit to give them a chance to put dollars into (or in this case, back into) our pocket.

Elapsed Time Changes Our Decision Process

This decision process, stay or exit, changes once the trade reaches the only-10-weeks-left mark. Now, ten weeks is usually adequate time for a market to move far enough to make our straddle profitable, but the knife's edge begins to approach our throat past this point, and the knife is being wielded by Sister Theta, who is completely merciless. The theta figure for our straddle at this point is typically somewhere between 0.7 and 1.5%, meaning that we can expect to lose about 1% *per trading day* of the time premium remaining. Worse, theta will begin rising slowly any time now, and the decay of time premium will accelerate. The only counters for the damage theta will wreak on our capital from this point onward are significant market movement, or a rise in the options' IVs, or both.

If the options' IVs are still well to the bottom of their 6-month range at this point in the trade, we should consider it unlikely that we will get any assistance here. If the past month's gross movement is atypically low when compared to our original historical study, we've got still more trouble. We're definitely in the trickbag if both these conditions are true at this point. If both these conditions obtain, we exit, and right now—no crossing our fingers and rubbing our lucky rabbit's foot and staying around. If just one of these undesirable conditions is present, and we can see no potential market-moving event (a government report or possible weather scare, for instance) on the immediate horizon, we'll exit the trade and accept the loss right away, unless one other set of conditions happens to apply.

If the options' IV has indeed risen somewhat over the first part of our trade, if the market has moved perhaps a third of the way toward a point of absolute profitability point even though its overall gross movement has been under par so far, we might employ a defense. In the JOX 90 straddle we're looking at, suppose we had bought the straddle on May 5 for 750 points with JOX trading at 89.60 and the IV of the November options at 14%. Suppose we had originally decided to accept 260 points of risk, but now it's July 15th and the orange juice market has been *really* slow. Suppose the market closed at 87.50 tonight, the options' IV has moved up all the way (cough) to 15%, and our straddle is now worth just 620 points.

Our original trading plan isn't threatened yet. Theta is hovering somewhere around 1.1% and 30 days from now will likely be sneaking up on 1.8–2%, implying a further loss to us, if the FCOJ market stays dead, of something like 130 points in time premium over the next 30 days. Finally, suppose that a major independent crop report on Florida OJ is due to be released in 10 days, and the Brazilian crop is a pretty good one according to the information we can obtain.

If the overall IV of the OJ options is now sufficient for the September 80-strike puts to be worth 90–100 points or more, we have a legitimate opportunity to either restore profitability to or reduce the loss in our position via a mildly risky defense. Let's say also that we've noticed a smallish rise in trading volume and the open interest has been crawling higher over the past week. These are normal enough during the run-up to an anticipated (and presumably respected) market report, so we should probably not draw much inference here, but at least some factors of the trade are working a little bit in our favor.

It's possible, though unlikely, that the upcoming report will cause a sharp move in OJ. If the market reacts negatively, we may find ourselves back in the profit column very quickly. If the report is neutral or moderately bullish, our straddle is going to lose a chunk of value equally quickly. Of course, if it's very bullish and OJ runs up 6 or 7 cents or more right away, we might end up profitable on the call side of the trade. Okay, so where's our risk over the next 11 days? In the neutral or moderately bullish case, right? Can we take out some insurance against this outcome? You bet we can.

Given all these conditions (and I've omitted some, but I figure you're not really interested in reading a futures market version of *War and Peace*), we can take worthwhile action. Let's look at writing exactly two September OJ 80-strike puts for each straddle we own, netting perhaps 160 points, 1.6 cents, for the pair. "What!?!" (Oh yes, I hear you screaming.) "What's this nonsense? 160 points in OJ is 240 lousy dollars, what the blazes is this supposed to defend against? What happens if the report is way bearish and JOX falls 10 cents? And, hey, didn't you say earlier that you don't trade in front of a report? This is bull!"

Calm down already. I don't *initiate* trades in front of a report, ever, but that's not what we're doing here. We're attempting to defend against an immediate and quite possible loss of capital. The more radically the market reacts to the report, the better off we are in both the immediate and the intermediate term, *even if* the reaction is to the downside. How does that grab you? Consider all the cases.

If our feared result, a neutral or mildly bullish market reaction, occurs, we can liquidate our straddle, temporarily accepting a loss. The time premium of the September puts we wrote for defense, which expire in mid-August, will most certainly decline in short order, and we'll have the choice of sitting with them until expiration if we wish, minimizing our loss and ending up close to breakeven. In this case, the likelihood of being able to watch these puts expire quietly is quite high. There tends to be a comparative news and event void after the market digests a major report, and the only real seasonal factor in play in OJ until mid-August is the off-chance of a hurricane scare, which would be very pleasant for our adjusted position.

If the market reacts very positively, the puts we wrote are toast, and we'll just keep the premium, thank you. The IVs of OJ options are enormously likely to increase for at least a little while after such a report, and that fact combined with a sizeable upside move in JOX should put our position into the black straightaway.

If the market reacts a little bit negatively, we're still better off than we were. Our straddle will be closer to profitability, maybe even actually profitable, and our *apparent* new downside risk point will be about 76.60, which gives us a lot of room to construct a defense should the market drop down to the 79–80 cent level.

Things become slightly interesting if the market drops 10 cents. Such an occurrence is distinctly not probable, both historically and because OJ is cheap in terms of its relative economic value and has been an indifferent-to-bearish market for a few years, but, as always, anything not provably impossible is possible. Even in this case, though, we can easily keep our risk well under control.

There are several constructive actions available to us, should we see such a sharp drop. We could liquidate our November 90 call for perhaps 70–90 points. We could repurchase our excess short September 80 put, converting our trade to a bearish put spread, for around 330–350 (the market is now 77.50 by our hypothesis, and 80–100 points time premium in the now front-month September option is about right). We could even turn around and write a September 75-strike put or a pair of September 70 puts, if the premiums of these and the other pertinent market factors are high enough to point toward this tactic. We might do nothing and wait a bit for a bounce, hardly a remote possibility after such a drop. And, certainly, we might elect to liquidate the whole position and accept the loss.

The point of the defense is that, in four cases of five we will improve our position to a greater or lesser extent, and in the fifth case we will still retain good opportunities to reduce our loss or return to profitability. In this fifth case, what we actually will do will depend, again, on taking another look around the market, and particularly the historical tendency of OJ between now, approximately July 26 by hypothesis here, and the expiration of the September options in mid-August.

The Battle of Midway—The Straddle Is Profitable; Now What?

When the straddle we've bought has become profitable, and the 10-weeks-left point at which theta will start becoming nasty is still some time away, we have a decision to make, and it's the usual one: fold 'em or hold 'em. Claim the profit, or try for more? I would dearly love to write down three easy rules for us to follow in order to make this decision, but I don't happen to know them. There are clearly some principles worth adhering to, though.

First, perform two more historical studies. The first runs from now (whenever "now" is in our trade) to the date our straddle expires. The second runs from now through whatever date is 9 weeks from expiration. If both studies indicate that the market is historically apt to continue in our now-profitable direction, and if we aren't already profitable to an above-average extent (as suggested by our original historical study of the strangle), let's sit for a bit. If short-term supply/demand factors appear to be favorable also, that's a bonus, but not necessary to our decision.

Our mission in this case is to retain or enhance profit in hand. Taking any action (and sitting still *is* an action) that is less than 3-to-1 in our favor from this point is just plain wrong. Clearly, the probability of success from here (that is, increased profit) is not well-defined for every action we might take, but this isn't an undesirable situation. If we can't approximate our continuing advantage for any given action, we simply won't take that action. If none of the possible set of actions offers us, even apparently, the degree of advantage we want, we'll just take our profit, and find another good trade. Reasonable?

Or, maybe, not so fast. Just because our trade began as a straddle in no way implies that it must remain so for all its life. Suppose that our historical studies from this date are moderately favorable toward our trade, toward the direction the market is now moving, but nothing to rave about. Perhaps current supply/demand considerations are also somewhat in our favor, too. We do have an option here (er, so to speak). We can consider converting the straddle to an option spread, biased in the market's current direction.

The mechanics of this conversion are a snap. Let's say that the market we're straddling has moved higher since we entered the trade. If we elect to convert the trade, we sell back the put option we originally bought, at a loss to be sure, but this sale still shifts capital back into our pocket. We'll complete the conversion by writing an OOM call that expires when or before our original long call does. If, in our example trade, JOX had moved to 102.00 by July 15, the strangle would have been trading at 1280–1350, perhaps higher, and the September orange juice (JOU) 105 call would have been priced at something like 240–270 points. Not a rich reward for writing the JOU 105 call, I grant you, but if we have reason to consider that orange juice is even a reasonable favorite to move higher between now and the expiration of the September options, this might be worth our examination.

Selling back our JOX 90 put probably nets $50 to $60 at this point, nothing really, and writing the JOU 105 call for 230 points net would add about another $200 to our side of the ledger, totaling perhaps $400 per original straddle after all our trading costs. This amount may be numerically small in the world of trading, but dismissing these dollars out of hand would be plain silly. They happen to represent about 34% of our original per-straddle capital.

No matter which way we decide, to attempt an enhancement or simply to accept the profit, on occasion we'll be wrong. When we accept our trading gain, sometimes the market will keep on moving, and we'll be tempted to kick ourselves for throwing away a chance at an exceptional profit. Resist the temptation! If a trading decision is sound, if it represents the best or nearly the best we can do at a given time and with a given set of information about the market we're trading, let it go. Traders wander into the "woulda, shoulda, coulda" game far too often, and where's the benefit? Second-guess yourself for the next X months or years? What an incredibly unprofitable idea.

If we elect to try to enhance the profitability of the trade by converting the straddle to a directional spread (bullish, in our example), and the market begins to move against our newly adjusted position, the same reasoning should apply, with one important exception. If the market begins to move in such a fashion that our *existing* profit is at risk of vanishing, we exit, period, stop, end, no discussion, and as fast as we can. Sell back the long side and repurchase the shorter-term September options we've written, or, if historical studies and current market conditions warrant, try to hold the short side of the spread until expiration. Once we've latched onto another trader's capital, we do not want to give it (all) back for any reason, at least as far as we are able to control the situation.

Take the Cash and Leave the Sound of Distant Drums

Sometimes, our metaphorical "Battle of Midway" can't or shouldn't be fought. In our continuing example, I finally did manage to buy several JOX 90 straddles on May 16, at 790 points, with the OJ market right near 90 cents. Oh, I overpaid a little, not a doubt of it, and regretted it, too. Gave myself the rare privilege of spending about 65 days just watching the orange juice market do nothing. JOX dithered within a 5-cent *total* range from mid-May to mid-July, and this, my friend, defines "dead in the water" perfectly. The straddle fumbled its way down to 650, then 630 and I spent my time trying to ignore this morticians' market and finding some profitable trades. Then, out of the blue, a report surfaced that, due to the low level of spring and early summer rainfall in Florida, the juice content in the Florida crop this year would be 12–15% lower than last year. JOX popped up to 101.20 in about 10 days and I couldn't get out of the trade fast enough, throwing back the straddles for between 1120 and 1160 points during this period.

Too quick to exit, you say, sold them out too cheaply? Maybe, and so far you'd be right, because JOX has moved right on higher, to 106.40 tonight, and looks as if it might keep on rising. That's fine with me, and good luck to the OJ bulls. I was losing capital, the market gave it back and tacked on a profit not much less than that originally anticipated. Now I should be complaining? Not a chance; I'm delighted. If JOX moves on up to 120.00 or into that neighborhood, I'll just shake my head ruefully and mark the experience down for next year: be a little greedier . . . but not much. Meantime, if the volatility of the options dips back down somewhat, there's no reason not to try this strategy again in the March options later in the year, is there? Perhaps a good time to try it might be in the low gross-volatility month of September, conditions warranting.

Well, we'll see about that shortly. Right now, let's have a look at ways of earning a trading profit when buying a straddle in one or another market is not a favorable proposition. If straddle buying is distinctly unfavorable at a given time, is there an opposed strategy, a sort of anti-complementary one if you will, that is? Such strategies do exist, and we'll examine one of them in the next chapter.

CHAPTER 9

Don't Just Do Something, Stand There

The Strangle

Then Joshua spake . . . and he said in the sight of Israel, "Sun, stand thou still" . . . And the sun stood still, . . .
—Joshua 10:12-13

A potentially GREAT strangle trader!
—SAJ

Think about buying straddles for a moment. In theory, we could buy an ATM straddle, say of 4 to 6 months' duration, in every futures market that has reasonably liquid options, perhaps 25 markets in all. If we held all these straddles until the respective markets' options expired, and if being profitable in this broad selection were an even-money proposition, we would expect over time to lose just our contest risk, true? What really would happen? Would that be the extent of our loss?

Not even close. Such a strategy would be deadly to our capital. Most of the time in such a trade, we'd be *heavy* losers. We might profit, occasionally, maybe. If there were a serious summer drought, we might see the all the grain markets rise substantially. Maybe there would be an oil shock, too, or a banking or currency crisis might set the IMM currency futures on fire. The problem with this sort of strategy is that we are wagering that not one, but several different events will occur that move prices around sharply. For us to turn a profit by buying a sizeable number of markets' ATM straddles, at least six or seven markets, perhaps more, would need to undergo substantial moves, and all in the same period of time.

What is far more likely to happen is that the majority of all our markets would move around somewhat, a few would see a significant market-moving event, and we'd lose on all the rest. We'd very likely end up thinking seriously about putting our remaining capital into CDs at the bank. The negatives in this strategy are astonishing. First, we have exit problems. If we hold all the straddles until expiration, one of each pair of options will by definition expire worthless, for clearly no market can be simultaneously above and below the striking price of our straddle. No problem, you say, we don't usually intend to hold straddles all the way to expiration in the first place. True enough, but if we sell off, say, all the straddles showing a loss after 90 days have passed, we impose on ourselves yet another trading condition, one that's more than a little arbitrary. If instead we exit on a case-by-case basis, we will create numerous extra trading decisions. Write it down: more trading decisions equal lower profit. Our exit problems vanish only if we can formulate a workable and general exit rule that applies to most or all the futures markets having tradably liquid options. Good luck trying to find that!

Second, if this buy every-straddle strategy were profitable, the previous chapter must have been very much in error in discussing the highly restrictive conditions necessary to profiting when buying straddles. It isn't. Third, as you undoubtedly expect, there's empirical evidence, too. Consider Table 9.1.

The table lists 22 markets, each of which have a December contract, and therefore markets such as soybeans, orange juice, and lumber aren't present. The table tracks the value of ATM December straddles, and omits markets like IMM British Pound futures where one side of the straddle isn't trading yet, as of June 28. The CBOT 30-Year Bond future was omitted because the December contract settled at 102-22 on June 28 and the ATM strike of the options, 103-00, isn't open for trading yet. The popular S&P 500 Index market was omitted because one straddle in this market usually costs $30,000 or more, rather beyond most retail traders' pocketbooks for a single straddle. The e-mini S&P 500 market was omitted for the lack of liquidity in its options.

In this study, the buy-every-straddle strategy proceeded as it usually does . . . it lost badly. The one positive note about the strategy over the period June 28 to November 15, 2002 is that the trader actually had a chance to cash out a profit in the middle of the trade. This is atypical. I keep a similar study four times a year, and this buy-every-straddle strategy has succeeded exactly once since December 1997 at expiration, and has shown a paper profit during *any* implementation of this strategy just five times, in each case only for a brief period.

A trader *might* be able to turn a profit using this strategy if he set an arbitrary profit exit point and an arbitrary loss exit point for each market, but you and I can easily agree, I think, that determining such points is an enormously difficult task. The task may actually be impossible in the general case, over a series of such trades, because both market conditions and option volatilities change over time, which would require the trader to develop new entry and exit points for each cycle of the trade.

TABLE 9.1 Interim Results—Straddle "All" Markets Strategy, 06/28/2002. All contracts are December 2002—$Chg rounded to nearest $

Market	Straddle Strike	June 28 Price	June 28 Straddle	July 19 Price	July 19 Straddle	July 19 $Chg	August 16 Price	August 16 Straddle	August 16 $Chg	September 13 Price	September 13 Straddle	September 13 $Chg	October 18 Price	October 18 Straddle	October 18 $Chg	November 15 Price	November 15 Straddle	November 15 $Chg
Canadian Dollar	66.00	65.69	2.18	64.53	2.50	+320	63.87	2.90	+720	62.83	3.19	+1010	63.42	2.70	+520	63.03	2.99	+810
Cocoa	1650	1639	251	1789	284	+330	1883	313	+620	2016	376	+1250	1910	276	+250	1901(e)	301	+500
Coffee	50.00	51.95	10.52	51.90	10.08	-165	50.35	6.44	-1530	61.60	12.35	+686	62.60	12.92	+900	67.85(e)	1786	+2753
H-G Copper	78.00	78.05	7.95	72.75	8.30	+88	68.25	11.05	+775	69.70	9.05	+275	69.25	8.85	+225	71.85	620	-438
Corn	240-0	243-4	33-6	244-6	32-4	-63	282-6	43-7	+506	276-2	37-4	+188	254-2	18-0	-788	242-0	5-4	-1413
Cotton #2	50.00	49.53	6.64	48.74	6.30	-170	45.64	6.69	+25	43.17	6.98	+170	44.45	5.64	-500	48.39(e)	1.62	-2510
Crude Oil	26.00	26.03	4.25	26.91	4.00	-250	27.55	4.18	-70	29.76	5.03	+780	29.60	3.85	-400	25.51	0.50	-3750
Euro Currency	98.00	98.47	6.30	100.70	6.03	-550	97.85	4.43	-2338	96.80	3.94	-2950	96.94	2.62	-4600	100.73	2.83	-4338
Gold NYM/COMEX	320.0	315.9	26.5	326.1	23.7	-280	315.4	23.5	-300	318.1	19.50	-700	313.3	13.30	-1320	320.9	4.5	-2200
Heating Oil #2	70.00	70.68	11.40	72.61	11.27	-55	75.22	11.39	-4	80.24	13.10	+714	80.87	11.50	+42	68.85	4.05	-3087
Japanese Yen	84.00	84.43	4.19	87.05	4.74	+688	85.53	3.80	-488	82.54	3.47	-900	79.92	4.39	+250	83.17	1.67	-3150
Lean Hogs	38.00	37.02	8.75	40.47	8.75	0	37.37	5.97	-1110	38.02	6.62	-850	41.12	5.55	-1280	45.75	8.10	-260
Live Cattle	66.00	66.72	5.72	68.85	5.92	+80	70.62	6.27	+220	72.42	7.12	+560	70.70	5.42	-120	72.97	7.07	+560
Natural Gas	3.900	3.876	.964	3.582	.981	+170	3.757	.810	-1540	4.110	.763	-2010	4.460	.745	-2190	3.984	.273	-6910
Oats	160-0	159-4	30-0	173-6	33-0	+150	186-4	35-2	+263	195-4	37-6	+388	192-4	33-2	+163	190-4	30-5	+31
Silver NYM/COMEX	5.000	4.883	.490	5.108	.431	-295	4.521	.614	+620	457.5	.545	+275	4.360	.654	+820	4.575	.475	-75
Soybean Meal	165.0	166.2	19.25	169.8	18.85	-40	177.6	21.10	+185	179.8	17.10	-215	170.7	8.60	-1065	164.4	2.90	-1635
Soybean Oil	19.00	18.89	2.10	20.29	2.34	+144	21.09	2.48	+228	20.26	1.55	-330	20.27	1.46	-384	22.36	3.37	-162
Swiss Franc	67.00	67.76	4.57	69.56	4.51	-75	67.30	3.24	-1663	66.45	2.87	-2125	66.22	1.98	-3238	68.89	2.09	-1850
10-Year Notes	106-0	105-29	4-18	108-035	4-22	+63	110-045	5-45	+1422	113-210	7-57	+3609	112-220	6-55	+2578	113-235	7-48	+3469
Wheat – Chicago	320-0	323-4	37-4	340-0	38-6	+63	361-0	44-1	+331	392-6	75-2	+1888	413-0	93-1	+2781	389-6	69-7	+1169
Wheat – KC	330-0	329-4	36-2	364-2	45-6	+475	396-6	68-0	+1588	448-4	118-6	+3625	479-4	149-5	+6688	432-4	102-5	+3319
Result to date						+628			-1540			+4724			-668			-18907
Less Entry Commission (22 straddles @ $30.00)						-660			-660			-660			-660			-660
Less Exit Commission (22 contracts @ $15.00)						-330			-330			-330			-330			-330
Less Slippage (est. @ $40 entry/$20 exit per mkt)						-1320			-1320			-1320			-1320			-1320
Approximate Net Result, to date						-1682			-3850			+2414			-2978			-21217

(e) December option expired before named date
Final settlement prices of straddle used

The difficulties here are compounded by the fact that, even though these are notionally 5- to 6-month straddles, the trader dares not own them for that length of time. As the table demonstrates quite clearly, Sister Theta begins wreaking her havoc on the options' time premiums after mid-September, and the trader must surrender a good deal of the remaining life of the options or face very dire consequences.

You can confirm these results for any implementation of this strategy any day you wish. Visit your local library and look up old issues of *Investor's Business Daily*, or consult the various exchanges' records, and you'll persuade yourself very quickly that this is a stunningly rotten way to employ your capital. Knowing this, however, is highly useful to us because it helps us find another profitable strategy. If buying a broad selection of straddles isn't profitable (and it isn't, at all), what about writing them?

Writing put-call pairs ATM, otherwise called "short straddling," is less evil but still unacceptable from the standpoint of both ROC and excessive trading risk. If the 1995 summer grain markets or the 2000–2001 energy markets or the summer-autumn 1998 currency markets should recur, we'd have considerable difficulty in meeting our profit goals over the whole set of straddles we've written. Still worse, constructing a defense when one of our short straddles begins moving sharply will require our adopting an accurate market view instead of letting normal market fluctuations work for us, as we'd much rather do. Nevertheless, most of the time, writing a given option is statistically more favorable to us than buying that option. As long as we can control our trading risk, we should be able to find at least one profitable strategy when we write a put and call together, as opposed to buying them.

Half a Loaf, and Frequently the Whole Thing— Strangling a Market

The approach we want to take in selling put-call pairs is to move away from ATM striking prices. In the best possible case, we'd like to apply the non-seasonal strategy *twice* in the same trade, to apply it in both directions in a single market. Outrageous? Fantasyland? Hardly. All we need to do is take our usual look at current volatilities and historical tendencies, because opportunities for such trades turn up every so often. When the historical gross price movement of a market is moving lower from month to month at some time during the year, and its options' IVs are not falling (or not rapidly), profitable examples of these trades will likely appear. Just as the tables in Appendix A are useful for helping us decide when to buy a particular straddle, they're also helpful in this strategy for selecting time frames within which to strangle a market.

A strangle, as described earlier, is the paired sale of an OOM put and an OOM call having the same expiration, and it's a highly advantageous strategy when we can meet certain not-very-restrictive conditions. The distance between the striking price of the call and that of the put is the *width* of the strangle. Oh, I know what you may be thinking right now, "Aw, what is this? You talk about writing WOOM options for a non-seasonal trade, and about being careful because good disciplined ones are a little hard to find. Now, I'm supposed to find what is basically a *double* non-seasonal? Why not throw in a four-leaf clover and an honest politician, too? And a unicorn, while you're at it. Sheesh!"

You surprise me. After all this time, now, out of the blue, you consider that I'm advocating some sort of Ponce DeLeon Memorial Trade, something wonderful if you can find it, but that doesn't actually exist? No chance. Such opportunities occur reasonably often. I've never tried to count them up, but I'd be willing to wager quite a tidy sum that we can locate about half as many good, disciplined strangle trades as we can non-seasonals over a year's time. Just read on and you'll see why this is so.

Writing a put-call pair with the put having its striking price below the market and the call having its strike above, a strangle, is approximately the logical inverse of buying a straddle. When we buy a straddle, we want a market to move somewhere over a longish period of time, don't care where, just move, drat you! When we write a strangle, we want a market to move either nowhere or only a little bit over a severely limited period of time. Why should a promising strangle trade be difficult to find? Haven't we agreed long since that, in many trades in our personal experience, a market has done nothing for quite a while—frequently irritatingly so? I believe we have. Why not then take advantage of this non-movement, provided we can determine that such non-movement is likely over a particular period? I can't think of a single reason.

Talk is cheap. How do we locate advantageous possibilities for a strangle?

Necessities for Strangling—Rope, Gloves, . . . uh, Volatility, Width, and Short Dates

If you're thinking that the preconditions for entering a strangle trade constitute an admixture of the preconditions for the non-seasonal strategy and the reverse of the preconditions for buying a straddle, you're exactly right. We'd love to find situations where, historically, we can select OOM striking prices of options to write, a put and a call, where *both* meet our criteria in the non-seasonal strategy. These situations come around from time to time, but they aren't at all essential for success in writing strangles. Why? Because we don't need the same amount of potential ROC in either option we write—we're writing two options here, not one, and we can (and should) select strikes even further away from the current market than we would choose for a non-seasonal trade.

We have a structural advantage when we write strangles. Specifically, one side of the strangles we'll select will expire worthless some gigantic majority of the time, well more than 95% of all cases (about two standard deviations), and even more frequently if we remain very disciplined in our selections. If the market threatens the other option we've written, we have available the identical defenses that we would apply to a non-seasonal option write. The only difference, really, between these two strategies is the frequency with which we may be required to employ a defense

In theory, we should have to employ a defense against the threatened side of a strangle about twice as often as we would when using the non-seasonal strategy. This frequency of defense is reasonable given the nature of the trade, for we're dealing with two simultaneous and opposed short option positions. However, when strangling a market, we have the relative luxury of selecting striking prices usually a bit further away from the current market price than in the non-seasonal strategy. This extra distance OOM reduces the likelihood that we'll have to defend one side of the trade. Also, as previously noted, we have two revenue sources, not one, and so these further-away strikes are perfectly convenient to use. We'll normally be able to start off with a larger potential profit in a strangle trade than we will in any disciplined straight option write. This flexibility also partially compensates us for the increased likelihood that we may have to defend one side of the trade.

The conditions we'd prefer to observe before writing a strangle are as follows:

1. Any market we propose to strangle should have a relatively high but declining SV, and we'll avoid markets whose SV is to the low end of the 6-month range. We'd prefer the IVs of the options to be highish, too, but this is not a necessary condition.
2. Volatility aside, we'll avoid strangling a market during months in which its historical gross movement, as indicated in Appendix A, is high.
3. Shorter-term strangle writes are more favorable for us than longer-term ones on a net-return-per-unit of time basis, and we'll avoid most strangles of a term longer than eight weeks, preferring instead 2- to 6-week terms.
4. If our historical analysis over the term of the strangle shows that we can actually generate a double, or bi-directional, non-seasonal trade, we'll accept it gladly, but we will not see these frequently and this condition is not a requirement.

5. Our potential ROC when we write a strangle should be on the order of 7–11% per month, net of costs, using our regular comfortable cushion of 3 or 2.5 times initial margin requirement in the trade.

6. Supply/demand conditions in the market we're examining must be benign, as far as we can tell, and we'll simply not even look at markets that may encounter high seasonal event risk over the term of a proposed strangle.

Why These Criteria Work in Our Favor

As always, these preconditions want some elaboration. If a market's SV is well to the lower end of its 6-month historical range, it's likely that the premiums of its options are a little stingier than we'd like to see. In order to generate our targeted 7–11% per month theoretical ROC in a low-SV market in such a case, we'll probably have to write options whose striking prices are closer to the current market than we'd like. This requirement will pretty much guarantee our having to defend one side of the strangle at some point. Defense is fine, and very useful to us when we conduct it carefully, but let's not seek trades that are more likely than usual to require a defense. Defense almost always costs either time or money, sometimes both, even though we may expect to make these dollars back, and more, over the term of the defense.

If we observe a market whose SV is relatively low, but whose options' IVs are relatively middling to high, and the IV is rising, let's just omit this market from consideration for writing strangles right now. We might learn something useful without risking a dime of our capital. Surely, there's some sort of risk present when the volatilities of a market and its options are in this rather odd relation, and, once again, we've no reason to guess at the cause or take a poorly defined risk by writing strangles here. This market might turn out to have been a profitable candidate for a straddle, but we'll have to observe subsequent market movement, and the presumable causes for it, before we know. I'm not a good guesser. If you are, you might attempt this. Let me know how you make out.

By the definition of a strangle, we prefer to employ this strategy in markets whose SV has been declining moderately over the past few days or couple of weeks. Certainly, it can't be to our advantage to attempt the usual sort of short strangle, with both the put and the call decently OOM, when a market is or is threatening to become *more* volatile, can it? Monitoring the recent volatility of a market is easy to do, and will contribute solidly to our bottom line as our observations allow us to shun markets having this rising volatility. True, we might get lucky, and the formerly rising SV might decline from here, but we're trading to win, not to get lucky. Let's wait for SV to begin declining *before* we act.

We always allocate enough margin capital for a comfortable cushion against adversity, and strangling presents no exception to this policy. An argument can be made that we should allot even more margin cushion than usual when strangling, on the grounds that we're more likely to have to defend the trade, ultimately. This view is plausible, because the margin requirement of the trade will undoubtedly have increased by the time we decide to defend, but this argument is generally self-negating. When we do apply a defense, the defense itself usually lowers our margin requirement. One hand washes the other, as it were.

Condition 6 applies with more force to strangling than it does to straight one-way option writing. In an ordinary option write, we'll select the term and direction of the trade deliberately, as best we can, to avoid known seasonal and other potential event risk. We can make this selection effectively in most markets in a one-way option write, and we don't mind at all if event risk works in our favor during the trade. When strangling, though, *all* event risk is evil, plain and simple, and its occurrence will be costly for us.

For example, most of the time, I don't want to strangle the CBOT 5-year notes through a meeting of the Federal Open Market Committee. The FOMC may tinker with the Fed Funds rate unexpectedly, or may *not* tinker with it when the market expects it, or may tinker in the opposite direction from that the market expects, threatening our strangle potentially three different ways. Do such developments surprise the interest rate markets frequently? No, they don't, because the interest rate futures markets are dominated by pros who usually have a good knowledge of and feel for what the Fed is likely to do. Nonetheless, who needs this kind of potential aggravation? No one I know.

Selecting Strangles—Possibilities, Possibilities

The preceding preconditions are valuable guideposts to choosing a market for our strangle, but they indicate practically nothing about how we should go about choosing the striking prices of the put and call we'll write. We have two of our favorite tools available for this task, historical tendency and SV, but we need a quick look at a feature of SV that I skipped over in Chapter 3.

Volatility is almost always quoted as an annual figure, and this convention can cause confusion from time to time. If we say that a market's 60-day SV is 20%, it really isn't that over the past 60 days. When we looked at SV in Chapter 3, you'll recall that the final step in the calculation was to annualize the result of the figure we had obtained to that point. Annualizing is reasonable, and it's traditional practice. The SV we obtain, 20% in our example, is the model's way of saying that, over a year's time, the market will end up within ±20% of tonight's price about 68.3%, or one standard deviation, of the time.

Well, that's fine if we're trading for a whole year, but not very helpful when we're strangling a market for three or four weeks. We want the non-annualized figure here, and to this end we'll simply leave off the last step of the calculation. The resulting short-term SV will be our first good indicator of the strikes of the options to write. Let's see if this notion helps us in practice, if perhaps our old friend the NYMEX natural gas market is a good candidate to strangle just now.

Under the Lens

NYMEX August 2002 natural gas (ticker symbol NGQ) settled at 3.245 on June 28, 2002. The August options will expire on July 26, in just 19 trading days. Prices have recently been a little soft in this market due to the well-advanced levels of gas in storage in both the United States and Canada at this time of year. Summer heat waves have been known to spike NGQ's price on occasion, but will likely have less effect this year (should one occur) because of the large amount of gas already on hand.

We check the market's SV and find that the non-annualized 19-day SV is 2.762%, rising a little over the past week, and the IV of the NGQ options is, interestingly, right in line with the SV. This alignment doesn't occur all that often in the NG market. The price of NGQ is 3.245, and 2.762% of this is 0.0896, or 8.96 cents. This figure is very disturbing for strangle writers who have some familiarity with the natural gas market. It's too low for the real world. The figure is indicating that there is about a 0.683 probability of NGQ ending up between 3.335 and 3.155 at option expiration. A theoretical 18-cent target range in natural gas in 19 trading days is *likely?* Hmmm, that's a little hard to believe. Pick up *Barron's* any weekend and check the weekly market movements; you'll immediately find out why we should cast a wary eye at this figure. The price range of natural gas for any *one* week, for just five trading days, is enormously likely to be larger than 18 cents. However, if that's what the model says, then that's what it says, and we've no business second-guessing it before acquiring more information.

Upon looking up the price history of natural gas, as shown in Table 9.2, we see that there is actually a pretty strong downward tendency in this market during July, and now we should start being quite skeptical about strangling natural gas at this time. We may well end up just trading this market using the non-seasonal strategy and writing WOOM calls, but let's keep examining the potential of a strangle a little longer.

The maximum interim decline in NGQ was 25.63% over this period in July 1996 (not in 2000, check the figures!), and this is a very hard number to deal with if we intend to write puts on this market today. On tonight's close, a 25.63% drop would indicate an historical potential for this market to move down to 2.413, and this sizeable move in 1996 began when prices were fully

TABLE 9.2   Seasonal Sell Study, Natural Gas, 1991–2001

Entry Date MOC	Entry Price	Interim High	Interim Low	Exit Date MOC	Exit Price	Gross Result	Cumulative Net Result
91-06-28	1.208	1.280	1.145	91-07-23	1.195	+0.013	+0.010
92-06-29	1.508	1.960	1.496	92-07-24	1.939	−0.431	−0.403
93-06-28	2.197	2.215	1.960	93-07-23	2.121	+0.076	−0.340
94-06-28	2.200	2.240	1.765	94-07-22	1.789	+0.411	+0.058
95-06-28	1.532	1.605	1.335	95-07-24	1.385	+0.147	+0.192
96-06-28	2.911	2.980	2.165	96-07-25	2.249	+0.662	+0.841
97-06-30	2.139	2.225	2.051	97-07-28	2.183	−0.044	+0.784
98-06-29	2.389	2.520	1.925	98-07-27	1.965	+0.424	+1.195
99-06-28	2.324	2.580	2.100	99-07-26	2.542	−0.218	+0.964
00-06-28	4.397	4.575	3.610	00-07-26	3.763	+0.634	+1.585
01-06-28	3.280	3.816	2.910	01-07-26	3.128	+0.152	+1.724

Average on 11 attempts: +0.157 dollars; stop w/loss of: 0.40 dollars

Gross Movement (dollars/MMBTU)
Avg Up 0.201   Max Up 0.536   Avg Dn 0.326   Max Dn 0.787

Notes: August natural gas (NYMEX), NGQ; sell on 06-28, "buy" as expires.

10% lower than this year. Not good. If we want anything approaching a double non-seasonal for our strangle, we'll have to write August puts with a striking price no higher than 2.35. One small problem with writing the NGQ 2.35 puts: they're worth a hot $10.00 apiece tonight, *before* any contest risk. We will be dollars out of pocket, after commissions, by writing these options? The devil we will. Strike three for this idea . . . we don't even need to look at the rest of the analysis of writing a strangle in this market right now. Writing the NGQ WOOM calls, cautiously, on a non-seasonal basis does look rather tasty though, wouldn't you say?

Can't Find if We Don't Look

The natural gas market isn't suitable for a strangle at this time. Are others? Summer is not usually the best time of year for strangling, because many markets have strong seasonal trends or high degrees of weather uncertainty. The grain and oilseed markets are nervous right now, for large parts of the North American grain belts are extremely short on moisture, and several crops are in or approaching critical development stages. Uncertainty in these markets is high, far too high for any but the greediest trader to attempt a strangle. The CME's meat markets are, as a rule, very difficult to strangle unless we're willing to accept a longer term than we prefer, perhaps 8 to 12 weeks. The other energy markets on NYMEX historically show strong seasonal tendencies from mid-summer through about Labor Day, making strangle writing unsuitably risky here. The gross movement tables in Appendix A are not encouraging for currencies, either—historically, we'd much rather buy straddles about a month from now than write strangles today. This year, too, the marked weakness of the dollar for most of this year argues forcefully against any sort of currency strangle at this time. Maybe a little later in the year.

That leaves us with metals, interest rate markets, and the soft markets. The FOMC is meeting on August 13, and ordinarily that event would eliminate the major CBOT interest rate markets and the CME Eurodollar contract from consideration. The September options in these markets don't expire until after this date, and will likely retain highish premiums until the Fed offers its newest wisdom. I really don't think the Federal Reserve will take any action at the meeting; the whole of the financial side of the administration appears to be paralyzed by the dive in the stock markets. Even if I'm right in this view, though, that doesn't help with finding a strangle, because the interest rate markets will tend to trade in the other direction from the S&P and DJIA indexes for a while. We might strangle the August options that expire 3+ weeks from tonight, but interest rate markets are trending smoothly higher right now. Let's not initiate a strangle in a trending market, ever, all right?

As for the soft commodities, it's high winter in Brazil, so forget about coffee. Cocoa is in the midst of a solid bull move, and strangling that market can't be correct just now. Cotton is subject to the same weather considerations as corn and soybeans, and I want exactly *no* part of that mess at this time. Orange juice is dead in the water and its volatility is way too low for us to strangle at this point. Metals and lumber don't seem at all promising to strangle at the moment; their respective historical price movements from this date can be quite large.

Well, rats. This happens occasionally: no market looks attractive to strangle here. The only the thing to do is have another look at the prospects, a little ways down the road. We never *have* to enter a trade, right? You bet that's right. The markets will still be there in two weeks or a month.

Defending Strangles—Just a Variation on the Non-Seasonal Technique

Methods of defending a strangle are essentially identical to those we use in defending a non-seasonal option write. We won't be writing low-width strangles ever, except occasionally in connection with the Endplay strategy we'll examine in Chapter 13. In the typical wide strangles written according to the preconditions set forth previously, if the market should move so as to threaten one of our written options, then the other option will now be WOOM, trading for just a pittance, and we can essentially ignore it regarding defensive considerations. When defense is necessary for a strangle, don't get fancy; defend the option whose striking price is being threatened just as you would if it were the only option you'd written in the trade.

There is an interesting and effective, but fairly aggressive, alternative strangle defense, sometimes called the "permanent strangle," which we'll look at in just a moment.

A Variation on Creating a Strangle— The Step-In

Some strategies allow us to enhance our potential gain during the trade without accepting noticeably more risk, or, in the worst case, no more than we had when we entered the trade. The non-seasonal is one of these. Suppose we've entered a 7-week non-seasonal option write in a market that historically rises somewhat over the seven weeks, but has never fallen more than 7% during that time, historically. We've written the puts whose strike is 12% or so below the current market price, notionally attempting to make 9.7% on capital over the 7 weeks, using 2.5 times initial SPAN requirement as our capital commitment. The trade proceeds beautifully, with the market rising 4.5% in 3 weeks' time, and we're perfectly happy with developments. Can we do better from here?

Sometimes we can. We should analyze the historical actions of this market over the time period remaining in the trade. Suppose that there aren't any obvious supply/demand risks in the trade's remaining four weeks this year, hardly a rare condition. Suppose it's also the case that this market is historically neutral or slightly negative from now until the expiration of the puts we've written. And, just to have a number, let's say that the maximum historical *rise* of this market has been 5% during these four weeks. Suppose also that the IVs (hence, as always, the premiums) of the call options that expire along with our short puts are still interesting, still worthwhile to write from the perspective of ROC. Why shouldn't we help ourselves to another piece of the pie?

Why not indeed . . . and this is easily done. We'll take a look at the premium of a call option whose strike is somewhat OOM from the now-current market price. If the premium of this option is worth our consideration and historical price movement and current events are on our side, let's step right in and write a few of these calls, in the process converting our original non-seasonal trade into a strangle. Naturally, there are a few things we want to observe before we take this step, or, step-in.

When we step into a so-far profitable trade and adjust the position, for any reason, our first goal is to minimize the chance of shooting ourselves in the foot and creating a problem (or, much worse, a loss) where there was none before. When we step into a strangle, as here, we will be just a bit paranoid about the strike of the option we elect to write. Opportunities to step in occur not infrequently in the currency markets. Let's have a look at a real-world example of such an opportunity in Japanese yen, summer 2002.

Stepping Out with the Step-In

I'd written several August Japanese yen 81.50 puts (ticker: JYQ), expiring August 9, in order to attempt to profit from the weakness of the U.S. dollar that was quite evident through most of early and mid-2002. The trade had proceeded in good order, without September yen futures (ticker: JYU), the underlying asset, ever approaching 81.50. By mid-session on July 22, with 14½ trading days until August expiration and JYU having moved favorably to 86.35, I stepped in and wrote a few JYQ 89.00-strike calls. Taken by itself, this was a disciplined non-seasonal action, as we see in Table 9.3, my usual non-seasonal study, from July 22 through option expiration on August 9.

If we can enhance our original notional ROC by 30–50% or more, under disciplined if not absolutely ideal conditions, we should strongly consider attempting some form of the step-in. The original notional ROC in writing the JYQ puts had been about 6.35% per month, and the trade was on track toward that goal. When the market moved smartly in my favor, and with only these 14-odd trading days remaining, SPAN requirement had dropped to $350 apiece for the puts. The capital commitment for the short puts, with cushion, had shrunk to $1,050 total per option, well down from the margin and cushion at the start.

The JYQ 89.00 calls were trading for 18 pips at that point, and now appeared to be a good time for a step-in. In no year had yen futures moved up 250 pips from here at this time of year (think—vacations!), even when yen ruled over the dollar in the mid-1990s. With no contrary information in hand, I elected to write these calls. The initial SPAN requirement moved up to $878 per strangle, and the capital commitment per option popped back up to $2,634 each, cushion included. However, the notional ROC increased well more than did the capital commitment. Net of costs, I was now trying to profit by $260 for each put plus $210 per call, or $470 net of costs, in the remaining 14½ trading days. This was a very decent notional enhancement, to 470/2634, or 17.8%. Pardon my opinionating, but that figure ought to be tasty enough for any trader, over less than a 3-week period. The ROC, in theory, was enhanced by more than 100%—probably I should have written the JYQ 90 calls instead of the 89s, in the interest of risk control.

TABLE 9.3 Seasonal Buy Study, Japanese Yen, 1990–2001

Entry Date MOC	Entry Price	Interim		Exit Date MOC	Exit Price	Gross Result	Cumulative Net Result
		High	Low				
90-07-23	67.52	68.63	66.27	90-08-09	66.77	−0.75	−0.800
91-07-22	72.49	73.78	71.75	91-08-09	73.06	+0.57	−0.280
92-07-22	78.78	79.15	77.93	92-08-10	78.14	−0.64	−0.970
93-07-22	94.16	96.08	92.83	93-08-09	95.32	+1.16	+0.140
94-07-22	101.51	102.72	98.50	94-08-09	98.99	−2.52	−1.310
95-07-24	115.01	115.72	109.42	95-08-09	109.71	−5.30	−2.760
96-07-22	93.73	94.65	92.62	96-08-09	92.83	−0.90	−3.710
97-07-22	87.41	88.1x	84.06	97-08-11	86.58	−0.83	−5.160
98-07-22	71.33	71.89	68.52	98-08-10	68.75	−2.58	−6.610
99-07-22	86.39	88.50	85.15	99-08-09	87.25	+0.86	−5.800
00-07-24	92.90	93.41	91.89	00-08-09	93.37	+0.47	−5.380
01-07-23	80.82	82.72	80.14	01-08-09	82.39	+1.57	−3.860

Average on 12 buys: 0.322 cent; stop w/loss of: 1.40 cent

Gross Movement (cents/100 yen)
Avg Up 1.108   Max Up 2.110   Avg Dn 1.914   Max Dn 5.590

Notes: September Japanese yen (CME/IMM), JYU; buy on 07-22, sell on 08-09.

Obviously, the profit isn't in pocket yet (I'm writing this in the evening of July 25, and JYU closed the day session at 86.32), but we can hardly dislike this situation, can we? There are statistically very fine chances of cashing both sides of the strangle, and even if defense becomes necessary, the defensive prospects are excellent, because all the written options are now short-dated and becoming shorter-dated every day.

Please understand that, assuming both sets of written options expire worthless on August 9, the real-world ROC in the completed trade isn't 17+%. Once again, to calculate our ROC figure accurately, we would have to calculate the SPAN requirement and our cushion for each day of the trade, find the average capital-in-use-per-day, divide the ultimate net profit by this number, and then convert it to a per-month figure. Save your effort, don't bother with this. This trade will have performed very well, and the total dollar profit figure will be quite enough detail.

Now, if yen would turn around and go straight south from tonight's price, requiring me to defend the original written puts, as the study in Table 9.3 suggests is possible, note that, even so, I'm *much* better off for having stepped into the strangle. Effectively, I'm taking two new risks by stepping in at this point. I'm risking a capital loss if yen zooms higher and I'm unable, for some curious reason, to take defensive action. There's also a risk of having to stay in the trade for another month if and when defense of the calls becomes necessary. Against this, the reward is a richly enhanced profit in the statistical majority of cases where yen stays below about 89.14 over the next 14 trading days, and a tidily improved result if the market would whipsaw back lower and I had not stepped in.

How does this trade turn out? How well does the step-in do? I'll put the result at the end of the chapter (I don't know yet, after all). Maybe this trade is a turkey just asking to be basted, and maybe I've stuck my head in the oven to watch, but I have much the long end of the odds, historically and statistically. We'll see.

Another Variation—The Permanent Strangle, the Counterpuncher's Delight

Take a very simple case. Pick a market with reasonably liquid options in all or most months and with a present volatility toward the middle of its 6-month range. Exclude from consideration coffee, soybeans, natural gas, all the usual native high-volatility suspects. Choose a market that is currently historically neutral, or only moderately bullish or bearish for the next couple or three months (whatever part of the year it happens to be when you do this). Find a decently disciplined strangle trade available in that market, according to our preconditions. The wider the strikes you can find, the better, but this time I want you to look at a trade of six to ten weeks' duration. Don't be a fanatic about selecting the strikes of the puts and calls to write, just be reasonable about it, based on historical studies and current supply/demand considerations, as best you can discover.

Here comes another piece of trading heresy. Ready? I don't care if you selected optimum strikes or mediocre ones, you should earn a profit. As long as the width of the trade is sufficient that the market hasn't ever (or only in very odd years) had an historical range that would threaten *both* strikes during the upcoming 6–10 week period, you should profit . . . either immediately or ultimately. You just won't necessarily collect all your profit in the original term of the trade.

What we're attempting to create here is nothing more or less than a money machine, and, bar some radical development in our chosen market, we should succeed at doing so practically every time, given only patience on our part. I call this variation the "permanent strangle," for we propose to carry on with this trade for as long as the market allows us to earn a profit or allow us to keep extending or regenerating the trade.

There are only two cases to examine over any cycle of this trade. Either the market stays in our selected range, and the options expire worthless, or we are required to defend one or the other position. In the first case, we say "Thanks very much," have a festive dinner with friends, and go and look to re-implement a similar trade in this or another market. In the second case, we defend. We accept profits on one side of the trade as it expires and reposition the strangle in the next month further out, or perhaps 2 months further out, if defense becomes necessary. This is a good place for the fission defense, for the aggressive trader. We will intend to reduce the size of each side of the position over time. We also will intend, as always, to write more option premium each time we defend, should defense be required. To this end, we must be prepared also to increase the size of the trade modestly if the market behaves perversely (well, from our standpoint) and we must engage in multiple defenses over several months.

Markets with reasonably liquid serial-month options are very useful to us in the event we must defend one side of the trade, so please keep this condition of contest in mind before establishing a permanent strangle trade, if the selected market doesn't happen to have 12 regular months.

Gentlemen, Start Your Strangle

In a step-by-step fashion, using statistically approximate option strikes and prices, here's what a permanent strangle trade might look like.

1. On December 9, we write a 60-day strangle in NYBOT March cocoa. The market price is 1720, and we write three strangles of 1400-strike puts and 2050-strike calls, collecting $310 gross, $280 net premium per strangle, total $840. Initial SPAN requirement is $746 per strangle, which we treble as usual, allotting $6,714 ($746 × 3 × 3 strangles) for the trade. This represents a notional 12.5% ROC overall, about 6.07% per month, compounded. The trade will end, if nothing too radical occurs in cocoa, on the first Friday in February. Unluckily for us (look, we don't need to consider a lucky result; in that case, we pocket the profit and there's no more to be said), the cocoa market starts edging upward. On January 4, March cocoa hits 1930.

2. The March 2050 calls we've written are now trading at 25, or $250, with just under 5 weeks left in their life. We repurchase the three calls and write a second strangle—possibly with just two lots of puts and calls, but perhaps three—this time writing the 1650 puts and the 2250 or maybe the 2300 calls. If we can stay in the March contract and write, net, as much or more premium as we've repurchased, that's great. If not, we'll move on and write this strangle in the April options, which offset

against the May contract. Cocoa being bullish right now, we'll assume that May cocoa futures are trading at $20/tonne under the March futures. In writing the April options, we might decide to move both the put and call strikes down a notch to compensate for this differential. Note that we are still short the March 1450 puts. Here, we'll assume the 1650/2250 strangle in April can be written for 41, or $410 gross, $380 net per lot, or $1,140 for three, versus our total repurchase cost of $265 per March call, or $795. Net to us, $345 on the defense, at least for now. Margin? Up somewhat, perhaps $1,000 total (I'm being pessimistic), since the original March puts are still on the books.

3. Well, drat. Cocoa turns right around, and by January 27, March cocoa is back to 1760, and May cocoa is, by rough assumption, trading at 1740. We have no intention of letting *any* of our written strikes be threatened, so we're going to adjust the position again, and our broker just loves this, naturally. We'll repurchase all the April 1650 puts, now trading at 35. We'll then, not surprisingly, write another strangle, $600 or $650 wide, in the May options, likely the 1450/2050. Our short March puts expire on the first Friday in February and are now WOOM and almost certainly toast. If we couldn't before, then by this time, we may be able to replace the premium we've repurchased by just writing two strangles here. If we must write three, so be it—when defending, we *always write at least as much premium as we repurchase*. Assume we write 3 May 1450/2050 strangles for 46, yielding $1,380 gross and $1,290 net, versus our total repurchase cost of $1,140, $170 net to us, whether temporarily or not we don't know.

4. Sigh, no rest for the weary. Three-plus weeks later, on February 20, May cocoa (the March puts have expired and their premium is now in our pocket) runs up to 1980, a new high. Where are we now? The March 1450 puts are gone, the second-phase April 1650s were repurchased, and we're short 3 May 1450 puts. On the call side, the original short March 2050s were repurchased, and we're short 3 April 2250s and 3 May 2050s. We'll repurchase the May 2050s and write a pair of strangles to replace the premium, almost certainly in the June options.

5. We need to do this for two reasons. Our position is now unbalanced, and the next written strangle will correct this. While being unbalanced isn't evil in itself, when we're strangling a market, we much prefer that our short put and short call positions are always equal or very close. Observe, though, that if we have defended in a disciplined fashion, and have each time written at least as much premium as we've repurchased, we have profit in hand and a fine potential for more, at every point during the trade. Our margin requirement will have increased from its level

at the start, but our cushion has not come anywhere near to being used up.

6. We continue along these lines, replacing threatened options with the same or, preferably, a lower number of strangles. We also prefer to keep the term of the newly written strangles as short as we can. If we can avoid moving another month further out in any cycle (while always writing more premium than we repurchase), we'll jump at the opportunity.

Once again, in our theoretical permanent strangle, I've taken completely negative assumptions about the behavior of the market in which we're involved. The movement of the market has caused us to adjust our position from three lots originally probably up to five, maybe six, at this point in the example, and we likely have only one profit (possibly two) in pocket, with another to be cashed out in about 2 weeks. All right, that's *why* I make negative assumptions; that's why I double-whipsawed this trade in our example here. The usual behavior of markets is much less inimical to us, and it's more useful for learning purposes to watch what happens when the market behaves negatively, because we learn how we can compensate for or avoid such adversity. When the market trades in a less unfriendly fashion, as it will do many times, we'll cash out completely in one or another early cycle of the trade, and have another look at that special gift our spouse has been hinting about.

When we attempt a permanent strangle, some large percentage of the time we will be much more richly rewarded than in our example, and more quickly, too. This trade ends when the market stays in our movable range and the most recently written strangles expire. The single key factor in this strategy is to keep the width of each successive strangle as wide as possible, generally as wide as or wider than the original strangle. If the trade has not ended by the time our market heads into an historically high-volatility period of the year, we will have to consider folding the trade. If, however, a period of rising volatility coincides with a seasonal tendency, we may just as easily convert the trade to a non-seasonal, wait a bit longer, and then cash it.

There is exactly no requirement that we use a fission defense in this strategy, replacing threatened options with new strangles. At any point that a fission defense appears undesirable, we can use roll or flip defenses at our pleasure for whichever short position is threatened. There will be numerous occasions when we'll prefer these defenses to the fission defense. If our historical studies indicate that, six weeks down the road, this market begins a strong upward seasonal, then we'll probably apply a flip defense if some of our short calls become threatened. If in the interim the market's movement comes to menace any of our short puts, we'll almost surely use a roll defense, move the striking prices out a month or two, and wait for the upward seasonal to commence.

Match the defense in each cycle of a permanent strangle to the current market situation, but keep looking ahead. These are *futures* markets after all. If we're strangling cocoa, and there are rumors of a *coup d'etat* in Ivory Coast or Ghana, seasonal tendency or not, I know I'm not going to write a whole lot of calls (read: absolutely zero) as part of a defense in that market until the dust settles. If we're strangling soybean oil, and it looks as if the Canadian canola crop is going to be enormous, and maybe the U.S. soybean crop also, writing puts as a defense simply isn't on the table.

There are a considerable number of other variations on the general strategy of strangling. Sometimes it will be desirable to strangle a market in an unbalanced fashion, writing more puts than calls, or the other way around. A creative but complex variation of the strategy is what I call the "universal" strangle, essentially the logical inverse of the inferior "buy-every-straddle" strategy, wherein we attempt wide-ish strangles on 10 or more different markets at once, typically for a term of 30 days or so. Here, we anticipate that normal market fluctuations will allow us to cash half or more of the positions in the first cycle. We'll defend the rest and intend to pick off the remaining positions one at a time via some flavor of the permanent strangle procedure, or through some other variation suitable to the specific market at the time defense becomes desirable.

Sheldon Natenberg, author of the outstandingly useful book *Option Pricing and Volatility*, calls strangling one of the most dangerous strategies that a trader can employ. It certainly can be, not a doubt of it. If the trader is nonchalant about selecting disciplined striking prices, less than scrupulously careful about watching for supply/demand surprises that may lie ahead, or decides that any of the preconditions for a disciplined strangle are not worth his time and attention, he's asking for a whole lot of trouble. Effectively, by doing any of these, the trader is courting external event risk, even in some sense daring it to show its face. This can never be part of trading to win. Don't do it.

Because the strangles we intend to write have, speaking broadly, shorter life spans than trades we might undertake when using a number of other strategies, we might be able to give ourselves yet another advantage here. Without violating any of our preconditions, we might decide to bias our selections toward a nearer expiration date and tend to be more reluctant about accepting strangle trades having a longer term. While I haven't any figures in hand to quantify this potential advantage, I do have the distinct impression from experience that the shorter-dated strangles I've traded over the years have succeeded, and usually without extended defense, more frequently than the longer-dated ones. It would be very nice to have collected a hefty, detailed history of all these trades, in order to see if my impression is accurate. For right now, though, I'll have to recommend that you simply consider this observation for what it may be worth.

Although profitable and disciplined strangles don't turn up as often as do our opportunities in the non-seasonal strategy, we should always be on the alert for them. Their property of almost always allowing us to cash some profit during each month, or each cycle of the trade if we must defend, is an extremely attractive feature. Option traders should not fail to appreciate the enhanced level of profitability that strangles offer. True, to employ this strategy and its variations effectively, we must hone our defensive skills, and I'm well aware that a lot of traders don't like to employ possibly complex defenses. Not a problem. If you are one such trader, there are strategies that are more suited to your temperament, and, just by very good luck, we'll examine one of these when you turn the page.

L'Envoi: September yen traded between 83.37 and 86.52 over the remaining 14 trading days to August 9. Both sides of the 81.50–89.00 strangle expired worthless.

CHAPTER 10

Hi-Yo, Yogi!

Riding the Bear

How low can you go?
—Ernest Evans (*Chubby Checker*, "Limbo Rock")

O ne of the nicer things about physical futures markets is that every so often they present an opportunity to traders that no other market can offer. If it turns out that a company is a fraud or it will not or cannot adapt to changes in the marketplace, the price of its shares will sooner or later go to pennies or to zero. In these cases, and in numerous others besides, dubious companies' bonds will also trade for a tiny fraction of face value. Government bonds? Hah! Far too often, default is the magic word regarding these. Not infrequently, the issuing government will accompany its default with a comforting message to debtholders, like "Bleep you, and the llama (or samovar, or camel, or elephant) you rode in on." Currencies? Don't get me started—any number of supposedly civilized countries literally *cancelled* their respective currencies in the last century and replaced them with wonderful new currencies, oh so trustworthy, we promise, this time will be different.

Bull. Pure, unadulterated, USDA-inspected, Grade A bull, with whipped cream and a cherry on top. If it's paper, it's only worth what the promise behind it is worth, and, if this promise is dubious or becomes so, then it's toilet paper.

In contrast, someone will *always* bid for corn, or cocoa, or coffee, or crude oil at some price, and this price won't be pennies either. In these markets, there is a price below which, even discounting incompetent governmental (pardon the redundancy) meddling and subsidy and other vote-buying distortions, selling will drop off markedly or even essentially cease. This fact offers us a chance to fatten up our trading accounts on occasion. Given a specific set of circumstances within a bear market, we'll jump right on and ride the bear . . . and not in the manner you might at first think.

Minimum Value—When Suppliers Won't Play

In physical futures markets, large numbers of participants, simply by bidding for or offering these markets' goods, engage in price discovery. For our purposes, their efforts here can be very helpful under certain circumstances. When there is too much of a physical commodity, we'll sooner or later see the famous bear market, and we've an excellent opportunity when such a bear market meets a few conditions. What will be the low price in December corn this year? I haven't a clue and have no intention of trying to guess it, for there's no need. Whether coffee or cocoa, cotton or crude, if a physical futures market is in considerable oversupply, the market itself will very kindly tell us when to make a dollar.

In any physical market, the economic notion of *minimum value* applies. There is a hard, objective price for the product, below which producers will sharply curtail production or stop producing altogether. No point in engaging in commercial activity if you can't turn a profit, is there? Clearly, this effective minimum value varies from producer to producer, and by market and year. Can we determine what this price area level is at a specific time, either actually or approximately?

We can get close to figuring this price point, but we need a little help. First and foremost, we want to observe a particular type of event that hints to us that minimum value is close at hand. I call this a trigger event. In late 1999, citizens of the Ivory Coast made the newswires worldwide, first by threatening to and subsequently by actually dumping great piles of low-grade cocoa in the streets and burning them. Evidently a number of growers were so frustrated/annoyed/furious at persistently low world cocoa prices that they ultimately decided such action was the only way to express their anger and/or plead for higher government subsidies.

Bingo. This is a dandy trigger event, nearly a perfect one. I couldn't put a hard number to it at the time, but minimum value was lurking somewhere in the current price neighborhood. When producers spontaneously begin destroying their own production, how in the world can the market price *not* be close to minimum value? Opportunities like this are certainly not everyday occurrences, but they come along sufficiently often that we ignore them only to our detriment.

Turning Facts into Dollars—How to Do It and Why It Works

Earning a profit in such situations is a remarkably likely result and involves applying an easy, straightforward strategy. We'll write short-dated puts immediately under the market and, for the most part, sit still. If the front-month cocoa futures are at a price of 780, we'll write the short-dated 750 puts; if the market is 820, we'll write the 800s, or just possibly the 750s if the potential ROC of the trade is satisfactory. If we're alert and a little bit nimble, we can occasionally manage to execute this trade profitably for several successive months.

"Aw, come on, Stu! First you say that when I write options, I should write 'em way out of the money, now you want me to snuggle the strike I write right up to the current market price. You can't have it both ways!" Oh yes I can, and I do. In usual option-writing strategies, we much prefer to write short- and shorter-dated options as far away from the market as is convenient and consistent with a positive expectation and a solid ROC. Here, we're not dealing with the usual case, though—we not only have Sister Theta on our team, we also have her little brother, human economic rationality, hitting right behind her in the lineup, and it gets better still. Batting behind human nature comes our long-time friend historical tendency—and he knows how to hit this pitcher, believe me. This lineup is trading's equivalent of the famed Yankees' "Murderer's Row" of old.

Theta's on our side because, in the bear market situation just described for cocoa, we'll elect to write short-dated puts, typically with four to eight weeks until expiration. Human nature is under contract to us this time because people won't produce, or won't deliver goods to market, if they earn nothing or nearly nothing in return. History is way in our favor because of a very interesting fact about bear markets in physical futures, one which admits of precisely no historical exception.

We have even one more thing going for us here. What is a market, ultimately? I claim—and I'm 100% willing to stake my capital on this definition, and economics professors who disagree be damned—that it is an anticipatory discounting mechanism of price. Yesterday's news is worth nothing, and today's little or nothing, save in extreme cases such as Hussein invading Kuwait on August 1, 1990. The market participants have discounted to a considerable extent whatever supply/demand information has been available, and ordinary news will have little effect on their or our future decisions. Under everyday circumstances, market participants in any market are engaged in two activities: making a profit and price discovery. Shall we assume, again under everyday circumstances, that the market participants collectively have somehow elaborately failed in their efforts at price discovery? You may, and feel free to do so. I won't.

When a market's price declines to a point at which producers become reluctant or refuse outright to produce or deliver goods to market, the market participants will pick up on this development almost immediately via their continuing price discovery efforts. En route to this point, those who have been following such a market will have sold as much as they care to sell. We sometimes hear analysts, traders, and even pundits describing a market as "sold out." Unlike the ordinary usage of this phrase, which means there's nothing left to be bought, in a trading context the phrase is used to indicate that market participants have sold all they want and are unwilling to sell more at current price levels. If there's little new selling to be expected in the near term, the market price will have a difficult time indeed in moving much lower.

History bears this out in very clear fashion. Bear markets can persist for years (for example, coffee from December 1999 to the present date, mid-2002). However, an enormously interesting thing happens, or rather does not happen, when a long-term bear market matures, as it were, and gets close to the point of being sold out. It may continue to work lower by dribs and drabs, making a new low every so often, but it never—and I mean not once I can find by looking through 25+ years of data in 20-odd physical futures markets—makes a sharp, spiky new low at this point. We'll have a detailed look at a recent example of this non-phenomenon throughout this chapter.

Entry Conditions—How Mature Is the Bear?

By writing puts when a long-term bear market is close to sold out, we are again anticipating what a market will not do in the near future. The question is now, "How can we recognize an advantageous entry point?" The preconditions for entry appear to be as follows:

1. The bear market, that is, the initial 20% decline from the top of the last upward move, must have begun not less than 4 months ago, and the longer ago, the better for us.
2. The total decline to date, measured from the top of the last upward move, should be not less than 40% of the price at that most recent top.
3. If the market we're examining does not have 12 regular months, then its serial month options must have sufficient liquidity to be tradable.
4. If the market we're examining is agricultural, we do not initiate the trade just before harvest season of the crop when a large harvest is forecast.
5. The 30-day SV of the market we're examining should have been declining, at minimum over the past 2 weeks, and preferably longer.

6. The market must not have undergone any 4% or larger daily decline over the past 2 weeks, and preferably longer.

7. There must occur an observable trigger event—some action taken by producers, governments, or both.

Now we see why opportunities to ride the bear are scarce. At any given time, some considerable percentage of all markets are moving upward or are doing not much of anything, and are thus excluded from consideration. Then, not all that many bear markets decline 40% or more from their last high. The not-right-before-harvest condition excludes some number of potential ursine excursions, NYBOT "C" coffee having been a perfect example in mid-2002. Finally, we do not intend, ever, to apply this strategy in any financial, currency, or index market. The whole reasoning behind the strategy is inapplicable to such markets, because there is no practical definition of the minimum value of paper promises, unless we allow zero.

If you happen to be a technically oriented trader and you have a satisfactory method of determining that a particular market is likely to be "putting in a bottom," as they say, feel free to substitute your favorite condition or set of conditions for condition 5. A market's SV doesn't always move lower toward the end of a huge, long-lasting bear market, just most of the time. Condition 6 is vital. If a market is still spiking around every few days, it's simply too early to try riding the bear. Wait for it.

If we have not observed a trigger event, something along the lines previously described for cocoa in 1999, I don't know what we're doing, but we aren't applying the ride-the-bear strategy as I understand it. If you have legitimate cause to believe that a bottom is about to be made in one of these extended bear markets, go right ahead and write some puts, and I certainly hope your decision is correct. The occurrence of a trigger event is my security blanket, though, and I pretty well insist on having it.

Condition 3 concerning regular/serial months of options wants a little more discussion. Some markets, the NYMEX energy contracts for instance, have a regularly traded futures contract for all 12 months of the year and an expiry of options associated with each month. For markets that do not have 12 regular months, the months in which there is no futures contract are called *serial months*. Some markets, NYBOT cotton and orange juice for example, in theory do have options available in their serial months, but good luck trying to trade them; these months' option volumes range from imperceptible to nil. We'll avoid these markets in this strategy. Some markets' option volumes are negligible in every month, CME pork bellies and NYBOT platinum to name two, and we've no use for these markets here, either. You may very reasonably be asking why we care about liquidity in the serial months of a market. There are two reasons: profit potential and defensive capability.

The Best of Both Worlds—Profit Each Month, or Walk Out on the Bill

What we really would like to do when we ride the bear is to stay right on his back, to turn a profit for several months in succession while a market puts in an extended bottom. Suppose we'd be required by the lack of liquidity or the complete non-existence of the next month's options to move our second, third, *n*th option write to the options 2 or 3 months away for each successive write. We'd almost surely earn a larger premium on the successive writes, but the premium, equally surely, would be net lower on a per-month basis and we'd have to contend with yet another condition.

When a bear market in physical goods exists, supplies are by definition too ample for the existing market demand. The price of each successive regular month futures contract will reflect this excess in the cost of interest, and of storing and insuring the goods for another 60 or 90 days or so, the well-known *carrying charge*. These successive months' prices will be higher than the nearby regular month contract, and this price structure may force us to make a decision whether to change the striking price of the next puts we write.

Serial month options are offset against the next regular month's futures. January and February options in cocoa, for example, are matched off against the March futures, just as are the March options. Liquid serial month options give us a sizeable opportunity advantage. If we would want to continue the trade while the underlying market keeps scraping along its bottom, their availability will have removed one variable from our decision-making process, namely, the striking price of the next options we'll write. If we begin riding the bear by writing the January puts in cocoa or coffee, say, then when or just before the January options expire, our decision process is very simple—do it again or call it a day. We usually won't have to examine which strike to write; the same strike we originally wrote will ordinarily be the one we'll want for the next write. Naturally, wanting and getting are not the same thing at all, and we may be required by market conditions to write a different strike, but whichever strike best meets our entry criteria will be all right with us.

Liquid serial month options also, beneficially, make defending our position easier should a defense become desirable. A hedge defense isn't possible when riding the bear because we have deliberately written a strike very close to the market price. A spread defense, creating a calendar time spread by purchasing puts in a further out month with the same striking price as the ones we wrote, presents more complications than it's worth, and usually restricts our future range of profitability far too tightly.

The usual defense in this strategy is a roll-out; buy back what we originally sold and then write some number of puts in the next month, or possibly two months, out. When we can and when the option premiums justify it, we'll prefer to roll out-and-down to a lower strike while the bear market piddles along near its bottoms. Our ability to do so will depend on the amount of life left in the puts we originally wrote and the comparative premiums of the two options at the time we decide to examine defensive possibilities.

On the Bear's Back—A Real-World Trade

For a practical example of riding the bear, we can look at a trade conducted over several months in the 1999–2000 cocoa market. Your favorite author managed the trade fairly well from November through August (I'd give myself about 65 or 70 marks out of 100, no more). At the time, I was just fooling with developing the ride-the-bear strategy, and if I had known then what I know now . . . well, never mind.

On November 12, 1998, NYBOT March 2000 cocoa, a 10 metric ton (tonne) contract, closed at 1648. The contract began a steady and protracted decline on continuing good supply news until the market reached 984 on May 28, 1999. In the next month, it bounced back to 1226 on June 21, then resumed its price erosion. The market broke 1000 again on August 18, and gave up another $150/tonne through early November.

At the time, I was involved in a non-seasonal trade, writing NYBOT cocoa calls, which, as we see above, was certainly a profitable idea over the preceding period. Then, reading over the newswires on November 12, I saw the story about Ivorians threatening to burn cocoa stocks. I hadn't analyzed the ride-the-bear strategy thoroughly at that point, but was willing to experiment a little bit, so I wrote a few February 2000 800-strike puts for $35/tonne, thus stepping into a strangle along the lines discussed in the previous chapter. As things turned out, I was too early, but only slightly. The market wasn't quite sold out.

February 2000 cocoa options on NYBOT offset against the March 2000 futures (ticker: CCH), and expire on the first Friday in January. March futures closed at 838 on November 12, and there were 53 days remaining until expiration of the February options. The trade was uneventful until December 22, when CCH took a dive down to 808. The short puts were now at $18. What to do? Repurchase the puts, roll 'em out, or sit still? I didn't have any empirical experience with this type of trade, but I had had six weeks to learn a little about market behavior toward the end of extended bear markets. I decided that, if CCH would trade below 800 the next day, I'd simply exit the trade.

It didn't. CCH opened sharply higher (for reasons I still haven't learned) on the last trading day before Christmas. It settled at 849 and the pressure was off the trade temporarily. Good news! I also had some time to think. Bad news! You can think yourself into more dumb trades, I swear, and I took this opportunity to do exactly that. I wrote several March 800 put options for $26/tonne, due to expire on February 4, 2000. I didn't write the reasoning in my trading notebook, so I can't really tell you why. At least nothing *too* evil happened subsequently.

The February puts expired tamely on January 7, and CCH wandered around in the low 800s for the rest of the month. On February 1, it popped below 800, with just three days until expiration of the March options. At least *this* situation I knew how to handle. CCH opened at 779, bounced up to 793, and I couldn't buy those short March puts back fast enough. I paid $25/tonne for them, losing commissions on the trade, and rolled the short March 800 put position into the May 750 puts for $18/tonne, thus breaking at least one of our trading conditions. However, I didn't have our handy list of preconditions at the time, I was learning by doing . . . and making a pretty fair hash of it, too. You'll notice that the April options got lost in the shuffle? They sure did. I forgot to write any of the April options. Just plain forgot.

Six days later, the market offered me a chance to rectify my error of not writing more premium than I repurchased, and, good news, cocoa's volatility had risen. I was able to write about 40% more May 750 puts at $23/tonne, with May cocoa (ticker: CCK) at 810, and the May options due to expire on the first Friday in April. Nothing much happened in the trade until the last day of February. CCK zipped down to 756 at one point, and I was faced with the same dilemma as in December, except this time there were 5 weeks until expiration, not 16 days.

Stage Two—Not Pretty So Far

Well, if sitting still was the right action once, it might well be the right action again. Besides, I'd had a lot of time to research this type of trade by now, and the research strongly indicated that the behavior of extended bear markets toward the bottom of the move is remarkably—remarkably!—consistent. Not to say that CCK *had to* turn around and go higher right here, right this minute, not at all—just that there was an excellent basis historically to say that it was unlikely to go sharply lower from here, having diddled around in the 755–850 area for 4 months. Better still, there was absolutely no news about supply increases threatening the market. My cash broker contact actually laughed when I called him to inquire on this point.

Darned if CCK didn't turn right around, too. By March 7, CCK was up at 859, and it popped up over 900 at one point during the month. I figured that this experimental trade was over. Low prices are always the cure for low prices, and cocoa seemed as if it might be returning to more usual price levels. The June cocoa puts that I wanted to write were simply not worth writing, at $3 and $9 for the 750 and 800 strikes, respectively. Well, I'd made a little profit and learned a few things, so it was worthwhile overall.

Not so fast. CCK tanked back down to 796 on March 28 and, while the June puts still weren't salable, the July 750s certainly were. I wrote several of them on the 29th for $21/tonne, with July cocoa (ticker: CCN) closing at 826. The May cocoa traded that day in a rather wide 796–833 range, and the May 750 puts were down to just $5/tonne. The May puts gave up the ghost quietly on the first Friday in April, and now I had two months to sit, and maybe at some point to try to write some August puts.

July cocoa was enormously cooperative, never dipping below 775, but on May 8, September cocoa (ticker: CCU), against which the August options offset, dropped down to 805 and I was able to write the August 750 puts, this time for $18/tonne. A brick here, a brick there, pretty soon you've got a house, right? Election season in the Ivory Coast brought some amount of civil strife, with 300-odd citizens getting killed, and this event was not a bearish factor for cocoa at all. It was, however, a risk factor . . . because I started thinking again. If there's civil strife, I (haha) reasoned, supply can't possibly rise and may very well decline. Cocoa trees might be torched, growers might be taken hostage, numerous menaces to normal cocoa supply were possible. On June 26, with CCU trading at 847, I wrote several September 800 (not 750, oops) puts for $26/tonne. There's a technical term for this action: greed.

The August puts expired on July 7, and CCU spent the rest of the month trading between 822 and 891. CCU was wandering around 850, and it looked like the September puts were going to end up worthless on August 4. Anyway, that's what it looked like on July 28, with 1 week left until expiration. The next week saw CCU do something it hadn't done in months, namely drop 8.6%. On expiration day, CCU opened at 791 and I had to pay $23/tonne to repurchase the 800 puts, breaking almost exactly even on the September write.

Was the Ride Worth It?

That ended the trade. In theory, I could have continued to ride the bear for a while longer, but that stiff drop was unnerving and I decided that an extra dose of caution was in order. As trades go, this wasn't a bad result at all. The February, May, July, and August puts all expired worthless. I lost most of the commissions on the March write and a few pennies in fees on the— frankly dumb—September write. All this netted out to about $910 profit per month over the six trades (a precise per trade figure isn't available because I didn't write the same number of options every month). The ROC of the whole mess turned out to be (notionally) 53.1% on an annualized basis. The actual figure was probably a bit better, because cocoa had spent a good portion of the term of the trade well away from the striking prices of the puts I'd written. Hardly spectacular, but acceptable enough for a trade in which I'd bungled a couple of times along the way.

How Can the Market Beat Us? Never Say Never, but . . .

Once we've selected a disciplined entry point and begun riding the bear, the only threats to our profitability are human error or a new spike low in the market. Given our preconditions, there is only one generic occurrence that might generate enough selling to produce such a spike. Such occurrences are historically extremely unlikely, and probably would consist of some legitimate scientific research emerging (as opposed to some ridiculous headline in the tabloid press) that indicates that demand for this market's product may or will be sharply lower in the *future.* In a foodstuffs market, this might be represented by an article in a respected publication, the *Journal of the American Medical Association* perhaps, that indicates the existence of a severe health hazard to consumers of our market's product.

Now, *Homo sapiens* have been eating the products of all the tradable edible agricultural markets for millennia, and while this possibility exists, especially given the unfortunate prosperity and ubiquity of the less than honest health-scare industry, it's exceptionally remote. Another such possibility would be the discovery of a useful alternate fuel for automobiles and—necessary condition—the announcement of plans to create the distribution infrastructure required to make this new fuel available to the mass market.

In either of these cases, whether the research ultimately pans out or not, just the announcement of it would likely send our market crashing lower, and we'd be in hell's own trouble. However, this outcome as described seems to me to be quite impossible. Why? Are we to believe that a legitimate piece of complex research such as just postulated will have no effect at all on the price of our market *prior to* its public announcement? Fiddle-dee-dee. Objective and independently duplicable research is practically impossible to hide in large, widely traded markets, particularly in regard to its putative future result. Some number of people will have or gain access to it and some of these folks will talk about it for any of a wide variety of reasons. (OK, OK, all you conspiracy theorists out there, I'll exclude all the folks in the sub-basement levels of Area 51.) Think it through. The market in which we might *otherwise* have been riding the bear, we won't actually be trading in—or, at least, not riding the bear in—because a rumor-driven market does not ever meet our entry qualifications, particularly the non-spike condition.

Let's Just Not Beat Ourselves

The second danger, much more likely, is that we will err seriously in deciding when to begin riding the bear. In the ideal case, we'll have been observing an extended bear market, one that's making or sneaking down toward multi-decade low prices, and we'll have an obvious trigger event in hand. These conditions aren't at all impossible to meet simultaneously; the cocoa market in 1999–2000 was a textbook case. They just don't all occur together frequently.

If, immediately or very soon after we enter the trade, we find out that we've goofed in selecting the entry point, we'll run for the exit. The indicator of our error will be a new spike low, perhaps a 4–5% or larger drop in a single day, and there's unfortunately no good way to combat or defend against this. If, however, the put options only have a week or less to live, we might have a defense. We'll have to review the supply/demand situation in our market again, to make as certain as possible that we haven't overlooked an important development in the market. We'll definitely want to consult our various informed sources (you are compiling a list of your sources and potential sources now, I hope), and learn whether today's sizeable drop was a one-off event and unlikely to recur . . . or something more serious.

Please permit a small digression here. A two-pronged approach is best in trying to evaluate the new market situation after a sharp dip. If possible, call a cash market broker for the supply/demand part of the question. These guys' living literally depends on their keeping abreast of the latest supply/demand developments in their market, and they're our first, best resource without question. This is completely reasonable if you consider the matter. Nestlé, Hershey's, Cadbury's, E. D. & F. Man and their cash market colleagues *should* know functionally everything going on in the cocoa market, shouldn't they?

Suppose that your cash market source says that there haven't been any developments, now what? Now we turn our attention to the exchange, in cocoa's case either NYBOT or LIFFE, and pick the brains of our broker's floor people and any other floor sources we've been able to acquire. It's likely enough that we won't be able to talk to our floor sources while the market's open; they're probably having quite a wild day themselves. Trying to pull them off the floor to answer a question is not only rude, it's a waste of your time and theirs. Just leave a polite message asking them to call you back when they can (that's why we have the 800 number, right? We try to put the odds in our favor all the time, in this case the odds that they'll call us back). Who knows, one of them might have time to call while the market is still open. It's not time wasted waiting for the callbacks, either; we can and should be using this time to check the newswires, just in case the market-moving event has accidentally been discovered by the financial press. End of digression—now back to solving our problem.

If none of our sources can add to our stock of information about what the devil is going on in the market, we exit, as quickly as we can. Dancing in the dark is a lot of fun; trading in the dark is a losing proposition all the time. Contrarily, if our floor sources indicate that, for example, some large traders got caught badly wrong and had to liquidate their long positions (unluckily for us, of course), we can, courtesy of the short remaining life of the puts we wrote, either sit still or roll them out or out-and-down. The major determining factor in our decision will be how far, if at all, the market has moved into-the-money relative to our puts' striking price.

Still in Our Favor

We do have what amounts to some built-in insurance when we select our starting point for riding the bear. We can to a degree ignore the actual price movement of the front month contract if the other preconditions have been fully met. If a trigger event has occurred—voluntary crop destruction or abandonment on a large scale, the shutting in of oil or gas wells, any action that patently restricts immediate or reduces future supply—we're right near the short-term minimum value of that market. We no longer need to watch for the "extended bear market" condition, because this condition *will* be in effect. If the bear market, given the conditions just named, is only of 3 months' duration to date when the trigger event occurs, the precondition of lasting 4 months or more has become irrelevant. The occurrence of a trigger event overrides the duration condition in the real world, and if the other preconditions are in line, we can merrily discard it and proceed with the trade.

The Ordinary Case—The Bear Nibbles On

When we're disciplined about selecting our starting point for riding the bear, it's entirely typical to see the market move somewhat lower over the first month, possibly below the strike of the our short puts. We've written the nearest strike puts and it is a bear market after all, and this is hardly an outrageous result. While we prefer not to see such a drop, such an event represents only an annoyance as opposed to a threat to our capital. If we entered the trade on a disciplined basis and cannot find any reason to believe an increase of supply is on its way, we'll sit very still, particularly if there are just a few days remaining in the life of the options we wrote.

We don't necessarily expect a bounce in the market, but what we do expect, given our entry conditions, is that further declines in our market will be both slow and small, if they occur at all, especially in our favorite case of the market being at or near long-time lows. We have another tasty little advantage here, too, courtesy of nothing less than the very nature of futures markets. As long as our dollar risk remains small and no new supply/demand factor appears, we actually don't care if our short puts go slightly into-the-money.

Fairly interesting, yes? Why don't we care? We took stock of the relative advantages futures markets offer us, compared to other broad markets, in Chapter 2. These weren't by any means all the advantages. In stock markets, if we write put options and they go into-the-money with weeks left until expiration, the owner of the options may decide to exercise his options early, that is, two or three weeks or more before the options expire. On exercising his option, he sells his shares, we put writers will have to pay for them, and he can earn interest on the dollars we pay him. As I write this, U.S. short-term interest rates are risibly low, and the put owner won't be terribly anxious to exercise early, but short-term interest rates won't be low forever, and the put owner will enthusiastically resume parking our dollars in his interest-bearing instruments when rates do rise.

In futures markets, put writers have no such hazard, for early exercise simply doesn't occur, barring the case where the put owner is an outright bozo. When an option is exercised, put or call, all that happens is that the writer is assigned a position in a futures contract. The option owner receives no dollars whatever; indeed, by exercising early, he cleverly costs himself at least one more commission per contract. He has exactly zero incentive to exercise his in-the-money options until the very end of the options' life.

Another Sandwich Out of the Picnic Basket

All right, the bear has kept nibbling on the market price, and the puts we've written have just a couple of days to live. What's our next move? There are several cases to check. If the options we've written are still a little bit OOM, I prefer to wait and try to give them a chance to expire worthless. If they appear to be expiring worthless, for example if cocoa is 11 dollars above our striking price with 90 minutes left to trade on expiration day, we should proceed with writing the next month's puts. Sure, there's a bit of risk in doing this, the market could tank 20 dollars or more in the last hour, but we once again are trying to give ourselves the long end of the odds.

If, instead, we would wait until the Monday after expiration (NYBOT cocoa options expire on a Friday, or on the day before if Friday is a holiday) to write the next month's puts, we might have a problem. Unless the market opens lower on Monday, we'll be very apt to find that the premium of the puts we want to write has dropped, sometimes annoyingly far, and they may no longer be worth our time and effort to write.

If the market has moved modestly upward from the date we entered the trade into the last week or so of the life of the options, a different action is warranted. When the exercise of our puts becomes extremely improbable, as in this case, we should accept a modest risk and go ahead and write the next month's puts, ending up with a double position for a few days, assuming that the ROC of the next write is satisfactory. Yes, we are vulnerable, if the market moves downward and into-the-money, to having to either repurchase the original puts or to roll them out and hold onto a double position for a month. If you don't like even the prospect of having a double-size position, you can alternatively buy back this month's short puts, ideally for 1 tick but probably for more. Other considerations aside, if we want to continue riding the bear, we *must* figure out how to write puts for the next cycle of the trade.

When this modestly rising market occurs instead with two or three weeks left until option expiration, we're in a bit of a bind. In extended bear markets, all options' time premiums decrease, in absolute dollar terms, sooner or later. Our dilemma is this: if we wait until the expiration of our current puts, the time premium on the next month's puts is likely to be so low that we don't want to bother writing them. If, contrarily, if we would take preemptive action, by writing the next month's puts while still holding our short position in the front month puts, we may be inviting trouble. The longer time frame, even as little as a week or 10 days longer, changes our risk/ reward picture, and the risk here is—what else?—capacity risk. If we have sufficient capital and cushion to support the larger position, that's fine. If we don't, or it's close, we'll be creating for ourselves what amounts to a Martingale, an ancient and unsound "system" involving doubling or tripling one's stake after a losing wager. This tactic of "doubling-up" has been notorious throughout history, having caught in its snares Dostoyevsky and Casanova among thousands of others, and we don't want any part of it.

Well, it's not enough, it's never enough to merely complain about a dilemma. What tactic *do* we employ when this situation arises? Easy. We ask ourselves this question, "Which path is riskier, overall?" and all of a sudden we don't have a dilemma any longer. We never *have to* enter a trade, right? You bet it's right, and as far as I'm concerned it's an absolute. If we can't write the next month's puts conveniently, and for the level of premium we want, we'll let our current short puts expire, bank the profit, and quit riding the bear for a while. A favorable market movement may restore our opportunity to resume our ride, but here's another of my trading axioms: *don't force a trade* (as I did when writing the September 2000 800 cocoa puts in the earlier example). Just like our insistence on entering a trade at *our* price, we should relentlessly insist that any continuation of a trade must conform to our specifications. If it doesn't, we'll find something else to trade.

Troublesome Cases

When our short puts have moved into-the-money with only a few days left in their lives, we'll simply roll them out, preferably out-and-down but possibly just out, to the next or the second month away. At least, that's what we'll intend to do. We might well run into the same difficulty previously described in the case of our puts expiring worthless. If there isn't enough premium available to us in the prices of options into which we might roll, we'll just buy back the written puts, put this trade into the history books, and look around for another opportunity.

There's one more case to examine, and it's our least favorite . . . which makes it the most important, because the principal portion of our task in writing options is to control risk at those times it rears its head. What do we do if the market moves more than a few ticks into-the-money? As discussed previously, given the entry conditions for this strategy, this result will obtain every so often, and we must consider it. The answer, or at least my answer, to the question of what to do is, "It depends on *how* the market has moved."

If the market dives right through our striking price within a few days or a week of entering the trade, or of any cycle of the trade, then we must admit we have erred and exit the trade ASAP. In contrast, if there's only a week or less remaining in the life of our short puts when the market dives down into-the-money, we might have an opportunity to roll out, or flip out, or out-and-down or out-and-up. Equally, after such an undesirable movement, we might very well not *want* to continue the trade. Our decision to continue on or not will hinge on the cause of this sharp drop in price.

We'll be more likely to see the other type of decline, a gradual but persistent move downward through the strike of our short puts. This is a sign that we were a little early when we selected our entry point or that a supply factor has changed during our trade, and this will happen to us occasionally. Fortunately, as long as we're prudent, this sort of market movement tends to be much more a nuisance than a problem.

Suppose we've written, in cocoa, some month's 750 puts for $20/tonne with five weeks until expiration. The market is at 785 tonight, but over two weeks it works downward to 754, and in the third week down to 728. I won't try to speak for you, but that's plenty far enough in-the-money for me. Speaking as a professional coward, 740 is probably the price at which I would have tried to take some action. The puts, let's say, have settled at 31 tonight. We can sit still, exit the trade, or roll out. Which do we prefer, and why?

Exiting the trade is an option, but I don't much like it in this situation. We'll lose 11 ticks at least, probably more like 14 or 15 after we wrestle with the bid-ask spread again, and of course two commissions per contract. That's an acceptably small loss, and by exiting the trade we'd obviously dispose of any further trading risk, but this action would be premature. We wouldn't be giving ourselves the chance to emerge with a profit. In this spot, I'm much more inclined to roll out, if not for one month then for two, repurchase the 750 puts and write the 700s if possible. Clearly, this decision will be contingent on a satisfactory level of time premium in the options I'd roll into, but if the premium is adequate, then I want that opportunity to profit.

Please note that, unless some market condition has changed during the three weeks we've been in this hypothetical trade, our relative risk in extending the trade by rolling out is really quite low if we properly observed the trading preconditions of this strategy. We're not bottom-picking when we ride the bear. We don't much care if the market continues lower, as long as it doesn't do so suddenly, because ultimately we will book a profit, or perhaps several profits. And, of course, the history of physical futures markets indicates very strongly that this feared sudden large downward thrust never actually does materialize.

Models, Margins, and Red Flags

You've probably observed that I haven't said a word about some topics that are usually quite important when discussing strategies and their application. Aren't we going to look at the data we can acquire from our pricing model? This time, we're not. When we're riding the bear, the model doesn't tell us very much about our risk or our potential for success. And, what about margin considerations and other factors?

The reason our model isn't too helpful here is straightforward. The model is derived, ultimately, from the theory that a market's next n ticks tend to be random, lognormally distributed, when n is large enough. It deals in terms of the probability of the future distribution of prices, with other things being equal or held constant. When we ride the bear, other things aren't equal in the first place, and we distinctly do not expect normal distribution of prices in future; in fact, we anticipate a very non-lognormal outcome. The underlying hypothesis of the strategy is that approximately 40–45% of the prices represented along the lognormal curve will simply not be seen in the near term. We believe we have a strong historical advantage due to a market's recent price activity, and we think we have a good idea about future price distribution . . . and our picture of it doesn't look anything like the model's price distribution curve.

In one sense, riding the bear resembles certain technical methods. We take action X because of price movement Y having occurred in the market, and looking for future market movement Z, which is in essence what technically oriented traders do. The comparison isn't exact, though, because we're again anticipating where a market is *not* likely to go, just as in the non-seasonal strategy, whereas the usual approach of the technician is to think more like most traders, that is, where a market *is* likely to go.

What about our capital considerations? The SPAN margin requirements are derived from the lognormal model, no matter what any market may be doing at any given time. This fact works in our favor. First, we're in a longish-term bear market and, when the price declines, the gross value of the futures contract obviously does too. SPAN uses gross contract value as one of its parameters, and our margin requirement from this component of the SPAN formulae will as a rule be declining moderately, in harmony with the market decline. This lessening of margin requirement will persist until or unless our market moves substantially into-the-money with regard to the options we've written.

Next, our market's volatility may have been doing many things while we've been riding the bear, but it almost surely hasn't gone up more than a point or two, and it surely hasn't gone well higher. Cocoa's SV, virtually throughout the trade we've discussed in this chapter, stayed within a very few points of its 6-month lows. SPAN uses market volatility in its calculations, too, and we won't be seeing any sharp margin increases from this component of the SPAN equations.

In short, unlike in other strategies, we don't have reason to worry about severe changes in our margin requirement. This relative freedom from worry allows us a good bit of latitude when we set up our amount of cushion. When riding the bear, I've been very comfortable over several trades by using a figure of 2 times the SPAN requirement. If you're not comfortable with this level of cushion, feel free to increase it proportionally, but when you watch how a ride-the-bear trade proceeds, you'll quickly see that there's little or no cause to be overgenerous in the amount of cushion you use (again, very much unlike many other strategies).

If the major potential threat to our capital in this strategy is a sharp spike lower, do we have any way to establish a sort of early-warning system? We do, and it's easy to use, but it's not exactly foolproof. What is usually the proximate cause of a large and sudden downward move in any market? The emergence of lots of selling, right? If we just monitor the daily volume of our market, we'll be able to tell very easily if the activity level in the market is rising. If volume and the open interest both rise, more or less steadily, over a couple of weeks, and we also observe the market steadily moving lower, these circumstances probably constitute a red flag that it's a little early to start riding the bear.

If someone has a whole lot of something to sell, he is not ordinarily likely to stand on a chair and yell out "Hey, I've got a lot of stuff to sell!" He'll try to dispose of his goods as smoothly as he can, in an effort to try not to disturb the market price too much. In large, liquid markets, the market can absorb amazing amounts of buying and selling, many times with only tiny movements in price. Our large seller won't need to be cagey in such a market. He can usually offer what he has or stand around and pick off bids until he's finished.

This is definitely not the case in smaller, less liquid markets, and we must be careful here. Cocoa, per our example, is not a large market as physical futures markets go. Often enough, a truly large seller will require a full day or two, perhaps up to a week or so, in order to complete his sale in one of these markets, assuming he is concerned with not knocking the market price markedly lower. This is the type of situation that our monitoring of volume and open interest can discover.

If the open interest in our market would be falling, our hypothetical large seller would clearly be liquidating a long position, and we can sit still, because he'll shortly be running out of goods to sell. When open interest is rising, he represents new selling. We may decide that this situation imputes a little more downside risk than we're willing to tolerate, and either not enter the trade or give the bear's back a rest by exiting our existing trade. What we can't detect in advance is a huge wave of selling, for instance a group of funds entering the market on the short side. How likely is this latter occurrence at or near the bottom of our presumably long-term and nearly sold out bear market?

If the market's price is somewhere within its normal historical range, this sort of price movement is possible and has occurred once in a while, the 1997 CBOT corn market being one example. However, when a market is flirting with long-time absolute lows, as was the situation in the cocoa example we've seen throughout this chapter, such waves of selling simply don't materialize. Who will be the sellers? Not producers—if we have a trigger event in hand, they're leaving or have already left the market. Commercial users? Hey, they're absolutely delighted. They're locking in future production costs very profitably by buying each dip in the market. Commodity funds? Nope, not them either. They're required (well, if they want to survive, at least) to produce profitable results for their clients, and they fully understand that selling cocoa at $700 per tonne, or coffee at 42.00 cents per pound, or oats for $1.02 per bushel aren't exactly wonderful ways to generate much, or any, profit.

When a bear market emerges in physical futures, and when it persists for several months, let's keep a sharp eye and an open mind. When there's just too much supply in a market, let's be patient and wait for the selling to dry up. Then, we'll ride the bear to our profit over a couple or several months, and we'll be quite pleased to be in a very low risk, low margin, high expectation, and high ROC trade, and with enormous flexibility on our side, too.

Perhaps it's more fun riding horses, or camels, or maybe even giraffes—I wouldn't know about that—but it's far more profitable to ride the bear when we have the chance.

So far, we've had a look at three strategies that don't depend on the existence of either bull or bear markets. Non-seasonals occur in both, and in neutral markets, too. Strangles? Well, we certainly prefer to apply them in markets that will remain neutral for a time. Straddles are approximately the inverse of strangles, applied to take advantage of rising option IVs and possibly also a sizeable market move.

Riding the bear, of course, depends on the pre-existence of a bear market, and I can hear you getting restless if you happen to be the most common species of trader—a bull. Something about human nature seems to just naturally love a bull market. "C'mon, haven't you got any strategies that we can use in bull markets?"

You bet I do. They're my favorite kind of markets, too . . . or, at least, the middle and the end of them are. However, I hate the whipsaw risk these markets typically pose. Trying to establish and maintain a straight long position in a bull market can be enormously frustrating, not to mention costly. Why not instead establish a position that will profit if the market moves higher, *and* when it doesn't?

How do we go about doing this? Turn the page.

CHAPTER 11

The King of Strategies

The Martian Ratio-Spread

Spread out! . . . (whap!) . . . Spread out some more!
—Morris Horwitz (Moe Howard)

U nder a few sets of conditions, the WOOM call options in a market can become startlingly well bid, insanely bid to all intents. Huge bull markets will frequently have this effect on prices, as will some impending market-moving events like certain reports when a market is in a state of high uncertainty, and like hurricanes any time. Smaller bull moves can have this effect also, in usually proportional degree. We're not concerned about how a market's call options came to be so overpriced, but we can usually create a profitable trade indeed when such overvaluation has occurred.

We can easily tell when the premiums of a market's WOOM calls are getting to be relatively well overpriced by simply watching their IVs and comparing these against their recent historical range and to the underlying market's SV. The principal timing indicator here is to watch for the underlying market's SV to begin declining while the IVs remain lofty or possibly even move higher for a week or 10 days. Alternately, if both measures are high relative to their recent ranges and SV begins falling faster than the option IVs, this, too, is a good wake-up call. There will be a reason for these changing volatilities, there's always at least one cause here. Supply/demand considerations may be beginning to migrate in favor of supply, or perhaps a pending weather event has dissipated or appears as if it will.

Spreading with an Attitude—The Ratio-Spread

A *ratio-spread* is a trade in which we purchase a call option and write some number of higher-strike call options against it. In a traditional ratio-spread, we buy an ATM or slightly OOM option, and we write two higher-strike OOM options of the same expiration against it, with the written options typically having too high an IV relative to the option we purchase. Or, we might buy five calls and write seven other calls against them. Traditionally, we try to take advantage of an apparent skew in today's option premiums, as compared to the computed fair values in our selected model.

Ratio-spreading is a time-honored strategy and works very well under either of two conditions. If the skew in the option premiums is pronounced, we might well profit just from the correction of this skew over the passage of time. If the underlying market moves moderately higher during the life of the options, the trade will almost certainly end up profitably. The traditional ratio-spreader obviously prefers to see both these conditions eventuate. From our unashamedly pragmatic standpoint, though, this strategy is a bit of a problem to execute.

Option pricing skews in near-the-money options vanish very quickly as a rule. There are lots of institutions and traders who look for these opportunities on a more or less continuous basis, and who have the computing power to locate them efficiently and speedily. You might have the time and computing power available (I don't), but the chances are very good that investment banks and funds have just a trifle more of both of these than you do. That's fine, not a problem at all. We don't need to play the game according to their rules. Additionally, this type of ratio-spread begins at a debit. While traditional ratio-spreaders are delighted when they can generate a credit from a (typical) 1-to-2 ratio-spread, they don't mind a bit entering the trade with a debit.

As is very clear by now, I *do* mind. I flat won't do that, except when buying straddles and in one strategy described in Chapter 12. Therefore, this strategy is off the table for me . . . or, at least this *version* of the strategy is. Here, we must gracefully part company with most of the folks who theorize and write about ratio-spreads, for we can do far, far better with our time and capital.

This Is Not Your Father's Ratio-Spread—
My Favorite Martian?

When the volatility of a market, having risen sharply in previous days, weeks, or months, begins to decline, we can look around for ways to implement our version of the ratio-spread. When the force or event(s) driving the volatility increase begins to subside, our mission becomes simple. If the rise in volatility was based on drought (coffee, October-November 1999), and it begins to rain in critical geographical areas, we're in. If the rise was based on the condition of some nation's economy, and this economy stops going in the tank (USD/MXN, the dollar versus the Mexican peso, early 1995), we're in. If the rise was based on political developments, and the feared politico-economic situation improves substantially (crude oil, January 1991), we're in. So, what does our version of the ratio-spread look like?

When I first showed my new methodology (new to me, anyway; someone undoubtedly has thought of this before) in ratio-spreading to a couple of other traders, one of them—gotcha, Don!—shook his head at me, rolled his eyes, and said "Man, that's *really* from Mars. You're gonna get killed with that." All right, if I'm a Martian then I'm a Martian, but obviously, he was somewhat incorrect in his evaluation. To paraphrase Mr. Twain, rumors of my death have been greatly exaggerated. Herewith, then, the Martian ratio-spread strategy. This is the single most consistently profitable strategy I've ever run across.

The usual ratio-spread trader is concerned with mispriced options ATM or moderately OOM, and he would prefer the market to be slightly bullish in its orientation. We Martians are also concerned with mispriced options, but only with WOOM- and WTBOOM-strike calls, and the farther OOM from the current market price the better. Occasionally we can locate absolutely excellent opportunities to exploit overpriced calls and the underlying IV situation by using these strikes.

The delightfully useful fact of the matter is, that, when call premiums get bid to very high levels, they tend to stay there for a while and the IVs of these options tend to decline fairly slowly over time. Some markets have taken a year and more before the premiums of its WOOM and WTBOOM calls have returned to historically typical levels. We might apply a non-seasonal trade in these situations, assuming our preconditions were fully met, but if we do take the simple non-seasonal trade when call option volatilities are way high, we might end up accepting more risk than we should. Let's not do that.

In its basic form, the Martian ratio-spread involves buying a WOOM call, typically with 3 to 6 months to live, and writing some number, generally from three to seven WTBOOM calls against them, with both (sets of) calls having the same expiration. We look for opportunities to use this strategy whenever and whyever call premiums have become wildly inflated. This situation might occur without a sharp bull move in the underlying market, but usually there will have been considerable upward price movement. We establish a spread position instead of a straight option writing position as insurance against a further sharp move in a known high-volatility market. In short, we hedge a little bit at the start of the trade, before we might need to. Whatever market developments originally caused option buyers to bid the WOOM calls to the sky may recur, which would seriously threaten our capital in a non-seasonal trade or in any other straight option writing strategy. We gain a secondary advantage, too. In this type of trade, where we begin with a hedged position, defending the trade will be substantially easier if a defense should come to be required.

Everyone Needs an Epiphany—December 1999

Throughout the last half of 1999, I'd had some success in writing OOM puts against the NYBOT coffee market, on a generally non-seasonal basis. Cashed every trade, and wasn't complaining a bit. The ROC of these trades was acceptable, even a little better than acceptable. I'd traded coffee before, for decades in fact, with indifferent success. When options on the coffee market became available after the CFTC re-legitimized them in 1984, life became a little easier and trading more profitable, but it was perfectly clear to me that, while profitable, the strategies I was employing were just adequate, no better.

While looking for information on the corn market one day in August 1999, I happened upon an Internet site, forum.ino.com. The participants on this site include a number of industry pros, cash and futures brokers, successful traders, unsuccessful traders, enthusiasts, novices, and a few gen-u-wine clowns . . . in general, a fascinating mix of people. Brazil's coffee-growing states were at the time enduring a fairly severe soil moisture deficit, possibly a precursor to a seriously damaging drought. In the next couple of months, the moisture situation worsened, which was very pleasant. I was busily writing OOM puts and banking solid profits each month.

Coffee kept moving higher as the rains stayed away, even though the market was enormously erratic and supplies in storage edged up a little bit. Day after day, the folks who posted on this forum kept becoming more and more bullish. From October 7th to the 13th, March 2000 coffee rose a remarkable 33.40 cents, from 87.95 to 121.35, with 22.05 cents of the move occurring on just the 13th. Now, I was loving this state of affairs, of course, having written a comparative flock of the December 1999 and January 2000 puts with strikes of 77.50 and 80.00 and 82.50. I noticed a curious thing about the messages on this trading forum; something like 9 in 10 of them had something to do with either NYBOT coffee or COMEX gold (which had just had a goldbug bull party, and was looking like it might have another at the time). At this point, the bullish posters on the forum were only raving about coffee going to $2.50.

Here's another of my tiresome little trading maxims: the public are *always* wrong, sooner or later. When Bernard Baruch started getting stock tips from shoeshine boys and cab drivers in 1929, so the story goes, he started selling. Baron Rothschild is supposed to have said, "When the blood is running in the streets, I buy." Doubtless some similar good stories will emerge from the recent tech/dot.com fiasco in the stock markets. Even if these stories are apocryphal, they reveal several valuable truths about markets, as far as I'm concerned.

All right. This forum represents a reasonable sample of retail traders' opinion, the "public" if you like, so now all I had to do was solve the problems of how and when to fade them. An outright short position in coffee was out of the question, far too risky and far too much margin required. In any case, a crop-wrecking drought *was* a distinct possibility, according to the cash coffee brokers whose ear I was bending. Rather than try to guess the market, I wrote a few more WOOM puts non-seasonally and started studying.

Meanwhile, March coffee was just berserk. Down to 93.90 by October 21, back up to new highs at 126.10 on November 12 and at 132.75 the next day. Now, the bulls were screaming about $3.00 coffee. Then, for a change of pace—change of pacemaker, more likely—the coffee market tanked out to 110.85 over the next 11 days (it rained a little bit in Minas Gerais and Sao Paulo, key coffee states). Two days later, it had turned around and made another new high for the move at 134.60, followed by touching 149.00 on December 2 and closing at 144.05 on the December 3. So help me, now I saw not one, but *five* different posters on the forum ranting about FOUR dollar coffee. If New York "C" coffee has ever reached that price, *ever*, I can't find it in my historical files. There just had to be a trade in here someplace.

I got lucky. I got very sick for a couple of weeks (talk about silver linings!), and the coffee market was off my mind. By the time I felt like trading again, it was Christmas week, not usually an auspicious time to embark on trades in wild markets because too many market participants are absent, and such a market can become even more distorted. However, I was watching the option premiums on and off, and something had struck me. Ordinarily, as we'll see in Chapter 12, there's a very clear signal that I look for at the end of raging bull markets. A little light bulb came on (only a 10-watter, but we all have to start someplace). I didn't *need* that signal, if I took a different perspective.

Staring Off the 10-Meter Platform—Trade or Fade?

Merry Christmas, ho, ho, ho. My family was thoroughly annoyed with me that year because I couldn't get these ideas out of my head. Call option prices in coffee were just insane, their IVs were out of sight, but these goofball market opinions about $3.00 and $4.00 coffee prices meant there actually *were* people willing to pay these outrageous premiums for call options with strikes $1.50 and more OOM. These strikes, have no doubt of it, were the textbook definition of WTBOOM. Finally, without having gotten in hand all the data that I wanted, on December 27, with May coffee trading at 124.20, I tried what I'd been thinking about. Bought a May coffee 210 call for 300 points, 3 cents (think about that!) and wrote eight May 300 calls for 120 points, net credit of about 597 points, with the options due to expire on April 14.

Now, even before you say anything, I'm going to tell you that you're absolutely right: this trade as executed was, putting it bluntly, stupid and far too risky. The ratio in this trade was too high, absolutely. As I've figured out since, 1-to-4 or 1-to-5 or 2-to-9 are statistically much more favorable ratios . . . but I didn't know that then.

However, I did do a couple of things correctly. I had checked the weather forecasts, especially what Brazilian ones I could locate, and January was universally predicted to be at least decently moist in the coffee states. The SPAN margin in the trade as entered was, if I recall correctly, $868, which I quadrupled, not trebled, on the grounds that I was flying blind, as it were, having had exactly zero experience with this strategy. I'd determined (via a marginally informed guess) a first defensive point in case the market started going cuckoo again. And, I'd checked the certified stocks in warehouses, and their changes over the past 6 weeks (up each week, which augured somewhat in favor of the trade). Further, the Central American coffee crop, most of which is deliverable against the New York contract (most Brazilian coffee is not), was apparently in fine shape, not a problem anywhere on the horizon.

The trade succeeded, not due to any cleverness on my part, of course. The CentAm crop was a fine one, and stocks in certified warehouses rose virtually every week for months. Brazil received some rainfall shortly after my entering the trade, then quite a bit more later on, and the IVs of the May coffee calls fell off a cliff within three weeks of entering the trade. I added to the position as coffee relaxed, using lower strike calls and a more conservative ratio (I finally figured that part out), and in April and May cashed out a tasty profit. Well, whoopee. Just a dumb trade that lucked out? I don't think so, because opportunities to use this strategy, absent my initial stupidity about reasonable ratios but otherwise on more or less exactly the same basis, appear several times a year.

The Journey to Mars—No Passport Required

Other markets have offered excellent Martian ratio-spreading opportunities since then, and not necessarily the most natively volatile ones, either. I'm ratio-spreading October and November natural gas as I write this, very profitably and with practically zero statistical risk. In December of last year and January of this year, COMEX silver offered good opportunities in ratio-spreads in the May and July options (and I almost never trade silver, either, because I don't understand the dynamics of that market).

As a follow-up to December 1999, the coffee market's call option premiums stayed high enough to employ successive Martian ratio-spreads for about another year (always excluding the summer months, just don't try this or any call writing strategy in coffee in the summer, period.) COMEX gold offered a fine ratio-spread trade in the June 2000 contract, but hasn't since. November or January soybeans may be offering a good trade right this minute, but not quite good enough for me to try this year . . . yet. If the weather stays dry in the Canadian prairies, there might develop an excellent opportunity to ratio-spread wheat or even the widely ignored CBOT oats market later this year. NYBOT cocoa has had a dandy run-up this year, and if it should continue to the point where the bulls get out of hand, I'll cheerfully lighten a few wallets with a good ratio-spread. When the WTBOOM option buyers come out of the woodwork waving fistfuls of cash, wait for them, *wait* for them, and then pick their pockets.

Your question now, reasonably enough, is what marks the opportunity to apply a profitable ratio-spread. The envelope, please . . .

1. We must have a market in which the premiums, hence the IVs, of the WTBOOM calls are, for lack of a better term, outrageous. We then wait a little for the SV of the market to begin to decline, which we take as suggesting that whatever situation created the rise in volatility in the first place is beginning to subside or has subsided.

2. We want to buy WOOM-strike calls as far as possible away from the current market and write WTBOOM calls as far as possible above the strike of the WOOMs, and the ratio of the WOOM-to-WTBOOM *premiums* for the strikes we select should be between 2-1 and 3-1.

3. The ratio of the *number* of WOOMs to WTBOOMs will be larger or smaller according to the relative strength of a market's options' IVs. If the market situation that prompted the explosion in option premiums has definitely passed, we will consider using ratios of 1-to-5 or 1-to-6. If the IVs are still well toward the high side of their 6-month range, then 1-to-4 or 1-to-3 is more prudent. The trade *MUST* begin at a healthy net credit.

4. The ratio between the number of written and purchased calls should be adjusted upward the further OOM the two strikes are from the current market price, and downward the closer they are, with 1-to-4 and 1-to-5 being typical.

5. Patience is a necessity. The terms of the best ratio-spreads I've seen (and traded) have been from 3½ to 6 months, but there's no particular reason to think that similar 2-month and 8-month ratio-spreads might not be equally successful, provided the other preconditions are in order.

6. SPAN margin requirement on ratio-spreads as described is *very* low as a rule, in absolute dollar terms. We must avoid taking too heavy a position, even if we mentally allot 3 or 4 times the SPAN figure for our margin cushion.

7. The notional ROC of a desirable ratio-spread should approximate 8%, net of costs per month, over the term of the trade, using treble or (better) quadruple SPAN initial margin. This ROC can easily be *much* higher, and will vary widely by market and current market IVs.

8. We must select a first defensive point before entering the trade. This point should be about 15–20% between the current market price and the lower strike of our pair of options. As always, we must not spend more on the first defense than we intended to make in the trade originally. We must not change a ratio-spread from a credit to a debit on the first defense.

9. If there is a doubt about whether or not to defend the trade at any given point, defend it, period, by buying an appropriate strike call or calls. We can always sell the defensive calls back later if the market turns back lower, and accept a modest loss while keeping the trade both intact and profitable, and while keeping our margin requirement and risk (capacity risk, mainly, here) manageable.

Just as the first step in a recipe for rabbit stew is to catch a rabbit, the first step in Martian ratio-spreading is to find a market that is suitable. This task is straightforward—all we have to do is consult a table of the IVs of various markets. Several times a year, we'll see one or another market's option IVs being bid well past the top of their current 6-month range. When we do, we start watching for the trigger condition of declining SV along with (ideally) market prices starting to move away from the apparent recent peak.

In physical futures markets, we also want to look for increasing supply, or at least the potential of increased supply clearly on the horizon. As it happens, I've never found a worthwhile ratio-spread in financial and currency markets, but that's not to say that such an opportunity won't occur—merely that it seems unlikely according to these preconditions. In these markets, for proper entry conditions (especially including outlandish call premiums) to exist, some government(s) somewhere would have to be in a state of panic, and the indicator of this would likely be a set of screaming headlines about the utter destruction of a country's economy. The problem here is obvious: absent World War III, no developed nation is likely to collapse in your and my lifetime because its trading partners can't afford to let it go under.

This fact implies directly that any Martian ratio-spreads we would undertake in a currency or interest rate market would be in a so-called developing nation . . . but these nations' bonds and currencies don't have viable futures markets, do they? Oops, we'd be forced to trust to the tender mercies of the interbank foreign exchange market and, gulp, customized options. Waiter, check please! Not on your life. I wouldn't try this strategy in the interbank forex market with *your* capital, let alone mine.

Side note: Barbara Rockefeller, a trader/analyst/author of strong opinions and thorough experience in all forms of currency dealing, once eviscerated the idea of retail trading in the interbank forex market very eloquently. I was looking for a way to take advantage of the collapse in South African Rand in 2000, but the CME/IMM S. A. Rand futures market is, frankly, necrotic. I had asked her about possibilities in the interbank market. Her reply? "Look, some futures brokers might be scumballs, but at least they're heavily regulated scumballs. You don't really want to deal with **un**-regulated scumballs, do you?"

She has her reasons for disdaining retail interbank forex trading, and perfectly good ones they are. For a long time, forex trading was, for all practical purposes, completely unregulated, the Wild West of the world of trading. Abuses were rampant; fraud was everywhere the trader turned. In 2001, the CFTC started taking American forex trading firms in hand and forcibly cleaning them up and, in several cases, making them guests of the taxpayer for extended periods. There aren't as many crocodiles as there used to be, at least domestically, but those that still exist would take a bite out of your leg just as soon as they would one out of your wallet. Who needs this kind of risk? Right. Not us.

Oddly, corrupt practice is not my principal reason for avoiding this market, because I have a more immediate one. The retail forex market doesn't even come close to meeting a condition we very much desire. It is *very* asymmetric. Larger accounts can execute certain orders that are disallowed for smaller ones. Options we might buy in a straddle have *no* secondary market whatever, zero resale liquidity; if we want to take profits in a straddle, we must exercise our options and liquidate the positions that result. Ugh! Writing options? Forget it. Can't be done, with most (all?) retail forex firms. They simply won't accept the order. What is this nonsense? We have zero, or highly limited, defensive possibilities, is that right? Right again. Two words: stay away.

Setting Up the Advantage—Selecting Strikes

A ratio-spread involves selecting two different call option strikes in the same month of expiration. Selecting the lower strike first is pretty much an art form, and it's more than a little dicey. In the best of all possible ratio-spreads, we'd love to see the market move up to or somewhat above the lower strike with just a week or two left until expiration. When this occurs (rarely), we will pocket a profit on both sides of the spread, which is always a lot of fun. We do want to leave some small chance for this result to happen, while at the same time leaving only the most miniscule statistical possibility that the market will go as far as the upper strike until we've defended/adjusted our position satisfactorily. Clearly, the wider the price differential between the two strikes of our trade, the more relatively likely this double profit will be, although it won't (or at least shouldn't) ever be a statistically likely outcome when we enter the trade. The rule here is safety first, then a dash of opportunism when and as available.

The better way to select our strikes is to choose the upper strike first. Set it at the maximum distance away from the current market price, consistent with our goals for ROC. One good way to locate a promising upper strike is to set up a dummy account in the PC-SPAN program. Then, begin the selection process by examining the highest WTBOOM strike in the options price table for a particular month that has a net premium of $150–200 (or more, of course, as in the coffee example), typically expiring in 4 or 5 months. Next, scan back down the table until reaching a strike having a *net* premium of 2 to 3 times the *net* premium of the upper strike option. We definitely must include commission cost when evaluating these strikes, for the calls that we'll write in this strategy will not ordinarily have super-high dollar premiums, and the Martian ratio-spread is fairly highly commission intensive compared to other strategies.

Having gotten this far, let's next check the SPAN initial requirement for a 1-to-4 trade using these two strikes, and multiply that number by 3. If the resultant notional return on capital meets precondition 7, this might be a good opportunity. There are still the other preconditions to check, and in any case the chance that our order(s) will be filled at tonight's closing prices is virtually nil. If the notional ROC isn't satisfactory, move the lower striking price up one notch and check the figures again. If it still isn't satisfactory, let's run another analysis based on writing one more call, making the ratio 1-to-5, or adjust the ratio to 2-to-9. Sometimes, we can ratchet the ratio up to 1-to-6, but the option IVs must have fallen off rather sharply from their recent highs before we consider this ratio, as noted in precondition 3. Move the parameters around, check the spreads a month further out, use your imagination in order to find an optimum combination. Typically, I'll have to run through a dozen or fifteen combinations of strikes and ratios and months in the market I'm examining before either finding a disciplined pair of strikes or deciding this strategy isn't suitable for this market at this time.

Conditions 3 and 4, concerning option IVs, are a bit redundant. Martian ratio-spreads aren't about picking tops, though, and we must insist on seeing at least the start of a decline in the market's volatility, preferably accompanied by some sort of modest downmove in the price, before using this strategy. The behavior of this market's options' IVs won't follow a hard-and-fast pattern. Sometimes IVs fall out of bed immediately when SV begins to decline, sometimes they stick around at lofty levels for awhile, sometimes they move down in tandem with IV as the market declines. When the IVs are toward the high end of their 6-month range, we'll probably be able to establish a good ratio-spread having a lower ratio; when they're not (they're still relatively high, regardless), we'll likely have to employ a higher ratio or else pass on the trade.

No matter what ratio and which strikes we ultimately select, if the trade cannot be established at a very clear net credit and with ROC in line with or better than required by our precondition, forget about it. When we're trading to win, the other trader's dollars start off in *our* pocket, not ours in his, save in two distinct strategies discussed elsewhere in the text.

Precondition 5 is unavoidable. If you don't favor trades with a term of three to six months, don't use this strategy. As mentioned, I've never seen a 2-month term in a worthwhile Martian trade. Not to say such a trade can't occur, but there are better ways to spend your time than looking for shorter-term Martian ratio-spreads, except in the markets having the very highest native volatility. Condition 6 is more vital in this strategy than in others. If the market moves so that we must defend the trade, our defensive tactic initially will be a hedge, and these get downright expensive when defending written calls in markets when option IVs (hence premiums) are at or moving toward nosebleed levels. SPAN requirement will also probably increase substantially under such conditions, to boot. Don't skimp on the margin cushion here, okay? If anything, you should probably increase it.

In the runaway parabolic bull market in NYMEX natural gas in late 2000, the margin requirement moved from $4,800 per contract up to $21,500(!) over about two months. Now, those figures are for one single futures contract, and a 1-to-4 Martian ratio-spread was a heck of a lot cheaper . . . but even so, its margin requirement rose some 450% in the same period, even after I'd applied one hedge defense. After a second hedge defense, the margin situation was again well under control, but the trade was now at a net debit, and stayed there for fully 32 days—very unpleasant. If ever there is a strategy in which we must not take too heavy a position, it is this one; a severe adverse move, even though we may and likely will profit in the end, will force us to put up more and more capital, sometimes a small fortune. Been there, done that, and you really don't want to duplicate the experience.

Defending Mars Against Invasion—Have Your Wallet Ready

We enter this type of ratio-spread knowing that the underlying market has recently been very volatile and attempting to take advantage of relatively overpriced WTBOOM calls. This situation of entry implies that, due to nothing more than normal price fluctuation in such an excitable market, it may become necessary to defend the trade more frequently than when we use other strategies. This has been the case for the Martian ratio-spreads I've traded. Defense, usually lasting a very few days, has been necessary (or, at least, I've undertaken a defense, not at all the same thing!) 13 times in 29 ratio-spreads I've traded since December 1999.

From the structure of the trade, long one WOOM call, short four or five calls many strikes further out, we have a lot of tactical room in which to plot our defense, so we have the clear advantage of flexibility. By being prudent about when we enter the trade, presumably at some little time after the market's SV has peaked, the only threats to the trade are a wicked upward move in the market and the reemergence of aggressive WOOM call buyers. We can't, or at least I can't, name all the circumstances that might get these folks frothing at the mouth again, but we can describe the features of the defense we will conduct when either of these does occur.

When and How to Defend

First, let's defend a little bit, a little bit early. Consider the coffee ratio-spread discussed previously. The May coffee market was at 124.20 on entry, and the lower strike in the trade was the 210. At the time, this being my first attempt at this style of ratio-spreading, I had originally thought to buy another call, perhaps a 240 strike, if May coffee moved a third of the way from 124 to 210, up to 152–153. The market never reached that level, but it turns out that my putative initial defense would have been a bit dilatory. We should take our first defensive action at between 15 and 20% of the distance between the market price on entry and our lower strike. This would have been somewhere around the 144 level.

This is a policy I've held to since, but I can't say that it's prevented any disasters. Instead, I've cost myself some capital with each of these 15–20% level defenses, bar one. Once again, we can improve on this tactic, if we think things through (which I was very slow in doing, but at least you won't have to pay this bit of tuition yourself). Just because we're defending a trade doesn't mean at all that we are despairing of its ultimate success, its ultimate validity if you will. What is our original market view in a Martian ratio-spread? It isn't bearish, it is a not-extremely-bullish view. What is the initial delta of our position? It's unquestionably negative, typically about 25 to 60% of one full contract, or −0.25 to −0.60. In theory, we'll lose some capital (presumably temporarily, a paper loss, or as my broker likes to call it, a "loan") if and as the market moves up early in the trade, well before theta begins to eat into the calls' remaining time premiums.

Well, how does this information help us decide when and how to defend? We refuse to turn the trade from a net credit to a net debit in our first defense, and we therefore know in advance the absolute maximum that we will pay for the first defensive call. As the market moves up 15–20% from its initial price, we want to examine the change in the total delta of our ratio-spread. Almost surely, total delta will have become more negative by this time, and we'd like to buy a defensive call that will return our total delta to close to its original level. Problem solved. We examine the table of our market's call prices and deltas and select the lowest-*priced* WOOM call whose delta (which is, again, a positive figure when we buy it, and will thus make our total delta less negative) will put the trade's total delta approximately back where we prefer.

So Far, So Good . . . Usually

Just as when we apply a hedge defense to a non-seasonal trade, if we undertake a hedge defense here and the market turns back around on us, we'll sell back the defensive option and accept a presumably modest loss. To date, I've accepted 12 of these modest losses . . . but I can hardly complain because, with one exception, all 29 ratio-spreads I've undertaken to date have ended up ultimately profitable. That one exception occurred when the market added two more whipsaws right around and through my initial defensive price level. Up again, defend again, whipsaw again. The series of losses finally put the trade into losing territory. Lots of fun, that was . . . su-u-ure it was. There's nothing to say except "That's the market for you." The overall 28-to-1 ratio of actual profitable ratio-spread trades to losers is very encouraging, though, and the dollar and percentage gains have been thoroughly enjoyable.

Perhaps I chose a poor defensive point in that multi-whipsaw trade due to chart considerations, or for other reasons. It's probably correct, even if not always possible, to avoid applying a defense at or near prices that are, effectively, obvious chart points for technical traders. It took a little while for your thick-headed author to understand that the change in the total delta of the position was likely the best indicator of when to defend and which option strike to buy for the defense. Generally speaking, the ratio-spread defenses that I've applied must have been correct in attitude at least, even if unsuccessful in their immediate result. I view these interim losses, one of them costing 120 points in loss per defensive option (way too much!) in the NYMEX unleaded gasoline market, as necessary insurance against a real live disaster. I'll pay for this insurance every time, and gladly, but I'll try in future not to go out of my way to give the floor 50–60 points more than necessary.

In actual experience, I've only been in one ratio-spread trade that required a second line of defense. I even applied a third, in a 1-to-4 trade. This happened in the January 2001 NYMEX natural gas futures market, and that was one scary market, my friend. The only truly smart way to have traded this puppy was to have liquidated all positions, disconnected the phone, and taken a vacation. When ratio-spreading, we don't intend to get involved with a runaway bull; we have *observed on entry* that the market volatility is declining and we consider it will continue to do so. Volatility was declining when I entered the ratio-spread in that market. Events overtook this trade, though, a shortage of supply and a brutally cold winter in high gas-consuming regions, plus the assorted machinations and fumblings of energy trading companies, politicians, and bureaucrats. Even if this trade did end up putting a good deal of money in my pocket—and it did—to this day I wish I'd never even seen it. Trading to *survive*, as was necessary in that market, is not trading to win.

Suitability—Round Up the Suspects

The inflation of options' IVs can theoretically occur in any market, from azuki beans to wheat, and probably in stamps, baseball cards, and Ming porcelain, too, but not all markets offer opportunities for Martian ratio-spreads. In some markets, call premiums can become wildly out of line relative to that market, but still not reach the quite high levels required for this style of ratio-spreading. Currencies and interest-rate bull markets, for example, typically will feature their call IVs below 20% even in a strong bull market, and while the WOOM and WTBOOM options' premiums will surely have risen, they won't likely be anywhere near the levels we want to see before employing this strategy.

I rarely trade stock-index markets, but I'd guess that in the late 1990s these markets offered some excellent Martian ratio-spread opportunities. (Once I acquire that historical database of option prices, I'm definitely going to hunt around for such occurrences). These markets, after all, could hardly have been much more bullish than they actually were, and SVs and the call options' IVs probably had some hefty spikes on occasion. Nonetheless, index futures probably are only rarely good candidates.

McMillan and other writers have commented on a long-lasting overvaluation in the call option IVs and premiums in certain markets, naming coffee, soybeans, and gold as prime examples. I don't really believe in a sort of long-term collective market psyche, but in these markets the evidence is incontrovertible. When the bull threatens to rumble, these markets' call premiums go absolutely bazoo. Natural gas, too. These are all excellent candidates for us, the "A" list so to speak, and these markets, along with silver occasionally, have offered the vast majority of the ratio-spreads I've entered in the past few years.

You might be tempted to think that NYMEX crude oil and heating oil would be markets to watch here also, and I would too. Maybe they are. I've never yet found a really good possibility in either of these, but who's to say I haven't just missed one when it was present? So, I'll keep looking, and perhaps a good, disciplined ratio-spread will turn up one day. Right around the time the bombs start falling on Iraq, as a guess.

I wouldn't doubt for a minute that CBOT corn had some dandy ratio-spread possibilities in 1995 when the market topped $5.00. Unfortunately, I wasn't looking for them then, and, barring some enormous weather disaster, the Congress has seen to it that giant bull markets in corn and other grains and oilseeds probably will be rare for several years. An example of lower than possibly expected IVs may be seen in the 2002 grain crops, seriously damaged by heat and drought, yet whose volatilities haven't spiked sharply enough to allow creation of a good Martian-style trade. Curiously, the CBOT oats market may become an exception to this situation, because some large fraction of the crop each year comes from Canada, Sweden, and Finland, which nations are (mostly) beyond the depredations of Congress, and this year's Canadian harvest is beset by all sorts of problems. A bad crop next year, too, and . . . who knows?

The various metals markets are half-yes, half-no. NYMEX/COMEX gold and silver offer us excellent ratio-spreads from time to time. NYMEX/COMEX copper might at some point, but opportunities here have been nonexistent for the last few years. The NYBOT platinum and palladium markets certainly meet the preconditions for ratio-spreading every so often, but their options are completely impossible to trade for the careful and practical trader. I can't see even trying to ratio-spread these two markets.

I haven't seen any ratio-spread opportunities in the CME meat markets, either, although other opportunities abound for option trading on these floors. This brings us to the softs markets, what we used to call "exotics" 30 years ago. Aside from NYBOT coffee (one of my favorites), CME lumber, NYBOT cocoa, and frozen concentrated orange juice will very likely present good opportunities from time to time and are very much worth keeping an eye on. The options markets in lumber and OJ are thinly traded as a rule, and our contest risk, particularly our slippage, will generally be higher than we want to see, but an opportunity is an opportunity, and not to be ignored out of hand.

We Don't Need—or Want—The Runaway Bull

One important point needs to be clearer than perhaps I've made it so far. While many traders consider a rip-snorting bull market as necessary for the sharply rising IVs we want to observe as the initial setup for a good ratio-spread, this is not the case. We distinctly do not require a long-lasting runaway bull market such as NYMEX natural gas in late 2000 or COMEX gold in late 1979. Any circumstance that sends SV higher and also causes WOOM call option premiums to rise apace is definitely good enough for our purposes.

From November 21, 2001 to January 9, 2002, NYMEX/COMEX May silver had a nice bull move, from 408.6 to 470.7 on a closing-price basis. I'm still not certain of the cause of the move—believe me, you can get more nonsense passing for information about gold and silver than about any two other markets you care to name, including dot.coms.

However, lo and behold, a few days later in January, the volatility situation in May silver met all our preconditions, with futures trading at $4.68. Being a suspicious sort (and not understanding the silver market too well), I waited a couple of days and only took a moderate position in a comparatively short-term ratio-spread. The strikes were 5.25 versus 6.25, 1-to-4, parking 3.6 cents, about $180 per spread, in my pocket on an initial SPAN requirement of $278. Everything I could learn—history, economic conditions, currency markets, too—seemed to be in favor of the trade, with the exception of rumor. For my money, if the cause of the rise in volatilities isn't fairly clear, I turn on the caution lights right away, and in any event we simply do not take overly heavy positions in ratio-spreads, no matter how much free trading capital we may have. Sooner or later, we usually (not always by any means) find out what did happen to cause this surge in volatility, but in the meantime we must keep capacity risk at a known and presumably very safe distance.

The trade turned out to be thoroughly dull, my favorite kind. Along the way, while the WOOM option premiums were still nicely inflated, I put on a similar trade in the July silver contract, using slightly higher strikes. This one wasn't quite as dull. Silver had another mild little upmove, and looked as if it might become obnoxious for a day or two. It didn't, fortunately. A couple of decent profits in hand over 5 months, no extravagant market movement, no defense required, no aggravation? Sounds pretty good to me.

Now, this wasn't good trading, or excellent trading, or brilliance in action or any such nonsense. It was simply trading to win. The opportunity was present, the preconditions were met, and the trade worked generally according to plan. Had defense been required, excellent resources were available. In the event of a sharp upward move in the May silver, say to $4.95 over two weeks, possibly before, I'd have bought one 5.75 or 6.00 May call and actually would have been rooting after that point for the market to continue moving higher.

I'm absolutely certain that constructive refinements to this strategy exist. Even though the Martian ratio-spread strategy has demonstrated its profitability over a couple of years, it can be improved. I'm working on it, and I'd welcome your suggestions . . . but in the meantime, earning 30 or 40% net ROC, or more, over three to five months when these opportunities show up is entirely satisfactory.

Practicality and Tacticality

You may be wondering about my assertion that 1-to-4 and 1-to-5 ratios in this strategy are, or are close to, optimum. From an *offensive* standpoint, they aren't; higher ratios are probably warranted. We probably can make higher profits with higher ratios, but we can also undergo endless pain on occasion, unless our trading pockets are quite deep. These ratios work best, and reasonably so in my view, because of *defensive* considerations. At the critical first defensive point, it has invariably been the case in my experience that we'll only need to purchase one defensive call in order to restore the trade to good order and cool out the trading risk inherent in a hot market. This apparent fact makes our trading lives much easier, because it isn't (or at least, hasn't been to date) any sort of problem to locate a defensive call whose premium is in compliance with one of our main principles of defense. Once more, we simply must not spend more to defend than we intended to make in the trade when we entered it . . . at the first defensive point. Suppose a ratio-spread turns up that has a huge differential between the two calls' striking prices, and the options' IV is well down from its highs. If, therefore, we reasonably consider that a 1-to-6 ratio is a good choice, then we should again defend a little bit, a little bit earlier, to accommodate our defensive philosophy and keep capacity risk on a firm, tight leash.

There's one last important tactical point that arises when using this ratio-spreading strategy, and it seems to some extent to be out of the trader's control. Which do we want: to send two separate orders to the exchange floor and wait/hope for both of them to be filled, or to put the whole trade on one ticket so that we have zero risk of only entering half the trade? Pretty easy question, right? Who needs or wants any extra risk, and nobody I know wants to end the day with only half their intended trade. So, we'll enter our order for establishing a ratio-spread on one ticket, correct? Well, maybe.

In the practical world, maybe we can place this unbalanced spread order on one ticket and maybe we can't, and the causes of this uncertainty aren't entirely clear. In the developing electronic markets, from the no-volume currency-cross contracts to the enormously popular CME e-mini S&P 500 contract, we can't. This circumstance isn't terribly important to option traders at this time, because options volume in every e-contract on every North American exchange ranges from non-liquid to non-existent. Presumably, this situation will be remedied as the exchanges' order-matching software improves, and as the exchanges come around to the notion of hiring market-makers to provide liquidity for options on popular and liquid e-contracts.

More to our purpose here, the fact of the matter is that our ability to enter ratio-spread orders on one ticket mostly depends on our brokerage. Some houses, including most discount houses of which I'm aware, simply won't accept the order as one item and insist on two tickets. Some houses will accept the order, but their exchange and clearing arrangements may result in the order being broken into two parts in order to be executed. I learned about this highly disadvantageous situation completely by accident.

I trade with REFCO, Inc., and I'm perfectly happy with their service and the executions I receive (although their back office could use a *lot* of work . . . sorry, folks, but that's this trader's considered view). However, it turns out that, in some of the NYBOT markets, coffee and orange juice to name two, REFCO does not use its own employees as filling brokers for option orders (at least), preferring to use the services of local firms that perform this function. There's nothing wrong with this arrangement, but it does lead to odd results. Some of its agency firms will accept one-ticket ratio-spread orders and some won't. How's a trader to know which situation prevails on a given day? Right. The trader doesn't know; he has to guess. What fun.

On some exchanges, executing unbalanced spreads on one ticket is not an issue. The floor traders on the Chicago Board of Trade are absolutely excellent executors of such orders. The floor traders on NYMEX are also extremely good. Nonetheless, in other markets, our net result is that we may have to enter ratio- and other unbalanced spread trades as two separate orders. We traders can handle this, of course, even if we may be muttering various unflattering comments under our breath.

In unbalanced spread trades that cannot, for whatever reason, be executed as one order, we will place the larger order first. If we're entering a 1-to-5 ratio-spread, we must unfailingly write the five WTBOOM options first, and only when filled on these enter our order to buy the WOOM option(s). To attempt to enter the two positions in the other sequence, buying the 1-lot and only then writing the 4- or 5-lot, is a very poor tactic and can on occasion be ridiculously costly.

Listen to the voice of experience here, because I did this . . . exactly once and never again. It was a very calm market, too, that day, or at least it was calm until two minutes after I'd bought the WOOM calls. The market took a nice swan dive off some convenient cliff, and I had to write the upper-strike calls for 45 points less, apiece, than intended. This is more slippage than *any* trader can tolerate, and this is the reason we must always execute the larger side first if we're required by situation to use two tickets to execute our spread. Always.

How frequently do good Martian ratio-spreading opportunities arise? Just as anything else in trading, it varies. We can go for months, even years I suppose, and not see a one. Then, five will turn up over 60 days. When we're trading to win, we have to look around regularly for these opportunities and not become annoyed or impatient if we're in a period where they're scarce. These opportunities will show up sooner or later, and all we have to do is stay prepared to jump on them when they do, and subsequently claim our very handsome profit.

Martian ratio-spreads can turn up at any time, but they *do* turn up almost inevitably at the end of the speculators' favorite type of market, the runaway parabolic bull. That's useful to know, and we'll tuck that little fact away for Chapter 12. You see, there's another excellent strategic approach toward carving out a set of tasty porterhouse steaks from such a bull market, *and* making the bulls pay the dinner check in the bargain.

What do you say to a little metaphorical side trip to sunny Spain?

Every Once in a While

The Picador

Will you have some [roast beef] rare, or the slice off the end?
—Robert A. Heinlein ("If This Goes On—")

I don't know the first thing about bullfighting. As far as I can tell from films, the object of the exercise is for a bunch of guys to chase a bull around a ring until he gets worn out, then stab him with a bunch of colored spears until he keels over. The guy who waves the cape around is the *matador* and the guys with the spears are called *picadores*, so they tell me. Well, to each his own. If I have to stab a dying bull, I'll do it in the markets, and I'll do it sitting down and not under a hot Spanish sun in the afternoon, thank you very much.

Big bear markets are persistent. Big bull markets are crazy, basically. Bear markets can and do become overdone, but big bull markets almost without exception become screamingly overdone at some point. I suspect this is due to a combination of human nature and the side effects of the admixture of emotions such markets produce, but that's just idle speculation. We're not concerned about why this situation occurs, but we do want to know how to profit from the end of, pardon my plagiarism, this irrational exuberance. Let's have a look at a very effective approach to fattening our trading accounts when the bull starts to bite the dust.

Bull markets result from fear. In physical commodities, this is the fear the users of a commodity have that they won't be able to acquire said commodity at acceptable prices (or, occasionally, at all) in the future, and they'd better buy the goods today. In interest rate markets, this is generally the fear that other asset values will decline and therefore existing fixed income instruments will become relatively more valuable, especially if interest rates are declining or about to decline. In currency markets, it's the fear that the economy of some nation is about to undergo substantial adversity or that the sundry governmental policies of that nation are about to become more bone-headed than usual. Such currency panics produce the well-known "flight to quality" and can, interestingly, have the effect of supercharging *other* nations' currency and interest rate markets, occasionally turning an ordinary bull market into a super-bull.

For our purposes, the existence of fear in a market is excellent (assuming, of course, that we ourselves aren't in that market right this minute). Fear is an emotion, and when considerable numbers of market participants become emotional, markets become distorted. The good news is that such distortions only infrequently last for long periods, and the even better news is that, just as in riding the bear, the market itself is going to give us a strong hint as to when to make a dollar. So, if this is true—and it is—when do we start pitching spears at the bull?

El Toro Grande—Runaway Parabolic Markets

In physical futures markets every so often, supply, demand, and market sentiment among the participants become so unbalanced that prices become bid to amazing levels. Usually, the bull move in such markets begins when the market participants realize the possibility of a supply shortage in future. Developments unfold and supply problems do begin to emerge, prompting users to begin to anticipate future needs in advance of their normal schedule, and also attracting speculative interest into this market. At some point, in addition to whatever degree of supply shortage actually exists, some number of market participants also begin trading on a perceived worse shortage in future, and that's when prices go wild. The daily price bar chart moves upward in a manner resembling the right-hand side of a parabola, margin requirements go to the moon, and people who have been caught short in this market begin thinking that the window ledge on the 35th floor looks mighty attractive.

As all this develops, you and I should be sharpening up our colored spears, because we're about to be handed a whole lot of money. These runaway parabolic markets all end, typically in a few weeks or months, and they almost invariably give a very clear signal to the watchful trader as to when to help himself to other traders' capital. We'll just sit around and watch, laughing with the bulls and commiserating with the bears (assuming they haven't availed themselves of a trip to the 35th floor yet).

By and by, and we simply don't care how long it takes, the bull market is going to top out. We are distinctly not going to attempt to time this action, or to anticipate it; it'll happen when it happens. The market will top out, begin heading lower, sometimes very sharply, and then, a little later, a couple of weeks or a month or two, the market *will* make a run at the old highs. If it makes new highs (rarely), we'll continue to watch and wait. If this secondary run-up fails, though, that's it—that's the end of the party, and it's time for us to become *picadores* and start to carve up the dying bull.

When exactly do we swing into action? We wait, specifically, for the third day down after the top of the secondary run-up. That's all, nothing fancy, and anyone can play. Furthermore, we discard the notion of statistical risk, and we park our pricing model in a desk drawer for a while, at least regarding this market. There's nothing at all normal or lognormal about price distribution under these conditions, and it will probably be quite some time before this tool will be useful again in this specific market.

Carving Up the Bull—The Knife to Select

I maintain, and have for years, that a successful trader is generally a professional coward, and this sentiment is at its truest during and just after parabolic markets. Statistical risk calculations are meaningless in such markets, and we will opt for an absolute and measurable dollar risk here. As far as I'm concerned, the single most cowardly way to slice up this kind of ailing bull is to apply a debit put spread, also called a bearish put spread. This is a structurally simple tactic that involves buying a put option, in this case having a strike moderately below the market, and selling exactly one other put, with a further OOM strike, that expires in the same month. All right, now how do we select an advantageous pair of puts for this spread?

The first thing we'll do is to stop looking at the nearby contract in our bull market. It's fun to watch, to be sure, but is definitely not the best place to make our profit. Once again, we must allow the other market participants some amount of time to fatten our wallets, and to this end we'll want to look at the put options in a regular month 2 to 4 months away, or even further out if the premiums are encouraging. The further-out futures contract will usually be lower in price than the nearby month most of the time under these assumed bull market conditions, but if it isn't, if instead it's a little higher, that's fine with us.

The put option we'll buy will have a striking price typically 3–10% under the current market price of the month we're watching. Which put we write will depend on our level of confidence in this strategy. I'm quite confident of its profitability, and I tend to write a put whose striking price is 3 or 4 strikes, even 5 strikes below the put I've bought. If you're less confident, then writing the put only 2 strikes below is a good compromise, because your capital commitment to the trade will be lower.

Our trade begins at a debit, which I don't much like (as you know very well by now), but its historical success is nothing short of astounding. I haven't ever found a (former) parabolic bull market that met our not-very-restrictive entry condition, where this strategy took more than 30-40 elapsed days to become profitable. This isn't too surprising, though, when you think about things for a moment, because we have strong tactical advantages when we're *picadores*.

First, our dollar risk is absolutely limited to the amount of the debit we incur on entry, plus our contest risk, of course. Second, there is effectively no margin requirement in our trade, and this fact itself represents another edge for us. Those traders who are still long in this bull market are at least beginning, at this point, to have major margin problems. The exchange has unquestionably raised margin requirements during the huge bull run, probably several times, and the volatility of the market is almost certainly up in the clouds, which will cause the SPAN procedure to produce an even higher margin figure for the bulls. This happy condition will continue to nudge some number of the remaining bulls in the market toward the exit, which, in turn, helps us along by the amount of induced selling thus created. What a shame, eh? Contrarily, our debit put spread isn't subject to any margin aggravation whatever.

Enhancement—It Gets Better from Here

Some strategies are just "there." We enter a statistically favorable trade, defend it perhaps 10–15% of the time, and simply cash out on the remaining occasions, end of story. The *Picador* strategy is not one of these. We usually have excellent chances to enhance our profit during the trade. Logically, this must be so.

Consider. We're in a trade that profits when the market moves lower. When the trade begins to become profitable, clearly our market view has been confirmed, at least so far. If a market is moving downward, it isn't moving upward, and if it isn't moving upward, we might begin to think about applying a non-seasonal approach to this market and writing short-dated WOOM or WTBOOM calls. The IVs of the calls are surely still high enough for this to be a nicely profitable endeavor, and this style of enhancement is perfectly viable. I prefer a more cautious approach . . . but I don't suppose that's any sort of surprise to you, is it?

Why not put on a ratio-spread instead? All the preconditions are almost certainly in line, and our chances of success must be very high. Now, we're not going to enter this ratio-spread recklessly—in a technical sense, this market is still probably a bull. If we can observe a couple of conditions, though, we're just giving money away by *not* attempting to enhance our picadorean profit.

The time to look at adding a ratio-spread to our position is just when our original debit spread becomes profitable. Additionally, we'd like to learn whether or not the initial severe supply problem in this market may be starting to correct itself, either through declining demand due to high prices or through the potential of increased supply over time due to an influx of physical goods. The place to look for a ratio-spread is above the now-faded top of the bull move, in options 3 to 6 months out, possibly even in the same month in which we own our debit put spread.

We neither need nor want to be bold when we enhance the trade. We want ratios of 1-to-3 or 1-to-4, never higher, as far above the old highs as feasible and with the largest differential between the strikes of the spread that we can achieve. Here, boldness equals greed, and to no purpose. We're already apparently on the way toward a good profit in our original trade, and adding a ratio-spread increases our risk in the event the bull resumes romping. Countering this is a very interesting historical fact: once past their peak, *parabolic bull markets do not ever regain the old highs after the secondary upmove fails*. Perhaps this has happened somewhere, sometime, but I can't find a single example of such an occurrence anywhere in my databases.

The *Picador* strategy, or rather, the *El Toro Grande* version of it, has a drawback and an inherent limiting factor. The drawback is that the initial put spread is very awkward to defend. We enter the debit put spread having a negative market view, which makes writing another, lower-strike, put in an attempt to recover all or part of our debit a rather self-contradictory action. Equally, if the market doesn't move lower for whatever reason after we've entered our put spread, writing calls is far too risky to even consider. From these considerations, if we haven't seen the downward market action we expect, over the first 25–35 days or half the life of the original put spread position, I suggest that we fold the trade and find another opportunity. We probably should also take a hard look at the particular dynamic of and resultant action in this market, with a view toward understanding why our trade didn't work this time, and toward improving the strategy in future. The good news when we fold the trade, though, is that our trading loss is quite small by definition.

The limiting factor is margin requirement. Our initial position, the debit put spread, is immune here, but any enhancement will expose us to what will unquestionably be an inflated requirement. We want to enhance the trade when possible, for this feature of the strategy is what makes it remarkably profitable. Moderate-ratio OOM/WOOM/WTBOOM ratio-spreads ordinarily have reasonable, even low margin requirements, but a recent runaway bull market is hardly "ordinary" in any sense of the word. We'll be putting up a fair amount of capital when we enhance the trade.

Did I say "enhancement," singular? If so, I misled you . . . sorry about that. Once the bull's back is provably broken, we'll almost certainly be able to replicate this strategy in subsequent months, even several times over perhaps a year or more, roughly along the lines of the coffee market example in Chapter 11. The whole trick to profiting very handsomely by becoming a *picador* for *El Toro Grande* is: start small and don't be early. If we wait to trade, or to enhance the trade, until we're as certain as possible that the bull is well-done hamburger, toast, *finito*, and this delay should cost us some dollars, so what? We're going to have a long time to exploit the bull's demise, banking profits in each cycle.

Toro Poco—More Frequent, Less Volatile

Another factor that limits the usefulness of *El Toro Grande* is that opportunities to implement it are rare. We absolutely must witness the occurrence of a runaway bull market before we can use it, and these come along, what, once every 3 or 4 years or so. Recently, we've had the 2000–2001 natural gas market, the 1995 grain markets, the 1994 lumber and coffee markets, coffee again in 1997 and a little bit in 1999, and probably a couple of others that I've forgotten just now. There haven't been very many in the past decade, in any case.

However, *El Toro Grande* has a little brother who shows up much more often. Mini-bull markets, or *toros pocos* as I call them, come along several times a year, and, usefully, in a wider variety of markets than the big bull. These opportunities can be somewhat more difficult to spot, and they're considerably more difficult to define in a general way, but let's give it a try. The first requirement, of course, is that a market be undergoing a bull move, a rather specific kind of bull move.

This condition varies a bit from market to market, but there is a useful rule of thumb available. Take the overall IV of a market's options on a named date. Here, let's say this figure is 35% on an annualized basis. If, over a month or six weeks, this market moves up half or more of that amount, in percentage terms, we have a possible candidate for a *toro poco* trade. Another condition we strongly want to observe is that this market's options' IVs have risen, right along with the price. We are distinctly not interested, in this strategy, in a market that is gradually working higher and taking its sweet time about it. Further, this bull move should not be a direct result of U.S. weather, and, if possible, of weather anywhere else, either. This precondition will be somewhat restrictive regarding markets such as soybeans, in which weather somewhere in the world is a factor in the market for the bulk of the year. Weather-driven markets are gamblers' markets, and we avoid them when we're trading to win.

Clearly, our parameter for minimum upward movement is an arbitrary number. No pretense about it, this degree of movement is not and cannot be the optimum amount for all markets. For markets that have high native volatility—our old friends coffee, natural gas, cocoa sometimes, lumber, maybe non-summer soybeans—the half-of-known-IV figure is just too low. These markets might move that much in a short time if someone sneezes twice on 8 consecutive days, and we'll want to see a larger move here, perhaps 70–75% of annualized IV within the same short time frame.

Tactics and Timing for *Toro Poco*

Our technique, trading tactics, and entry timing in the mini-bull market differ from those we use in *El Grande*, because the premise of the trade is different. When we're dealing with the big bad bull, we want the market itself to tell us when to push the button. For *toro poco*, all we want to do is to gain some assurance that the present market isn't going to become a runaway. Naturally, we never want to be in the position of trying to pick tops (or bottoms either, in other strategies), and to this end we'll look for a development or an event that indicates the mini-bull won't become parabolic. Again, I have no quarrel with technical methods for determining a likely entry point in this strategy, but I don't use them. Give me an old-fashioned supply/demand development every time. I might also draw an inference in the event of a rapid drop in the open interest in the market, which would presumably suggest that the traders on the long side are exiting their positions and pocketing their gains.

We may want a different trading approach here also. Establishing debit put spreads is a sound and cautious tactic and is a favorite to succeed, given that our market view is even close to accurate. If we use this tactic, we'll tend to buy a put with a striking price just under the market and write a put two strikes below that, maybe three strikes if the put premiums are encouraging, that is, high. We also have the choice of taking a more aggressive stance without increasing risk too much. We can establish a ratio-spread below the market, then look to enter ratio-spreads above the market later on as the market begins to soften up.

"Huh? How can you put on a ratio-spread below the market?" A fair question. In almost all cases, we use calls in ratio-spreads because the premiums of OOM call options can and do become wildly skewed, offering us an opportunity for an excellent ROC. In this strategy, and it's one of very few occasions, we'll use puts in the lower half, the put half, of the trade. We may have to resort to a 1-to-4 ratio in the puts here, because, as with any option writing strategy, we *insist* on an initial credit. Also, when entering ratio-spreads, we insist that the striking prices of the two options in the spread be as widely separated as we can manage.

In the other half of the trade, the calls, we should have little difficulty establishing a disciplined ratio-spread in the OOM calls, for this market's call options' IVs are almost surely in the upper part of their 6-month range. Two other details apply here. First, we will not establish the call ratio-spread when the call IVs are at or very near the top of their recent range. We'll wait until they've cooled off a bit, and we prefer in the best case to witness a topping-out or decline in SV and in the market price, too. Second, we will establish exactly two call ratio-spreads for each put ratio-spread, once our topping condition has been observed.

In a mini-bull market, provided I've reasonable confidence from a supply/demand standpoint that a runaway bull is unlikely (or *very* unlikely, better still), I prefer enhancing the trade with low-ratio call ratio-spreads nicely above the market, ideally using a 1-to-3 ratio. Given that the call IVs of a mini-bull market's options have increased while the market has been moving higher, this tactic appears to offer the best overall expectation. This approach retains good chances of returning a very healthy profit if the market continues moving higher, (but not running away), and also if the bull gives up the ghost shortly.

One remaining thing is different about the call ratio-spreads we'll employ in the mini-bull market. We want to shorten up the term of the trade, to no more than eight to twelve weeks, and five or six weeks is preferable if we can arrange it (this latter effort can be difficult, by the way). When we ratio-spread over this shorter term, we must accept that we will not usually be able to find worthwhile premiums in options with striking prices *way* out-of-the-money, as we would in a typical ratio-spread. That's all right; we'll take what the market gives us in terms of striking prices that meet our conditions. Much more important here is the differential between the striking prices, in the call portion of the trade. This we maximize, period.

Defense Against Getting Gored by the Mini-Bull

We have established a fairly complex position, and you might tend to think that defending it, when necessary, would also be complex. It isn't really. Our defense here will be nothing more than a combination of defenses we've previously applied.

Defending the put half of the trade if the mini-bull dies and the market turns lower is a snap. Assume that the put half of our trade is in fact a 1-to-4 ratio-spread. If the market moves down to the strike of the put we own, we'll roll exactly two of the short puts out-and-down, at any point in the first two-thirds of the term of the trade. If the market persists in going lower, we'll roll or flip out the remaining excess short put, preferring the flip defense to the roll, and we'll sit quietly with the remaining single bearish put spread and defend the two further-out short puts later if required. Additionally, in this case, we'll sell back our long calls at a point we deem convenient, but not in the first couple of weeks of the trade. Why hold onto the long calls, after all? By hypothesis here, the calls we've written are now WOOM or nearly so, not just OOM (assuming we selected a reasonable strike to write), and will by this time be heavy favorites to expire meekly now that the market has turned downward. If the market continues still lower, we'll buy exactly one put at some convenient strike above the strike of the rolled-out puts, and replicate this defense in later months if need be.

Defending the call side of the trade if the market keeps moving up is a little different, but only a little. Rolling calls out-and-up during an insistent bull market can be, as noted before, fairly dicey and very aggravating in terms of committing more time and more capital to the defense than we'd like. I'm instead much more inclined either to exit the trade or to flip the calls into some number of puts at some OOM or WOOM strike in the next one or two months further out. In our hypothetical 1-to-3 call ratio-spreads, I prefer to flip one of the short calls in each ratio-spread if the market moves about two-thirds of the way from its initial price (the price on the day we entered the trade) toward the strike of the long call. The remaining excess short call(s) will be flipped when the market moves above the strike of the long calls. And, being consistent, I'll sell back the long put too, probably a little before I flip the second set of calls.

These are reasonable and likely profitable defenses over the first two-thirds of the trade, but when the trade becomes very short-dated, the timing of the defense changes a bit. Yes, we'll still sell back the long put if the market has moved up, and the long calls if the market has worked lower. However, we should at least try to sit with the possibly threatened short position for a little while longer before flipping the excess shorts, a day or two or three, in order to attempt to allow Sister Theta to gobble up some more of the remaining time premium. Make no mistake about it though, if the market won't give us those extra days and keeps moving in whichever direction it's now headed, we must defend the threatened side of the trade along the lines just indicated, and right quickly too.

Never Take Your Eye Off the, Er, Bull

The various shades of defense are not particularly important of themselves; we apply defense as necessary. What is important is that we keep our eye on the bull. Whether in *El Toro Grande* or *toro poco*, one premise of the trade is that the bull market, great or small, will not resume violently. If the premise happens to be incorrect, which it historically never has been for the big bull given our adherence to the entry condition, but might be so for the mini-bull, we take steps —immediamente—to limit our risk. In a violently moving market, the principle of self-preservation when wrong is simple: bail or fail. If we're wrong in a trade in such a market, no matter the strategy we're using, we must admit it right this minute and take an appropriate action to preserve our capital. We have precisely zero interest in becoming bullfighters.

At bottom, this decision process for defense works out to be a matter of nothing other than our good judgment. After all, we would not enter a trade in which we did not have an historical or statistical advantage, or both, at the point of entry. Doubtless, a couple or three times in ten trials, we will make a less-than-optimum selection of option strikes, or the market's behavior will contradict our view. Such eventualities are not problems, unless we let them become so. To minimize these occurrences, we simply exercise a good degree of caution when we enter the trade, and, not surprisingly, by doing so we also generate better results.

Actually, given only that we've been disciplined in selecting an entry point, the problems we are likely to encounter are much more tactical than strategic. Curiously too, the big bull, *El Grande*, is less likely to expose us to tactical snags than is his little brother. When a runaway bull market has failed, as long as we refrain from being greedy, it is literally child's play to turn a profit. *Toro poco*, though, as a rule is a product of less-well-defined market conditions, which, in turn, make our subsequent market decisions somewhat more difficult.

Now, I don't want to misrepresent anything to you. The few opportunities I've had to spear a fading runaway bull market as it starts to die have proceeded exactly as outlined, very profitably and with well-controlled risk. My practical experience with defending *El Toro Grande* is exactly zero. The defensive tactics previously discussed are therefore only theoretical. In the next such trade, if defense becomes necessary, I'll probably defend even more conservatively than indicated here.

Enhancement to *toro poco* trades is situationally less dangerous, assuming only that we can establish the call ratio-spreads with a nice, wide differential between the striking prices. Defense in an enhanced trade, at least theoretically, should be an easier proposition, and to my experience to date, it usually is. However, one trade, in May 1999 soybeans in late 1998 caused some problems on defense. I was a little early in enhancing the trade, and May soybeans rose a dime or so above the recent *toro poco* high. Margin requirement approximately tripled in about a week, using up the initial cushion, and out the window I could see our old nemesis, capacity risk, coming down the street. I was a little lucky in that I had some extra free capital in the account at the time, only because I hadn't happened to find very many good trades over the preceding month. My fault entirely, of course; I was both a little early and a little greedy even when entering the trade. I did not—and this is a mistake, pure and simple, don't do it—wait for the market's volatility to begin to decline. Had I simply been disciplined in entering and enhancing the trade, the capacity risk monster would never have made it into town, let alone been strolling along my street. Two weeks later, the mini-bull became seriously arteriosclerotic and I was able to scramble out of the trade with a tiny profit. Not worth the aggravation, I guarantee you.

This is definitely not the way to implement or enhance a *toro poco* trade. A disciplined trader would have waited until the market volatility started declining, entered the trade as described, and cashed out both sides, perhaps having to roll out one or two put options for a month, a minor nuisance. A dandy profit was there for the taking, but the greedy trader, your humble servant, didn't even get a sniff of it . . . and didn't deserve it, either.

Wait for the Wildness

The last chapter of Peter Bernstein's scholarly and marvelously readable book, *Against The Gods: The Remarkable Story of Risk* (Wiley, 1998) is titled, "Awaiting the Wildness." When we want to be *picadores*, we want to first await the wildness in a market, then await the beginning of its passing, and then help ourselves to a hefty profit. You may wonder a little bit that this chapter is comparatively short, but there you have the reason for it: the necessary conditions for our becoming *picadores* are summed up perfectly in the previous sentence and need little if any elaboration. Let the traders in a market become optimistic, even fantastically so, then let their ardor subside . . . and then stab them and the dying bull in the knee, in the heart, and especially in the wallet. Several times.

Now, I fully understand that most of the strategies I've written about, up to this point, do in fact require some—sometimes a lot of—patience on your part to implement successfully. This probably shouldn't be much of a surprise. After all, I've mentioned several times that we must allow the market participants a little time to fatten our trading accounts. Do I ever apply short-term strategies? Sure, just not frequently. I discuss one of my favorites in the next chapter.

Here's one of my favorites.

CHAPTER 13

Pay Me after Lunch

The Endplay

You can observe a lotta things by watchin'.
Lawrence Peter "Yogi" Berra

In 1962, Edward O. Thorp wrote a remarkable book, *Beat the Dealer* (Random House), the first of its kind as far as I know. He programmed an extensive computerized analysis of the game of blackjack (no mean feat in the 1960s, I assure you—we've all been spoiled by PCs by now). The book is partly a very readable analytical commentary and partly a series of tales about his and his colleagues' adventures in attempting to put their computer-generated strategies into practice.

One of the anecdotes in the book concerns an evidently very sharp chap who figured out, without any computerized assistance, a strategy to generate an enormous statistical advantage at certain times in blackjack, provided that a couple of conditions existed. Hmm, that sounds familiar, doesn't it? Thorp titled this strategy "The Endplay" because the possibility of employing it occurs when there are only a few cards remaining in the deck or the dealing shoe. Casinos ultimately learned of this strategy and prohibited it, in effect testifying to its validity. Now, we're not blackjack players (at least not principally, I sincerely hope), but the good news is that there is a nearly perfect correlate strategy available to us in our trading.

Nature Abhors a Vacuum—We Don't

What causes a market's price to change? An influx of traders acting on presumably new information, correct? When the market participants are unsure of what might happen in the near term in their market—in other words, when the quantity and quality of available and pending information is insufficient for the participants' decision-making process, the more immediately volatile that market tends to be. Examples of this are trivially easy to find. Perhaps the best-known examples in futures are in the grain markets from late spring to mid-late summer. Will it rain or won't it, will the high-pressure ridge move east or west or maybe south, can the commercial interests squeeze the July contract? Questions like these abound, and absolutely *nobody* has the answers, so everyone is nervous and the volatility of these markets increases right along with the uncertainty as such questions arise. I'll take a pass every single time on trying to trade markets that are in this condition. "'That ain't my style,' said Casey," in the famous poem, and good luck to you if these types of markets are your style.

Ah, but what happens when the situation is reversed? What if, at some specific time, there is exactly zero weather disruption or other external event risk to be feared? What if there is no immediate supply/demand news to materialize for a few days or longer? And what if, in the ideal case, the politicians are on vacation? In such a situation, wouldn't the volatility of such a market decline in very short order? This result would seem very likely, wouldn't you say? Let's sweeten the pot a bit. Suppose we have this type of temporary news and event vacuum in a market, and also suppose the nearby options only have a day or two left until they will expire. If such a market also has a high native volatility or its options' IVs are high at the moment, we ought to be able to fatten our trading account tidily and very quickly.

We can realistically take one of two paths in this case. We can attempt to determine in which direction our news-vacuum market is likely to move in the next day or day and a half. We'll write OOM puts if we think it is more likely to move up, or OOM calls if we hold the opposite market view. Alternately, we may decide that the market will be essentially dead in the water for the remaining day or two of the options' lives, and accordingly write an OOM strangle.

As always, there are trade-offs between the two approaches. Writing a strangle will usually offer us a superior ROC compared to simply writing a put or a call, but the strangle has two possible risk points, the straight option write only one. The strangle is more capital-efficient in that we will many times be able to write options with striking prices further away from the market in order to earn the same or more premium as writing a single option, and our margin requirement will therefore be smaller. Writing a strangle, though, increases our likelihood of having to defend the trade, of sitting in a modified trade for a month or more. If we are not inclined, due to historical price movement at this time or to current market conditions, to stay in a particular market for an extended defense, we should prefer writing the single option or looking for a different market to trade. When we don't object to staying in the market with a defensive position after our options expire, the strangle would seem to be statistically the better tactic. When we are correct about the postulated news/weather/event vacuum, the market we're interested in really does tend to calm down and to hand us our trading profit right away.

Structural Difficulties and Restrictive Markets— Forewarned Is Forearmed

There are two inherent difficulties with the endplay strategy. In order for an endplay to be worth our time, capital, and effort, we are required to deal generally in high-volatility markets. This condition isn't undesirable on its face. High-volatility markets offer us excellent opportunities at various times, but also pose a higher degree of basic market risk in the possibility of an untimely and radical price movement. The success of the endplay strategy is dependent on our being correct in our view that a market is about to see a news and event vacuum for a day or two. If we err, if some serious market-moving development occurs, we must defend or exit the trade immediately. This possibility of error implies that we must do something I detest, namely, watch the market closely over the term of the trade.

Watching a market may be to a trader's advantage. It's almost essential if your approach to trading involves swing trading or scalping. I've nothing against these methods, as long as they generate a profit for you, but I have a different advantage: I know that I'm no damned good at them. Unfortunately from my point of view at least, the nature of the endplay strategy may require very short-term trading as a defensive tool. We'll see one such situation later in this chapter.

The second difficulty involves margin requirement and the rules of option expiration, but fortunately this difficulty exists in only a few markets. Some markets settle their contracts and options for cash. We don't care about these here; cash settlement eliminates such concerns along these lines. For markets that settle their contracts via delivery, it's a different story. Now, most of these latter markets' options expire well before the notice-of-delivery period begins (when exchange margin requirements begin to rise, and we don't really want any part of delivery/redelivery, as noted earlier). These markets are very convenient for an endplay trade, assuming only that the necessary event/news vacuum exists. Grain and oilseed markets' options expire well before delivery becomes a consideration, but rarely offer us an opportunity except during weather-driven markets, and these are all yours, my friend. I won't touch them. The softs markets—coffee particularly, but occasionally cocoa and cotton too—present an occasional opportunity for us, and these markets' options also expire well before the delivery period. CME meat markets are impossible regarding this strategy. Forget about them. The problems are too numerous to list. The COMEX/NYMEX gold market occasionally allows a good endplay, but we're talking about once or twice in two or three years.

I haven't yet found a worthwhile endplay trade in the interest rate markets, bonds, notes, Eurodollars, LIBOR, and so forth, but if these markets' volatility stays as historically high as it is this minute, something may turn up. Sadly, from an option writing standpoint, these markets' absolute level of volatility is low. I would suggest, without any practical experience here, that the one-sided version of the endplay will work better in these markets than the strangle. We're likely to have to set the striking prices for a strangle far too narrowly, and, consequently, to have to defend the trade more often than we'd like. The IMM currencies, despite their relatively low overall volatility, offer good one-sided endplays from time to time, but be prepared to attempt to make just $100–200 net per lot, rarely more.

Fun and Games in the Big Apple—When *Is* the Trade Over?

This brings us to the energy markets, which undoubtedly offer us more opportunities for endplay trades than any other class of market. However, we must be even more alert than usual when attempting an endplay in these markets, because the rules of the New York Mercantile Exchange are a little bit odd regarding option expiration. What happens with expiration, in most months in the NYMEX energy contracts, is really quite fascinating . . . until you put your capital at risk.

As Yogi Berra once famously said, "It ain't over 'til it's over," and nowhere, *nowhere*, in the world of trading does this amusing tautology apply more than in option expiration on most of the NYMEX energy contracts. If you aren't a serious option trader, option writer especially, you might very reasonably believe that when an option stops trading, it has expired by rule. Your view is perfectly sensible, but now, my friend, welcome to New York.

Options on NYMEX energy contracts stop trading at the close of the market on their scheduled last trading day. So far, so good, and utterly normal. But, by rule, they can be exercised by the owner of the options for another couple of hours after the close. This extension still isn't a problem for option writers. Fine, allow the option owners to exercise away, and more power to them. The "gotcha" condition comes now. Unless the last trading day for the options happens to be a Friday, the after-market NYMEX ACCESS session opens for trading *before the exercise period elapses*. In plain English, if we've written an option that has, notionally, expired out-of-the-money, but only by just a little bit at the market close, then, during the ACCESS session, the market can (and does occasionally, bet your life!) move so that the written option is now in-the-money. The $64,000 question is now: will this option be exercised, and will we be assigned a position?

The answer is: probably, because almost every brokerage employs the so-called 1-tick rule. To protect careless traders who forget about options they own, virtually all brokerages will exercise the option on behalf of the client if it is even one tick in-the-money (ITM), unless they have received instructions from the client to the contrary. Good for the brokerages; they're looking out for the client's interests. It doesn't help us, though. If the option we've written does move into the money early in the ACCESS session, we may have a problem. The ugly part is that this problem *can't usually be resolved.*

What we'd like to do in this case, when the option we've written has moved into the money after the market close, is wait until the last few minutes before the option can no longer be exercised. If it's ITM, we'll buy a future to offset against a short call being exercised or sell a future to clear off a short put that might be exercised. If we do so, then, when the option is exercised, we'll be assigned the opposite position, and we'll end up flat, out of the market, which is exactly what we want. In theory, that's the way things will proceed. Would that matters were so straightforward.

In *any* market that has an afternoon after-market session, occasionally, the after-hours market will move so that our short option is just a little bit ITM, 5 points perhaps in crude oil, or a half-cent in natural gas. Here's a question for you: will the owner of the option exercise it under these conditions? "Hey, you said the brokerage automatically exercises ITM options at expiration! What's the deal here? Of course the option will be exercised." I did say that, it's absolutely true, and the brokerage will indeed exercise the option . . . unless the client has told them not to. There's absolutely nothing to stop a trader from placing an order with his broker something like "Exercise 2 CLZ 25.00 calls at expiration, only if CLZ is above 25.07." Orders like this are fairly common, and, if you consider the point for a moment, you'll see why.

Some considerable fraction of the traders who buy options either don't want the underlying futures position or don't have enough trading capital to hold the position. If the option they own is only a tiny amount ITM, it may well be the case that exercising their option and trading out of the futures position costs more than it's worth to them, and they'll simply abandon the option. This is where our problem originates. At expiration, the exchange matches up long and short option positions, generally according to the length of time the long/short position has been held, and then doles out the assignment notices. If the trader who owns the option we sold simply abandons the position, we won't know about it, usually, until tomorrow morning. In short, *we will not know if we have a position* in the market, and this is major-league bad news. The overnight session, whether on ACCESS, on

CME's GLOBEX2, or even conceivably on CBOT/Eurex' A/C/E session, might kick us in the head with a sharp move in our market, when we don't even know for certain whether we're still involved in the market.

In the event we find ourselves in this nasty situation, we must try to find out from our broker's back-office people whether we have been assigned a position. This is not necessarily easy to do. The back-office people, on option expiration day in any market, have an extended workday matching up exercises and assignments, and quite naturally want to get home as quickly as possible afterwards. When the last assignment notice is posted, they're out the door immediately, so our finding out about our particular position is a matter of timing and, to some extent, of luck. If we're unable to talk to them, all we can do is guess whether we have a position. Get out your lucky silver dollar and flip it . . . and hope you call it correctly.

Fortunately, this situation will occur only once or twice a year when we employ the endplay strategy. In my experience in a half-dozen or so of these cases, it seems to be about a 2-to-1 favorite that the very slightly ITM option will in fact be exercised, but this data sample is far too tiny to generalize into a firm rule, so be very careful. If one of your short options is right smack on top of its striking price near the close on its last trading day, I'd strongly consider buying it back with a market-on-close order or something similar, no matter how much I loathe market orders when trading options. Doing this will probably cost several points in contest risk, but the extremely undesirable case of *not knowing* if you have a position, a little later on if the market moves adversely, can cost a heck of a lot more.

More Fun and Games—Digitalis, Anyone?

In one NYMEX market, we must also contend with what I call the phantom heart-attack margin call. Every month, the natural gas contract expires on the next business day after its associated options expire. Here, we're not concerned with exercise and assignment. Suppose we've written five 3.00 natural gas calls, and the market has obligingly stayed down around 2.90. The options expire, we pocket the profit, and everyone's happy except the guy who bought the options, right?

Not quite. When we receive our daily trading and equity statement overnight via e-mail or fax, we find our margin requirement has increased by upwards of $30,000—I am *not* kidding here—and we may find ourselves receiving a margin call from our broker. What?! We don't have more positions now than we did yesterday; we have fewer, in fact exactly none in this month's contract! This can't be right, can it? Sadly, it can be and is. What happens is that the brokerage takes an extra day to clear expired options positions off their books, so, even though we don't *have* any natural gas position, we are still charged margin requirement as if we did have. And, it gets worse. The next trading session is the last trading day for this month's natural gas, true? Last-day margin requirement in a delivery-settled market like natural gas does exactly one thing: it goes straight up, and hugely, because the brokerage wants to make certain the trader can handle any delivery/redelivery situations that materialize.

Don't worry, I hear you. You're absolutely right, too. We don't have a position, why the devil are we being charged *any* margin when we're entirely out of the market? This is crazy, but that's the way it is. The good news here is that I know of no experienced broker in the world who will give you any trouble about this phantom margin call, and if you know of one who does, don't trade with him or his firm. Just ignore it. This goofy margin situation clears up by itself, always and every time, the very next business day.

Pardon the lengthy discussion of these topics, but knowledge of these unusual conditions concerning option expiration is, frankly, essential if you intend to use the endplay strategy in your trading. I'd have done you no service at all by omitting it. For that matter, I'd have done myself no favor by omitting it and having you swear at me the first time you ran afoul of any of these tawdry little details.

Filling Out the Deposit Slip—Preconditions for the Endplay

So much for negativity. The preconditions for a good endplay trade are remarkably straightforward and easily met, and here they are:

1. Option expiration must be no more than two day sessions away when we write the options, whether using the one-sided approach or the strangle, and the less time remaining, the better for us.

2. The IVs of the nearby options in this market must be high. If the market has natively very high absolute volatility (natural gas, coffee, etc.), we still prefer that the present IV be in the upper half of its 6-month range. If the market has only middling-highish native volatility (cocoa, soybeans, crude oil, etc.), we insist that the IVs be near the top end of their 6-month range.

3. In the strangle approach to endplays, ROC net of costs should be at least 3% of double the initial SPAN margin requirement. In the one-sided approach, net ROC should be at least 2% of double initial SPAN requirement.

4. If the market can be strongly affected by overnight weather developments, and one or more such developments are even possible in the next

2–3 days, do not use the endplay strategy at this time in this market. This strategy is completely dependent on our being very confident that there exists a short-term news/event vacuum in our selected market.

5. If there is any supply/demand news pending in a market in the next 2–3 days, or better still 4–5 days, do not use the endplay strategy. The endplay strategy works best when the trade is entered a day or two after a scheduled supply/demand report or other significant information has reached the market, and the news/event vacuum is now present.

6. Don't be greedy. Attempting to make 8–10% or more, while possible, gives away the structural advantage of the trade. Select the strike(s) of the endplay as far away from the current market as possible, consistent with the goals for ROC.

Condition 1 is part of the definition of the strategy. Don't adapt it by extending the trade to three or four days, because more time until expiration means more possibility of external events intruding on the trade. Condition 2 is likewise vital, particularly for the strangle approach. If option IVs are low, strangle-style endplays will need to be defended much more often than we'd like, which defeats the purpose of the trade. Sure, we'll defend if necessary, but, once again, we do not want to seek out trades that we are more likely to have to defend. Lower IVs are acceptable in the one-sided approach, as long as you've a reasonable measure of confidence that your view of the market's direction over a day or two isn't considerably off the mark. Use non-seasonal reasoning here: you don't need to be right to make a profit, merely not significantly wrong.

Conditions 3 is included because a considerable number of traders consider a 2–3% return on a trade to be not worth their while. Two or three per cent over a year? I agree completely. But, 2 or 3 per cent over 1 or 2 days? How greedy are these traders, anyway? If we were able to find enough trades yielding 2% over 2 days, consecutively throughout a year's time, we'd be staring at a 1,161% total ROC at the end of the year. Maybe I'm missing something here, but that's certainly enough for me. Condition 6 applies here, too. As in other option writing strategies, keep the strikes of the written options as far from the current market price as feasible, the more so given the modest ROC requirement.

Condition 4 is somewhat amorphous, but still easily implemented. For example, the natural gas market is notoriously affected by certain weather conditions—an extended nationwide heat wave in the summer, prolonged cold as we saw in the winter of 2000–2001, or the advent of a hurricane near the production areas in the Gulf of Mexico. If any of these exist, or might come to exist within 48 hours, don't enter an endplay trade. If they don't, then go ahead. Condition 5 is really the key to this strategy. In an endplay, the occurrence of new news is either outright evil, in the straddle approach, or halfway risky, in the one-sided approach. The less likely that new information will appear in the marketplace over the 1–2-day term of the trade, the more likely the trade is to succeed.

Markets that have regularly scheduled weekly or monthly releases of supply/demand data are considerably more likely than other markets to be good candidates for endplays. This is why the NYMEX energy markets tend to offer more opportunities to apply this strategy. For crude oil, heating oil, and gasoline, the major weekly reports and their times of release are well-known and, even more importantly, well trusted by the market participants. By mid-morning every Wednesday, the market has digested the weekly API and DOE supply/demand figures, and if the current month options expire on that Thursday or Friday, we have the potential for a good endplay trade. The natural gas figures, now also from DOE/EIA, are released Thursday morning, and, if the front-month options expire on Friday or Monday, we may be able to spot a good opportunity. Keep in mind that it is entirely to our advantage to seek out Friday expirations in all these markets, in order to avoid even possibly being snagged by the NYMEX contracts' odd conditions at option expiration.

C-Y-A in the Old Endplay—Defense

Defense in an endplay trade comes in two flavors, one less undesirable than the other. (All defense is undesirable, from a profit and ROC standpoint, but, just as mother told you to, so also eat your broccoli because it's good for you, and defense is good for your capital, ultimately.) The first is immediate—how we'll try to defend if we'd want to keep our trade expiring as planned, in just a day or two. Usually, in an endplay, the striking price(s) of the options we've written are much closer to the market than in other option-writing strategies. This factor makes a hedge defense using options very difficult. Moving the goalposts is also not feasible, for the option(s) that are further OOM than the one(s) we've written are only worth pennies at this point.

A time-spread defense can be very useful in this case. The usual condition for this defense must be in force: the option(s) we buy to create a time spread must have significantly lower IV than the current IV of the options we originally wrote. Fortunately, this is not an uncommon situation at all, but we must watch one other parameter of this defense closely. Assume we're in an endplay in September natural gas (ticker: NGU), and one of our written options is the September 2.80 put. Assume also that the price of September NG is 2.82, and the price of October NG is 2.86. To defend properly with a time spread, we should purchase, 1-for-1 (or perhaps 3- or 4-for-5, depending on comparative IVs), the October 2.85 put, not the 2.80 put. This will be expensive, and this purchase will certainly violate our policy of not spending more on a first defense than the trade is worth. Nevertheless, if the two options' IVs are correctly aligned for our purposes, this will be an excellent defense as a rule, unless the market reverses sharply. This reversal must occur almost immediately in order to be costly to us, though, and this necessary immediacy, and its usual non-occurrence due to the presumable news and event vacuum, should work to our advantage.

We have one other choice if we want to try to keep to the original expiration date of the trade. In this example, we're clearly concerned about the market falling well below 2.80. If we have 3 or more lots in the trade, we can usually do well for ourselves by defending with futures, again, an action that is against our normal policy. Just as with the spread defense, we will distinctly improve our position unless the market reverses sharply. Typically, something between a 1-to-3 and a 1-to-5 futures-to-options ratio in defense is what we'll want, but, unfortunately, each case in the real world is unique.

Of course, even notwithstanding the very short time frame of an endplay trade, sitting for even an hour or two in a trade that appears to be working against us can be an eternity. We may, and reasonably, consider that the risk of an adverse market movement is too high in either of these defenses. We may readily decide that an extended defense is the best choice, and we have our familiar tactical tools available, the roll and the flip, or some combination of the two. If we elect to roll or to flip, we'll select the appropriate options for the next cycle of the trade according to the conditions described in Chapter 7.

I mentioned the fission defense earlier. This defense is a combination of rolling and flipping, and, when executing this defense, we also reduce the size of our position. Suppose we've written five options in an endplay, and the market is threatening our position. We can repurchase the written options and write either three or four strangles, as wide as we can manage, in the next month further out. As always, we must make certain that we write more premium than we repurchase. Here's a practical, if not entirely wonderful, example of the fission defense in a real-world endplay trade.

Gentlemen, Start Your Endplay

Our market: NYMEX natural gas. The contract: initially June 2002 (ticker: NGM). The date: Thursday, May 23, 2002. Option expiration date: Tuesday, May 28, 2002, after Memorial Day. Sometimes, we have to contend with 3-day weekends, whether we like it or not.

NGM was trading at 3.462 late in the day session on Thursday the 23rd, and, in accordance with the endplay strategy, I wrote seven strangles, selecting the June 3.30 puts and 3.65 calls that were to expire the following

Tuesday. Given the Memorial Day holiday, there were about two trading days remaining in the life of the June options, depending on how you choose to count the overnight ACCESS session on NYMEX on Monday night June 27. I received a gross total of 4.0 cents, $400 for each pair, about $370 net. NGM had reacted rather negatively after the weekly storage statistics that the EIA published on Thursday morning, but it seemed to have steadied up around the 3.46 level, with the day session starting to run out.

The market weaseled a little lower toward the close of the session, finally settling at 3.438. Friday's shortened trading session was predictably dull. Hey, why not take a 4-day weekend, eh? Lots of floor traders do exactly this on holiday weekends and the trading volume tends to shrink noticeably on the Friday before the weekend. Volume or no volume, the market kept sneaking lower, setting 9 cents down to 3.347. I had established a small defense by selling a couple of NGM futures very late in the session on Friday at 3.33. Boy, am I slick or what? Now, I'm holding *two* losing positions. I found myself using some very choice descriptive terms to myself in the mirror. The ACCESS session on Monday night was equally dull, but the market kept edging lower, down to 3.29 at one point before I decided I had to get some sleep. Monitoring trades overnight is definitely not my favorite hobby, but sometimes it's necessary, unfortunately.

The profitability range of the trade, as entered, was between about 3.266 and 3.684, all costs paid. Obviously, I wanted the market in the best case to finish between 3.30 and 3.65 on Tuesday. Let's let the short options expire worthless, as always . . . if possible. Forget about that. The market, as ever, did no such thing. Tuesday morning, expiration day, saw the market open at 3.27 (mutter, grumble), and at one point early in the day it traded down to 3.255. I wasn't in terrible shape in the trade. It was still slightly profitable at 3.255, but I was sitting on a whole pile of risk, and I hate that.

Rather than hope/gamble that NGM would bounce back up over 3.30, I applied a fission defense to the 5 naked 3.30-strike puts, repurchasing them for 3.8 cents each as the market diddled around 3.275–3.280 with a couple of hours left in the day session. The other 2 short 3.30 puts were covered by the 2 short NGM futures. No brilliance involved, I guarantee you. This move was merely risk reduction, in combination with trying to retain some of the profit potential of the position.

Now, please note that I could easily have decided to accept the loss of, basically, commissions on the 5-lot I repurchased. Total loss on these would have been $5 \times (4.0 - 3.8) \times 100$, or +$100, less 15 commissions @ $15, –$225, for a net of –$125 minus a few dollars in floor fees. Accepting this loss, probably, was the intelligent thing to do. What, me intelligent? Only occasionally, I'm sorry to say. If the market would remain below 3.30, the remaining two lots in the trade, given the two futures sold, would have had the following result. I'd have been +$400 × 2 on these two short option strangles, less 4 commissions, –$60, plus 3 cents each on the two futures, or $(3.0 \times 2) \times 100$ = $600, less 4 more commissions on the futures, another –$60, for a net of +$840 on these last two. Net for the whole trade? Roughly, +$710 with all costs paid.

Extended Defense—Another Month in the Muck

Did I do this? Don't be silly. I elected to extend the defense. Why? I haven't any idea, and I must have realized the general stupidity of my actions, too, because there isn't a single line in my trading notebook about it.

After finding out where several strikes of the July options were quoted by the floor, and crunching a few numbers for a statistical analysis, a good (cough . . .) defensive possibility emerged. I wrote the July NG (ticker: NGN) 2.85 puts and July 4.00 calls, but only *four* pairs apiece, not five, for 7.3 cents the pair. This is the idea behind a fission defense: turning one position into two opposed and smaller ones. Could this defense be wrong (aside, of course, from my sappy notion of not accepting a profit in hand and getting on to other opportunities)? Absolutely, because natural gas might easily pop back up 10 cents or more in any given hour. Given the market's behavior over the three previous days, this development didn't appear likely, but who knows about any given 1-hour period in the natural gas market, eh?

The result that did occur represented $2,920 gross premium for the four pairs sold, less 5 times 3.8 cents, or $1,900 gross premium repurchased, less 13 commissions, $195 (4 pairs equals 8 lots sold, plus 5 lots repurchased). This works out to $825, net of all costs, plus the proceeds of the original trade. NGM ended at 3.285 at the market close, the two remaining short 3.30 puts were exercised by their owner, thus assigning two long NGM positions to me, which offset against the two NGM shorts I held. OK, we're flat, no position left in June natural gas, and sitting with a position in July. Good position, or bad? A worthwhile defense or not?

Let's run the numbers. Original credit: 7 times 4.0 cents, $2,800, less 14 commissions. First defense: sold 2 NGM futures at 3.33, with 2 more commissions. Repurchased 5 NGM 3.30 puts at 3.8 cents, or –$1,900, and 5 more commissions. Wrote 4 NGN 4.00 calls and 4 NGN 2.85 puts, gross credit $2,920, with 8 commissions. The two remaining short 3.30 puts were assigned, giving me a long position of 2 NGM futures, which offset neatly against the two NGM short futures at 3.33. Gross profit on futures and the assigned puts, $600, less 2 more commissions.

Bottom line: + $2800 – $1900 + $600, minus 31 commissions at $15.00, or $465, equaling about $1,035 net in pocket on Wednesday, May 29. Former position: short 7 NGM 3.30 puts, short 7 NGM 3.65 calls, short 2 NGM futures.

Former differential between the put strike and the call strike, the width, 3.65 – 3.30 = 35 cents. New position: 4 July NG strangles, width 4.00 – 2.85 = 115 cents. New position expires in 28 days.

Disadvantages in applying the defense: refusal to take a good profit in hand (very bad, don't do it!), having to sit for another month and tie up some amount of capital, and possibly be required by market movement to apply another defense to one or the other side of the remaining trade. Advantages to the defense: now only dealing with four lots as opposed to five (or seven, depending on how you count), margin requirement significantly lower (4 very wide strangles versus 7 narrow ones plus 2 short futures), hard dollars in hand, and more profit yet to be earned, potentially.

While the natural gas market can become ridiculously erratic at times, supply and demand didn't look particularly conspiratorial at this point, there having been an historically high level of gas in storage, and demand having been staying moderate. Weekly injections into storage continued to be quite decent, even relatively high on a nationwide temperature-adjusted basis. The remaining July position was probably more risky to the downside than the upside, whether considering a possible summer heat wave or not. This risk profile was acceptable, because excellent defensive possibilities existed if NG moved sharply lower, had the trade required a second month's defense. With profit in hand and a lower gross risk due to the now-smaller position, though having to stay in the market for another month, I was about as happy as the proverbial clam, except, of course, for having been just plain dumb in applying the defense in the first place. All defenses should work out so well.

"Aw, that was a lucky outcome," you might be scoffing, "I'm glad you made a profit, but that was a fluke and you're just picking out a good case to show off." Lucky, you say, that NGM moved lower after I'd sold futures, and the short futures position became profitable? Not a chance in the world. You're forgetting about time and its effect on the return earned on capital.

In terms of ROC, I strongly preferred that NGM had moved a little higher. I'd cheerfully have forgone half or so of the initial potential profit in the trade, roughly $1,300, had NGM moved 6 cents higher after I'd sold the futures. Had it done so, I almost surely wouldn't have considered applying a defense and sitting for another month. Remember the extremely limited time span over which this trade occurred, just 5 total days and only about 2 actual trading days, and the yet more limited time during which I was short the futures? Which would you prefer: about $1,100 profit in hand in 5 days' time, or $2,400 or so in 5 weeks? Yep, I thought so. Me, too.

Had NGM run up 6 or 7 cents, I'd have exited the short futures position, taken that loss, and would have had the remaining profit in the original position in my pocket by Wednesday, May 29, with all the margin capital freed up and available. Trade as you like, of course, and my best wishes for your profitability, but I will *always* accept half a loaf, especially when I can obtain that half a loaf in 95% or more of all cases, and in just a day or two. Except, of course, when the old brain isn't operating. Sigh.

What do you say, my friend? Is there any part of this result you *don't* like (barring, naturally, my error in not accepting the immediate profit)? Do you want even better news? Believe it or not, this wasn't a superior result at all. In terms of ROC, endplays ordinarily do significantly better, because we usually collect all our profit in a very few days. How did the defensive July position turn out? Both sides expired worthless, thanks, but it wouldn't have mattered if they had not. One side was going to expire worthless—it would have taken an almost unimaginable market movement to threaten *both* 2.85 and 4.00 in 20 trading days, given the supply/demand conditions then obtaining in the market. And, by the way, yes, I would indeed have defended the threatened side of the remaining July trade, had such a threat developed.

The endplay strategy is, just as any other, not about outsmarting the market, but about trying to locate and enter a high-expectation, high-ROC trade when the terms of doing so are in our favor. The existence of a news and event vacuum is absolutely essential to the success of the trade, and the premiums of the options must remain high or highish right down to the last little part of their lives. News vacuums tend to occur after previously scheduled supply/demand reports, but the release date of these reports may or may not be near a given market's option expiration. When they are, we may have an opportunity for a good solid endplay.

Nor can we afford to forgo checking a market's options' IV. In the past couple of months (July, August 2002) in natural gas, the IVs (hence, as always, the premiums) of the options haven't been nearly suitable for trying an endplay trade. The gold market seems to be warming up, though, and perhaps an opportunity will occur here before the end of the year. IVs are rising right now in the grain markets, but who knows whether option pricing will be suitable to an endplay for the September options. We watch, we wait, maybe we pounce. The next opportunity will come along in its own good time.

CHAPTER 14

Filling in the Cracks

Ideas, Understanding, and Winning

There is no substitute for victory.
—General of the Army Douglas MacArthur

In the best of all worlds, what we'd like to do is examine a large number of strategies that we might employ and rank them for effectiveness, relative ease of use, relative risk-to-reward, and frequency of applicability. I wanted to include detailed discussions of three more strategies we haven't examined yet, but deadlines loom. (Trust me, if you intend to be an author, do *not* irritate your editor!) We'll have to settle for a short glance at these ideas.

The permanent strangle has a one-directional relative called the fadeaway, which is easy to implement, easy to defend, profitable, and applicable quite frequently. In fact, any given option write can be converted into a fadeaway trade most of the time, if desired. We compute 80% of the distance from the market's initial price to the strike of the option we've written, and if the market, at any time before the last week or so of the trade, touches that point, we apply a roll-out defense. Just one condition on the defense this time: we must roll further away from the market, no rolling into an equidistant strike in the next month (or two months) further out. We may need to repeat this defense once, twice, or more. Sooner or later, the position expires and we bank our profit. This strategy is similar to what is usually called "rolling for credits," differing in that this approach always deals with OOM or WOOM options, is much less capital-intensive, and is unlikely ever to turn into a Martingale, even accidentally. This seems a better strategy for writing puts than writing calls, because we won't even have the possibility of having to contend with a runaway bull market.

Another useful but sometimes tricky strategy I call, aptly enough, "the bookie." It consists of combining the purchase of a straddle and the sale of two or three OOM-WOOM strangles of a nearer expiration than that of the straddle. We might buy a December Swiss franc straddle (ATM, of course) when option IVs are in the middle of their 6-month range, and then write 2 October strangles, 350 or 400 pips wide, which options also offset against the December futures. The idea behind the trade is to exploit the differential in volatility or time decay per unit of time remaining in the written options versus the long side of the trade. Ultimately, we'd want to let our hypothetical written October options expire or replace them with November options at a convenient point, and later on repeat the process, rolling the strangles (or, more likely, one side of the strangle) into December options. We prefer to enter this kind of trade when the next couple of months are historically neutral, as regards the gross movement of the underlying market. Defense usually consists of rolling all or all minus one of the threatened written options out-and-away from the market, or selling off the unsuccessful half of our straddle purchase at a convenient point, typically right when we roll the options.

Coattailing a squeeze is a situational option-buying strategy. If there appears to exist the possibility of a short squeeze developing in some month in a physical futures market, we'll buy near-the-money calls in the *next* regular month. We don't buy calls in the month that may be about to be squeezed for two reasons. First, the options in the potential squeeze month probably will have expired by the time the squeeze materializes, if in fact it does. Second, ATM and near-the-money options in the squeeze month, even if available, are likely to be both expensive and subject to being heavily chewed on by Sister Theta. By moving out to the next regular month, we avoid this potential problem. If the squeeze doesn't materialize, we'll sell back the calls, trying to limit our loss to perhaps 15–20% of capital. If it does, we attempt to stay in the trade until we've made 30–40% or more net ROC. We also reserve the right, if the market does run higher, to write a higher-strike call, convert the trade to a bullish call spread, and recapture all or most of our premium expense, reducing risk considerably and potentially enhancing the trade in the bargain.

An Open Mind Plus Understanding Plus Discipline Equals a Full Wallet

When we're trading to win, few abstract things are more valuable to us than keeping an open mind. You might want to make the case that doing this is valuable in any endeavor, but it's *really* an essential in trading. This applies equally to markets and to methods. I mentioned earlier that I'd trade in any market in which I thought I understood how to profit, and that's exactly true. Similarly, I've a very open mind regarding strategies and methodology. If some strategy works, or seems to have worked in analytical studies, and if I at least generally understand the rationale behind the strategy, I'll give it a try. As for markets, historically, I'm an absolutely terrible grain trader, but I'm still completely open to ideas on how to trade those markets success-fully. I prefer to write options as a means of generating profit because I un-derstand to at least a modest extent the structure and dynamic of futures options, because I'm comfortable with the process, and, of course, because I do very well at it. Does this preference imply that I reject other strategies, those not involving options? Not for a moment.

Lots of opportunities don't lend themselves very well to option trading, or can be much better implemented by trading futures contracts. One such, which has persisted throughout most of 2002 and might last for another 6 months or more, has to do with interest rates. Early in 2002, the wise men were busily speculating as to when Mr. Green Beans (my private name for the Chairman of the Federal Reserve Board, after the old Captain Kangaroo character) would get around to raising the overnight Fed Funds rate. It be-came evident rapidly that conditions in the economy were so iffy that rais-ing this rate was not a pleasing prospect, and Mr. Green Beans (correctly, in my view, but who cares about my view) has sat on his hands to date. Know-ing that the Fed is not going to do something is every bit as valuable as know-ing what it's about to do and when it will be doing it.

If overnight rates aren't going to move higher, then I think we would readily agree with each other that 90-day rates aren't going to move much or perhaps at all higher, over the same period. The CME Eurodollar contract is a 90-day rate strip. Due to the earlier prevailing market view that short-term rates were about to rise, the spreads between the 2003 contracts and the 2002 contracts had become very wide, more than 100 basis points, up-wards of one full per cent, in the June 2003/December 2002 spread. You don't have to be a Fortune 500 firm's chief economist (heck, you don't even need to know any more economics than a Congresscritter, i.e., virtually none), to see that these spreads had to change, had to become narrower, *as long as the Fed continued doing nothing*. As time passes, the closer to ex-piration a Eurodollar contract becomes, the more its price tends to move right toward the current Fed Funds rate, less a small discount. The only thing that will alter this price action is a perception on the part of the market par-ticipants that the Fed is *about* to start changing the Fed Funds figure, but it was exactly the opposite perception that market participants held during this period.

Ah, but, there's really no good way to take advantage of this situation with options. Trading the ordinary futures spread is far superior, and much more profitable. Over the eight weeks ending August 5, 2002, the June 2003/December 2002 spread narrowed from 108½ to 38 basis points, a terrific move. The nicest thing about this trade was that exactly no timing was required. Had you undertaken the trade virtually any day in that period, you would have profited . . . without a single option in the mix. I managed to pocket a few dollars in this little enterprise, and wouldn't hesitate to try to do so again if the Federal Reserve continues to take no action at the next meeting and Eurodollar spreads remain somewhat wide.

The point here is not that you and I make a profit, or do not, on a particular type of trade. The point is that if, say, swing trading is your preferred style, to state baldly that "I don't trade options, because . . ." of whatever reasons, is a good sign of a closed mind, and a sure sign that you aren't earning as much profit as you might, and likely should, make. It's the same for me. I trade futures positions only rarely because I've more confidence and better results in trading options. However, if an opportunity in an asset trade or asset spread is present and I (mostly, at least) understand it, and can get good indications of its likely success through research, I'll jump on it like a starving man on a deluxe pizza.

An open mind enhances our chances for success, but it's the understanding of an opportunity that puts profit into our trading accounts. Absent our understanding of at least the main part of a market's mechanism and its supply/demand considerations, how in the world can we attempt in some reasonably organized fashion to make a profit trading in it? For example, I've been looking at the CME Grade III Milk market for more than a year. If you've never run across this market, I wouldn't be at all surprised, for it isn't a high-volume one, somewhat of a backwater as such things go.

This market's options, rather surprisingly, are considerably more liquid than are those in a number of much higher-profile futures markets and would appear to be very much worth trading, but how? The terms of the futures contract are readily obtainable at the CME's Internet site, but that's not much help. Why do the options sometimes expire *after* the named month, nearly a unique situation in markets? Is the market completely dominated by commercial interests, or is there some participation by the public? How wide are the bid-ask spreads? Is there just one options market-maker on the floor, or a half dozen? These and numerous other questions need to be answered before a rational trader can enter this market. That's my next project after sending this text off to the publisher, and it will probably take some little time to gather the information necessary to understand this market's basics well enough to attempt to trade in it.

Randomness and Options—Markets Are Efficient . . . Aren't They?

Want to get into an argument? Neither do I, but sometimes we're going to have no choice when we're talking with traders and especially with academics. I made a huge mistake in one of these conversations in 1974, right about when the grain, oilseed, and sugar markets were going crazy for the second year in a row. A bunch of us—brokers and traders, the treasurer of the company, several other folks, and, gulp, an economics professor—were sitting around jawing after another huge bull day. I happened to mention the notion of efficient markets, and that I thought the current-day markets weren't operating very efficiently. From the reaction to this remark, you'd have thought I'd called someone's mother a Nazi hooker.

Our company's treasurer, a real stuffy type, started a discourse about market efficiency being necessary to market continuity. The professor (an absolutely *terrible* trader, and *not* my client, thank you) weighed in with a bunch of polysyllabic academic duckspeak, the gist of which was that I didn't know what I was talking about. One of my buddies, not too politely, asked the professor why, if he knew what *he* was talking about, he was such a rotten trader, and suggested that maybe knowledge of economic theory had no relation to trading success. One of our floor guys pointed out, pointedly, to the treasurer that these big bull markets weren't continuous anyway, citing the seven limit-up days followed by eight limit-down days in the cotton market the previous year. (The exchanges were just starting to adopt expandable daily limits at that time, but fixed limits were still more or less the norm except in grain markets.) The discussion heated up considerably and went downhill pretty quickly after that, with all the people who actually dealt in the markets lined up opposite all the theorists and executives and executive-wannabees. At least no one threw a punch at anyone, and that's the best I can say about this little soiree.

Now, you've seen me argue frequently in this text that the introduction of new information into a market changes the minds of some/most/all market participants and induces them to take actions that lead to a change in that market's price. Presumably, this change will be toward the post-new-information now theoretically correct market price. This process is, in essence, the basis of what is usually called efficient market theory, and so you might reasonably think that I'm a student or a devotee of this theory. I'm not, at all, and the reasons why not are both straightforward and potentially profitable to us.

Just because some proportion of the traders in a market act on a piece of information and the market price subsequently moves somewhere doesn't for a microsecond imply that the resulting price is the correct one, the price suggested by efficient market doctrine. I'd be very willing to accept that the new price is less incorrect than the former one, but the notion that the new price is correct is absolute poppycock. If, after some new information is introduced into the market, the new price of corn is 2.85/bushel, give me one even marginally plausible reason why that price is correct, and not 2.82½ or 2.85¼ or 2.87. Right, you can't. Don't fret about it, the efficient market crowd can't, either.

For that matter, you've probably seen many occasions yourself on which a new, post-new-information-into-the-market price cannot possibly be correct, in any reasonable usage of that word. Local traders frequently search for price levels at or near which lots of stop-loss orders are entered, and try on occasion to run the stops, make them execute all at once, if possible, and thereby profit from the resulting abrupt short-term market movement. They're pretty talented at doing so, too, which makes placing stop-loss orders in certain markets a rather risky proposition for the trader. Would you, or anyone, claim that, after a big batch of stops has been run and the market has moved an extra 80 points (or whatever amount), that this resultant price is correct, even though it's likely enough to snap back to previous levels very quickly? Of course you wouldn't—we all realize that this is a short-term market distortion that will right itself rapidly in all likelihood. So, where, during such a period of action in a market, is the correct price?

The best we can say is that, over time, a market will *tend* to move toward its correct price, the price at which it would be if every market participant had perfect information about the market, and probably roughly equal capital too. Consider the conditions, though. Huh, whazzat? Perfect information? Equal capital? When does this fantasy occur? Wake me when it does, okay?

The point of this discussion is that, as far as traders are concerned, there is rarely if ever a determinable *correct* price for a market. Ordinarily, the most accurate observation we can make about a market's correct price at any given time is that "it's around here somewhere." The size of the price range implied by this "somewhere" increases or decreases along with the market's very short-term SV. If the market is jumping all over the place, "somewhere" is larger, maybe much larger, and the converse is true if the market is very quiet. If you're interested in physics, this concept of "somewhere" bears a certain theoretical kinship to Werner Heisenberg's famed uncertainty principle, although, continuing the comparison, Heisenberg's principle is impeccably dressed in an academic tuxedo, whereas "somewhere" is much less formal, lounging around in jeans and a sweatshirt.

What does all this have to do with trading? Stated baldly, the notion of a market's correct price being "somewhere" is one of the considerations that impel me to prefer trading options to trading assets. "Somewhere" represents an extra chunk of randomness, and in most markets, to my observation, there's quite enough of that to satisfy anyone. The asset trader is almost always trading in the neighborhood of "somewhere," and his capital is much more subject to severe short-term fluctuation, as the market wanders around "somewhere" seeking the correct price, than is the capital of the disciplined option trader.

This is, of course, largely a philosophical view and subject therefore to all kinds of objections. Not about capital fluctuation; that's for all practical purposes inarguable—all you need to do to confirm it is compare the monthly brokerage statements of a disciplined asset trader with those of a disciplined options trader. There is, however, at least a small set of empirical data to support the notion of relative steadiness of profit resulting from disciplined options trading. The available set of data is too small to be a valid statistical sample, but it is large enough, I think, to be really rather suggestive.

Real-World Results—Proof of the Pudding?

I've traded in the markets for decades, and for a considerable number of years very indifferently. Beginning in the 1990s, I started studying various features of risk in a semi-formal way, and began systematically to discard ideas and strategies that either embodied too much risk or were unsatisfactory for other reasons. By 1996, I'd come firmly to the conclusion that the trader can do best for himself by dealing principally in options, due to the wide variety of insurance and risk-reduction features that options offer.

A couple of years later (I'm pretty deliberate about these things), it seemed clearly to be the case that event risk in the stock markets was simply too dominating a factor to be overcome, if I were sincerely interested in generating steady, as opposed to more erratic event-driven, profit. By mid-2000, I had functionally left the stock markets to the bubble boys and the one-way market advocates (and I'm sure they haven't missed me . . . nor have I missed them). By March of 2001, I was dealing solely in options on futures markets, using the strategies discussed throughout this text.

Traders aren't, or shouldn't be, interested in hitting home runs; that's Barry Bonds' job. Prudent bankers and competent bookmakers, those who are best overall at making money with money, have no use for financial home runs. They make their profit a bit at a time, steadily, daily, weekly . . . inexorably. I've exactly no interest in trading contests, or being top dog or a champion trader or whatever. If you enjoy that sort of thing, that's great, my very best wishes to you, and I hope you win. I want to generate profit in the steadiest possible fashion, just somewhat more quickly than bankers and bookies; 6% per month here, 4% there, occasionally 9–10% if such an opportunity presents itself. If some opportunity requires four months to put 18% net ROC in my pocket, that's fine with me. You can have the whole cheesecake, I'll just take a forkful every so often.

Does this attitude, do these strategies and similar ones, succeed? Judge for yourself. I trade three accounts right now, one mine and the other two small partnerships involving friends and business associates. As I mentioned in the Preface, I'm just a retail trader.

The Fly-By-Night Trading Partners (I like whimsical names for partnerships) were organized in March 1995, originally with a plan to trade in listed stock options. We weren't notably successful in this, turning $25,000 original capital into $20,420.80 by April 15, 2001, at which point the partners agreed that we should instead attempt to apply the strategies discussed herein, and to deal almost solely in futures options henceforth. Another partner joined us in July 2001, his contribution raising the effective capitalization of the partnership from April 15, 2001 to $25,420.80.

Account equity improved to $33,539.04 by December 31, 2001 and, as of the close of business December 31, 2002 was $56,475.49, just 3.86% below the partnership's best equity level of $58,656.02, attained on November 26, 2002. The maximum peak-to-trough interim loss, or drawdown, in the partnership's equity was a 31.32% loss, from August 13 to August 26, 2002. The largest drop under the partnership's "initial" equity on April 15, 2001 was to $17,357.92 on October 29, 2001, an unpleasant but modest 17.69%. Our average capital from April 15, 2001 to December 31, 2002 was $24,109.07, and the overall ROC for the partnership from April 15, 2001 to December 31, 2002 was therefore 134.25%, or 64.41% on a compounded annualized basis.

Consolidated Chaos, another partnership, was established on November 15, 2001, with an initial capitalization of $45,000. Two new partners joined, in January 2002 and February 2002 respectively, contributing between them another $20,000 in capital. At the close of business on December 31, 2002, the partnership equity was $101,310.17, unfortunately 21.64% down from its best level of $123,242.14 attained on July 26, 2002. This is entirely my fault. ConChaos, as the partners call it, was entirely too successful in the first half of 2002, and I subsequently became undisciplined, even a little careless, in selecting trades for about 30 days, costing the partners a bunch of equity for no reason. Well, only temporarily, but another lesson learned

ConChaos' average capital to December 31, 2002 was $62,037.03% and the overall ROC over 13½ months was 63.31%, or 54.65% on a compounded annualized basis. The maximum drawdown for the partnership occurred between July 26 and August 26, 2002, a figure of 36.11% due almost completely to my lack of trading discipline over that period. The largest drop under initial equity occurred right at the start, with account equity falling 9.63% to $41,046.52 on November 30, 2001. Fortunately, the partners don't seem *too* annoyed about our less than optimum results to date, but I do wonder what to make of the blindfold and the package of cigarettes they sent me, ostensibly as a Christmas present.

My personal account is somewhat less clear regarding its results, because I use it as a sort of piggybank, withdrawing capital from it occasionally, as convenient. By January 2001, I'd ceased applying any trading strategies except the ones discussed in the text (and their cousins), but still held several positions based on inferior strategies, which positions, perversely enough, made a healthy profit during the month. But, bad news rising, some of these positions weren't due to expire until various times in February and March.

These remaining positions resulting from inferior strategies were not sound—far too low in positive expectation—and I've not employed such strategies since. At the start of 2001, my account held a ridiculously large amount of written option premium, and I was sailing *far* too close to the wind regarding margin usage as a percentage of equity, waiting around for Sister Theta to gobble up these excess premiums. She (mostly) obliged, fortunately for me and even more fortunately given the inferior strategies and dicey margin situation. Here, for what they're worth, are the results from January 31, 2001 through December 31, 2002. Frankly, I'd be cautious about accepting this account's results as being as indicative as those of the two partnership accounts.

The account equity at the close of business December 31, 2000 was $47,335.84. Through January 2001, things went very well, with the equity on January 25 reaching $66,831.22. On that date, after a considerable number of options had expired and the account's margin usage was back down to about 14% of equity, I withdrew $45,000 to apply to a different investment—and, looking back, I should clearly have left that sum right where it was. Dummy! At the close of business January 31, 2001, account equity was $20,748.01. The remaining positions in the account that were based on poor strategies performed very badly in February and March. The now-depleted account saw (gasp, choke) a drawdown of 40.91% from February 1 to March 22, 2001, the worst I've endured since applying the strategies herein on a consistent and (presumably, cough . . .) disciplined basis. Once again, I had to learn the hard way. Inferior strategies, sooner or later, bring with them their own punishment for the trader.

The equity in the account, with no further additions or withdrawals, reached $34,580.70 on December 31, 2001 and improved to $58,841.11 by December 31, 2002, implying ROC of 183.59% over the 23 months, or 72.26% as a compounded annualized figure. The best equity level was $61,338.97, attained on August 13, 2002. The largest drop under the beginning equity was when total equity fell to only $13,141.02 on March 22, 2001.

Please note that, for the results based on the methodology and strategies I've advocated here to be proven statistically valid, similar or better results will need to be produced for the next two, three, perhaps even four years. That's fine with me. In fact, for an objective conclusion about the merits of the methodology and these strategies, it's entirely necessary. Candidly, these trading results weren't nearly as good as they could have been, and likely should have been.

I'm all too aware of the assorted strategic and tactical errors I've made over the past two years. I won't mention any further the sundry delusions and, not unlikely, madnesses that I indulged in during this period. They're depressing in retrospect, and I detest the attitude of "woulda, coulda, shoulda." A far better attitude for traders is *"Excelsior!"*—onward and upward! Fortunately, my departures from practicality and discipline have been rare, and ideally will become rarer still over time. The acquisition of discipline in any field of endeavor is a cumulative process; the more we practice it today, and next week, and next month, the more habitual it becomes for us.

Well, no doubt, we'll soon see how things turn out in future futures (er, so to speak), but I suppose these results are acceptable for a part-time retail trader. The trick, of course, for you and me and any trader, is to keep improving all the component factors necessary to successful trading: our tactics, our strategies, our methodological approach, our knowledge and understanding of markets, and our trading discipline.

Method Generates Strategy and Strategy Trumps Tactics

In our chosen endeavor, there is only one overriding consideration: trading to win is about making a profit. Everything else, *absolutely everything else*, is just a sideshow. If, theoretically, you might earn X% profit by applying strategy Y in a particular situation, but in the real world you only manage to earn half of X%, this isn't a problem. The trade is or has been profitable, it's proceeded generally according to plan, and you've had the chance to observe your strategy in action. Very possibly, while observing the trade, you've spotted a way to improve the strategy, and I surely hope you've been looking for such improvements. If it became desirable or even necessary to defend the trade, you've gained an opportunity to sharpen your defensive tactics, preserve your capital, and practice keeping trading risk under tight rein. All these situations, all these outcomes, are in one way or another advantageous. Some more than others, certainly, but none of us wants to pay too much tuition for a course in Markets 203a and 203b, right?

Strategy trumps tactics every time. You might be the finest tactical trader in the world, but your profitability is still subject to the methods you use to select your strategies. If your methodology involves reading chicken entrails or tea leaves, and you profit by employing the strategies these imply, then, by all means, do it. Let the rest of the traders laugh while you visit the bank regularly, what do you care? Somewhat more likely, I imagine, you'll adopt or develop other less exotic but equally or more successful methods. If your method and your strategic approach(es) to that method work for you, that's all that need be said.

There is obviously no single methodology and no single set of strategies within a methodology for making money with money. There are dozens of profitable methodologies, but what is the common ground among these? Just this: they attempt to minimize risk, to exploit a (presumably) well-defined situation, to establish a discipline for entering and exiting trades, to set oneself up to claim a healthy return on capital over any given period, and at all times to keep the expectation in any particular trade in the plus column. To these ends, the trading strategies that I've described here work very well for me. It wouldn't be a bit surprising if these strategies would work as successfully or even better for you, and I wouldn't wonder for a moment that you'd be able improve on them, or discover highly advantageous variations on their respective themes.

As Ethel Barrymore used to say, "That's all there is, there isn't any more." I hope you've enjoyed this little examination of one profitable broad methodology and philosophy of trading, and that you've run across several (or, better still, a lot of) useful and profitable ideas, strategies, and tactics in the text. If you decide you'd like to kick around some of these notions, or others, may I invite you to visit the Internet site forum.ino.com, where I can frequently be found theorizing about trading and generally lowering property values. Or if, you consider these strategies to be false-to-fact or nonsense, let's discuss those views too.

No matter what else, healthy profits and good trading to you!

Studies of Historical Gross Movement in Selected Markets, 1990–2002

Those who do not learn from history . . .
—George Santayana

. . . had better not trade futures and options.
—SAJ

I find the use of historical gross movement in the evaluation of potential straddles and strangles to be invaluable. This appendix presents linear gross movement studies for 30 of the most popular North American futures markets in the accompanying tables. There are any number of ways to apply these data to your trading.

Clearly, if we're looking into these two strategies, the tables will indicate months in which the purchase of straddles has historically been advantageous or disadvantageous, and we can also easily see spans of months over which writing strangles is likely to have been profitable. Buying December Australian dollar straddles in July is historically a definite winner *if* you can manage to do so—this is a notably thin market. Writing 1-month NG strangles in the spring and early summer, more than $1.00/MMBTU wide, has been a huge winner ever since the great bull market of 2000–2001, and looks to be profitable for the next few years if certain structural problems in that market cannot be resolved. You can easily spot numerous potential opportunities by examining the tables.

This sort of analysis, though, as noted in the text, is only one of the factors to consider when straddling or strangling a market. Please don't skimp on your analysis of the other preconditions! The overall success of applying these strategies depends at least as much on current supply/demand conditions and present-day market volatility as on historical tendency. Also, your own research well may turn up other useful, and subsequently profitable, preconditions. After all, the more research you do, the more likely you are to find another means of generating an extra advantage in setting up a trade, and I wish you the best results possible.

The tables herein are also somewhat useful for evaluating non-seasonal trades. They do not, however, replace a specific historical analysis of a definite period, for few non-seasonals begin and end conveniently on month boundaries. I'd suggest using these tables merely as a shortcut to locating interesting non-seasonal ideas, and then refining the trading idea from that point using an historically-based entry/exit analysis.

These tables are completely straightforward, but a brief note is in order. They represent, once again, a whole-month analysis. Thus, the computed results for, say, NYMEX crude oil in March, are computed from the May crude oil contract's daily data. The March crude contract expires in February, and so cannot be used. The April contract expires in March, and does not afford us the entire month of March for the calculations.

The "Average" columns are computed as follows: for a March result, I took the settlement price on the appropriate futures contract on the last trading day in February, and computed the intraday highs and lows, both in total points of movement and percentage of price change, all through March. Then, I just repeated this calculation over 12 or 13 years and took the arithmetic mean of the March results. Use either analysis you prefer, gross points or gross percentage of movement.

CME/IMM Australian Dollar December 1989 Through May 2002 (0.01 = $10.00)

	Years	Average Up	Average % Up	Average Down	Average % Down	Average Range	Average % Range
Jan	13	1.74	2.72	2.04	2.85	3.78	5.57
Feb	13	1.61	2.47	1.88	2.65	3.49	5.11
Mar	13	1.29	1.90	1.18	1.82	2.46	3.72
Apr	13	1.71	2.56	1.31	2.08	3.03	4.64
May	13	2.07	3.19	1.72	2.57	3.79	5.76
Jun	12	1.38	2.15	1.32	1.92	2.71	4.06
Jul	12	1.53	2.27	1.18	1.66	2.70	3.92
Aug	12	2.00	2.96	1.92	2.79	3.92	5.75
Sep	12	1.22	1.76	1.48	2.37	2.70	4.13
Oct	12	1.57	2.36	2.26	3.45	3.83	5.81
Nov	12	1.45	2.20	2.33	3.49	3.78	5.69
Dec	13	1.24	1.90	1.26	1.83	2.50	3.72

CME/IMM British Pound December 1989 Through May 2002 (0.01 = $6.25)

	Years	Average Up	Average % Up	Average Down	Average % Down	Average Range	Average % Range
Jan	13	5.07	3.21	2.60	1.58	7.67	4.79
Feb	13	3.90	2.44	3.07	1.92	6.97	4.35
Mar	13	2.88	1.89	3.62	2.13	6.50	4.02
Apr	13	3.77	2.50	3.40	1.98	7.16	4.47
May	13	4.65	3.02	3.90	2.32	8.54	5.34
Jun	12	3.32	2.03	3.02	1.91	6.33	3.95
Jul	12	5.19	3.17	2.39	1.50	7.58	4.67
Aug	12	6.47	3.93	3.25	2.05	9.71	5.98
Sep	12	4.64	2.95	4.22	2.38	8.87	5.34
Oct	12	5.99	3.73	4.33	2.37	10.32	6.09
Nov	12	5.99	3.69	5.26	2.93	11.25	6.62
Dec	13	4.54	2.89	2.32	1.39	6.86	4.27

CME/IMM Canadian Dollar December 1989 Through May 2002 (0.01 = $10.00)

	Years	Average Up	Average % Up	Average Down	Average % Down	Average Range	Average % Range
Jan	13	0.95	1.29	1.17	1.57	2.12	2.86
Feb	13	0.90	1.25	1.23	1.61	2.13	2.86
Mar	13	0.55	0.75	0.91	1.25	1.46	2.00
Apr	13	0.92	1.27	0.98	1.35	1.90	2.62
May	13	1.07	1.51	0.95	1.30	2.02	2.81
Jun	12	0.71	0.98	0.52	0.70	1.23	1.68
Jul	12	0.90	1.21	0.72	1.01	1.62	2.21
Aug	12	1.02	1.32	1.08	1.52	2.11	2.84
Sep	12	0.90	1.26	1.06	1.39	1.95	2.65
Oct	12	1.19	1.64	1.27	1.70	2.46	3.33
Nov	12	1.04	1.42	1.43	1.93	2.47	3.35
Dec	13	0.80	1.11	0.94	1.29	1.74	2.39

NYBOT Cocoa December 1989 Through June 2002 (1.00 = $10.00)

	Years	Average Up	Average % Up	Average Down	Average % Down	Average Range	Average % Range
Jan	13	59.85	6.40	89.54	7.26	149.38	13.66
Feb	13	78.62	8.59	115.38	9.35	194.00	17.95
Mar	13	82.15	7.27	67.08	5.72	149.23	12.99
Apr	13	85.08	7.13	104.54	8.77	189.62	15.89
May	13	95.46	8.20	61.54	5.36	157.00	13.56
Jun	13	89.00	7.67	95.46	8.20	184.46	15.86
Jul	12	84.17	7.76	61.83	4.79	146.00	12.55
Aug	12	79.17	7.47	83.42	6.70	162.58	14.17
Sep	12	65.42	6.22	63.67	5.12	129.08	11.34
Oct	12	65.08	6.25	82.92	6.53	148.00	12.78
Nov	12	73.50	7.11	108.67	8.83	182.17	15.94
Dec	13	52.38	4.28	69.31	5.87	121.69	10.15

NYBOT Coffee "C" December 1989 Through June 2002 (0.01 = $3.75)

	Years	Average Up	Average % Up	Average Down	Average % Down	Average Range	Average % Range
Jan	13	11.33	10.53	8.31	8.92	19.64	19.45
Feb	13	14.41	13.19	9.27	9.88	23.68	23.07
Mar	13	8.94	9.08	7.60	6.40	16.53	15.48
Apr	13	9.97	9.28	9.01	8.51	18.98	17.79
May	13	17.43	13.71	6.39	6.43	23.82	20.14
Jun	13	15.04	13.30	13.43	11.98	28.47	25.28
Jul	12	18.05	15.01	7.86	7.29	25.91	22.29
Aug	12	14.21	12.06	8.55	8.78	22.76	20.83
Sep	12	6.51	5.92	11.23	10.06	17.75	15.98
Oct	12	5.75	7.09	15.94	13.26	21.70	20.35
Nov	12	6.95	8.38	17.75	13.96	24.70	22.34
Dec	13	9.66	8.80	6.22	5.88	15.88	14.68

NYMEX/COMEX High-Grade Copper December 1989 Through April 2002 (0.10 = $25.00)

	Years	Average Up	Average % Up	Average Down	Average % Down	Average Range	Average % Range
Jan	13	3.65	3.66	6.72	6.43	10.37	10.09
Feb	13	4.14	4.38	6.25	5.99	10.39	10.37
Mar	13	5.33	5.37	2.02	2.00	7.35	7.37
Apr	13	6.32	6.68	4.20	4.12	10.51	10.81
May	12	5.43	5.24	5.76	6.17	11.19	11.41
Jun	12	7.83	7.61	7.60	7.66	15.43	15.27
Jul	12	5.73	5.79	3.83	3.82	9.56	9.61
Aug	12	6.03	5.73	3.66	3.60	9.68	9.33
Sep	12	3.31	3.49	5.84	5.61	9.15	9.11
Oct	12	2.31	2.44	7.94	7.64	10.25	10.08
Nov	12	5.22	5.11	7.85	7.62	13.07	12.73
Dec	13	3.71	3.69	4.39	4.27	8.10	7.95

CBT Corn December 1989 Through June 2002 (1.00 = $50.00)

	Years	Average Up	Average % Up	Average Down	Average % Down	Average Range	Average % Range
Jan	13	12.02	4.72	8.27	3.41	20.29	8.13
Feb	13	13.40	5.05	7.83	3.31	21.23	8.36
Mar	13	11.40	4.50	7.44	2.80	18.85	7.31
Apr	13	18.58	6.20	11.52	4.48	30.10	10.68
May	13	14.50	5.11	10.77	4.22	25.27	9.34
Jun	13	13.15	4.37	20.79	7.98	33.94	12.35
Jul	12	17.00	6.78	21.29	8.13	38.29	14.91
Aug	12	13.04	5.76	24.19	8.98	37.23	14.74
Sep	12	7.52	3.17	12.58	4.84	20.10	8.00
Oct	12	11.46	4.77	15.90	5.91	27.35	10.68
Nov	12	13.73	5.72	17.71	6.68	31.44	12.40
Dec	13	8.17	3.08	7.40	3.04	15.58	6.12

NYBOT Cotton #2 December 1989 Through June 2002 (0.01 = $5.00)

	Years	Average Up	Average % Up	Average Down	Average % Down	Average Range	Average % Range
Jan	13	4.27	6.51	3.72	5.79	7.99	12.30
Feb	13	5.81	8.59	4.50	7.10	10.31	15.69
Mar	13	3.45	5.44	3.04	4.33	6.49	9.77
Apr	13	3.90	5.40	4.24	6.46	8.14	11.87
May	13	3.86	5.81	3.78	5.58	7.64	11.39
Jun	13	4.43	6.90	6.65	9.51	11.08	16.41
Jul	12	2.07	3.36	4.33	6.14	6.41	9.50
Aug	12	1.72	2.92	6.34	9.02	8.06	11.94
Sep	12	2.48	3.63	6.15	9.27	8.63	12.89
Oct	12	2.58	3.93	3.22	5.33	5.80	9.26
Nov	12	2.69	4.62	4.13	6.52	6.83	11.14
Dec	13	2.39	3.40	2.88	4.55	5.27	7.94

NYMEX Light Sweet Crude November 1989 Through May 2002 (0.01 = $10.00)

	Years	Average Up	Average % Up	Average Down	Average % Down	Average Range	Average % Range
Jan	13	1.78	8.42	1.68	7.44	3.46	15.86
Feb	13	1.33	6.20	1.19	6.19	2.52	12.38
Mar	13	2.11	11.33	0.99	4.79	3.10	16.13
Apr	13	1.49	7.53	1.14	5.22	2.63	12.75
May	13	1.49	6.82	1.18	5.70	2.66	12.52
Jun	12	1.25	5.93	1.40	6.93	2.65	12.86
Jul	12	1.16	5.91	1.02	4.69	2.18	10.60
Aug	12	2.42	10.95	0.76	3.96	3.17	14.91
Sep	12	2.74	11.83	1.18	4.91	3.92	16.74
Oct	12	1.36	5.30	2.26	9.13	3.62	14.43
Nov	13	1.45	6.62	1.73	8.01	3.18	14.63
Dec	13	1.03	5.26	2.01	8.55	3.04	13.80

CME Feeder Cattle November 1989 Through April 2002 (0.01 = $5.00)

	Years	Average Up	Average % Up	Average Down	Average % Down	Average Range	Average % Range
Jan	13	2.01	2.66	1.92	2.43	3.93	5.09
Feb	13	1.94	2.60	2.16	2.71	4.10	5.31
Mar	13	1.38	1.76	2.09	2.83	3.47	4.59
Apr	13	1.93	2.60	2.28	3.29	4.20	5.89
May	12	1.66	2.31	2.36	3.07	4.02	5.38
Jun	12	2.98	4.14	1.97	2.54	4.96	6.68
Jul	12	4.13	5.65	1.69	2.17	5.82	7.83
Aug	12	1.54	2.08	2.13	2.66	3.67	4.74
Sep	12	2.27	2.98	1.39	1.73	3.67	4.70
Oct	12	1.63	2.11	1.68	2.16	3.31	4.28
Nov	13	1.58	2.04	2.07	2.59	3.66	4.63
Dec	13	2.19	2.76	2.63	3.38	4.82	6.14

NYMEX/COMEX Gold December 1989 Through November 2002 (0.10 = $10.00)

	Years	Average Up	Average % Up	Average Down	Average % Down	Average Range	Average % Range
Jan	13	7.92	2.302	11.45	3.271	19.37	5.573
Feb	13	10.58	3.277	7.00	2.042	17.58	5.320
Mar	13	5.97	1.771	14.06	4.070	20.03	5.841
Apr	13	7.59	2.368	7.84	2.234	15.43	4.602
May	13	10.69	3.333	6.15	1.895	16.84	5.228
Jun	13	6.32	2.015	9.34	2.702	15.65	4.717
Jul	13	7.35	2.060	8.28	2.618	15.64	4.678
Aug	13	8.32	2.488	11.10	3.144	19.33	5.632
Sep	13	14.42	4.875	6.85	1.970	21.27	6.845
Oct	13	7.36	2.256	13.83	4.023	21.19	6.279
Nov	13	5.75	1.668	7.05	2.142	12.79	3.810
Dec	13	5.18	1.463	9.37	2.703	14.45	4.166

NYMEX Heating Oil #2 November 1989 Through May 2002 (0.01 = $4.20)

	Years	Average Up	Average % Up	Average Down	Average % Down	Average Range	Average % Range
Jan	13	4.63	7.90	5.76	9.35	10.39	17.25
Feb	13	3.39	5.88	3.51	6.61	6.90	12.49
Mar	13	4.78	9.76	2.51	4.66	7.29	14.42
Apr	13	3.79	6.82	2.39	4.16	6.17	10.98
May	13	3.22	5.42	3.00	5.58	6.22	11.00
Jun	12	2.53	5.74	3.03	5.67	5.56	11.41
Jul	12	2.82	5.32	2.66	4.53	5.48	9.84
Aug	12	8.29	13.33	2.01	3.78	10.30	17.11
Sep	12	6.62	10.27	3.39	4.93	10.01	15.20
Oct	12	3.63	4.84	6.21	8.92	9.84	13.76
Nov	13	4.72	7.43	4.61	7.49	9.33	14.92
Dec	13	4.28	7.47	5.35	7.91	9.62	15.38

CME/IMM Japanese Yen December 1989 Through May 2002 (0.01 = $12.50)

	Years	Average Up	Average % Up	Average Down	Average % Down	Average Range	Average % Range
Jan	13	1.53	1.89	3.87	4.38	5.40	6.26
Feb	13	2.39	2.88	3.64	4.07	6.03	6.95
Mar	13	2.40	2.59	2.64	3.26	5.04	5.85
Apr	13	3.08	3.24	2.86	3.54	5.94	6.78
May	13	3.43	3.78	3.08	3.77	6.51	7.55
Jun	12	2.13	2.43	2.00	2.35	4.13	4.78
Jul	12	2.26	2.65	2.41	2.62	4.67	5.27
Aug	12	2.59	3.10	3.22	3.27	5.81	6.36
Sep	12	2.55	3.15	1.84	1.96	4.39	5.11
Oct	12	3.64	4.81	2.06	2.18	5.69	6.99
Nov	12	3.47	4.57	2.82	3.04	6.29	7.61
Dec	13	1.57	1.88	2.06	2.38	3.63	4.26

CME Live Cattle December 1989 Through June 2002 (0.05 = $20.00)

	Years	Average Up	Average % Up	Average Down	Average % Down	Average Range	Average % Range
Jan	13	3.45	4.83	1.39	2.04	4.85	6.88
Feb	13	2.19	3.03	1.53	2.14	3.72	5.16
Mar	13	2.57	3.49	1.84	2.56	4.41	6.05
Apr	13	1.42	2.12	2.39	3.53	3.81	5.65
May	13	1.07	1.56	3.44	4.98	4.51	6.55
Jun	12	1.78	2.66	1.26	1.85	3.03	4.52
Jul	12	2.92	4.38	1.91	2.79	4.83	7.17
Aug	12	1.41	2.08	2.25	3.18	3.66	5.26
Sep	12	1.64	2.41	2.73	3.83	4.37	6.24
Oct	12	1.78	2.61	1.61	2.27	3.38	4.88
Nov	12	1.95	2.82	1.73	2.45	3.68	5.27
Dec	13	2.06	2.91	1.90	2.76	3.95	5.67

CME Live/Lean Hogs December 1989 Through June 2002 (0.05 = $20.00)

	Years	Average Up	Average % Up	Average Down	Average % Down	Average Range	Average % Range
Jan	13	2.59	6.11	2.39	4.86	4.98	10.97
Feb	13	2.40	4.99	2.42	4.46	4.83	9.45
Mar	13	3.77	7.83	3.12	5.54	6.89	13.37
Apr	13	3.28	5.62	2.21	3.70	5.49	9.32
May	13	3.69	6.54	3.38	5.68	7.07	12.22
Jun	13	2.69	4.65	2.53	4.47	5.22	9.12
Jul	12	2.78	5.44	2.46	4.48	5.24	9.93
Aug	12	1.78	3.85	3.49	6.70	5.27	10.54
Sep	12	2.54	5.56	3.37	6.52	5.91	12.08
Oct	12	1.97	4.14	3.22	6.51	5.19	10.66
Nov	12	1.44	2.96	4.30	9.36	5.74	12.32
Dec	13	1.84	3.96	2.63	5.60	4.47	9.55

CME Random Length Lumber November 1989 Through May 2002 (0.01 = $11.00)

	Years	Average Up	Average % Up	Average Down	Average % Down	Average Range	Average % Range
Jan	13	19.79	7.10	19.07	5.92	38.86	13.01
Feb	13	31.72	11.80	17.25	5.20	48.98	17.01
Mar	13	20.27	6.68	16.48	4.76	36.75	11.45
Apr	13	21.01	7.73	30.91	8.60	51.92	16.32
May	13	20.18	6.87	19.41	6.30	39.59	13.17
Jun	12	23.28	8.14	28.88	8.82	52.15	16.96
Jul	12	16.42	5.33	24.58	8.63	41.00	13.96
Aug	12	22.20	7.59	23.51	8.24	45.71	15.83
Sep	12	12.87	4.20	31.94	10.50	44.81	14.70
Oct	12	11.83	3.96	38.94	13.01	50.78	16.97
Nov	13	23.41	7.82	11.17	4.38	34.58	12.21
Dec	13	28.34	9.61	15.26	5.92	43.60	15.53

NYMEX Natural Gas May 1991 Through June 2002 (0.001 = $10.00)

	Years	Average Up	Average % Up	Average Down	Average % Down	Average Range	Average % Range
Jan	10	0.300	12.40	0.544	15.34	0.844	27.74
Feb	10	0.238	9.79	0.139	6.17	0.377	15.97
Mar	10	0.318	14.41	0.090	3.45	0.408	17.86
Apr	10	0.267	10.50	0.123	4.78	0.390	15.28
May	11	0.223	9.10	0.251	7.99	0.474	17.09
Jun	11	0.211	7.56	0.256	10.02	0.467	17.57
Jul	10	0.107	5.73	0.296	11.26	0.403	16.99
Aug	10	0.312	12.86	0.248	10.09	0.560	22.95
Sep	10	0.331	12.78	0.141	6.08	0.472	18.86
Oct	10	0.308	10.72	0.249	8.24	0.557	18.96
Nov	10	0.388	11.63	0.313	11.61	0.701	23.24
Dec	10	0.651	18.62	0.235	10.66	0.886	29.28

NYBOT Frozen Concentrated Orange Juice November 1989 Through June 2002 (0.05 = $7.50)

	Years	Average Up	Average % Up	Average Down	Average % Down	Average Range	Average % Range
Jan	13	9.85	8.85	8.20	7.92	18.05	16.78
Feb	13	8.52	7.47	9.64	9.39	18.16	16.86
Mar	13	7.63	7.72	1.82	1.78	9.44	9.50
Apr	13	6.95	7.08	4.43	4.48	11.38	11.56
May	13	8.85	9.18	3.54	3.12	12.38	12.31
Jun	13	7.55	8.01	6.95	5.65	14.49	13.66
Jul	12	4.74	4.50	6.53	6.18	11.27	10.68
Aug	12	6.41	6.82	7.66	7.16	14.08	13.98
Sep	12	4.65	4.62	7.17	6.43	11.82	11.05
Oct	12	9.97	9.44	10.89	9.51	20.86	18.95
Nov	13	7.14	7.33	4.25	3.80	11.39	11.13
Dec	13	10.12	10.56	8.72	7.79	18.83	18.35

CBT Oats December 1989 Through June 2002 (1.00 = $50.00)

	Years	Average Up	Average % Up	Average Down	Average % Down	Average Range	Average % Range
Jan	13	6.96	4.54	10.10	6.81	17.06	11.35
Feb	13	9.35	6.03	11.35	7.83	20.69	13.86
Mar	13	8.15	5.99	5.27	3.45	13.42	9.44
Apr	13	15.04	9.76	11.63	6.82	26.67	16.58
May	13	12.02	8.28	12.04	7.17	24.06	15.45
Jun	13	10.60	7.88	17.46	11.16	28.06	19.04
Jul	12	14.77	11.09	9.48	6.74	24.25	17.83
Aug	12	9.58	7.59	13.92	9.82	23.50	17.41
Sep	12	6.98	5.25	6.25	4.18	13.23	9.43
Oct	12	11.60	8.47	5.65	3.69	17.25	12.16
Nov	12	13.69	9.58	11.29	8.07	24.98	17.65
Dec	13	5.88	3.80	6.83	4.53	12.71	8.33

NYMEX/COMEX Silver December 1989 Through November 2002 (0.10 = $5.00)

	Years	Average Up	Average % Up	Average Down	Average % Down	Average Range	Average % Range
Jan	13	25.20	5.316	20.60	4.148	45.80	9.464
Feb	13	33.04	6.380	17.21	3.674	50.25	10.054
Mar	13	22.46	4.994	27.23	5.068	49.69	10.062
Apr	13	23.42	4.952	24.27	4.639	47.69	9.591
May	13	27.51	5.670	26.15	4.678	53.65	10.349
Jun	13	19.68	4.163	20.84	4.139	40.52	8.302
Jul	13	19.72	4.028	22.14	4.596	41.86	8.624
Aug	13	17.85	3.671	31.99	6.416	49.85	10.087
Sep	13	32.02	6.928	17.42	3.512	49.44	10.439
Oct	13	10.92	2.381	34.05	6.767	44.96	9.148
Nov	13	18.12	3.962	18.04	3.836	36.15	7.798
Dec	13	12.68	2.851	17.83	3.707	30.51	6.558

CBT Soybean Oil January 1990 Through April 2002 (0.01 = $6.00)

	Years	Average Up	Average % Up	Average Down	Average % Down	Average Range	Average % Range
Jan	13	0.95	4.64	0.83	3.58	1.78	8.22
Feb	13	0.77	3.92	1.08	4.66	1.85	8.58
Mar	13	1.40	7.03	0.57	2.44	1.97	9.47
Apr	13	1.29	6.51	0.72	3.17	2.02	9.68
May	12	1.12	5.12	1.17	5.04	2.29	10.16
Jun	12	1.05	5.17	1.74	7.26	2.78	12.42
Jul	12	1.41	6.83	1.22	5.57	2.64	12.40
Aug	12	0.89	4.38	1.02	4.73	1.90	9.11
Sep	12	0.96	4.42	0.72	3.50	1.68	7.92
Oct	12	0.77	3.42	1.00	4.78	1.76	8.20
Nov	12	1.34	5.98	1.08	4.99	2.42	10.96
Dec	12	0.88	3.84	0.91	4.37	1.79	8.22

CBT Soybean Meal January 1990 Through April 2002 (0.10 = $10.00)

	Years	Average Up	Average % Up	Average Down	Average % Down	Average Range	Average % Range
Jan	13	7.47	4.41	7.61	4.15	15.08	8.56
Feb	13	6.80	3.83	11.42	6.22	18.22	10.05
Mar	13	10.06	5.76	4.62	2.52	14.68	8.28
Apr	13	12.59	6.84	3.71	2.09	16.30	8.92
May	13	10.78	6.01	4.45	2.28	15.23	8.29
Jun	13	11.66	6.90	7.99	3.81	19.65	10.72
Jul	12	13.95	7.42	9.31	5.18	23.26	12.60
Aug	12	11.21	6.24	8.35	4.51	19.56	10.75
Sep	12	8.72	4.78	7.14	3.80	15.86	8.58
Oct	11	10.09	5.88	7.72	3.88	17.81	9.76
Nov	11	11.09	6.34	8.28	4.18	19.37	10.52
Dec	12	5.60	2.98	7.21	4.11	12.81	7.09

CBT Soybeans November 1989 Through June 2002 (1.00 = $50.00)

	Years	Average Up	Average % Up	Average Down	Average % Down	Average Range	Average % Range
Jan	13	21.94	3.90	19.85	3.43	41.79	7.33
Feb	13	18.38	3.20	24.67	4.22	43.06	7.42
Mar	13	27.94	4.92	11.10	1.87	39.04	6.79
Apr	13	33.37	5.52	40.10	7.59	73.46	13.11
May	13	28.94	4.87	21.94	3.47	50.88	8.34
Jun	13	25.46	4.64	37.06	5.64	62.52	10.28
Jul	12	44.38	7.35	35.13	5.90	79.50	13.25
Aug	12	30.08	5.39	28.73	4.84	58.81	10.23
Sep	12	21.90	3.79	19.04	3.21	40.94	7.00
Oct	12	23.19	4.01	39.15	6.48	62.33	10.49
Nov	13	26.54	4.53	11.23	1.96	37.77	6.49
Dec	13	26.48	4.45	15.37	2.75	41.85	7.20

NYBOT Sugar #11 October 1989 Through June 2002 (0.01 = $11.20)

	Years	Average Up	Average % Up	Average Down	Average % Down	Average Range	Average % Range
Jan	13	0.91	9.13	0.70	7.71	1.61	16.83
Feb	13	0.82	7.66	0.97	11.13	1.79	18.79
Mar	13	0.80	8.64	0.38	4.07	1.18	12.71
Apr	13	0.91	10.70	0.85	8.94	1.76	19.64
May	13	0.71	8.85	0.57	4.91	1.28	13.76
Jun	13	1.37	17.85	0.74	5.88	2.11	23.72
Jul	12	0.63	6.70	0.76	7.86	1.39	14.56
Aug	12	0.70	7.77	0.86	8.49	1.56	16.26
Sep	12	0.70	7.70	1.00	9.79	1.70	17.48
Oct	13	0.52	5.37	0.41	4.50	0.94	9.87
Nov	13	0.76	7.58	0.42	4.71	1.19	12.29
Dec	13	0.72	7.29	0.45	4.76	1.17	12.05

CME/IMM Swiss Franc December 1989 Through May 2002 (0.01 = $12.50)

	Years	Average Up	Average % Up	Average Down	Average % Down	Average Range	Average % Range
Jan	13	2.21	3.25	2.15	2.99	4.36	6.24
Feb	13	1.80	2.66	2.93	4.05	4.73	6.71
Mar	13	1.55	2.16	1.84	2.67	3.39	4.82
Apr	13	2.04	2.92	2.38	3.40	4.42	6.32
May	13	2.52	3.69	2.38	3.40	4.90	7.09
Jun	12	1.54	2.25	1.75	2.49	3.30	4.75
Jul	12	2.81	4.07	2.11	3.03	4.91	7.10
Aug	12	3.73	5.44	2.22	3.09	5.94	8.53
Sep	12	2.83	4.01	1.50	2.04	4.32	6.04
Oct	12	3.70	5.17	1.46	1.98	5.16	7.16
Nov	12	2.73	3.83	2.24	3.01	4.97	6.85
Dec	13	2.27	3.31	1.15	1.62	3.42	4.92

CBT U.S. Treasury 10-Year Notes December 1990 Through May 2002 (0.01 = $10.00)

	Years	Average Up	Average % Up	Average Down	Average % Down	Average Range	Average % Range
Jan	13	2.05	1.94	1.49	1.42	3.54	3.36
Feb	13	2.30	2.20	1.82	1.68	4.11	3.89
Mar	13	0.95	0.91	2.01	1.88	2.96	2.79
Apr	13	1.13	1.09	2.15	2.02	3.28	3.10
May	13	1.16	1.12	2.20	2.06	3.36	3.18
Jun	12	1.75	1.67	0.80	0.76	2.56	2.43
Jul	12	2.51	2.40	0.67	0.64	3.18	3.04
Aug	12	3.44	3.31	0.77	0.73	4.21	4.04
Sep	12	1.87	1.73	0.88	0.84	2.75	2.57
Oct	12	2.94	2.73	1.23	1.16	4.17	3.90
Nov	12	2.84	2.70	0.95	0.89	3.80	3.60
Dec	13	1.68	1.60	1.24	1.16	2.92	2.76

CBT U.S. Treasury 30-Year Bonds December 1990 Through May 2002
(0.01 = $10.00)

	Years	Average Up	Average % Up	Average Down	Average % Down	Average Range	Average % Range
Jan	13	2.74	2.61	2.37	2.21	5.11	4.81
Feb	13	3.06	2.99	2.59	2.28	5.66	5.27
Mar	13	1.29	1.22	2.84	2.68	4.14	3.90
Apr	13	1.42	1.36	3.31	3.10	4.74	4.46
May	13	1.54	1.48	3.48	3.24	5.01	4.72
Jun	12	2.46	2.33	1.19	1.13	3.65	3.46
Jul	12	3.55	3.38	1.15	1.07	4.70	4.45
Aug	12	4.92	4.72	1.32	1.26	6.24	5.98
Sep	12	2.21	2.03	1.63	1.56	3.85	3.59
Oct	12	3.83	3.49	1.40	1.33	5.23	4.83
Nov	12	4.03	3.81	1.90	1.75	5.93	5.56
Dec	13	2.49	2.39	1.75	1.60	4.24	4.00

NYMEX RFG II Unleaded Gasoline November 1989 Through May 2002 (0.01 = $4.20)

	Years	Average Up	Average % Up	Average Down	Average % Down	Average Range	Average % Range
Jan	13	5.29	8.66	3.86	6.37	9.15	15.03
Feb	13	3.95	5.78	3.63	6.21	7.58	11.99
Mar	13	6.26	10.69	2.65	4.34	8.91	15.02
Apr	13	4.74	7.03	3.56	5.19	8.30	12.22
May	13	4.37	6.36	3.67	5.40	8.04	11.76
Jun	12	2.55	3.94	5.17	7.88	7.72	11.82
Jul	12	3.89	6.76	3.23	5.03	7.12	11.79
Aug	12	8.24	13.12	4.03	6.39	12.27	19.51
Sep	12	5.28	8.04	3.91	5.99	9.19	14.03
Oct	12	3.70	5.58	5.04	7.37	8.74	12.96
Nov	13	3.17	5.15	4.49	7.73	7.66	12.88
Dec	13	3.34	6.19	4.83	7.57	8.16	13.76

CBT Soft Red Winter Wheat December 1989 Through June 2002 (1.00 = $50.00)

	Years	Average Up	Average % Up	Average Down	Average % Down	Average Range	Average % Range
Jan	13	22.06	6.33	17.31	4.97	39.37	11.30
Feb	13	15.42	4.27	21.54	6.50	36.96	10.77
Mar	13	16.58	5.58	13.96	3.96	30.54	9.54
Apr	13	32.96	8.50	16.65	5.05	49.62	13.55
May	13	17.10	5.04	19.67	5.33	36.77	10.37
Jun	13	16.65	5.29	31.52	8.45	48.17	13.75
Jul	12	18.71	5.69	24.85	7.39	43.56	13.08
Aug	12	18.42	6.03	25.04	7.42	43.46	13.45
Sep	12	13.04	3.91	15.48	4.58	28.52	8.49
Oct	12	21.63	6.61	18.96	5.42	40.58	12.03
Nov	12	21.25	6.55	24.23	7.02	45.48	13.57
Dec	13	14.40	3.97	11.75	3.56	26.15	7.53

KCBT Hard Red Winter Wheat December 1989 Through June 2002 (1.00 = $50.00)

	Years	Average Up	Average % Up	Average Down	Average % Down	Average Range	Average % Range
Jan	13	19.42	5.28	14.35	4.08	33.77	9.37
Feb	13	18.85	4.97	17.12	5.00	35.96	9.97
Mar	13	14.73	4.57	11.29	3.08	26.02	7.66
Apr	13	36.73	9.00	14.29	4.17	51.02	13.18
May	13	17.54	4.76	18.04	4.50	35.58	9.26
Jun	13	21.77	6.65	29.19	7.22	50.96	13.87
Jul	12	16.73	4.99	26.38	7.36	43.10	12.34
Aug	12	16.71	5.35	27.71	7.65	44.42	12.99
Sep	12	14.90	4.44	13.33	3.63	28.23	8.06
Oct	12	23.83	7.11	17.06	4.70	40.90	11.81
Nov	12	25.02	7.56	20.00	5.50	45.02	13.05
Dec	13	12.94	3.45	10.88	3.20	23.83	6.65

Distribution of Contract Highs and Lows in Selected Markets, 1980–2002

In addition to historical gross movement, another type of study that has been very useful to me over the years, particularly as an adjunct to non-seasonal analysis, is a distribution study of when various markets make their yearly highs and lows. I imagine that someone must have published this or a similar study, but I've never seen it . . . so here it is, tables for the same 30 markets that appear in Appendix A. There are a couple of good ways to use these data, but, before we check on them, a few notes about the tables are in order.

These are not whole-month studies, as other studies in the text have been. These are actual month; if a contract in a market made its high on the last trading day of the contract, then that's the way it's scored in the accompanying tables. In the other style of studies, as in Appendix A for example, I omitted data from late in the life of the contract to avoid introducing skews into the gross movement figures.

The letters down the left-hand side of the tables are the standard futures contract month designators:

F, January	G, February	H, March	J, April
K, May	M, June	N, July	Q, August
U, September	V, October	X, November	Z, December

The month names across the top of the tables are the months in which the highs and lows occurred. The numbers within the table are the numbers of times contract highs or lows occurred in the named month (the column).

If we look at, say, March NYBOT cocoa in February, the G row, we see that this contract has made its lifetime high during February twice, and its lifetime low on four occasions. This example is a trifle deceiving, for these tables only consider the last year in the life of the contracts in calculating contract lifetime highs and lows. This policy may be a tiny bit distortive for markets whose contracts can live for years—bonds and notes, crude oil, and so forth—but this restriction was chosen to keep in line with our definition of trading as a capital commitment lasting no longer than one year.

One good way of deriving useful information from the tables is to look across the rows. When you see a string of three or four months in which the contract never or almost never makes a contract high, it's reasonable to include this fact in your analysis if you are considering writing call options on a non-seasonal basis. Naturally, this will be just a supplementary condition for the other parts of a non-seasonal analysis. September Canadian dollar is a good example of not making contract highs during the summer months. Similarly, if a string of consecutive months constitutes the majority of the time that a contract has made lifetime highs or lows, writing options non-seasonally in the *other* direction may be a profitable move, if other historical and present-day market conditions are in line. July heating oil offers an example of this bunching of contract highs during the first three months of the year.

There are several other inferences that may be drawn from these tables. August gold, for instance, makes its lifetime low in September, that single month, about half the time, but does so only infrequently after that point. We might well consider this to be an indicator that writing longish-dated August puts after September has passed is a worthwhile idea, other market conditions concurring. There's never any one right way to apply a set of data to trading, and the trader should—once again—keep an open mind as to whether and how a particular data set, as here, may be put to profitable use.

Please note that some markets did not exist in 1980 (Australian dollar, natural gas) and therefore contain fewer year's data.

CME/IMM Australian Dollar (AD)

		Jan	Feb	Mar	Apr	May	Jun	Jul	Aug	Sep	Oct	Nov	Dec
H	Hi	0	3	3	0	1	3	0	1	0	2	0	3
	Lo	4	1	2	1	0	1	1	1	2	0	2	1
M	Hi	0	1	1	1	3	4	2	0	0	1	0	2
	Lo	3	0	0	1	2	3	0	1	1	1	2	1
U	Hi	2	0	2	1	1	0	0	2	4	1	0	2
	Lo	2	1	1	1	0	2	1	2	3	1	0	1
Z	Hi	2	0	3	1	1	0	0	0	1	3	0	4
	Lo	0	1	3	1	1	2	1	1	1	0	2	2

CME/IMM British Pound (BP)

		Jan	Feb	Mar	Apr	May	Jun	Jul	Aug	Sep	Oct	Nov	Dec
H	Hi	1	4	2	5	2	0	0	0	1	2	1	4
	Lo	2	3	2	1	2	3	3	3	2	1	0	0
M	Hi	1	1	1	2	2	2	2	1	4	2	2	2
	Lo	0	2	1	2	2	5	1	2	4	2	1	0
U	Hi	2	1	2	3	1	0	1	1	4	2	1	4
	Lo	0	4	2	0	1	2	3	4	2	2	1	1
Z	Hi	4	3	1	3	0	0	0	0	1	4	4	2
	Lo	1	4	0	2	1	2	3	3	1	1	3	1

CME/IMM Canadian Dollar (CD)

		Jan	Feb	Mar	Apr	May	Jun	Jul	Aug	Sep	Oct	Nov	Dec
H	Hi	3	2	2	4	2	1	2	1	1	1	2	1
	Lo	2	2	5	3	4	1	1	2	0	0	2	0
M	Hi	1	1	1	2	2	2	5	2	2	1	2	1
	Lo	1	3	0	3	3	3	2	4	2	0	1	0
U	Hi	1	1	1	1	1	0	1	2	2	8	3	1
	Lo	1	3	1	2	2	1	1	3	1	3	2	2
Z	Hi	7	2	3	0	2	0	0	1	0	2	3	2
	Lo	6	3	0	1	1	1	1	2	0	1	3	3

NYBOT Cocoa (CC)

		Jan	Feb	Mar	Apr	May	Jun	Jul	Aug	Sep	Oct	Nov	Dec
H	Hi	0	2	0	3	4	1	3	2	3	1	0	2
	Lo	1	4	7	2	1	2	0	0	1	0	2	1
K	Hi	0	2	0	2	1	7	2	1	3	1	0	2
	Lo	1	2	2	2	6	1	0	1	2	0	2	2
N	Hi	0	2	0	0	2	2	1	5	6	1	1	1
	Lo	0	1	1	1	1	10	2	1	1	0	2	1
U	Hi	2	3	0	0	2	1	3	0	0	7	2	1
	Lo	0	1	1	1	0	5	1	5	3	0	1	3
Z	Hi	8	1	0	0	2	2	2	0	3	0	1	2
	Lo	3	1	2	1	0	4	2	1	1	0	3	3

NYBOT Coffee "C" (KC)

		Jan	Feb	Mar	Apr	May	Jun	Jul	Aug	Sep	Oct	Nov	Dec
H	Hi	2	2	3	5	3	1	1	1	1	0	1	2
	Lo	1	2	3	6	0	1	4	1	1	2	1	0
K	Hi	2	2	1	0	3	6	2	1	1	0	1	3
	Lo	1	1	0	4	3	4	5	1	0	3	0	0
N	Hi	2	1	1	0	5	2	1	4	3	0	0	3
	Lo	1	0	0	1	0	2	9	3	3	2	0	1
U	Hi	3	1	1	0	3	1	1	2	2	5	0	3
	Lo	1	1	0	2	0	1	2	4	5	4	0	2
Z	Hi	6	2	3	0	3	0	1	0	0	1	0	6
	Lo	3	2	0	1	0	1	3	1	2	2	2	5

NYMEX/COMEX High-Grade Copper (HG)

		Jan	Feb	Mar	Apr	May	Jun	Jul	Aug	Sep	Oct	Nov	Dec
F	Hi	3	5	3	2	0	0	0	3	2	1	0	1
	Lo	6	2	0	2	0	2	1	2	1	1	1	2
H	Hi	1	1	5	5	2	1	1	2	2	1	0	1
	Lo	4	1	4	4	0	3	1	2	1	1	0	1
K	Hi	1	2	3	0	5	2	3	2	2	1	0	1
	Lo	2	0	1	0	6	7	1	2	1	1	0	1
N	Hi	1	2	2	0	1	3	5	5	3	0	0	0
	Lo	2	0	0	1	2	4	5	4	1	2	0	1
U	Hi	2	2	1	1	1	1	1	1	7	5	0	0
	Lo	2	0	0	1	1	4	1	1	5	7	0	0
Z	Hi	4	2	4	1	1	1	0	2	3	0	0	4
	Lo	3	1	0	2	1	3	1	1	1	1	3	5

CBT Corn (C)

		Jan	Feb	Mar	Apr	May	Jun	Jul	Aug	Sep	Oct	Nov	Dec
H	Hi	1	0	1	5	2	5	3	2	0	2	1	0
	Lo	1	4	2	1	1	3	2	3	1	1	2	1
K	Hi	1	0	2	0	3	9	4	1	0	1	1	0
	Lo	2	4	3	0	2	4	3	1	0	1	1	1
N	Hi	1	0	2	0	0	2	5	7	0	2	1	2
	Lo	0	2	1	0	0	3	11	3	0	1	1	0
U	Hi	2	0	3	0	2	3	2	1	2	3	2	2
	Lo	0	0	1	0	0	2	5	5	5	0	4	0
Z	Hi	4	1	4	1	1	4	2	2	0	0	1	2
	Lo	2	0	1	0	0	2	2	4	1	2	4	4

NYBOT Cotton #2 (CT)

		Jan	Feb	Mar	Apr	May	Jun	Jul	Aug	Sep	Oct	Nov	Dec
H	Hi	0	2	2	3	3	4	1	3	2	0	1	0
	Lo	0	5	1	4	1	1	0	4	1	1	1	2
K	Hi	0	0	2	2	4	8	1	2	2	0	1	0
	Lo	1	3	1	3	1	3	1	4	1	1	1	2
N	Hi	0	1	2	0	3	3	4	4	2	2	1	0
	Lo	1	2	1	2	0	2	7	5	0	1	1	0
V	Hi	1	0	2	1	3	3	1	3	2	0	4	1
	Lo	0	0	0	0	0	0	1	5	3	4	5	3
Z	Hi	4	0	2	0	3	2	1	4	2	0	0	3
	Lo	3	2	0	0	0	1	1	3	1	2	5	3

NYMEX Light Sweet Crude (CL)

		Jan	Feb	Mar	Apr	May	Jun	Jul	Aug	Sep	Oct	Nov	Dec
F	Hi	0	2	1	1	1	1	1	2	0	3	3	3
	Lo	1	5	1	0	0	1	2	0	0	2	1	5
G	Hi	6	0	2	0	1	1	1	2	0	4	1	0
	Lo	5	0	3	2	0	0	2	0	0	2	0	4
H	Hi	4	2	0	1	2	1	1	2	0	4	1	0
	Lo	3	3	0	4	1	0	2	0	0	2	0	3
J	Hi	2	0	5	0	3	1	1	1	0	4	1	0
	Lo	3	2	3	0	4	1	1	0	0	2	0	2
K	Hi	1	1	2	5	0	3	1	0	0	4	1	0
	Lo	3	2	3	0	0	3	1	0	0	2	0	4
M	Hi	1	1	1	2	4	0	2	1	1	4	1	0
	Lo	3	2	2	0	1	0	3	1	0	1	1	4
N	Hi	1	1	0	0	3	6	0	1	1	4	1	0
	Lo	2	2	2	0	0	3	0	3	0	1	1	4
Q	Hi	1	1	0	0	2	2	6	0	1	5	1	0
	Lo	2	2	1	1	0	2	6	0	1	2	1	1
U	Hi	1	0	0	0	2	1	1	7	0	6	1	0
	Lo	2	2	1	1	0	1	4	2	0	2	1	3
V	Hi	1	0	1	1	3	1	0	3	5	0	4	0
	Lo	2	3	1	1	0	1	4	1	2	0	2	2
X	Hi	0	0	1	1	2	1	0	3	2	6	0	3
	Lo	3	3	1	1	0	1	3	0	1	3	0	3
Z	Hi	2	0	1	1	2	1	1	2	1	6	2	0
	Lo	3	4	1	1	0	1	2	0	0	3	4	0

CME Feeder Cattle (FC)

		Jan	Feb	Mar	Apr	May	Jun	Jul	Aug	Sep	Oct	Nov	Dec
F	Hi	10	2	0	4	0	1	1	0	1	1	0	2
	Lo	2	2	2	3	2	3	0	2	2	1	0	3
H	Hi	6	4	1	5	0	2	1	0	1	1	0	1
	Lo	2	0	4	4	3	2	0	2	0	0	1	4
J	Hi	3	3	2	4	3	3	2	0	1	1	0	0
	Lo	1	0	3	5	2	6	1	1	0	0	0	3
K	Hi	2	3	1	0	6	4	3	0	1	1	1	0
	Lo	1	0	1	4	5	5	0	1	0	0	1	4
Q	Hi	1	2	0	0	0	2	3	8	3	1	1	1
	Lo	0	0	0	4	1	1	3	1	4	5	0	3
U	Hi	3	2	1	0	0	1	3	6	3	1	1	1
	Lo	1	0	0	4	1	2	1	0	3	4	2	4
V	Hi	1	2	1	0	0	1	3	4	4	3	1	2
	Lo	0	0	0	4	1	0	1	1	6	0	4	5
X	Hi	2	2	1	1	0	1	2	3	4	1	3	2
	Lo	1	0	0	5	0	0	1	2	4	1	1	7

NYMEX/COMEX Gold (GC)

		Jan	Feb	Mar	Apr	May	Jun	Jul	Aug	Sep	Oct	Nov	Dec
G	Hi	3	1	9	2	1	2	2	0	1	1	0	0
	Lo	4	8	3	1	0	2	0	2	1	0	1	0
J	Hi	3	1	1	1	6	4	2	1	1	1	1	0
	Lo	3	1	6	5	1	2	0	1	1	0	1	1
M	Hi	3	1	0	0	2	0	7	2	3	2	1	1
	Lo	1	1	3	2	1	8	2	2	1	0	0	1
Q	Hi	2	1	0	0	1	0	1	1	11	2	2	1
	Lo	0	1	2	1	0	4	2	7	3	0	1	1
V	Hi	4	2	0	0	1	0	1	0	3	1	8	2
	Lo	0	1	1	1	0	2	0	4	5	4	3	1
Z	Hi	9	3	1	3	0	0	1	0	3	1	0	1
	Lo	0	2	1	1	1	3	0	2	3	0	4	5

NYMEX Heating Oil #2 (HO)

		Jan	Feb	Mar	Apr	May	Jun	Jul	Aug	Sep	Oct	Nov	Dec
F	Hi	0	2	1	1	1	2	1	2	0	3	4	5
	Lo	1	3	2	0	0	1	2	1	1	2	0	9
G	Hi	8	0	3	0	1	2	1	1	0	4	2	0
	Lo	9	0	3	1	0	1	2	1	0	2	0	3
H	Hi	5	3	0	2	3	1	1	1	1	2	3	0
	Lo	3	6	0	2	0	2	3	1	0	2	0	3
J	Hi	4	0	4	0	4	1	1	2	1	2	2	1
	Lo	2	3	6	0	2	2	2	1	0	2	0	2
K	Hi	4	0	2	1	0	4	3	1	2	2	2	1
	Lo	3	2	6	0	0	4	2	1	0	2	0	2
M	Hi	3	0	1	1	4	0	4	1	2	4	1	1
	Lo	3	2	5	0	1	0	5	1	0	3	0	2
N	Hi	3	0	1	2	1	3	0	4	3	3	1	1
	Lo	2	3	6	0	0	3	0	5	0	2	0	1
Q	Hi	3	0	1	1	1	2	3	0	3	6	0	2
	Lo	1	3	3	0	0	4	6	0	1	3	0	1
U	Hi	1	1	1	0	2	1	1	6	0	8	0	1
	Lo	1	3	2	0	0	3	4	4	0	4	0	1
V	Hi	1	1	1	0	2	2	1	2	6	0	5	1
	Lo	2	3	2	0	0	3	3	3	3	0	2	1
X	Hi	0	2	1	1	2	2	1	2	1	7	0	3
	Lo	2	3	2	0	0	3	2	3	1	3	0	3
Z	Hi	2	1	1	1	2	2	1	2	0	5	5	0
	Lo	2	4	3	0	0	2	1	1	2	2	5	0

CME/IMM Japanese Yen (JY)

		Jan	Feb	Mar	Apr	May	Jun	Jul	Aug	Sep	Oct	Nov	Dec
H	Hi	5	1	3	4	1	3	0	1	0	1	2	1
	Lo	1	4	3	3	3	2	2	1	2	0	1	0
M	Hi	4	0	1	1	2	1	4	3	1	1	2	2
	Lo	2	1	0	4	0	5	4	3	1	0	2	0
U	Hi	3	0	1	1	2	0	2	2	2	5	3	1
	Lo	2	1	0	4	0	2	1	4	4	3	1	0
Z	Hi	4	1	1	1	2	1	1	1	2	3	3	2
	Lo	3	1	1	3	1	2	0	2	2	0	2	5

CME Live Cattle (LC)

		Jan	Feb	Mar	Apr	May	Jun	Jul	Aug	Sep	Oct	Nov	Dec
G	Hi	3	10	2	1	1	0	1	1	0	1	1	1
	Lo	0	3	4	2	3	1	0	1	3	1	0	4
J	Hi	1	1	4	10	2	0	1	0	0	1	1	1
	Lo	0	0	3	4	6	1	1	1	1	0	1	4
M	Hi	2	2	3	2	3	3	4	1	0	1	1	0
	Lo	0	1	1	2	3	4	3	0	0	3	0	5
Q	Hi	3	1	1	2	1	1	1	9	2	0	1	0
	Lo	0	0	0	2	2	3	2	3	2	3	2	3
V	Hi	4	1	2	2	0	0	1	4	1	5	1	1
	Lo	0	0	0	3	3	1	1	1	5	1	3	4
Z	Hi	5	0	0	0	0	0	2	1	2	1	4	7
	Lo	5	0	0	3	2	1	0	0	3	1	2	5

CME Live/Lean Hogs (LH)

		Jan	Feb	Mar	Apr	May	Jun	Jul	Aug	Sep	Oct	Nov	Dec
G	Hi	3	1	3	4	2	3	0	0	2	1	1	2
	Lo	1	2	3	2	0	2	2	4	1	1	1	3
J	Hi	3	1	3	4	5	3	0	0	1	0	1	1
	Lo	1	0	2	3	3	2	2	4	1	0	1	3
M	Hi	3	0	1	5	5	4	2	0	0	0	1	1
	Lo	1	0	2	2	2	2	4	5	0	1	0	3
N	Hi	3	0	1	3	5	0	5	3	0	0	1	1
	Lo	1	1	1	2	1	0	4	7	1	1	1	2
Q	Hi	3	0	2	1	3	2	0	8	0	1	0	2
	Lo	1	1	1	1	0	1	5	1	5	2	1	3
V	Hi	4	0	1	1	3	1	0	2	4	5	0	1
	Lo	1	1	1	1	0	2	4	1	4	2	3	2
Z	Hi	4	0	0	3	1	2	0	0	3	4	0	5
	Lo	4	1	1	1	0	2	3	1	2	2	1	4

CME Random Length Lumber (LB)

		Jan	Feb	Mar	Apr	May	Jun	Jul	Aug	Sep	Oct	Nov	Dec
F	Hi	4	7	2	0	2	2	2	0	0	1	0	2
	Lo	4	3	1	0	0	1	3	3	1	1	3	2
H	Hi	4	3	3	3	3	2	2	0	0	1	0	1
	Lo	2	2	4	4	1	0	4	2	0	1	2	0
K	Hi	1	4	3	2	4	4	3	1	0	0	0	0
	Lo	0	2	2	1	6	3	3	0	1	2	2	0
N	Hi	1	2	4	1	4	2	2	5	0	0	1	0
	Lo	2	1	1	1	1	4	2	4	2	3	1	0
U	Hi	1	4	1	1	2	2	2	1	3	1	4	0
	Lo	4	1	0	0	1	0	3	4	5	3	1	0
X	Hi	4	3	2	0	1	3	2	1	0	0	2	4
	Lo	2	1	0	0	2	1	2	1	3	4	4	2

NYMEX Natural Gas (NG)

		Jan	Feb	Mar	Apr	May	Jun	Jul	Aug	Sep	Oct	Nov	Dec
F	Hi	0	1	0	2	0	0	0	1	1	3	0	3
	Lo	1	2	0	0	0	0	1	0	0	0	0	7
G	Hi	2	0	2	1	0	1	0	1	1	2	0	1
	Lo	7	0	2	0	0	0	1	0	0	0	0	1
H	Hi	1	2	0	1	0	1	0	1	2	2	0	1
	Lo	4	4	0	1	0	0	1	0	0	0	0	1
J	Hi	1	1	3	0	0	2	0	1	1	1	0	1
	Lo	4	3	1	0	1	0	1	0	0	0	0	1
K	Hi	1	0	1	4	0	3	0	1	0	0	0	1
	Lo	4	2	1	1	0	1	1	0	0	0	0	1
M	Hi	1	0	0	4	3	0	1	2	0	0	0	0
	Lo	1	2	1	0	2	0	4	0	0	0	0	1
N	Hi	1	0	0	3	1	4	0	2	0	1	0	0
	Lo	2	2	1	0	1	4	0	0	0	1	0	1
Q	Hi	1	0	0	3	1	2	2	0	2	1	0	0
	Lo	2	1	0	0	0	1	5	0	1	1	0	1
U	Hi	1	0	0	1	1	0	3	4	0	2	0	0
	Lo	3	1	1	0	0	1	1	4	0	1	0	0
V	Hi	1	1	0	2	1	0	1	1	3	0	2	0
	Lo	3	2	0	0	0	1	1	1	3	0	1	0
X	Hi	1	1	0	2	1	0	1	1	1	4	0	0
	Lo	2	3	0	0	0	1	2	0	1	2	0	1
Z	Hi	2	1	0	2	0	0	0	1	1	2	3	0
	Lo	3	2	0	0	0	1	2	0	0	0	4	0

NYBOT Frozen Concentrated Orange Juice (JO)

		Jan	Feb	Mar	Apr	May	Jun	Jul	Aug	Sep	Oct	Nov	Dec
F	Hi	5	7	1	0	1	1	0	0	1	1	3	2
	Lo	6	2	2	1	0	1	2	1	1	3	1	2
H	Hi	2	2	3	3	0	1	1	3	1	2	1	3
	Lo	1	7	3	3	0	1	2	0	0	1	2	2
K	Hi	3	0	0	2	4	2	1	2	2	3	1	2
	Lo	1	3	3	5	1	3	1	1	0	1	1	2
N	Hi	2	0	1	2	3	0	2	4	1	3	1	3
	Lo	2	3	1	1	0	3	4	5	0	1	1	1
U	Hi	4	0	0	1	3	0	1	1	1	5	2	4
	Lo	2	2	1	0	0	2	4	3	2	4	1	1
X	Hi	3	1	1	0	2	0	0	0	1	2	3	9
	Lo	2	1	5	0	0	2	2	1	2	4	2	1

CBT Oats (O)

		Jan	Feb	Mar	Apr	May	Jun	Jul	Aug	Sep	Oct	Nov	Dec
H	Hi	1	2	0	7	4	3	0	0	1	1	3	0
	Lo	2	7	3	2	1	2	1	1	1	0	1	1
K	Hi	0	1	1	1	1	11	2	1	0	1	3	0
	Lo	2	4	2	3	2	4	1	1	1	0	1	1
N	Hi	1	1	0	3	3	1	3	4	1	2	1	2
	Lo	1	1	1	0	1	5	8	2	0	0	2	1
U	Hi	3	1	0	2	2	1	0	0	4	5	2	2
	Lo	0	1	2	0	1	3	4	7	1	1	2	0
Z	Hi	4	2	2	4	3	1	0	0	1	0	1	4
	Lo	0	2	3	0	1	2	2	1	2	2	3	4

NYMEX/COMEX Silver (SI)

		Jan	Feb	Mar	Apr	May	Jun	Jul	Aug	Sep	Oct	Nov	Dec
F	Hi	2	7	4	0	1	1	1	1	0	0	0	0
	Lo	8	4	0	0	2	1	0	0	0	1	0	1
H	Hi	1	3	1	7	5	1	1	0	3	0	0	0
	Lo	2	3	8	3	1	1	1	1	0	0	0	2
K	Hi	1	2	1	0	3	6	2	3	3	0	1	0
	Lo	1	3	2	2	6	2	2	1	1	0	0	2
N	Hi	1	3	1	0	2	0	1	9	4	0	1	0
	Lo	0	3	2	0	1	3	7	5	1	0	0	0
U	Hi	2	6	1	0	2	0	0	1	0	7	3	0
	Lo	0	2	2	0	2	1	2	5	4	2	1	1
Z	Hi	7	4	3	0	2	1	1	1	1	0	0	2
	Lo	0	3	1	1	2	1	1	0	0	1	5	7

CBT Soybean Oil (BO)

		Jan	Feb	Mar	Apr	May	Jun	Jul	Aug	Sep	Oct	Nov	Dec
F	Hi	2	2	1	3	3	3	2	1	1	0	1	2
	Lo	7	2	1	1	0	1	2	1	1	1	0	4
H	Hi	3	0	3	4	4	2	2	2	1	0	1	0
	Lo	4	4	4	1	0	2	3	1	1	1	0	1
K	Hi	0	0	1	2	6	6	4	2	0	0	1	0
	Lo	2	2	3	1	4	3	1	2	1	2	0	1
N	Hi	0	0	0	1	5	0	7	6	1	0	1	0
	Lo	0	2	1	1	1	1	7	3	2	3	0	0
Q	Hi	0	0	0	1	5	0	5	2	6	0	2	1
	Lo	1	2	0	1	1	0	4	8	2	3	0	0
U	Hi	0	0	1	1	5	1	5	1	2	4	2	0
	Lo	1	2	0	1	1	0	4	4	4	5	0	0
V	Hi	0	0	2	1	5	1	5	1	2	0	3	2
	Lo	0	2	0	0	2	0	4	2	2	5	5	0
Z	Hi	3	1	4	1	3	1	1	2	2	0	1	3
	Lo	2	2	1	1	0	1	4	1	1	3	2	4

CBT Soybean Meal (SM)

		Jan	Feb	Mar	Apr	May	Jun	Jul	Aug	Sep	Oct	Nov	Dec
F	Hi	1	3	2	2	2	3	1	2	1	0	1	3
	Lo	4	4	0	0	0	2	3	1	1	1	2	3
H	Hi	1	0	3	5	2	4	1	2	0	0	2	2
	Lo	0	2	8	2	0	3	3	1	0	2	1	0
K	Hi	0	0	1	1	4	7	4	2	0	0	2	1
	Lo	0	2	6	2	4	1	2	2	0	2	1	0
N	Hi	0	0	1	1	3	2	3	6	1	1	3	1
	Lo	0	2	3	1	0	2	7	4	0	2	0	1
Q	Hi	0	0	1	1	3	2	2	3	4	1	3	1
	Lo	0	2	1	1	0	0	4	8	2	2	0	1
U	Hi	0	0	1	0	3	2	1	1	4	3	5	1
	Lo	0	2	1	0	0	1	4	4	4	2	2	1
V	Hi	1	0	1	1	3	3	1	1	2	3	5	1
	Lo	0	3	1	0	0	1	4	3	2	4	4	0
Z	Hi	4	0	2	2	2	2	1	1	3	0	2	2
	Lo	1	3	1	0	0	2	4	2	1	1	4	2

CBT Soybeans (S)

		Jan	Feb	Mar	Apr	May	Jun	Jul	Aug	Sep	Oct	Nov	Dec
F	Hi	1	3	2	2	1	6	2	1	2	0	2	0
	Lo	3	3	0	1	0	2	3	4	0	3	2	1
H	Hi	2	0	1	5	1	7	2	1	1	0	2	0
	Lo	2	5	2	2	1	3	3	1	0	1	2	0
K	Hi	0	0	0	1	4	8	5	1	1	0	2	0
	Lo	1	4	1	3	1	4	3	2	0	1	2	0
N	Hi	1	0	0	0	4	2	4	5	3	0	3	0
	Lo	1	2	0	2	0	1	9	4	0	1	2	0
Q	Hi	1	0	0	1	3	2	4	1	6	0	4	0
	Lo	0	2	0	2	0	0	5	9	2	2	0	0
U	Hi	1	0	0	0	4	3	1	1	5	3	2	2
	Lo	1	1	0	2	0	0	3	4	6	4	1	0
X	Hi	1	0	2	0	1	5	2	1	2	0	2	6
	Lo	0	2	0	2	0	1	3	3	0	5	4	2

NYBOT Sugar #11 (SB)

		Jan	Feb	Mar	Apr	May	Jun	Jul	Aug	Sep	Oct	Nov	Dec
H	Hi	2	1	0	7	2	1	1	0	3	1	2	2
	Lo	3	6	0	5	3	2	0	2	0	1	0	0
K	Hi	2	1	4	4	0	5	2	0	0	2	1	1
	Lo	3	1	1	7	0	4	1	3	1	0	1	0
N	Hi	1	0	1	2	3	7	0	5	0	1	1	1
	Lo	4	1	2	1	3	4	0	6	1	0	0	0
V	Hi	2	0	1	2	2	1	2	2	4	0	5	1
	Lo	2	2	2	1	2	1	0	2	5	1	4	0

CME/IMM Swiss Franc (SF)

		Jan	Feb	Mar	Apr	May	Jun	Jul	Aug	Sep	Oct	Nov	Dec
H	Hi	2	2	2	6	2	1	1	0	1	3	1	1
	Lo	2	2	4	2	1	2	2	5	0	1	1	0
M	Hi	2	1	0	1	4	0	4	1	0	5	3	1
	Lo	0	2	1	3	3	5	1	2	2	0	3	0
U	Hi	2	1	0	1	1	0	0	2	4	5	4	2
	Lo	0	2	0	2	2	0	4	3	4	1	3	1
Z	Hi	10	4	1	1	0	1	0	0	2	3	2	2
	Lo	5	1	3	1	2	0	3	3	1	1	1	5

CBT U.S. Treasury 10-Year Notes (TY)

		Jan	Feb	Mar	Apr	May	Jun	Jul	Aug	Sep	Oct	Nov	Dec
H	Hi	2	2	7	0	1	0	1	1	0	3	1	1
	Lo	1	0	1	5	2	5	1	1	1	1	1	0
M	Hi	1	2	3	2	1	4	0	0	0	3	1	2
	Lo	1	0	0	0	4	2	5	3	2	1	1	0
U	Hi	0	1	2	0	1	1	2	3	5	2	0	2
	Lo	0	0	2	1	4	3	0	1	1	4	2	1
Z	Hi	1	1	2	1	1	0	0	1	0	3	3	7
	Lo	3	0	3	3	4	3	0	1	0	2	1	0

CBT U.S. Treasury 30-Year Bonds (US)

		Jan	Feb	Mar	Apr	May	Jun	Jul	Aug	Sep	Oct	Nov	Dec
H	Hi	5	1	5	2	1	2	1	0	0	2	1	2
	Lo	1	1	2	7	3	4	0	0	1	2	1	0
M	Hi	2	1	3	2	1	5	4	0	0	2	1	2
	Lo	1	1	1	1	4	2	8	1	1	2	1	0
U	Hi	1	0	2	1	1	2	1	1	7	7	0	1
	Lo	1	1	0	1	2	1	1	2	4	8	3	0
Z	Hi	4	0	2	1	1	1	0	1	1	2	2	7
	Lo	4	1	4	1	3	2	0	2	1	1	1	2

NYMEX RFG II Unleaded Gasoline (HU)

		Jan	Feb	Mar	Apr	May	Jun	Jul	Aug	Sep	Oct	Nov	Dec
F	Hi	0	0	2	0	0	1	1	1	1	2	2	6
	Lo	0	1	2	1	0	3	2	0	0	2	0	5
G	Hi	7	0	1	0	1	1	1	0	0	3	2	0
	Lo	5	0	1	1	0	2	2	0	0	2	0	3
H	Hi	4	3	0	1	1	1	1	0	0	3	2	0
	Lo	1	4	0	1	1	2	2	0	0	2	0	3
J	Hi	2	0	5	0	1	2	1	0	0	3	2	0
	Lo	1	2	4	0	2	2	1	1	0	2	0	1
K	Hi	2	0	2	6	0	2	0	1	1	1	2	0
	Lo	2	2	4	0	0	3	2	1	0	2	0	1
M	Hi	1	0	0	1	8	0	1	1	1	2	2	0
	Lo	1	2	4	0	1	0	3	3	0	2	0	1
N	Hi	2	0	0	1	4	5	0	1	0	3	1	0
	Lo	1	2	3	0	0	4	0	1	0	3	0	3
Q	Hi	0	0	0	1	2	2	8	0	1	2	1	0
	Lo	1	3	3	0	0	1	5	0	1	2	1	0
U	Hi	0	0	0	3	2	1	1	6	0	3	1	0
	Lo	2	3	2	0	0	2	4	1	0	1	2	0
V	Hi	0	0	1	1	1	1	1	1	9	0	2	0
	Lo	2	4	1	0	0	2	2	1	3	0	2	0
X	Hi	0	0	1	0	2	1	1	0	4	6	0	2
	Lo	1	5	1	0	0	2	2	1	0	4	0	1
Z	Hi	2	0	1	1	1	1	1	0	2	2	6	0
	Lo	1	5	0	1	0	2	2	0	0	2	4	0

CBT Soft Red Winter Wheat (W)

		Jan	Feb	Mar	Apr	May	Jun	Jul	Aug	Sep	Oct	Nov	Dec
H	Hi	2	4	3	5	4	1	0	1	0	2	0	0
	Lo	1	7	2	5	0	1	2	2	0	0	0	2
K	Hi	1	2	1	1	2	10	0	3	0	2	0	0
	Lo	3	4	2	2	3	2	5	1	0	0	0	0
N	Hi	2	2	1	2	1	1	1	8	0	3	0	1
	Lo	0	2	1	2	0	3	8	5	1	0	0	0
U	Hi	2	2	1	2	1	0	1	2	3	6	1	1
	Lo	0	2	1	1	0	3	4	3	3	5	0	0
Z	Hi	5	2	1	3	3	0	0	1	1	2	0	4
	Lo	2	1	1	2	0	1	2	2	4	1	3	3

KCBT Hard Red Winter Wheat (KW)

		Jan	Feb	Mar	Apr	May	Jun	Jul	Aug	Sep	Oct	Nov	Dec
H	Hi	1	3	1	5	6	2	0	1	0	2	0	1
	Lo	3	3	2	4	0	1	3	3	0	1	1	1
K	Hi	1	2	0	1	4	8	1	4	0	1	0	0
	Lo	1	1	3	3	4	4	3	1	0	1	1	0
N	Hi	2	2	0	2	2	1	1	7	0	3	1	1
	Lo	0	1	0	0	0	3	9	6	2	1	0	0
U	Hi	1	2	0	1	3	1	1	2	2	5	3	1
	Lo	1	1	1	0	0	3	4	5	3	3	1	0
Z	Hi	6	2	0	2	3	1	0	1	1	2	0	4
	Lo	2	1	1	1	0	2	2	3	2	1	2	5

Index

Illustration and table page references are *italic*.